Reliure serrée

A SURVEY OF THE Estate of France,

AND

Of some of the adjoyning ILANDS:

TAKEN

In the Description of the principal Cities, and chief Provinces; with, The *Temper*, *Humor* and *Affections* of the People generally; And an exact accompt of the Publick Government in reference to the *Court*, the *Church*, and the *Civill State*.

By *PETER HEYLYN*.

Published according to the Authors own Copy, and with his consent, for preventing of all False, Imperfect, and Surreptitious Impressions of it.

LONDON,

Printed by *E. Cotes* for *Henry Seile*, and are to be sold at his Shop over against St. *Dunstans* Church in *Fleetstreet*, M. DC. LVI.

Robert Butler

TO THE RIGHT HONOURABLE THE Lord Marquesse OF DORCHESTER.

I Here present unto your Lordship the *Fruits*, if not the Follies also, of my younger daies, not published now, if the audaciousnesse of some others had not made that *necessary* which in my own thoughts

thoughts was esteemed *unseasonable*. The reasons why I have no sooner published these Relations, and those which have inforced me to do it now, are laid down in the following Preface, sufficient (as I hope) both to excuse and justifie me with ingenuous men. But for my boldnesse in giving them the countenance of your Lordships name, I shall not study other reasons then a desire to render to your Lordship some acknowledgement of those many fair expressions of esteem and favour, which your Lordship from my first coming to *Westminster*, hath vouchsafed unto me. Your known abilities in most parts of learning, together with the great respects you have for those which pretend unto it, enclined you to embrace such opinion of me, as was more answerable to your

own

own goodnesse then to my desert, and to cherish in me those Proficiencies, which were more truly in your self. And for my part, I alwaies looked upon your Lordship as a true Son of the Church of *England*, devoted zealously to her Forms of worship, the orthodoxies of her Doctrine, and the Apostolicism of her Government; which makes me confident that these pieces will not prove unwelcome to you, in which the superstitions & innovations of the two opposite parties, are with an equal hand laid open to your Lordships view. Nor shall you find in these Relations, such matters of compliance only with your Lordship in point of Judgement, as promise satisfaction unto your intellectuall, and more noble parts; but many things which may afford you entertainments of a different nature, when you are either spent with study, or wearied with affairs of more near importance. For here you have the principallest Cities and fairest Provinces of *France* presented in as lively colours, as my unpolished hand could give them; the Temper, Humour and Affections of the People, generally deciphered with a free and impartial Pen; the publick Government of the whole, in reference to the Court, the Church, and the Civil State, described more punctually then ever heretofore in the *English* Tongue; some observations intermingled of more ancient learning, but pertinent and proper to the businesse which I had in hand. You have here such an accompt also of some of the adjoyning Islands (the only remainders of our Rights in the Dukedome of *Normandy*)

mandy) that your Lordship may finde cause to wonder, how I could say so much on so small a subject, if the great alterations which have hapned there in bringing in and working out the *Genevian Discipline*, had not occasioned these enlargements. Such as it is, it is submitted with that Reverence to your Lordships Judgement, which best becometh

My Lord,

Your Lordships most humble

And most devoted Servant,

Pet. Heylyn.

The Authors Preface to the Reader.

IT may seem strange unto the Reader, that after so large a volume of *Cosmography*, in which the world was made the subject of my Travels, I should descend unto the publishing of these *Relations*, which point at the estate only of some neighbouring places: or that in these declining times of my life and fortunes, I should take pleasure in communicating such *Compositions*, as were the products of my youth, and therefore probably not able to endure the censure of severer age. And to say truth, there are some things in this *publication*, whereof I think my self obliged to give an account to him that shall read these papers, as well for his satisfaction as mine own discharge; as namely touching the occasion of these several Journeys, my different manner of proceeding in these Relations, the reasons why not published sooner, and the impulsions which have moved me to produce them now.

For the two first, the Reader may be pleased to know, that as I undertook the first Journey, in the company of a private friend, only to satisfie my self in taking a brief view of the pleasures and delights of *France*; so having pleased my

self

self in the sight thereof, and in the observation of such things as were most considerable, I resolved to give my self the pleasure of making such a character and description of them, as were then most agreeable to my present humour, at what time both my wits and fancies (if ever I was master of any) were in their predominancy. I was then free from all engagements, depending meerly on my self, not having fastned my relations upon any one man, in order to my future preferment in Church or State, and therefore thought of nothing else then a self-complacency, and the contentment of indulging to mine own affections. This made me to take that liberty in decipheting the tempers, humours, and behaviours of the *French* Nation generally, which to a grave judgement may seem too luxuriant, and to have more in it of the *Satyrist*, then is consistent with an equall and impartiall character. But in the midst of so much folly (if the Reader shall vouchsafe it no better name) there is such a mixture of more serious matters, as makes the temperature of the whole be more delightfull, according to that saying of *Horace* in his Book *de Arte Poetica*:

Omne tulit punctum, qui miscuit utile dulci.

That is to say,

He hits on every point aright,
Who mingleth profit with delight.

III.   The other Journey being undertaken almost four years after, in attendance on the Earl of *Danby*, is
fashioned

To the Reader.

fashioned after a more serious and solemn manner. I had then began to apply my self to the Lord Bishop of *London,* and was resolved to present the work to him, when it was once finished, and therefore was to frame my style agreeably unto the gravity and composednesse of so great a Prelate. My design was to let him see in the whole body and contexture of that discourse, that I was not altogether uncapable of managing such publick businesse, as he might afterwards think fit to entrust me with; and it succeeded so well with me, that within a short time after he recommended me unto his Majesty for a Chaplain in ordinary, and by degrees employed me in affairs of such weight and moment, as rendred my service not unusefull to the Church and State; however mistaken by some men, who think all matters ill conducted, which either passe not through their own hands, or are not managed by their sinister and precipitate counsels. This makes the style and language of the second Journey to be so different from the first. The indiscretion would have been impardonable, if I had come before such a person in so light a garb, as might have given him a just occasion to suppose, that I had too much of the Antick, and might be rather serviceable to his recreations, then to be honoured with employments of more weight and consequence.

If it be asked, why these Relations were not published assoon as they passed my hands, and might be thought more seasonable, then they are at this present; the Answer in a manner may prevent the question. The last discourse, being written, and intended purposely as a Present to that great Prelate whom before I spoke of, could not with any fitnesse, be communicated to the

pub-

To the Reader.

publick view, without his consent. For having tendred it unto him, it was no more mine, and not being mine, I had no reason to dispose otherwise of it, as long as the property thereof was vested in him by mine own free act. But he being laid to sleep in the bed of peace, I conceive my self to have gotten such a second right therein, as the *Granter* hath many times in Law, when there is no Heir left of the *Grantee* to enjoy the gift, and consequently to lay any claim unto it. And being resolved, upon the reasons hereafter following, to publish the first of these two Journals, I thought it not amisse to let this also wait upon it, second in place, as it had been second in performance and course of time.

V. So for the first Journey, being digested and committed unto writing for mine own contentment, without the thought of pleasing any body else; the keeping of it by me did as much conduce to the end proposed, as if it had been published to the view of others. And I had still satisfied my self in enjoying that end, if the importunity of friends (who were willing to put themselves to that charge and trouble) had not drawn some copies of it from me. By means whereof it came unto more hands then I ever meant it, and at the last into such hands, by which it would have been presented to the publick view without my consent; and that too with such faults and errors, as *Transcripts* of necessity must be subject to when not compared with the Original, or perused by the Author. And had it hapned so, as it was like enough to happen, and hath hapned since, the faults and errors of the Copy, as well as of the Presse, would have passed for mine; and I must have been thought accomptable for those

trans-

To the Reader.

transgressions which the ignorance and unadvisednesse of other men would have drawn upon me. And yet there was some other reason, which made the publishing of that Journal when first finished by me, not so fit nor safe, nor so conducible to some ends, which I had in view. I had before apply'ed my self unto his Majesty, when Prince of *Wales*, by Dedicating to him the first Essayes of my *Cosmographie*; and thereby opened for my self a passage into the Court, whensoever I should have a minde to look that way. And at the time when I had finished these *Relations*, the *French* party there were as considerable for their number, as it was afterwards for their power: and the discourse fashioned with so much liberty, and touching (as it might be thought) with so much *Gayete de coeur* upon the humours of that people, might have procured me no good welcome; and proved but an unhandsome harbinger, to take up any good lodging for me in that place, when either my studies should enable, or my ambition prompt me to aspire unto it. Which causes being now removed, I conceive the time to be more seasonable now, then it was at the first, and that these papers may more confidently walk the open streets, without giving any just offence to my self or others.

For though perhaps it may be said, that I have made too bold with the *French*, and that my character of that people, hath too much of the *Satyrist* in it, as before was intimated; yet I conceive that no sober minded man either of that Nation or of this, will finde himself aggrieved at my freedome in it. The *French* and other forein Nations make as bold with us, not sparing to lay open our wants and weaknesses, even without occasion, and offering them by such multiplying Glasses to the sight of others, as render them far greater then indeed they are. Men of facetious fancies and scoffing wits (as the *French* generally are) must not expect to be alwaies on the offering hand, but be content to take such money as they use to give; there would be else no living neer them, or conversing with them. *Hanc veniam petimusq; damusq; vicissim*, in the Poets language. Besides the reader must distinguish betwixt the inclinations of nature, and corruptions in manners. Natural inclinations may be described under a free and liberal character, without any wrong unto the Nations which are so described: nor is it more to the dishonour of the *French*, to say that they are airy, light, *Mercurial*, assoon lost as found; then to the *Spaniard*, to be accounted slow, and *Saturnine*, lofty and proud, even in the lowest ebb of a beggerly fortune. The temperature of the soyle and air, together with the influences of the heavenly bodies, occasion that variety of temper and affections in all different Nations, which can be no reproach unto them, when no corruption of manners, no vice in matter of morality is charged upon them. *Hinc illa ab antiquo vitia, et patriæ forte durantia, qua totas in historiis gentes aut commendant aut notant*, saith a modern but judicious Author. The present *French* had not been else so like the *Galls* in the *Roman* stories, had not those influences, and other naturall causes before remembred, produced the same natural inclinations, and impulsions in them, as they had effected in the other; their own *Du Bartas* saith as much touching this particular, as he is thus translated by *Josuah Sylvester*.

To the Reader.

O see how full of wonders strange is nature,
Sith in each climate, not alone in stature,
Strength, colour, hair; but that men differ do
Both in their humours, and their manners too.

The Northern man is fair, the Southern foul;
That's white, this black; that smiles & this doth scowl.
The one blithe and frolick, the other dull & froward,
The one full of courage, the other a fearful coward.

Much lesse would I be thought injurious to the female sex, though I have used the like freedome in my character of them. I doubt not but there are amongst them, many gallant women, of most exemplary virtue, and unquestioned chastity; and I believe the greatest part are such indeed; though their behaviour at first sight might, to a man untravelled, persvade the contrary: But general characters are to be fitted to the temper and condition of a people generally, unto the *Genera singulorum*, as *Logicians* phrase it, though possibly (as there are few general Rules without some exceptions) many particular persons both of rank and merit, may challenge an exemption from them:

Queis meliore luto finxit præcordia Titan.

To whom the heavens have made a brest
Of choicer metall then the rest.

And it is possible enough I might have been more sparing of that liberty which I then gave unto my self, were there occasion to make a second character of them

them at this present time; or had I not thought fit to have offered this discourse without alteration, as it first issued from my pen. Our *English* women at that time were of a more retired behaviour then they have been since, which made the confident carriage of the *French Damosels*, seem more strange unto me, whereas of late the garbe of our women is so altered, and they have so much in them of the mode of *France*, as easily might take off those misapprehensions, with which I was really possessed at my first coming thither. So much doth custome alter the true face of things, that it makes many things approvable, which at the first appeared unsightly.

VIII. In the next place it may be said that this short Journall deserves not to be called *A SURVEY OF THE STATE OF FRANCE*, considering that it only treateth of some particular Provinces, and of such Towns and Cities only in those Provinces, as came within the compasse of a personal view. But then it may be said withall, that these four Provinces which I passed thorow, and describe, may be considered as the *Epitome* of the whole, the abstract or compendium of the Body of *France*: the Isle of *France* being looked on as the mother of *Paris*, *Picardie* as the chiefest *Granary*, and *La Beause* as the nurse thereof; as *Normandy* is esteemed for the Bulwark of all *France* it self by reason of that large Sea-coast, and well fortified Havens, wherewith it doth confront the *English*. And if the rule be true in *Logick* (as I think it is) that a Denomination may be taken from the nobler parts; then certainly a *Survey* of these four Provinces, the noblest and most considerable parts of all that Kingdome, may be entituled without any absurdity the Survey of *France*.

For

To the Reader.

For besides that which hath been spoken, it was in these four Provinces that *Henry* the 4. did lay the scene of his long war against the *Leaguers*, as if in keeping them assured or subjected to him the safety of the whole Kingdome did consist especially. For though the war was carried into most other Provinces as the necessity of affairs required, yet it was managed in those Provinces by particular parties. Neither the King himself, nor the Duke of *Mayenne* (the heads of the contending Armies) did act any thing in them except some light velitations in *Champagne*, and one excursion into *Burgundie*; the whole decision of the quarrels, depending principally, if not wholly, in the getting of these. The Duke of *Parma* had not else made so long a march from the Court of *Bruxels*, to raise the Kings Army from the siege of *Reven*; nor had the King mustered up all his wit and power to recover *Amiens*, when dexterously surprized by a *Spanish* stratagem. And if it be true, which the *French* generally affirm of *Paris*, that it is the Eye, nay the very Soul of all *France* it self; I may with confidence affirm, that I have given more sight to that Eye, more life and spirit to that Soul, then hath been hitherto communicated in the English Tongue. The Realm of *France* surveyed in the four principal Provinces, and the chief Cities of the whole, gives a good colour to the *title*, and yet the title hath more colour to insist upon, then the description of these Cities, and those principal Provinces, can contribute towards it. For though I have described those four Provinces only in the way of Chorography, yet I have took a general and *a full Survey of the State of* France, in reference to the Court, the Church, and the Civil State, which are the three main limbs of all *Bodies Politick*, and took it in so full a manner, as I think none, and am assured that very few have done before me.

IX. If it be said that my stay was not long enough to render me exact and punctual in my observations: I hope it will be said withall, that the lesse my stay was, my diligence must be the greater, and that I husbanded my time to the best advantage. For knowing that we could not stay there longer, then our money lasted, and that we carried not the wealth of the *Indies* with us, I was resolved to give my self as little rest, as the necessities of nature could dispense withall; and so to work my self into the good opinions of some principal persons of that nation, who were best able to inform me, as might in short space furnish me with such instructions, as others with a greater expence both of time and money could not so readily attain. By this accommodating of my self unto the humours of some men, and a resolution not to be wanting to that curiosity which I carryed with me, there was nothing which I desired to know (and there was nothing which I desired not to know) but what was readily imparted to me both with love and chearfulnesse. *Cur nescire pudens prave quam discere mallem?* I alwaies looked upon it as a greater shame to be ignorant of any thing, then to be taught by any body; and therefore made such use of men of both Religions, as were most likely to acquaint me with the counsels of their severall parties. Nor was I purse-bound when I had occasion to see any of those Rarities, Reliques, and matters of more true antiquity, which either their Religious Houses, Churches, Colledges, yea, or the Court it self could present unto me. Money is never better spent,

To the Reader.

spent then wen it is layed out in the bnying of knowledge.

X.

In the laſt place it may be ſaid that many things have hapned both in the Court and State of *France*, many great revolutions and alterations in the face thereof, ſince I digeſted the Relation of this Journey for my own contentment; which makes this publication the more unſeaſonable, and my conſent unto it ſubject to the greater cenſure: which notwithſtanding I conceive that the diſcourſe will be as uſefull to the ingenuous Reader, as if it had gone ſheet by ſheet from the *Pen* to the *Preſſe*, and had been offered to him in that point of time when it took life from me. The learned labours of *Pauſanias* in his Chorography of *Greece*, are as delightful now to the ſtudious Reader, as formerly to the beſt wits of *Rome* or *Athens*. Nor need we doubt, but that the deſcription of the *Netherlands* by *Lewis Guicciardine*, and of the Iſles of *Britain* by our famous *Camden*, will yeeld as great profit and contentment to future Ages, as to the men that knew the Authors. The Realm of *France* is ſtill the ſame, the temperature of the air and ſoyl the ſame, the humours and affections of the people ſtill the ſame; the Fractions of the Church as great, the Government as Regal or deſpotical now, as when the Author was amongſt them. The Cities ſtand in the ſame places which before they ſtood in, and the Rivers keep the ſame channels which before they had, no alteration in the *natural* parts of that great body, and not much in the *politick* neither. The change which ſince hath hapned by the Death of the King, being rather in the perſon of the Prince, then the form of Government. Affairs of State then maniged by a Queen-

Mother

Mother, and a Cardinal favourite, as they are at this present. The King in his Majority then, but not much versed or studied in his own concernments, as he is at this present; the Realm divided then into parties and factions (though not into the same factions) as it is at this present; and finally, the *English* then in as high esteem, by reason of the alliance then newly made between the Princes, as they can possibly be now, by reason of the late concluded peace betwixt the Nations. Nor hath there hapned any thing not reconcilable to the present times, but the almost miraculous birth of the King and his Brother, after 20 years barrennesse, and the mariage of the Monsieur with *Montpensiers* Daughter, contrary to the generall expectation of all that people, and for the first (I think I may be bold to say) of the world besides.

XII. These reasons as they may excuse this publication, in reference to the work it self, so there is one which serves to justifie it in respect of the Author; that is to say, the manifesting of this truth to all which shall peruse these papers, that he is still of the same Judgement, and opinion in matters of Religion, Gods worship, and the government of holy Church, of which he was 30 years agoe, when the Relation of the first Journey was fashioned by him; that he hath stood his ground in all those revolutions both of Church and State, which have hapned since; that he now holds no other *Tenets*, then those to which he hath been principled by education, and confirmed by study; and finally that such opinions as he holds, be they right or wrong, he brought to the Court with him, and took not from thence. So that whatsoever

other

other imputation may be charged upon him, he cannot be accused for a time-server, but alwaies constant to himself, in all times the same; *Qualis ab incepto processerit*, in the Poets language, the same man then as now without alteration. Compare my late book upon the *Creed*, with these present *Journals*, and it will easily be seen, that in all points wherein I have occasion to declare my Judgement, I am nothing altered; that neither the temptations of preferment, nor that great turn both in the publick and my own affairs which hath hapned since, have made me other then I was at the very first.

It's true in reading over these papers as they were sent to the Presse, I found some things which I could willingly have rectified as they passed my hands; but that I chose rather to let them go with some *Petit errors*, then alter any thing in the Copy, which might give any the least occasion to this misconceit, that the work went not to the Presse, as it came from my pen, but was corrected by the line and levell of my present Judgement. And for such *petit errors*, as then scaped my hands, being they are but *petit errors*, they may the more easily be pardoned by ingenuous men. But howsoever being *errors*, though but *petit* errors, I hold it necessary to correct them, and shall correct them in this order as they come before me.

XIII.

Normandy bounded on the South with L' Isle de France] Not with the *Isle of France* distinctly and properly so called, occasioned by the circlings of the *Seine* and the *Marne*, in which *Paris* standeth; but by that part of *France*, which is called commonly *France Special*, or the *Proper France*, as being the first fixed seat of the *French* Nation, after their first en-

p. 4. l. 17.

b 3   trance

trance into *Gaul*; which notwithstanding may in some sense, be called the Isle of *France* also, because environed on all sides with some river or other, that is to say, with the *Velle* on the East, the *Eure* on the West, the *Oise* on the North, and a vein Riveret of the *Seine* on the South parts of it.

P. 5. l. 10. *The name* Neustria] Not named so in the time of the *Romans*, when it was reckoned for a part of *Gallia Celtica*, as the words not well distinguished do seem to intimate; but when it was a part of the *French* Empire, and then corruptly so called for *Westria*, signifying the West parts thereof: the name of *Westria* or *Westenrick*, being given by some to this part of the Realm of *West France*, as that of *Austria* or *Ostenric* to a part of East *France*.

Ibid. l. 17. *By the permission of* Charles the Bald] Not so, but by the sufferance of *Charles* the *Simple*, a weaker Prince, and far lesse able to support the Majesty of a King of *France*. For though the *Normans* ransacked the Sea coasts of this Countrey during the reign of *Charles* the *Bald*, which lasted from the year 841 to the year 879. yet *Charles* the *Bald* was not so simple nor so ill advised, as to give them livery and seisin of so large a Province. That was a businesse fit for none but *Charles* the SIMPLE, who began his reign in the year 900. and unto him the words foregoing would direct the Reader, where it is thus told us of these *Normans, anno* 900. they first seated themselves in *France*, &c. which relates plainly to the reign of *Charles* the *Simple*, in the beginning whereof they first setled here, though *Rollo* their chief Captain was not honoured with the title of Duke of *Normandy* untill 12 years after.

For

To the Reader.

For the most part of a light and sandy mould] mista- P. 7. l. 26.
ken in the print for a *light* and *handy*, that is to say, of a more easie tillage, then the rest of those Kingdomes. Which words though positively true of the Countrey of *Norfolk*, are to be understood of *Normandy*, comparatively and respectively to the rest of *France*; for otherwise it would ill agree with the following words, where it is said to *be of a fat and liking soyle*, as indeed it is, though not so fat and deep as the Isle of *France*, *La Beauſe*, or many others of the Southern Provinces.

The French *custome giving to all the sons an equality* P. 8. l. 17.
in the Estate] which must be understood of the Estates of meaner and inferiour persons, and not of those of eminent, and more noble Families, which have been altered in this point; The Lands and Honours passing undivided to the eldest sons, the better to support the dignity of their place and titles; as many Gentlemen of *Kent* have changed their old tenure by Gavelkinde into Knights service, for the same reason, and obtained severall Acts of Parliament to make good that change.

For when Meroveus *the Grandchilde of* Pharamond] P. 34. l. 2.
so he is said to be by *Rufener*, as eldest son of *Clodian* the son of *Pharamond*; but *Paradine*, the best Herald of all the *French*, speaks more doubtfully of him, not knowing whether he were the son or next kinsman of *Clodian*, and others (whose authority I have elsewhere followed) make him to be the Master of the Horse to *Clodian*, whose children he is said to have dispossessed of the Crown, and transferred the same unto himself.

The

To the Reader.

P. 125. l. 15. *The reason of the name I could not learn amongst the people*] That is to say, not such a reason of the name, as I then approved of, my conceit strongly carrying me to the *Bellocassi*, whom I would fain have setled in the Countrey of *La Beause*, and from them derived that name unto it. But stronger reasons since have perswaded the contrary, so that leaving the *Bellocassi* near *Baieux* in the Dukedome of *Normandie*, we must derive the name of *La Beause*, and *Belsia*, by which it is severally called by the *French* and *Latines*, from the exceeding beautifulnesse of that flourishing Province, that which the *Latines* call *Bellus* in the Masculine, and *Bella* in the Feminine Gender, being by the *French* called *Bell* and *Beau*, as it after followeth.

P. 164. l. 1. *Picardie is divided into the higher, which containeth the Countreys of* Calice *and* Bologne, *&c.*] That *Picardie* is divided into the *higher* and the *lower*, is a Truth well known, though I know not by what negligence of mine they are here misplaced, that being the lower *Picardie* which lyeth next the sea containing the Countreys of *Calais*, and *Bologne*, with the Towns of *Abbeville*, and *Monstreuille*; and that the higher *Picardie*, which lieth more into the Land in which standeth the fair City of *Amiens*, and many other Towns and Territories else where described.

P. 207. l. 30. *Both these were born unto the King by Madam* Gabriele *for her excellent beauty surnamed* La Belle] Madam *Gabriele* is brought in here before her time, and being left out, the sense will run as currently; but more truly thus. *Both these were born unto the King by the Dutchesse of* Beaufort, *a Lady whom the King, &c.*

And

To the Reader.

And for the children which she brought him, though they are named right, yet (as I have been since informed) they are marshalled wrong, *Cæsar* Duke of *Vendosm* being the eldest; not the younger son. And as for Madam *Gabriele*, she was indeed the King best beloved Concubine, one whom he kept not only for his private chamber, but carried publickly along with him in the course of his wars. Insomuch that when the Duke of *Biron* had besieged *Amiens* (being then lately surprized by the *Spaniards* as before was intimated) and was promised succours by the King with all speed that might be; the King at last came forwards with Madam *Gabriele*, and a train of Ladies to attend her: which being noted by the Duke, he cryed aloud with a great deal of scorn and indignation, *Behold the goodly succours which the King hath brought us.* A Lady in great favour, but in greater power, to whom the character was intended, which by mistake, is here given to the Dutchesse of *Beaufort*, though possibly that Dutchesse also might deserve part of it.

When the Liturgie was translated into Latine by Doctor Mocket] Not by him first translated, as the words may intimate, it having been translated into *Latine* in Queen *Elizabeths* time. But that Edition being worn out, and the Book grown scarse, the Doctor gave it a Review, and caused it to be reprinted together with Bishop *Jewels Apologie*, the Articles of the Church of *England*, the Doctrinal points delivered in the Book of *Homilies*, with some other pieces, which being so reviewed and published, gave that contentment to many sober minded men of the *Romish* party which is after mentioned.

P. 243. l. 1.

c   In

To the Reader.

XIV. In the Relation of the second Journey, I finde no mistakes, requiring any Animadversions, as written in a riper judgement, and with greater care, because intended to a person of such known abilities. Nor was I lesse diligent in gathering the materials for it, then carefull that it might be free from mistakes and errors; not only informing my self punctually in all things which concerned these Islands, by persons of most knowledge and experience, in the affairs and state of either, but with mine own hand copying out some of their Records, many whole Letters from the Councel and Court of *England*, the whole body of the *Genevian* Discipline obtruded on both Islands by *Snape* and *Cartwright*, the Canons recommended by King *James* to the Isle of *Jarsey*, besides many papers of lesse bulk and consequence, out of all which I have so enlarged that discourse, that if it be not μὲιζον ἐν ἐλαχίσῳ, it comes very near it. Certain I am that here is more delivered of the affairs of these Islands and on their accompt, then all the Authors which have ever written of them being layed together, can amount unto. For in pursuance of this part, I have took a *full survey* of those Islands which I went to visit, together with such alterations in Religion as have hapned there, both when they were under the Popes of *Rome*, and the Bishops of *Constance*, as since they have discharged themselves from the power of both. The Reformation there being modelled according to the *Genevian* Platform, occasioned me to search into the beginning, growth, and progresse of the *Presbyterian* government with the setling of it in these Islands; together with the whole body of that Discipline as it was there setled,

led, and some short observations on the text thereof, the better to lay open the novelty, absurdity, and ill consequents of it. That done I have declared by what means and motives the Isle of *Jarsey* was made conformable in point of discipline and devotion to the Church of *England*, and given the Reader a full view of that body of Canons which was composed and confirmed for regulating the affairs thereof in sacred matters; and after a short application tending to the advancement of my main design, do conclude the whole.

Lastly, I am to tell the Reader, that though I was chiefly drawn to publish these *Relations* at this present time, for preventing all impressions of them, by any of those false copies which are got abroad; yet I am given to understand, that the first is coming out (if not out already) under the Title of *France painted out to he life*: but *painted* by so short a *Pensil*, as makes it vant much of that *life* which it ought to have. By whom and with what *colour* that piece is *painted* thus without my consent, I may learn hereafter. In the mean time, whether that Piece be printed with, or without my name unto it, I must protest against the wrong, and disclaim the work, as printed by a false and imperfect copy, deficient in some whole Sections, the distribution of the books and parts, not kept according to my minde and method, destitute also of those *Explications* and *Corrections*, which I have given unto it in my last perusal in this general Preface; and finally containing but one half of the work which is here presented. Faults and infirmities I have too many of mine own, *Nam vitiis nemo sine nascitur*, as we know who said; and therefore would not charge my

self

To the Reader.

self with those imperfections, those frequent errors and mistakes which the audaciousnesse of other men may obtrude upon me: which having signified to the Reader, for the detecting of this imposture, and mine own discharge, I recommend the following work to his favourable censure, and both of us to the mercies of the Supreme Judge.

Lacies Court in *Abingdon*,
April 17. 1656.

Books lately printed and reprinted for *Henry Seile*.

Doctor *Heylyn's Cosmography*, in fol.
Twenty Sermons of Dr. *Sanderson's, ad Aulam, &c.* never till now published.
Dr. *Heylyn's* Comment on the Apostles Creed, in fol.
Bishop *Andrewes* holy Devotions, the 4 Edition, in 12.
Martiall in 12. for the use of *Westminster* School.
John Willis his Art of Stenography or Short writing, by spelling Characters, in 8. the 5th Edition: together with the Schoolmaster to the said Art.

SYLLABUS CAPITUM:
OR,
The Contents of the Chapters.

NORMANDIE;
OR,
THE FIRST BOOK.

The Entrance.

THe beginning of our *Journey.* The nature of the *Sea.* A farewell to *England*.

CHAP. I.

NORMANDY in generall; the Name and bounds of it. The condition of the Antient Normans, and of the present. Ortelius

His character of them examined In what they resemble the Inhabitants of Norfolk. The commodities of it, and the Government. pag. 4.

CHAP. II.

Dieppe, the Town, strength and importance of it. The policy of Henry IV. not seconded by his Son. The custome of the English Kings in placing Governours in their Forts. The breaden God there, and strength of the Religion. Our passage from Dieppe to Roven. The Norman Innes, Women, and Manners. The importunity of servants in hosteries. The sawcie familiarity of the attendants. Ad pileum vocare, what it was amongst the Romans. Jus pileorum in the Universities of England, &c. p. 9.

CHAP. III.

ROVEN a neat City; how seated and built; the strength of it. St. Katharines mount. The Church of Nostre dame, &c. The Indecorum of the Papists in the severall and unsutable pictures of the Virgin. The little Chappell of the Capuchins in Boulogne. The House of Parliament. The precedency of the President and the Governor. The Legend of St. Romain, and the priviledge thence arising. The language and religion of the Rhothomagenses, or people of Roven. p. 19.

CHAP. IV.

Our journey between Roven and Pontoyse. The holy man of St. Clare and the Pilgrims thither. My sore eyes. Mante, Pontoyse, Normandy justly taken from King John. The end of this Booke. p. 26.

FRANCE

The Contents.

FRANCE specially so called;
OR,
THE SECOND BOOK.

CHAP. I.

France in what sense so called. The bounds of it. All old Gallia not possessed by the French. Countries follow the name of the most predominant Nation. The condition of the present French not different from that of the old Gaules. That the heavens have a constant power upon the same Climate, though the Inhabitants are changed. The quality of the French in private, at the Church, and at the table. Their language, complements, discourse, &c.
p. 33.

CHAP. II.

The French Women, their persons, prating and conditions. The immodesty of the French Ladies. Kissing not in use among them; and the sinister opinion conceived of the free use of it in England. The innocence and harmelesnesse of it amongst us. The impostures of French Pandars in London, with the scandall thence arising. The peccancy of an old English Doctor. More of the French Women.

The Contents.

Women. Their Marriages, and lives after wedlock, &c. *An Elogie to the* English *Ladies.* p. 41.

CHAP. III.

France *described. The valley of* Montmorancie, *and the Dukes of it.* Mont-martre. *Burials in former times not permitted within the walls. The prosecuting of this discourse by manner of a journall, intermitted for a time. The Town and Church of* St. Denis. *The Legend of him, and his head. Of* Dagobert *and the Leper. The reliques to be seen there. Martyrs how esteemed in* St. Augustine's *time. The Sepulchres of the* French *Kings, and the treasury there. The Kings house of* Madrit. *The Qeen Mothers house at* Ruall, *and fine devices in it.* St. Germains en lay, *another of the Kings houses. The curious painting in it.* Gorramburie *Window: the Garden belonging to it, and the excellency of the Water-works. Boys* St. Vincent de Vicennes, *and the Castle called* Bisester. p. 50.

CHAP. IV.

Paris, *the names and antiquity of it. The situation and greatnesse. The chief strength and Fortifications about it. The streets and buildings. King* James *his laudable care in beautyfying* London. *King* Henry *the fourths intent to fortifie the Town. Why not actuated. The Artifices and wealth of the* Parisians. *The bravery of the Citizens described under the person of a Barber.* p. 64.

CHAP. V.

Paris *divided into four parts. Of the* Fauxburgs *in generall. Of the Pest-house. The Fauxburg and Abbey of* St. Germain. *The Queen Mothers house there. Her purpose never to reside*

The Contents.

in it. The Provost of Merchants, and his authority. The Armes of the Town. The Town-house. The Grand Chastellet. The Arcenall. The place Royall, &c. The Vicounty of Paris. And the Provosts seven daughters. p. 73.

CHAP. VI.

The University of Paris, and Founders of it. Of the Colledges in general. Marriage when permitted to the Rectors of them. The small maintenance allowed the Scholars in the Universities of France. The great Colledge at Tholoza. Of the Colledge of the Sorbonne in particular; that and the House of Parliament, the chief Bulwarks of the French liberty. Of the Polity and Government of the University. The Rector and his precedency; the disordered life of the Scholars there being. An Apologie for Oxford and Cambridge. The priviledges of the Scholars, their degrees, &c. p. 80.

CHAP. VII.

The City of Paris seated in the place of old Lutetia. The Bridges which joyn it to the Town and University. King Henry's Statua. Alexander's injurious policy. The Church and revenues of Nostre Dame. The Holy water there. The original making and virtue of it. The Lamp before the Altar. The heathenishnesse of both customes. Paris best seen from the top of this Church: the great Bell there never rung but in time of Thunder: the baptizing of Bels, the grand Hospital and decency of it. The place Daulphin. The holy Chappel and Reliques there. What the Antients thought of Reliques. The Exchange. The little Chastelet. A transition to the Parlament. p. 90.

d CHAP.

The Contents.

CHAP. VIII.

The Parliament of France when begun; of whom it consisteth. The dignity and esteem of it abroad; made sedentarie at Paris, appropriated to the long robe. The Palais by whom built, and converted to seats of Justice. The seven Chambers of Parliament. The great Chamber. The number and dignity of the Presidents. The Duke of Biron afraid of them. The Kings seat in it. The sitting of the Grand Signeur in the Divano. The authority of this Court in causes of all kinds; and over the affaires of the King. This Court the main pillar of the Liberty of France. La Tournelle, and the Judges of it. The five Chambers of Enquestes severally instituted, and by whom. In what cause it is decisive. The forme of admitting Advocates into the Courts of Parliament. The Chancellour of France and his Authority. The two Courts of Requests, and Masters of them. The vain envy of the English Clergy against the Lawyers. p. 104.

CHAP. IX.

The Kings Palace of the Louure, by whom built: The unsuitablenesse of it. The fine Gallery of the Queen Mother. The long Gallery of Henry IV. His magnanimous intent to have built it into a quadrangle. Henry IV. a great builder. His infinite project upon the Mediterranean and the Ocean. La Salle des Antiques. The French not studious of Antiquities. Burbon house. The Tuilleries, &c. p. 113.

La BEAUSE;

The Contents.

La BEAUSE;
OR,
THE THIRD BOOK.

CHAP. I.

Our Journey towards Orleans, *the Town, Castle, and Battail of* Mont l'hierrie. *Many things imputed to the* English *which they never did.* Lewis *the* 11. *brought not the* French *Kings out of wardship. The town of* Chartroy, *and the mourning Church there. The Countrey of* La Beause *and people of it.* Estampes. *The dancing there. The new art of begging in the Innes of this Countrey.* Angerville. Tury. *The sawcinesse of the* French *Fidlers. Three kindes of Musick amongst the Antient. The French Musick.* p. 121.

CHAP. II.

The Country and site of Orleans *like that of* Worcester. *The Wine of* Orleans. *Presidial Towns in* France, *what they are. The sale of Offices in* France. *The fine walk and pastime of the* Palle Malle. *The Church of St.* Croix *founded by Superstition and a miracle. Defaced by the* Hugonots. *Some things hated only for*

their

The Contents.

their name. The Bishop of Orleans, and his priviledge. The Chappell and Pilgrims of St. Jacques. The form of Masse in St. Croix Censing an Heathenish custome. The great siege of Orleans, raised by Joan the Virgin. The valour of that woman: that she was no witch. An Elogie on her.   p. 131.

CHAP. III.

The study of the Civill Law revived in Europe. The dead time of learning. The Schools of Law in Orleans. The œconomie of them. The Chancellour of Oxford antiently appointed by the Diocesan. Their methode here, and prodigality in bestowing degrees. Orleans a great conflux of strangers. The language there. The Corporation of Germans there. Their house and priviledges. Dutch and Latine. The difference between an Academie and an University.   p. 145.

CHAP. IV.

Orleans not an University till the comming of the Jesuites. Their Colledge there by whom built. The Jesuites no singers. Their laudable and exact method of teaching. Their policies in it. Received not without great difficulty into Paris. Their houses in that university. Their strictnesse unto the rules of their order. Much maliced by the other Priests and Fryers. Why not sent into England with the Queen; and of what order they were that came with her. Our return to Paris.   p. 152.

PICARDIE;

The Contents.

PICARDIE;
OR,
THE FOURTH BOOK.

CHAP. I.

Our return towards England. *More of the* Hugonots *hate unto Crosses. The town of* Luzarch, *and St.* Loupæ. *The Country of* Picardie *and people. The Picts of* Britain *not of this Country. Mr.* Lee Dignicoes *Governour of* Picardie. *The office of Constable what it is in* France. *By whom the place supplied in* England. *The marble table in* France, *and causes there handled.* Clermount, *and the Castle there. The war raised up by the Princes against* D'Ancre. *What his designes might tend to, &c.* p.162.

CHAP. II.

The fair City of Amiens; *and greatnesse of it. The* English *feasted within it; and the error of that action; the Town how built, seated and fortified. The Citadell of it, thought to be impregnable. Not permitted to be viewed. The overmuch opennesse of the* English *in discovering their strength. The watch and form of Government*

The Contents.

in the Town. Amiens a Visdamate: to whom it pertaineth. What that honour is in France. And how many there enjoy it, &c. p. 169.

CHAP. III.

The Church of Nostre Dame in Amiens. The principall Churches in most Cities called by her name. More honour performed to her then to her Saviour. The surpassing beauty of this Church on the outside. The front of it. King Henry the sevenths Chappel at Westminster. The curiousnesse of this Church within. By what means it became to be so. The sumptuous masking closets in it. The excellency of perspective works. Indulgences by whom first founded. The estate of the Bishoprick. p. 175.

CHAP. IV.

Our Journey down the Some, and Company. The Town and Castle of Piquigni, for what famous. Comines censure of the English in matter of Prophecies. A farewell to the Church of Amiens. The Town and Castle of Pont D'Armie. Abbeville how seated; and the Garrison there. No Governour in it but the Major or Provost. The Authors imprudent curiosity; and the curtesie of the Provost to him. The French Post-horses how base and tyred. My preferment to the Trunk-horse. The horse of Philip de Comines. The Town and strength of Monstreuille. The importance of these three Towns to the French border, &c. p. 183.

CHAP.

The Contents.

CHAP. V.

The County of Boulonnois, *and Town of* Boulogne *By whom Enfranchized. The present of Salt Butter. Boulogne divided into two Towns. Procession in the lower Town to divert the Plague. The forme of it. Procession and the Letany by whom brought into the Church. The high Town Garrisoned. The old man of* Boulogne; *and the desperate visit which the Author bestowed upon him. The neglect of the English in leaving open the Havens. The fraternity* De la Charite, *and inconveniency of it. The costly Journey of* Henry VIII. *to* Boulogne. *Sir* Walt. Raleighs *censure of that Prince condemned. The discourtesie of* Charles V. *towards our* Edward VI. *The defence of the house of* Burgundy *how chargeable to the Kings of England.* Boulogne *yeilded back to the French; and on what conditions. The curtesie and cunning of my Host of* Bovillow. p. 192.

FRANCE

The Contents.

FRANCE GENERAL;
OR,
THE FIFTH BOOK.

Describing the Government of the Kingdom generally, in reference to the Court, the Church and the Civill State.

CHAP. I.

A transition to the Government of France in generall The person, age and marriage of King Lewis XIII. *Conjecturall reasons of his being issuelesse.* Iaqueline Countesse *of* Holland *kept from issue by the house of* Burgundy. *The Kings Sisters all marryed; and his alliances by them. His naturall Brethren, and their preferments. His lawfull Brother. The title of Monsieur in* France. *Monsieur as yet unmarried; not like to marry* Montpensiers *daughter. That Lady a fit wife for the Earl of* Soissons. *The difference between him and the Prince of* Conde *for the Crown, in case the line of* Navarre *fail. How the Lords stand affected in the cause. Whether a child may be born in the 11 month. King* Henry IV. *a great lover of fair Ladies.* Monsieur Barradas *the Kings favorite, his birth and offices. The omniregency of the Queen Mother; and the Cardinall of* Richileiu. *The Queen Mother a wise and prudent woman.* p. 204.

CHAP.

The Contents.

CHAP. II.

Two Religions struggling in France, like the two twins in the womb of Rebecca. The comparison between them two, and those in the general. A more particular survey of the Papists Church in France, in Policie, Priviledge and Revenue The complaint of the Clergy to the King. The acknowledgment of the French Church to the Pope meerly titular. The pragmatick sanction, Maxima tua fatuitas, and Conventui Tridentino, severally written to the Pope and Trent Councell. The tedious quarrell about Investitures. Four things propounded by the Parliament to the Jesuites. The French Bishops not to medle with Fryers, their lives and land. The ignorance of the French Priests. The Chanoins Latine in Orleans. The French not hard to be converted, if plausibly humoured. p. 216.

CHAP. III.

The correspondency between the French King and the Pope. This Pope an Omen of the Marriages of France with England. An English Catholicks conceit of it. His Holinesse Nuncio in Paris. A learned Argument to prove the Popes universality. A continuation of the allegory between Jacob and Esau. The Protestants compelled to leave their Forts and Towns. Their present estate and strength. The last War against them justly undertaken; not fairly managed. Their insolencies and disobedience to the Kings command. Their purpose to have themselves a free estate. The war not a war of Religion King James in justice could not assist them more then he did. First forsaken by their own party. Their happinesse before the war. The Court of the edict. A view of them in their Churches. The commendation which the French Papists give to the Church of England. Their Discipline and Ministers, &c. p. 229

CHAP.

The Contents.

CHAP. IV.

The connexion between the Church and Common wealth in generall. A transition to the particular of France. The Government there meerly regall. A mixt forme of Government most commendable. The Kings Patents for Offices. Monopolies above the censure of Parliament. The strange office intended to Mr. Luynes. The Kings gifts and expences. The Chamber of Accounts. France divided into three sorts of people. The Conventûs Ordinum nothing but a title. The inequality of the Nobles and Commons in France. The Kings power how much respected by the Princes. The powerablenesse of that rank. The formall execution done on them. The multitude and confusion of Nobility. King James defended. A censure of the French Heralds. The command of the French Nobles over their Tenants. Their priviledges, gibbets and other Regalia. They conspire with the King to undoe the Commons. p. 246.

CHAP. V.

The base and low estate of the French Paisant. The misery of them under their Lord. The bed of Procrustes. The suppressing of the Subject prejudiciall to a State. The wisdome of Henry VII. The Forces all in the Cavallerie. The cruell impositions laid upon the people by the King. No demain in France. Why the tryall by twelve men can be used only in England. The Gabell of Salt. The Popes licence for wenching. The Gabell of whom refused, and why. The Gascoines impatient of Taxes. The taille, and taillion. The Pancarte or Aides. The vain resistance of those of Paris. The Court of Aides. The manner of gathering the Kings moneys. The Kings revenue. The corruption of the French publicans. King Lewis why called the just. The monies currant in France. The gold of Spain more Catholick then the King. The happinesse of the English Subjects. A congratulation unto England. The conclusion of the first Journey. p. 258.

GUERN-

The Contents.

GUERNZEY and JARSEY;
OR,
THE SIXTH BOOK.

The Entrance.

(1) *The occasion of, &c.* (2) *Introduction to this work.* (3) *The Dedication,* (4) *and Method of the whole. The beginning, continuance of our voyage; with the most remarkable passages which happened in it. The mercenary falsnesse of the* Dutch *exemplified in the dealing of a man of warre.* p. 179.

CHAP. I.

(1) *Of the convenient situation, and* (2) *condition of these Islands in the generall.* (3) Alderney, *and* (4) Serke. (5) *The notable stratagem whereby this latter was recovered from the* French. (6) *Of* Guernzey, (7) *and the smaller Isles neer unto it.* (8) *Our Lady of* Lehu. (9) *The road, and* (10) *the Castle of* Cornet. (11) *The Trade, and* (12) *Priviledges of this people.* (13) *Of* Jarsey, *and* (14) *the strengths about it.* (15) *The Island why so poor and populous.* (16) Gavelkind, *and the nature of it* (17) *The Governours and other the Kings Officers. The* (18) *Politie, and* (19) *administration of justice in both Islands.* (20) *The Assembly of the Three Estates.* (21) *Courts Presidiall in* France *what they are.* (22) *The election of the Justices,* (23) *and the Oath taken at their admission.* (24) *Of their Advocates or Pleaders, and the number of them.* (25) *The number of Attorneys once limited in* England. (26) *A Catalogue of the Governours and Bailiffs of the Isle of* Jarsey. p. 292.

The Contents.

CHAP. II.

(1) *The City and Diocesse of* Constance. (2) *The condition of these Islands under that Government.* (3) *Churches appropriated what they were.* (4) *The* Black Book of Constance. (5) *That called* Dooms day. (6) *The suppression of Priors Aliens.* (7) Priours Dative, *how they differed from the* Conventuals. (8) *The condition of these Churches after the suppression.* (9) *A* Diagram *of the Revenue then allotted to each severall Parish, together with the Ministers and Justices now being.* (10) *What is meant by* Champarte *desarts and French* querrui. (11) *The alteration of Religion in these Islands.* (12) *Persecution here in the days of Queen* Mary. *The Authors indignation at it, expressed in a Poeticall rapture.* (13) *The Islands annexed for ever to the Diocese of* Winton, *and for what reasons.* p. 313.

CHAP. III.

(1.) *The condition of* Geneva *under their Bishop.* (2) *The alteration there both in* Politie, *and* (3) *in Religion.* (4) *The state of that Church before the coming of* Calvin *thither.* (5) *The conception,* (6) *birth, and* (7) *growth of the* New Discipline. (8) *The quality of* Lay-elders. (9) *The different proceedings of* Calvin, (10) *and* Beza *in the propagation of that cause.* (11) *Both of them enemies to the Church of* England. (12) *The first entrance of this Platforme into the Islands.* (13) *A permission of it by the Queen and the Councell in St. Peters and St. Hillaries.* (14) *The letters of the Councell to that purpose.* (15) *The tumults raised in* England *by the brethren.* (16) Snape *and* Cartwright *establish the new Discipline in the rest of the Islands.* p. 327.

CHAP. IV.

The Discipline Ecclesiasticall, *according as it hath been in practise of the Church after the Reformation of the same, by the Ministers, Elders and Deacons of the Isles of* Guernzey, Jarsey, Serke, *and* Alderney; *confirmed by the authority and in the presence of the Governours of the same Isles in a Synod holden in* Guernzey *the 28 of*

The Contents.

of June 1576. *And afterwards revived by the said* Ministers *and* Elders, *and confirmed by the said Governours in a Synod holden also in* Guernzey *the* 11, 12, 13, 14, 15, *and* 17. *days of* October, 1597. p. 338.

CHAP. V.

(1.) *Annotations on the* Discipline. (2) *N. place in it for the Kings Supremacy.* (3) *Their love to Parity, as well in the State as in the Church.* (4) *The covering of the head a sign of liberty.* (5) *The right hand of fellowship.* (6) *Agenda, what it is in the notion of the Church; The intrusion of the Eldership into Domestical affairs.* (7) *Millets case.* (8) *The brethren superstitious in giving names to children.* (9) *Ambling Communions.* (10) *The holy Discipline made a third note of the Church.* (11) *Marriage at certain times prohibited by the* Discipline. (12) *Dead bodies anciently not interred in Cities.* (13) *The Baptism of bels.* (14) *The brethren under pretence of* scandal, *usurp upon the* civil Courts. (15) *The* Discipline *incroacheth on our Church by stealth.* (16) *A caution to the Prelates.* p. 364.

CHAP. VI.

(1) *King* James *how affected to this Platform.* (2) *He confirms the* Discipline *in both Islands.* (3) *And for what reasons.* (4) *Sir* John Peyton *sent Governour into* Jarsey. (5) *His Articles against the Ministers there.* (6) *And the proceedings thereupon* (7) *The distracted estate of the Church and Ministery in that Island,* (8) *They refer themselves unto the King.* (9) *The Inhabitants of* Jarsey *petition for the* English Discipline. (10) *A reference of both parties to the Councell.* (11) *The restitution of the Dean.* (12) *The* Interim *of* Germany *what it was.* (13) *The* Interim *of* Jarsey. (14) *The exceptions of the Ministery against the Book of* Common-prayer. (15) *The establishment of the new* Canons. 378.

CHAP. VII.

The Canons and Constitutions Ecclesiasticall for the Church Discipline of Jarsey; *together with the Kings Letters Patents for the authorising of the same.* p. 390.

CHAP. VIII.

1) *For what cause it pleased his Majesty to begin with* Jarsey. (2) *A representation of such motives whereon the like may be effected in the Isle of* Guernzey. (3) *The indignity done by a Minister hereof to*

The Contents.

the *Church of England.* (4) *The calling of the Ministers in some reformed Churches how defensible.* (5) *The circumstances both of time and persons how ready for an alteration.* (6) *The grievances of the Ministery against the Magistrates.* (7) *Proposals of such means as may be fittest in the managing of this design.* (8) *The submission of the Author and the work unto his Lordship. The conclusion of the whole. Our return to* England. p. 412.

ERRATA.

Besides the errors of the Copy, the Reader is of course to look for some from the Presse, which the hast made for preventing the false impressions, hath more increased then any negligence of the Workman, which the Reader is desired to amend in this manner following.

Page 4. l. 17. r. *Le Main.* p. 5. l. 23. r. *locorum.* p. 7 l. 15. r. *qui.* p. 10. l. 22. r. *the predecessor to the same Henry.* p. 11. l. 17. del. *in.* p. 13. l. 18. r. *pace.* ibid. l. 35. r. *iyred* p. 19. l. 16. r. *Evenlode.* p. 31 l. 8. r. *fourth.* p. 39. l. 25. *& p.* 108. l. 9. r. *interview.* p. 49. l. 3. r. *then.* ibid. l. 4. r. *as at.* ibid. l. 9. r. *her own thoughts.* p. 52. l. 1. r. *Cumye.* p. 60. l. 28. r. *En lay.* ibid. l 35. r. *Troys.* p. 69. l. 26. del. *now.* p. 95. l. 17. r. *born.* p. 56. l. 19 r. *abolished.* p. 99. l. 20. r. *Treasurer* p. 100. l. 1. r. *visible.* p. 121. l. 12. r. *Chastres.* p. 123 l. 1. r. *as much bugged.* ibid. l. 16. r. *I shall hereafter shew you.* p. 125. l. 17. r. *Rou.* p. 127. l. 14. r. *Angerville.* p. 132. l. 12. r. *Angiers.* p. 138 l. 9. r. *kk.* p. 139. l. 15. r. *antient times.* ibid. l. 20. r. *quam disfumigantibus.* p. 143 l. 12. r. *Belbis* p. 147. l. 2. r. *meti.* p. 150. l. 27. r. *many.* p. 153. l. 6. r. *mouth.* ibid. l. 3. r. *same.* p. 158 l. 9. r. *monred.* p. 162. l. 11. r. *Les Dguieres.* p. 163. l. 10. r. *Beuie.* ibid. l. 13. r. *Troyes.* p. 167. l. 27. r. *Ancre.* p. 170. l. 18. r. *adeo.* ibid. l. 19. r. *fidei.* p. 175. l. 9. r. *messing* p. 185 l. 17. del. *do.* ibid. 36. r. *nor* p. 190. l. 3. del *my* ibid. l. 33. r. *Beckes.* p. 199. l. 10. r. *Lorreur.* p. 206. l. 8. r. *Franc.* p. 208. l. 1. r. 60000 p. 211. l. 14. del. *each of.* p. 213 l. 8. to these words *already mentioned,* add, *and Madam Gabrielle the most beloved of all.* p. 220. l. ult. r. *Aix.* p. 222. l. 38 r. *no other* p. 223. l. 7 & l. 31 r. *investiture.* ibid. l. 18. r. *Henry* IV. ibid. l. 34. r. *Henry* I. p. 225. l. 10. r. *sanctio.* ibid. l. 23. r. *lasse.* p. 230. l. 19. r. *fair.* p. 231. l. 3. r. *to come.* ibid. l. 6 r. *greatest act.* cap. 235. l. 3 del. *into* p. 242. l. 4 r. *Le Chastres* p. 244. l. 33. r. *Systematicall.* p. 248. l. 27. r. *passes.* p. 261. l. 24. del. *for.* p. 272. l. 13 r. *brud.* p. 273. l. ult. r. *Vitrey.* p. 274. l. 1. r. *purest metal.* p. 288. l. 28. r. *Peitor.* p. 298. l. e. & 302. l. 16. r. *Armir.* p. 304. l. 33. r. *Suxmay.* p. 306. l. 10. r. *manter.* p. 311. l. 8 del. *a Cross engraved O.* p. 314. l. 9. r. *Vicome.* p. 320. l. 8. r. *painsit.* ibid. l. 2. r. *koner.* p. 323. l. 34. r. *ence.* p. 325. l. 7. r. *sall.* p. 330. l. 36. r. *Bartilier.* p. 337. l. 11. r. *titulary.* ibid. l. 17 r. *Painsset.* p. 354. l. ult. r. *iham they* p. 368 l. 35. r. *propounded* p. 374 l. 10 r. *tellum.* p. 381. l. 14. r. *vacancy* p. 384. l. 3 & l. 31. & p. 386. l. 15. *Misservi.* p. 385. l. 17. r. *Olivier.* ibid. l. 34. r. *St. Martini.* p. 387. l. 31. r. *interes* p. 393 l. 9. r. *cure.* p. 401. l. ult. r. *rols.* p. 417 l. 11. del. *hath* p. 425 l. 3. r. *ceremoniall.* ibid. l. 35. r. *be said unto him.* ibid. l. 38. r. *Bshop.* p. 471. l. 8. r. *clamor.* p. 422. l. 13. r. *charge.* p. 423. l. 30. r. *sic.* ibid. l. 34. r. *scol.*

THE RELATION

Of the FIRST

JOURNEY:

CONTAINING

A SURVEY of the STATE

OF

FRANCE.

TAKING IN

The Description of the principal Provinces, and chief Cities of it; The Temper, Humors and Affections of the people generally; And an exact account of the Publick Government, in reference to the *Court*, the *Church* and the *Civill State*.

By *PET. HEYLYN.*

London, Printed 1656.

A SURVEY OF THE STATE of FRANCE.

NORMANDY;
OR,
THE FIRST BOOK.

The Entrance.

The beginning of our Journey. The nature of the Sea. A farewell to England.

ON Tuesday the 28 of *June*, just at the time when *England* had received the chief beauty of *France*, and the *French* had seen the choise beauties of *England*; we went to Sea in a Bark of *Dover*. The Port we aimed at, *Dieppe* in *Normandy*. The hour three in the afternoon. The winde faire and high, able, had it continued in

B that

that point, to have given us a waftage as speedy as our longings. Two hours before night it came about to the Westward, and the tide also not befriending us, our passage became tedious and troublesome. The next day being dedicated to the glory of God in the memory of St. *Peter*, we took the benefit of the ebb to assist us against the wind; this brought us out of the sight of *England*, and the floud ensuing compelled us to our Anchor.

I had now leasure to see Gods wonders in the deep; wonders indeed to us which had never before seen them: but too much familiarity had made them no other then the Sailers playfellowes. The waves striving by an imbred ambition which should be highest, which formost. Precedencie and supereminencie was equally desired, and each enjoyed it in succession. The winde more covetous in appearance, to play with the water, then disturb it, did only rock the billow, and seemed indeed to dandle the Ocean: you would at another time have thought that the seas had only danced to the winds whistle; or that the Winde straining it self to a Treble, and the Seas by a Diapason, supplying the Base, had tuned a *Caranto* to our ship. For so orderly they rose and fell according to the time and note of the Billow, that her violent agitation might be imagined to be nothing but a nimble Galliard filled with Capers. This nimblenesse of the waves and correspondency of our Bark unto them, was not to all our company alike pleasing: what in me moved only a reverend and awfull pleasure, was to others an occasion of sicknesse, their heads gidie, their joynts enfeebled, their stomachs loathing sustenance, and with great pangs avoiding what they had taken; in their mouths nothing might have been so frequent as that of *Horace*,

Illi robur & æs triplex
Circa pectus erat, qui fragilem truci
Commisit pelago ratem.

Hard was his heart, as brasse, which first did venture
In a weak ship, on the rough Seas to enter.

Whether

Whether it be, that the noisome smels, which arise from the saltnesse and tartnesse of that region of waters, poysoneth the brain; or that the ungoverned and unequall motion of the ship, stirreth and unsetleth the stomach, or both; we may conjecture with the Philosophers, rather then determine. This I am sure of, that the Cabbins and Decks were but as so many Hospitals or Pesthouses filled with diseased persons, whilest I and the Mariners only made good the Hatches. Here did I see the Scalie nation of that Kingdom solace themselves in the brimme of the waters, rejoycing in the sight and warmth of the day; and yet spouting from their mouths such quantity of waters, as if they purposed to quench that fire which gave it. They danced about our Vessell, as if it had been a moving May-pole; and that with such delightfull *decorum*, that you never saw a measure better troden with lesse art. And now I know not what wave bigger then the rest tossed up our ship so high, that I once more saw the coast of *England*. An object which took such hold on my senses, that I forgot that harmlesse company which sported below me, to bestow on my dearest mother, this (and for ought I could assure my self, my last) farewell.

England *adiew, thy most unworthy sonne*
Leaves thee, and grieves to see what he hath done.
What he hath done, in leaving thee the best
Of mothers, and more glorious then the rest
Thy sister-nations. Had'st thou been unkind;
Yet might he trust thee safer then the wind.
Had'st thou been weak; yet far more strength in thee,
Then in two inches of a sinking tree.
Had'st thou been cruell; yet thy angry face
Hath more love in it, then the Seas imbrace.
Suppose thee poor; his zeal and love the lesse,
Thus to forsake his Mother in distresse.
But thou art none of these, no want in thee;
Only a needlesse curiositie
Hath made him leap thy ditch. O! let him have
Thy blessing in his Voyage: and hee'l crave

The Gods to thunder wrath on his neglect,
When he performs not thee all due respect;
That Nemesis her scourge on him would pluck,
When he forgets those breasts which gave him suck:
That Nature would dissolve and turn him earth,
If thou beest not remembred in his mirth.
May he be cast from mankind, if he shame
To make profession of his mothers name.
Rest then assur'd in this, though sometimes hee
Conceal, perhaps, his faith, he will not thee.

Chap. I.

NORMANDY, *in generall; the Name and bounds of it. The condition of the Antient Normans, and of the present.* Ortelius *character of them examined. In what they resemble the Inhabitants of* Norfolk. *The commodities of it, and the Government.*

The next ebb brought us in sight of the Sea-coast of *Normandy*, a shore so evenly compassed and levelled, that it seemeth the work of Art, not Nature; the Rock all the way of an equall height, rising from the bottom to the top in a perpendicular, and withall so smooth and polished, that if you dare believe it the work of Nature, you must also think, that Nature wrought it by the line, and shewed an art in it above the imitation of an Artist. This wall is the Northern bound of this Province; the South parts of it being confined with *Le Mainde la Beausse*, and *L' Isle de France*; on the East it is divided from *Picardie* by the River of *Some*; and on the North it is bounded with the Ocean, and the little River *Cremon*, which severeth it from a corner of of *Britain*. It extendeth in length from the beginning of the 19 degree of longitude, to the middle of the 23. *viz.* from the Cape of St. *Saviour* West, to the Port-town of St *Valerie* East. For breadth, it lyeth partly in the 49, partly in the 50 degree of Latitude; so that reckoning 60 miles to a degree, we shall finde it to contain 270 *English* miles in length; and 60 *English* miles in breadth, where it is narrowest.

Amongst the Antients it was accounted a part of *Gallia Celtica*; the name *Neustria*. This new title it got by receiving into it a new Nation. A people which had so terribly spoyled the Maritime Coasts of *England*, *France*, and *Belgium*, that, *A furore Normannorum*, was inserted into the Letanie. Originally they were of *Norway*, their name importeth it. *Anno* 800, or thereabouts, they began first to be accounted one of the Plagues of *Europe*: 900 they seated themselves in *France* by the permission of *Charles* the *Balde*, and the valor of *Rollo* their Captain. Before this, they had made themselves masters of *Ireland*, though they long held it not, and *anno* 1067 they added to the glory of their name by the conquest of *England*: You would think them a people, not only born to the warres, but to victory. But, *Ut frugum semina mutato solo degenerant, sic illa genuina feritas eorum, amœnitate mollita est*; *Florus* spake it of the *Gaules* removed into *Asia*: it is applyable to the *Norwegians* transplanted into *Gallia*: yet fell they not suddenly, and at once into that want of courage which now possesseth them. During the time they continued *English*, they attempted the Kingdom of *Naples* and *Antioch*, with a fortune answerable to their valour. Being once oppressed by the *French*, and inslaved under that *Monarchie*; they grew presently crest-fain; and at once lost both their spirits, and their liberty.

The present *Norman* then, is but the corruption of the Antient; the heir of his name, and perhaps his possessions, but neither of his strength, nor his manhood. *Bondage*, and a fruitfull soil, hath so emasculated them, that it is a lost labour to look for *Normans* even in *Normandy*. There remaineth nothing almost in them of their progenitours, but the remainders of two qualities, and those also degenerated, if not bastards; a *penurious pride*, and an *ungoverned doggednesse*. Neither of them become their fortune, or their habite; yet to these they are constant. Finally, view him in his rags and dejected countenance, and you would swear it impossible that these snakes should be the descendents of those brave *Heroes*, which so often triumphed over both Religions, foiling the *Saracens*, and vanquishing the *Christians*.

But, perchance, their courage is evaporated into wit, and then the change is made for the better. *Ortelius* would seem to perswade us to this conceit of them; and well might he do it, if his words were Oracles: *Le gens* (saith he, speaking of this Nation) *sont des plus accorts & subtils, d' esprit de la Gaule*. A character, for which the *French* will little thank him; who (if he speak truth) must in matter of discretion give precedency to their Vassals. But as *Imbalt* a *French* leader said of the *Florentines* in the fifth book of *Guicciardine*, *Non sapeva dove consistesse lingegne tanto celebrate de Fiorentini*; so may I of the *Normans*. For my part I could never yet find, where that great wit of theirs lay. Certain it is, that as the *French* in generall, are termed the Kings Asses, so may these men peculiarly be called the *Asses of the French*, or the *veriest Asses of the rest*. For what with the unproportionable rents they pay to their Lords on the one side, and the immeasurable taxes laid upon them by the King on the other, they are kept in such a perpetuated course of drudgery, that there is no place for wit or wisdome left amongst them. Liberty is the Mother and the Nurse of those two qualities; and therefore the *Romans* (not unhappily) expressed both the conditions of a *Freeman*, and a *discreet and modest personage*, by this own word *Ingenuus*. Why the *French* King should lay a greater burden on the backs of this Nation, then their fellowes, I cannot determine. Perhaps it is, because they have been twice conquered by them, once from King *John*, and again from *Henry* VI. and therefore undergo a double servitude. 'It may be, to abate their naturall pride and stubbornnesse. Likely also it is, that being a revolting people, and apt to an apostasie from their allegiance, they may by this meanes be kept impoverished, and by consequence disabled

from

from such practises. This a *French* Gentleman of good understanding told me, that it was generally conceited in *France*, that the *Normans* would suddenly and unanimously betray their Countrey to the *English*, were the King a *Catholick*.

—— But there is yet a further cause of their beggerlinesse and poverty, which is their litigiousnesse and frequent going to law (as we call it.) *Ortelius*, however he failed in the first part of their character, in the conclusion of it hath done them justice. *Mais en generall* (saith he) *ils sont sçavans au possible en proces & plaideries*. They are prety well versed in the quirks of the Law, and have wit more then enough to wrangle. In this they agree exactly well with the Inhabitants of our Country of *Norfolk*: *ex infima plebe non pauci reperiuntur* (saith Mr. *Camden*) *quin si nihil litium sit, lites tamen ex ipsis juris apicibus serere calleant*. They are prety fellowes to finde out quirks in Law, and to it they will whatsoever it cost them. Mr. *Camden* spake not this at randome or by the guesse. For besides what my self observed in them at my being once amongst them, in a Colledge progresse, I have heard that there have been no lesse then 340 *Nisi prius* tryed there at one Assizes. The reason of this likenesse between the two Nations, I conjecture to be the resemblance of the site, and soil; both lie upon the Sea with a long and a spacious Coast; both enjoy a Countrey *Champain*, little swelled with hils, and for the most part of a light and sandy mould. To proceed to no more particulars, if there be any difference between the two Provinces, it is only this, that the Countrey of *Normandy*, and the people of *Norfolk*, are somewhat the richer.

For, indeed, the Countrey of *Normandie* is enriched with a fat and liking soil; such an one, *Quæ demum votis avari agricolæ respondet*, which may satisfie the expectation of the Husbandman, were it never so exorbitant. In my life I never saw Corn-fields more large and lovely, extended in an equall levell almost as far as eye can reach. The Wheat (for I saw little Barley) of a fair length in the stalke, and so heavy in the ear, that it is even bended double. You would think the grain had a desire to kisse the earth its mother, or that it purposed by making it self away into the ground, to save the Plough-man his next years labour. Thick it groweth, and so perfectly void of weeds, that no garden can be imagined to be kept cleaner by Art, then these fields are by Nature. Pasture ground it hath little, and lesse Meddow, yet sufficient to nourish those few Cattel they have in it. In all the way between *Dieppe* and *Pontoyse*, I saw but two flocks of Sheep, and them not above 40 in a flock. Kine they have in some measure, but not fat nor large, without these there were no living for them. The Nobles eat the flesh, whilst the Farmer feeds on Butter and Cheese, and that but sparingly. But the miserable estates of the *Norman paisant*, we will defer till another opportunity. Swine also they have in prety number, and some Pullen in their back sides; but of neither an excesse. The principall River of it is *Seine*, of which more hereafter; and besides this I saw two rivulets *Rebec* and *Renelle*.

In matter of Civill Government, this Countrey is directed by the court of *Parliament* established at *Roven*. For matters Military, it hath an Officer like the Lieutenant of our shires in *England*, the Governor they call him. The present Governor is Mr. *Le duc de Longueville*, to whom the charge of this Province was committed by the present King *Lewis* XIII. *anno* 1619. The Lawes by which they are governed are the Civill or Imperiall, augmented by some Customes of the *French*, and others more particular which are the *Norman*. One of the principal'st is in matters of inheritance; the *French* custome giving to all the Sons an equality in the estate, which we in *England* call *Gavelkind*; the *Norman* dividing the estate into three parts, and thereof allotting two unto the eldest brother, and a third to be divided among the others. A law which the *French* count not just: the younger brothers of *England* would think the contrary. To conclude this generall discourse of the *Normans*; I dare say it is as happy a Country as most in *Europe*, were it subject to the same Kings, and governed by the same Laws, which it gave unto *England*.

CHAP.

Chap. II.

Dieppe, the Town, strength and importance of it. The policy of Henry IV. *not seconded by his Son. The custome of the* English *Kings in placing Governours in their Forts. The breaden God there, and strength of the Religion. Our passage from* Dieppe *to* Roven. *The Norman Innes, Women, and Manners. The importunity of servants in hosteries. The sawcie familiarity of the attendants.* Ad pileum vocare, *what it was amongst the* Romans. Jus pileorum *in the Universities of* England, &c.

JUne the 30. at 6 of the clock in the morning, we landed at *Dieppe*, one of the Haven-towns of *Normandy*; seated on an arme of the Sea, between two hils, which embrace it in the nature of a Bay. This secureth the Haven from the violence of the weather, and is a great strength to the Town against the attempts of any forces which should assault it by Sea. The Town lying within these mountains, almost a quarter of a mile up the channell. The Town it self is not uncomely, the streets large and wel paved, the houses of an indifferent height, and built upright without any jettings out of one part over the other. The Fortifications, they say, (for we were not permitted to see them) are very good and modern; without stone, within earth: on the top of the hill, a Castle finely seated, both to defend the Town, and on occasions to command it. The Garrison consisteth of 60 men, in pay no more, but when need requireth, the Captain hath authority to arme the Inhabitants. The present Governour is the Duke of *Langueville*, who also is the Governour of the province, entrusted with both those charges by *Lewis* XIII. *anno* 1619. An action in which he swarved somewhat from the example of his father; who never committed the military command of a Countrey (which is the office of the Governour) and the custody of a Town of war or a Fortresse, unto one man. The Duke of *Biron* might hope as great a curtesie from that King, as the most deserving of his Subjects. He had stuck close to him in all his adversities, received many an honourable scar in his service; and indeed, was both *Fabius* and *Scipio*, the Sword and Buckler of the *French* empire. In a word, he might have said to this *Henry*, what *Silius* in *Tacitus* did to *Tiberius*, *Suum militem in obsequio mansisse, cum alii ad seditiones prolaberentur; neque duraturum Tiberii imperium, si iis quoque legionibus cupido novandi fuisset*: yet when he became *petitioner* to the King for the Citadell of *Burg*, seated on the confines of his government of *Bourgogne*, the King denied it. The reason was, because Governours of Provinces which command in chief, *ought not to have the command of Places and Fortresses within their Government*. There was also another reason & more enforcing, which was, that the Petitioner was suspected to hold intelligence with the Duke of *Savoy*, whose Town it was. The same *Henry*, though he loved the Duke of *Espernon*, even to the envy of the Court; yet even to him also he used the same caution. Therefore when he had made him Governor of *Xaintoigne* and *Angoulmois*, he put also into his hands the Towns of *Metz* and *Boulogne*; places so remote from the seat of his Government, and so distant one from another, that they did rather distract his power, then increase it.

The Kings of *England* have been well, and for a long time versed in this maxime of estate. Let *Kent* be one of our examples, and *Hampshire* the other. In *Kent* at this time the Lieutenant (or as the *French* would call him, the Governor) is the Earl of *Mountgomerie*; yet is *Dover* Castle in the hands of the Duke of *Buckingham*; and that of *Quinborough* in the custody of Sir *Edward Hobby*: of which the one commandeth the Sea, and the other the Thames, and the Medway. In *Hampshire*, the Lieutenant is the Earl of *South-Hampton*: but the government of the Town and Garrison of *Portesmouth*, is entrusted to the Earl of *Pembroke*: neither is
there

there any of the least Sconces or Blockhouses, on the shore-side of that Countrey, which is commanded by the *Lieutenant.*

But King *Lewis* now reigning in *France*, minded not his Fathers action; when at the same time also he made his confident Mr. *Luines* Governor of *Picardie*, and of the Town and Citadell of *Amiens.* The time ensuing gave him a sight of this State-breach. For when the Dukes of *Espernon, Vendosme, Longueville, Mayenne* and *Nemours,* the Count of *Soisons* and others, sided with the Queen Mother against the King; the Duke of *Longueville* strengthned this *Dieppe*; and had not Peace suddenly followed, would have made it good, maugre the Kings forces. A Town it is of great importance, King *Henry* IV. using it as his *Asylum* or City of refuge, when the league was hottest against him. For, had he been further distressed, from hence might he have made an escape into *England*; and in at this door was the entance made for those *English* forces which gave him the first step to his throne. The Town hath been pillaged and taken by our *Richard* the first, in his war against *Philip Augustus*; and in the declining of our affaires in *France*, it was nine monthes together besieged by the Duke of *York*, but with that successe, which commonly attendeth a falling *Empire.* The number of the Inhabitants is about 30000, whereof 9000 and upwards are of the Reformation, and are allowed them for the exercise of their religion, the Church of *Arques*, a Village some two miles distant; the remainders are Papists. In this Town I met with the first *Idolatry*, which ever I yet saw, more then in my Books. *Quos antea audiebam, hodie vidi Deos*, as a barbarous *German* in *Vellejus* said to *Tiberius.* The Gods of *Rome*, which before I only heard of, I now saw, and might have worshipped. It was the *Hoaste*, as they call it, or the *Sacrament reserved*, carryed by a couple of *Priests* under a *Canopie*, ushered by two or three torches, and attended by a company of boyes and old people which had no other imployment. Before it went a Bell continually tinkling, at the sound whereof all such as are in their houses, being warned that then their God goeth by them, make some shew of reverence; those which meet it in the street, with bended knees

knees and elevated hands doing it honour. The *Protestants*, of this Bell make an use more religious, and use it as a warning or watch-peal to avoid that street through which they hear it coming. This invention of the Bell hath somewhat in it of *Turcisme*, it being the custome there at their *Canonicall* houres, when they hear the criers bawling in the steeples, to fall prostrate on the ground wheresoever they are and kisse it thrice, so doing their devotions to *Mahomet*. The carrying of it about the streets hath, no question, in it a touch of the *Jew*, this ceremony being borrowed from that of carrying about the Arke on the shoulders of the *Levites*. The other main part of it which is the *Adoration*, is derived from the *Heathens*, there never being a people but they, which afforded divine honors to things inanimate. But the people indeed, I cannot blame for this Idolatrous devotion, their consciences being perswaded, that what they see passe by them, is the very body of their Saviour. For my part, could the like belief possesse my understanding, I could meet it with greater reverence, then their Church can enjoyn me. The Priests and Doctors of the people are to be condemned only, who impose and inforce this sin upon their hearers. And doubtlesse there is a reward which attendeth them for it. Of standing it is so young, that I never met with it before the year 1115. Then did Pope *Innocent* ordain in a Councell holden at *Rome*, that there should be a *Pix* made to cover the Bread, and a Bell bought to be rung before it. The Adoration of it was enjoyned by Pope *Honorius*, anno 1226. both afterward encreased by the new solemn feast of *Corpus Christi* day; by Pope *Urban* the IV. anno 1264. and confirmed for ever with multitudes of pardons, in the Councell of *Vienna*, by *Clement* the V. anno 1310. Such a punie is this great God of the Romans. *Lactantius* in his first Book of *Institutions* against the *Gentiles*, taxeth the wise men of those times of infinite ridiculousnesse, who worshipped *Jupiter* as a God, *Cùm eundem tamen Saturno & Rhea genitum confiterentur*, Since themselves so perfectly knew his originall. As much I marvell at the impudencie of the *Romish* Clergie, who will needs impose a new God upon their people, being so well acquainted with his cradle. It

CHAP. II. *a Journey into France.* 13

It is now time to go on in our journey to *Roven.* The Cart stayeth, and it is fit we were in it. Horses we could get none for money, and for love we did not expect them. We are now mounted in our Chariot, for so we must call it. An *English* man would have thought it a plain Cart, and if it needs will have the honour of being a Chariot, let it; sure I am it was never ordained for triumph. At one end was fastned three carcasses of horses, or three bodies which had once been horses, and now were worne to dead Images; had the *Statua* of a man been placed on any one of them, it might have been hanged up at an Inne door, to represent St. *George* on horseback, so livelesse they were, and as little moving; yet at last they began to crawle, for go they could not. This converted me from my former Heresie, and made me apprehend life in them: but it was so little, that it seemed only enough to carry them to the next pack of houndes. Thus accommodated we bid farewell to *Dieppe,* and proceeded with a space so slow, that me thought our journey unto *Roven* would prove a most perfect embleme of the motion of the ninth sphere, which is 49000 years in finishing. But this was not our greatest misery. The rain fell in us through our tilt, which for the many holes in it, one would have thought to have been a net. The durt brake plentifully in upon us, through the rails of our Chariot: and the unequall and ill proportioned pase of it, startled almost every bone of us. I protest, I marvell how a *French* man durst adventure in it. Thus endured we all the diseases of a journey, and the danger of three severall deaths, drowning, choaking with the mire, and breaking on the wheel; besides a fear of being famished before we came to our Inne, which was six *French* miles from us. The mad Duke in the Play, which undertook to drive two snailes from *Millaine* to *Musco,* without staffe, whip or goade; and in a braverie dared all the world to match him for an experiment: would here have had matter to have tryed his patience.

On the left hand we saw *Arques,* once famous for a siege laid about it by our *Richard* the first; but raised spredily by the *French.* It is now (as before I told you) the Parish

C 3 Church

Church of the *Dieppe* Protestants. Their Preachers Mr. *Corteau*, and Mr. *Mondenis*, who have each of them an yearly stipend of 40 l. or thereabouts; a poor pay, if the faithfull discharge of that duty were not a reward unto it self, above the value of gold and silver. To instance in none of those beggerly Villages we past through, we came at last unto *Tostes*, the place destinated to be our lodging; a Town somewhat like the worser sort of Market-towns in *England*. There our *Charetier* brought us to the ruines of an house, an Ale-house I should scarce have thought it, and yet in spight of my teeth it must be an Inne, yea and that an honorable one, as *Don Quixotes* hoste told him. Despair of finding there either Bedding or Victuals, made me just like the fellow at the gallowes, who when he might have been reprieved on condition he would marry a wench which there sued for him, having viewed her well, cryed to the hangman *to drive on his Cart*. The truth is, *I' eschappay la tomnere et rencheus en l' eschair*, according to the *French* proverb; I fell out of the frying-pan into the fire. One of the house (a ragged fellow I am sure he was, and so most likely to live there) brought us to a room somewhat of kindred to a Charnel-house, as dark and as dampish. I confesse it was paved with brick at the bottom, and had towards the Orchards a prety hole, which in former times had been a window, but now the glasse was all vanished. By the little light which came in at that hole, I first perceived that I was not in *England*. There stood in this Chamber three beds, if at the least it be lawfull so to call them; the foundation of them was of straw, so infinitely thronged together, that the wool-packs which our *Judges* sit on in the Parliament, were melted butter to them: upon this lay a medley of flocks and feathers sowed up together in a large bag; (for I am confident it was not a tick) but so ill ordered, that the knobs stuck out on each side, like a crab-tree cudgell. He had need to have flesh enough that lyeth on one of them, otherwise the second night would wear out his bones. The sheets which they brought us, were so course, that in my conscience no Mariner would vouchsafe to use them for a sail; and the coverlet so bare, that if a man would undertake to reckon the threads, he need not misse

one

one of the number. The napperie of the Table was sutable to the bedding, so foul and dirty, that I durst not conceive it had been washed above once; and yet the poor clothes looked as briskly as if it had been promised for the whole year ensuing, to scape many a scouring. The napkins were fit companions for the clothes, *Unum si noveris, omnes nosti*. By my description of this *Inne*, you may guesse at the rest of *France*; not altogether so wretched, yet is the alteration almost insensible.

Let us now walke into the *Kitching*, and observe their provision. And here we found a most terrible execution committed on the person of a pullet; my Hostesse (cruell woman) had cut the throat of it, and without plucking off the feathers, tore it into pieces with her hands, and after took away skin and feathers together, just as we strip Rabbets in *England*: this done, it was clapped into a pan, and fryed into a supper. In other places where we could get meat for the Spitte, it useth to be presently broached, and laid perpendicularly over the fire; three turns at the most dispatcheth it, and bringeth it to the Table, rather scorched then roasted. I say where we could get it, for in these rascally Innes, you cannot have what you would, but what you may; and that also not of the cheapest. At *Pontoyse* we met with a Rabbet, and we thought we had found a great purchase; larded it was, as all meat is in the Countrey, otherwise it is so lean, it would never endure roasting. In the eating it proved so tough, that I could not be perswaded, that it was any more then three removes from that Rabbet which was in the Ark. The price half a Crown *English*. My companions thought it over deer, to me it seemed very reasonable; for certainly the grasse which fed it, was worth more then thrice the money. But to return to *Tostes*.

And it it time; you might, perchance, else have lost the sight of mine Hostesse, and her daughters. You would have sworne at the first blush, they had been of a bloud; and it had been great pity had it been otherwise. The salutation of *Horace*, *Omatre pulchra filia pulchrior*, was never so unseasonable as here. Not to honour them with a further character

character, let it suffice that their persons kept so excellent a *decorum* with the house and furniture, that one could not possible make use of *Tullies Quàm dispari dominaris domina*. But this is not their luck only. The women not of *Normandy* alone, but generally of all *France*, are forced to be contented with a little beauty; and she which with us is reckoned with the vulgar, would amongst them be taken for a Princesse. But of the *French* women, more when we have taken a view of the Dames of *Paris*; now only somewhat of their habit and condition. Their habit in which they differ from the rest of *France*, is the attire of the head, which hangeth down their backs in the fashion of a Vail. In *Roven* and the greater Cities, it is made of linen, pure and decent; here, and in the Villages, it cannot possible be any thing else then an old dish-clout turned out of service, or the corner of a tablecloth reserved from washing. Their best condition is not alwayes visible. They shew it only in the mornings, or when you are ready to depart, and that is their begging; you shall have about you such a throng of those ill-faces, and every one whining out this *dity, Pour les servants*, that one might with greater ease distribute a dole at a rich mans Funerall, then give them a penny. Had you a purpose to give them unasked, their importunity will prevent your speediest bounty. After all this impudent begging, their ambition reacheth no higher then a *Sol*; he that giveth more out-biddeth their expectation, and shall be counted a spend-thrift.

But the principall ornaments of these Innes, are the men-servants, the raggedest regiment that ever I yet looked upon. Such a thing as a *Chamberlaine* was never heard of amongst them, and good clothes are as little known as he. By the habit of his attendants, a man would think himself in a Gaol; their clothes either full of patches, or open to the skin. Bid one of them wipe your boots, he presently hath recourse to the curtains, with those he will perhaps rub over one side, and leave the other to be made clean by the guest. It is enough for him, that he hath written the coppy. They wait alwayes with their hats on their heads, and so also do servants before their masters: attending bare-headed, is as much out

of

of fashion there, as in *Turkey*: of all *French* fashions, in my opinion, the most unfitting and unseeming. Time and much use reconciled me to many other things, which at the first were offensive; to this unreverent custome, I returned an enemy. Neither can I see how it can choose but stomach the most patient, to see the worthyest signe of liberty usurped and profaned by the basest of slaves. For seeing that the *French paisantrie*, are such infinite slaves unto their Lords and Princes, it cannot be, but that those which are their servants, must be one degree at the least, below the lowest condition.

Certainly among the antients, this *promiscuous covering* of the head, was never heard of. It was with them the chief sign of freedome, as is well known to those which are conversant with Antiquity. The *Lacenes* a people of *Peloponnesus*, after they had obtained to be made free denizens of *Lacedemon*, in signe of their new-gotten liberty, would never go into the battail *nisi pileati*, but with their hats on. Amongst the *Africans*, as it is written in *Alexander ab Alexandro*, the placing of a hat on the top of a spear, was used as a token to incite the people to their liberty, which had been oppressed by Tyrants; *Per pileum in hasta prepositum, ad libertatem proclamari*. But amongst the *Romans*, we have more variety. The taking off of the hat of *Tarquinius Priscus* by an Eagle, and the putting of it on again, occasioned the *Augur* to prophesie unto him the Kingdom, which fell out accordingly. In their sword playes, when one of the Gladiators had with credit slain his adversary; they would sometimes honour him with a Palm, sometimes with the Hat. Of these the last was the worthyer, the Palm only honouring the Victor, this also enfranchizing the receiver; therefore conferred commonly on him which had killed most men in the Theatres. Hence the complaints of *Tertullian, lib. de Spectaculis, cap. 21. Qui insigniori cuiquam homicidæ leonem poscit, idem gladiatori atroci rudem petat (rudis* was an other token of enfranchisement*) & pileum premium conferat*. In their common *Forum*, or *Guildhall*, when they purposed to manumit any of their servants; their custome also was, after the *Lictor* or *Sergeant* had registred the name of the party manumitted,

D

mitted, to shave his head and give him a cap, whence according to *Rosinus, ad pileum vocare,* is to set one at liberty.

Erasmus in his *Chiliades,* maketh the Hat to be the signe of some eminent worth in him that weareth it; *Pileus* (saith he) *insigne spectatæ virtutis.* On this he conjectureth that the putting on of caps on the heads of such as are created *Doctors* or *Masters,* had its originall. In the Universities of *England* this custome is still in force; the putting on of the cap being never performed, but in the solemn *Comitia,* and in the presence of all such as are either auditors or spectators of that dayes exercise. When I was *Regent,* the whole house of *Congregation* joyned together in a Petition to the Earl of *Pembroke,* to restore unto us the *jus pileorum,* the licence of putting on our Caps, at our publick meetings; which priviledge, time and the tyranny of the *Vicechancellors,* had taken from us. Among other motives, we used the solemn form of creating a Master in the Acts, by putting on his cap: and that that signe of liberty might distinguish us which were the *Regents,* from those boyes which we were to govern: which request he graciously granted. But this *French* sawcinesse hath drawn me out of my way. An impudent familiarity, which I confesse did much offend me: and to which I still professe my self an open enemy. Though *Jack* speak *French,* I cannot endure *Jack* should be a *Gentleman.*

CHAP.

Chap. III.

ROVEN *a neat City; how seated and built; the strength of it. St.* Katharines *mount. The Church of* Nostre dame, &c. *The indecorum of the Papists in the severall and unsuitable pictures of the* Virgin. *The little Chappell of the* Capuchins *in* Boulogne. *The House of* Parliament. *The precedencie of the* President *and the* Governor. *The Legend of St.* Romain, *and the priviledge thence arising. The language and religion of the* Rhothomagenses, *or people of* Roven.

July the first we set on for *Roven*. In 10 hours our Cart dragged us thither, the whole journey being in all six leagues *French*: admirable speed! About three of the clock in the afternoon we had a sight of the Town, daintily seated in a valley on the River *Seine*. I know not any Town better situate, *Oxford* excepted, which indeed it much resembleth; I mean not in bignesse, but situation: It standeth on all sides evironed with mountains, the North excepted, and hath a large and pleasant walk of meadowes by the river side, to the South-east-ward; as *Oxford* hath towards *Eveley*. It is seated on the principall river of *France*, distant from the *Metropolis* of that Country 50 miles *English*, or thereabouts; as *Oxford* on the *Thames*, and from *London*. Watered also it is with two small rivulets, *Robec* and *Renelle*, as the other with *Charwell* and *Eventede*. The difference is, that *Oxford* is seated somewhat higher on the swelling of an hill, and a little more removed from those mountains which environ it: and that the rivers which run through some part of *Roven*, do only wash the precincts of the other. The buildings are in some places wood, in some stone, in other both; the houses without juttings or

D 2 overlets,

overlets, four ftories high, and in the front not very beautifull. The moſt promiſing houſe which mine eye met with, was that of Mr. *Boniface*, who being of obſcure parents, and having raiſed himſelf a fortune in the wars, againſt the *League*, here built a receptacle for his age. It is faſhioned after the manner of new buildings in *London*, compoſed all of dainty white ſtone, ſquare and poliſhed. On the partition between the firſt ſtory and the ſecond, it hath theſe words engraven, *Vi & Virtute. Martis opus. Tentanda via. Amore & armis*: a motto ſutable to his riſing.

The other buildings of note are the bridge (for I as yet omit the Houſe of Parliament and the Churches) and the Town wall by it. The bridge, whilſt it was all ſtanding, was thought to have been the faireſt and ſtrongeſt piece of that kinde in all *France*. It conſiſteth of twelve arches, large and high: there now remain but ſeven of them, the reſt being broken down by the *Engliſh* in the falling of their affairs in *France*, the better to make good the Town againſt the *French*. The river is here about the breadth of the *Thames* at *Fulham*. Between the River and the Town wall, is the Exchange or meeting place of the Merchants, paved with broad and even peble. In breadth up to the wall-ward 30 yards, in length 100; a fine walke in fair weather. All along the banke ſide lay the ſhips, which by reaſon of the broken bridge come up thither, and on occaſions higher: a good turn for *Paris*. The wall for the length of 100 yards, is as ſtraight as one may lay a line, of a juſt height, and compoſed of ſquare and excellent ſtones, ſo cunningly laid, that I never ſaw the ſides of a Noble mans houſe built more handſomely. But it is not only the beauty of the wall which *Roven* delighteth in, there muſt ſomewhat alſo be expected of ſtrength: to which purpoſe it might ſerve indifferently well, were there ſome addition of earth within it. It is well helped on the outſide by the breadth and depth of the ditches; but more by St. *Katherines* fort ſeated on a hill at the Eaſt ſide of it. A Fort, which were it ſtrengthned according to the modern art of fortifying, would much aſſure the Town, and make it at once, both a ſlave and a commander. The *Marſhall D' Ancre*, when he was *Lieutenant* here

for

for the Queen mother, began to fortifie this mountain, *Quilleboeufe*, and other places of importance; but upon his death they were all rased: what were his projects in it, they know best which were acquainted with his ambition. Certainly the jars which he had sowen amongst the Princes one with the other, and between them and the King: shew that they were not intended for nothing.

There are in *Roven* 32 Parish Churches, besides those which belong to Abbies and Religious houses, of which the most beautifull is that of St. *Audoin* or *Owen*, once Archbishop of this City. The seat and Church of the Archbishop is that of *Nostre dame*, a building far more gorgeous in the outside, then within. It presents it self to you with a very gracious and majesticall front, decked with most curious imagery, and adorned with three stately Towers. The first *La tur de beurre* (because it was built with that money which was raised by Cardinall D'. *Amboyse*, for granting a dispensation to eat butter in the Lent): and a third built over the porch or great door, wherein is the great Bell so much talked of. Within it is but plain and ordinary, such as common Cathedrall Churches usually are, so big, so fashioned. Behinde the high Altar, at a pillar on the left had, is the remainder of the Duke of *Bedfords* Tomb: which for ought I could discerne, was nothing but an *Epitaph* some three yards high in the pillar. I saw nothing in it, which might move the envie of any Courtier to have it defaced, unlesse it were the title of *Regent du Royaume de France*, which is the least he merited.

Somewhat Eastward, beyond this is our Ladies Chappell, a prety neat piece, and daintily set out. There standeth on the top of the screen, the image of the Virgin her self, between two Angels. They have attired her in a red mantle, laced with two gold laces, a handsome ruffe about her neck, a vail of fine lawne hanging down her back, and (to shew that she was the Queen of heaven) a crown upon her head: in her left arme she holds her son in his side-coat, a black hat and a golden hatband. A jolly plump Ladie she seemeth to be, of a flaxen hair, a ruddy lip, and a chearefull complexion.

Twere well the Painters would agree about limming of her, otherwise we are likely to have almost as many Ladies, as Churches. At *Nostre dame* in *Paris*, she is taught us to be browne, and seemeth somewhat inclining to melancholie. I speak not of her different habit, for I envie not her changes of apparell. On'y I could not but observe how those of St. Se-pulchres Church, *en la Rue* St. *Dennis*, have placed her on the top of their Skreen, in a Coape, as if she had taken upon her the zeal of *Abraham*, and were going to make a bloudy sacrifice of her Son. They of *Nostre dame* in *Amiens*, have erected her *Statua* all in gold, with her Son also of the same mettle in her armes; casting beams of gold round about her, as the Sun is painted in its full glory: strange Idolatries! On the contrary, in the Parish Church of *Tury*, in *La Beausse*, she is to be seen in a plain petticoat of red, and her other garments correspondent. In my minde this holdeth most proportion to her estate, and will best serve to free their irre-ligion from absurdity. If they will worship her as a nurse, with her childe in her arme, or at her brest, let them array her in such apparell, as might beseem a Carpenters wife; such as she may be supposed to have worn before the world had taken notice, that she was the mother of her Saviour. If they needs must have her in her estate of glory, as at *Amiens*; or of honour (being now publickly acknowledged to be the *blessed-est among women*) as at *Paris*, let them disburden her of her child. To clap them thus together, is a folly, equally worthy of scorne and laughter. Certainly had she but so much liber-ty, as to make choice of her own clothes, I doubt not but she would observe a greater *decorum*. And therefore I com-mend the *Capuchins* of *Boulogne*, who in a little side-chappell consecrated unto her, have placed only a handsome fair looking-glasse upon her Altar, the best ornament of a female closet: why they placed it there, I cannot say, only I conceive it was, that she might there see how to dresse her self.

This Church is said to have been built (I should rather think repaired) by *Raoul* or *Rollo*, the first Duke of *Norman-dy*; since it hath been much beautifyed by the *English* when they were Lords of this Province. It is the seat of an
Arch-

Archbishop, a Dean and fifty Canons. The Archbishop was instituted by the authority of *Constantine* the Great, during the sitting of the Councell of *Arles*. *Anidian* who was there present, being consecrated the first Archbishop. The Bishops of *Sees, Aurenches, Constance, Bayeux, Lysieux* and *Eureux*, were appointed for his Diocesans. The now Archbishop is said to be an able Scholar, and a sound Statesman; his name I enquired not. The revenues of his Chair are said to be 10000 crowns: more they would amount to, were the Countrey any way fruitfull of Vines; out of which the other Prelates of *France* draw no small part of their *intrads*.

The *Parliament* of this Countrey, was established here by *Lewis* XII. who also built that fair Palace wherein Justice is administred, *anno* 1501. At that time he divided *Normandy* into seven *Lathes*, *Rapes*, or Bailliwicks, *viz. Rouen, Caux, Constentin, Caen, Eureux, Gisors,* and *Alençon*. This Court hath Supreme power to enquire into, and give sentence of all causes within the limits of *Normandy*. It receiveth appeals from the inferior Courts of the Dutchie unto it, but admitteth none from it. Here is also *Cour des Estux*, a Court of the generall Commissioners, also for Taxes; and *La Chambre des Aides*, instituted by *Charles* VII. for the receiving of his Subsidies, Gabels, Imposts, &c. The house of Parliament is in form quadrangular, a very gratefull and delectable building; that of *Paris* is but a Chaos or a Babell to it. In the great hall (into which you ascend by some 30 steppes or upwards) are the seats and desks of the *Procurators*; every ones name written in *Capital letters* over his head. These *Procurators* are like our *Atturnies*, to prepare causes and make them ready for the *Advocates*. In this Hall do suitors use either to attend on, or to walke up and down and confer with their pleaders. Within this hall is the great Chamber, the tribunall and seat of justice, both in causes Criminall and Civill.

At domus interior regali splendida luxu
Instruitur: —— As *Virgill* of Queen *Dido's* dining roome.

Camber so gallantly and richly built, that I must needs confess selfe it far surpasseth all the rooms that ever I saw in my life. The Palace of the *Louure* hath nothing in it comparable. The feeling all inlaid with gold, and yet did the workmanship exceed the matter. This Court consisteth of two *Presidents*, twenty *Counsellors* or Assistants, and as many *Advocates* as the Court will admit of. The prime *President* is termed *Ner de Riz*, by birth a *Norman*: upon the Bench, and in all places of his Court, he taketh the precedence of the Duke of *Longueville*: when there is a convention of the three Estates summoned, the Duke hath the priority.

We said even now, that from the sentence of this Court there lay no appeal; but this must be recanted, and it is no shame to do it: St. *Austin* hath written his *Retractations*; so also hath *Bellarmine*. Once in the year there is an appeal admitted, but that for one man only, and on this occasion: There was a poysonous Dragon not far from *Roven*, which had done much harme to the Countrey and City. Many wayes had been tryed to destroy him, but none prospered; at last *Romain*, afterwards made a Saint, then Archbishop of the Town, accompanied with a theef and a murderer, whose lives had been forfeited to a sentence, undertaketh the enterprise; upon sight of the Dragon the theef stole away, the murderer goeth on, and seeth that holy man vanquish the Serpent, armed only with a Stole (it is a neck habit, sanctifyed by his Holinesse of *Rome*, and made much after the manner of a tippet) with this Stole tied about the neck of the Dragon, doth the murderer lead him prisoner to *Roven*. To make short work, the name of God is praised, the Bishop magnifyed, the murderer pardoned, and the Dragon burned. This accident (if the story be not *Apocrypha*) is said to have hapned on *holy Thursday*. *Audoin* or *Owen*, successor unto St. *Romain*, in memory of this marvellous act, obtained of King *Dagobert* the first (he began his reign *anno* 632) that from that time forwards the *Chapitre* of the Cathedrall Church, should every *Ascension* day have the faculty of delivering any malefactor, whom the lawes had condemned. This that King then granted, and all the following Kings even to this time have successively confirmed it. I omit the ceremonies and solemnities wherewith this prisoner is

taken

taken from his irons, and restored to liberty. It is not above nine years agone, since a *Baron* of *Gascoyne* took occasion to kill his wife, which done, he fled hither into *Normandy*; and having first acquainted the *Canons* of *Nostre dame* with his desire, put himself to the sentence of the Court, and was adjudged to the wheel. *Ascension-day* immediately coming on, the *Canons* challenged him, and the Judge, according to the custome, caused him to be delivered. But the *Normans* pleaded that the benefit of that priviledge belonged only to the natives of that Province; and they pleaded with such fury, that the Baron was again committed to prison, till the Queen Mother had wooed the people, *pro ea saltem vice*, to admit of his reprievall.

I deferred to speak of the language of *Normandy*, till I came hither, because here it is best spoken. It differeth from the *Parisian*, and more elegant *French*, almost as much as the *English* spoken in the *North*, doth from that of *London* or *Oxford*. Some of the old *Norman* words it still retaineth, but not many. It is much altered from what it was in the time of the *Conqueror*, few of the words in which our lawes were written being known by them. One of our company gave a *Litleton's tenure*, written in that language, to a *French* Doctor of the Lawes; who protested that in three lines, he could not understand three words of it. The religion in this Town is indifferently poized, as it also is in most places of this Province. The *Protestants* are thought to be as great a party as the other, but far weaker, the Duke of *Longueville*, having disarmed them in the beginning of the last troubles.

E

CHAP.

Chap. IV.

Our journey between Roven *and* Pontoyse. *The holy man of St.* Clare *and the Pilgrims thither. My sore eyes.* Mante, Pontoyse, Normandy *justly taken from King* John. *The end of this Booke.*

July the second we take our farewell of *Roven*, better accommodated then we came thither; yet not so well as I desired. We are now preferred *ab Asinis ad equos*, from the Cart to the Waggon. The *French* call it a Coach, but that matters not; so they would needs have the Cart to be a Charlot. These Waggons are the ordinary instruments of travell in those Countries; much of a kin to *Gravesend*'s barge. You shall hardly finde them without a knave or a Giglot. A man may be sure to be merry in them, were he as certain to be wholesome. This, in which we travelled, contained ten persons, as all of them commonly do; and amongst these ten, one might have found *English*, *Scots*, *French*, *Normans*, *Dutch*, and *Italians*, a jolly medley; had our religions been as different as our Nations, I should have thought my self in *Amsterdam* or *Poland*; if a man had desired to have seen a Brief or an Epitome of the World, he would no where have received such satisfaction, as by looking on us. I have already reckoned up the severall Nations, I will now lay open the severall conditions. There were then to be found amongst these ten passengers, men and women, Lords and serving men, Scholars and Clowns, Ladies and Chambermaids, Priests and Laie-men, Gentlemen and Artificers, people of all sexes and almost all ages. *If all the learning in the world were lost, it might be found again in* Plutarch, so said *Budæus*. If all the Nations in the world had been lost, they might have been found again in our Waggon, so I. Seriously I think our

Coach

Coach to have been no unfit reprefentation of the Ark. A whole world of men and languages might have grown out of it.

But all this while our Waggon joggeth on, but fo leifurely, that it gave me leave to take a more patient view of the Countrey, then we could in the Cart. And here, indeed, I faw fufficient to affect the Countrey, yea to dote on it, had I not come out of *England*. The fields fuch as already I have defcribed, every where befet with Apple-trees, and fruits of the like nature. You could fcarce fee any thing which was barren in the whole Journey. Thefe Apples are both meat and drink to the poor *Paifant*. For the Country is ill provided with Vines (the only want I could obferve in it) and Beer is a good beverage at a Gentlemans table, Sider then, or Perry are the poor mans Claret; and happy man is he, which once or twice a week can afpire fo high above water. To proceed, through many a miferable Village (*Burghs* they call them) and one Town fomewhat bigger then the reft, called *Equille*; we came that night to St. *Claire* 10 *French* miles from *Roven*, a poor Town god wot, and had nothing in it remarkable, but an accident. There dwelt a monk there, grown into great opinion for his fanctity, and one who had an efpeciall hand upon fore eyes; yet his ability herein was not generall, none being capable of cure from him but pure Virgins. I perfwade my felf *France* could not yield him many patients: and yet from all parts he was much fought unto. Hope of cure and a charitable opinion, which they had of themfelves, had brought to him divers diftreffed Damofels; which, I am confident, had no intereft in his miracle. In the fame Inne (Alehoufe I fhould fay) where we were to be harbored, there had put in a whole convoy of thefe *Ladies errant, Pilgrims* they called themfelves, and had come on foot two dayes journey to cleer their eye-fight. They had white vailes hanging down their backs, which in part covered their faces; yet I perceived by a glimpfe, that fome of them were paft cure. Though my charity durft allow them maids, it was afraid to fuppofe them Virgins: yet fo far I dare affure them they fhould recover their fight, that when they came home, they fhould see their folly. At that time, what with too much watching on shipboard, what with the tartnesse of the water, and the violence of the winde, working upon me for almost 40 houres together whilst I lay on the Hatches: mine eyes had gotten a rheum and a rednesse: my Hostess (good woman) perswaded me to this holy Eye-wright, but I durst not venture Not that I had not as good a title to my Virginity as the best there: but because I had learned what a grievous sentence was denounced on *Abaziab* king of *Israel*, for seeking help of *Belzebub* the god of *Eckron*. When I hap to be ill, let my amendment come on Gods name. *Mallem semper profanus esse, quam sic religiosus*, as *Minutius Falix* of the *Roman* Sacrifices. Let my body rather be still troubled with a sore eye, then have such a recovery to be a perpetuall eye-sore to my conscience. Rather then go in Pilgrimage to such a Saint, let the Papists count me for an Heretick. Besides, how durst I imagine in him an ability of curing my bodily eyes, who had for above 70 years been troubled with a blindnesse in the eyes of his soul? ———*Thou fool* (said our Saviour almost in the like case) *first cast out the beam out of thine own eye, and then shalt thou see clearly to cast out the mote out of thy brothers eye.*

The next morning (*July* 3) I left my pilgrims to try their fortunes, and went on in our journey to *Paris*, which that day we were to visite. My eyes not permitting me to read, and my eares altogether strangers to the *French* chat, drave my thoughts back to *Roven*; and there nothing so much possessed me, as the small honour done to *Bedford* in his monument. I had leasure enough to provide him a longer Epitaph, and a shorter apologie against the envie of that Courtier, which perswaded *Charles* the VIII. to deface the ruines of his Sepulchre: Thus.

So did the Fox, the coward'st of the beard,
Kick the dead Lyon, and profane his beard.
So did the Greeks, about their vanquisht host,
Drag Hectors reliques, and torment his ghost.
So did the Parthian slaves deride the head
Of the great Crassus now betrayed and dead:

To whose victorious sword, not long before,
They would have sacrific'd their lives, or more.
So do the French assault dead Bedfords spright,
And trample on his ashes in despight.

But foolish Curio cease, and do not blame
So small an honor done unto his name:
Why grievest thou him a Sepulchre to have,
Who when he liv'd could make all France a grave?
His sword triumph'd through all those Towns which lie
In th' Isle, Maine, Anjoy, Guyen, Normandie.
Thy fathers felt it. Oh! thou worst of men,
(If man thou art) do not endevour then,
This Conquerour from his last hold to thrust,
Whom all brave minds should honour in his dust.

But be not troubled Bedford; thou shalt stand
Above the reach of malice, though the hand
Of a French basenesse may deface thy name,
And tear it from thy marble, yet shall fame
Speak loudly of thee and thy acts. Thy praise
A Pyramis unto it self shall raise,
Thy brave atchievements in the times to come,
Shall be a monument above a Tombe.
Thy name shall be thy Epitaph: and he
Which once reads Bedford, shall imagin thee
Beyond the power of Verses, and shall say
None could expresse thy worthes a fuller way.

Rest thou then quiet in the shades of night,
Nor vex thy self with Curio's weaker spite:
Whilest France remains, and Histories are writ,
Bedford shall live, and France shall Chronicl' it.

Having offered this unworthy, yet gratefull sacrifice, to the *Manes* of that brave *Heros*: I had the more leasure to behold *Mante*, and the Vines about it, being the first that ever I saw. They are planted like our Hop-gardens, and grow up by the helps of poles, but not so high. They are kept with little
cost,

cult, and yeeld profit to an husbandman sufficient to make him rich, had he neither King nor Landlord. The Wine which is pressed out of them, is harsh and not pleasing: as much differing in sweetnesse from the Wines of *Paris* or *Orleans*, as their language doth in elegancy. The rest of the *Norman* wines, which are not very frequent, as growing only on the frontiers towards *France*, are of the same quality. As for the Town of *Marte*, it seemeth to have been of good strength before the use of great Ordinances; having a wall, a competent ditch, and at every gate a draw-bridge. They are still sufficient to guard their Pullen from the Fox, and in the night times to secure their houses from any forain burglary. Once indeed they were able to make resistance to a King of *France*, but the *English* were then within it. At last on honorable termes it yeelded, and was entred by *Charles* VII. the second of *August*, anno 1449. The Town is for building and bignesse, somewhat above the better sort of Market Towns here in *England*.

The last Town of *Normandy* toward *Paris* is *Pontoyse*, a Town well fortifyed, as being a borderer, and one of the strongest bulwarks against *France*. It hath in it two fair Abbies of *Maubuissin* and St. *Martin*, and six Churches Parochiall, whereof that of *Nostre dame* in the Suburbs is the most beautifull. The name it derives from a bridge, built over the river of *Oyse*, on which it is situate, and by which on that side it is well defended; the bridge being strengthned with a strong gate, and two draw-bridges. It is commodiously situate on the rising of an hill, and is famous for the siege laid before it by *Charles* VII anno 1442 but more fortunate unto him in the taking of it. For having raised his Army upon the Duke of *Yorks* coming to give him battail with 6000 only; the *French* Army consisting of double the number; he retired or fled rather unto St. *Denis*; but there hearing how scandalous his retreat was to the *Parisians* even ready to mutiny; and that the Duke of *Orleans* and others of the Princes, stirred with the ignominiousnesse of his flight, began to practise against him; he speedily returned to *Pontoyse*, and maketh himself master of it by assault. Certainly to that fright he owed the getting of this Town, and all *Normandy*, the *French* by that
door

door making their entrie unto this Province; one of which at last they thrust the *English*, anno 1450. So desperate a thing is a frighted coward.

    This Countrey had once before been in possession of the *English*, and that by a firmer title then the sword. *William* the *Conqueror* had conveied it over the Seas into *England*, and it continued an Appendix of that Crown, from the year 1067 unto that of 1204. At that time, *John* called *Sans terre*, third son unto King *Henry* II. having usurped the estates of *England* and the *English* possessions in *France*, upon *Arthur* heir of *Brétagne*, and son unto *Geofry* his elder brother; was warred on by *Philip Augustus* King of *France*, who sided with the said *Arthur*. In the end *Arthur* was taken, and not long after was found dead in the ditches of the Castle of *Roven*. Whether this violent death happened unto him by the practise of his Uncle, as the *French* say, or that the young Prince came to that unfortunate end in an attempt to escape, as the *English* report, is not yet determined. For my part, considering the other carriages and virulencies of that King, I dare be of that opinion, that the death of *Arthur* was not without his contrivement. Certainly he that rebelled against his Father, and practised the eternall imprisonment and ruine of his Brother, would not much stick (this being so speedy a way to settle his affaires) at the murder of a Nephew. Upon the first bruit of this murder, *Constance* mother to the young Prince, complaineth unto the King and Parliament of *France*; not the Court which now is in force, consisting of men only of the long robe, but the Court of the *Pairrie* or 12 Peeres, whereof King *John* himself was one, as Duke of *Normandy*. I see not how in justice *Philip* could do lesse then summon him, an homager being slain, and a homager being accused. To this summons *John* refused to yeeld himself, a Counsell rather magnanimous then wise, and such as had more in it of a *English* King then a *French* Subject. *Edward* III. a Prince of finer metall then this *John*, obeyed the like warrant, and performed a personall homage to *Philip* of *Valoys*, and it is not reckoned amongst his disparagements. He committed yet a further errour or solecisme in State, not so much as sending any of his people to supply his place, or plead his cause. Upon this non-appearance, the Peers proceed

ceed to sentence, *Il fut par Arrest de la dite cour* (saith *Du Chesne*) *condamné pour atteint & convaincu du crime de parricide, & de felonie*; Parric de for killing his own Nephew; and Felony for committing an act so execrable on the person of a *French Vassal*, and in *France*. *John du Serres* addeth a third cause, which was contempt, in disobeying the Kings commandment. Upon this verdict the Court awarded, *Que toutes les terres qu'il avoit par de là demoureroient acquises & confisquees a la Couronne, &c.* A proceeding so fair and orderly, that I should sooner accuse King *John* of indiscretion, then the *French* of injustice. When my life or estate is in danger, let me have no more sinister a tryall. The *English* thus outed of *Normandy* by the weaknesse of *John*, recovered it again by the puissance of *Henry*; but being held only by the sword, it was after 30 years recovered again, as I have told you. And now being passed over the *Oyse*, I have at once freed the *English* and my self of *Normandy*; here ending this Book, but not that dayes journey.

The End of the First Book.

A

A SURVEY OF THE STATE of FRANCE.

FRANCE specially so called.

OR,

THE SECOND BOOK.

CHAP. I.

France in what sense so called. The bounds of it. All old Gallia not possessed by the French. Countries follow the name of the most predominant Nation. The condition of the present French not different from that of the old Gaules. That the heavens have a constant power upon the same Climate, though the Inhabitants are changed. The quality of the French in private, at the Church, and at the table. Their language, complements, discourse, &c.

July the third, which was the day we set out of St. *Claire*, having passed through *Pontoyse*, and crossed the river, we were entred into *France*: *France* as it is understood

in

in its limited sense, and as a part only of the whole, for when *Meroveus*, the Grandchild of *Pharamond*, first King of the *Franci* or *Frenchmen*, had taken an opportunity to passe the *Rhine*, having also during the wars between the *Romans* and the *Gothes*, taken *Paris*; he resolved there to set up his rest, and to make that the head City of his Empire. The Country-round about it, which was of no large extent, he commanded to be called *Francia* or *Terra Francorum*, after the name of his *Frankes* whom he governed. In this bounded and restrained sense, we now take it, being confined with *Normandy* on the North, *Champagne* on the East, and on the West and South with the Province of *La Beausse*. It is incircled in a manner with the *Oyse* on the Northwards, the *Eure* on the West, the *Velle* on the East, and a veine riveret of the *Seine* towards the South; but the principall environings are made by the *Seine*, and the *Marne* a river of *Campagne*, which constitute that part hereof which commonly and *all' Isle d'*, is called by the name of the Isle of *France*, and within the main Island makes divers little petty Isles, the waters winding up and down, as desirous to recreate the earth with the pleasures of its lovely and delicious embraces.

This Isle, this portion of *Gaul*, properly and limitedly styled *France*, was the seat of the *Francs* at their first coming hither, and hath still continued so. The rest of *Gallia*, is in effect rather subdued by the *French*, then inhabited: their valour in time having taken in those Countries which they never planted: so that if we look apprehensively into *Gaule*, we shall finde the other Nations of it, to have just cause to take up that complaint of the King of *Portugall* against *Ferdinand* of *Castile*, for assuming to himself the title of *Catholick King of Spain*; *Ejus tam non exigua parte penes reges alios*, as *Mariana* relateth it. Certain it is, that the least part of all *Gallia* is in the hands of the *French*, the *Normans*, *Britons*, *Biscainers* or *Gascons*, the *Gothes* (of *Languedoc* and *Province*) *Burgundians*, and the antient *Gaules* of *Poictou*, retaining in it such fair and ample Provinces. But it is the custome (shall I say) or fate of lesser and weaker Nations, to lose their names unto the stronger; as wives do to their husbands, and the smaller rivers to the greater. Thus we see the little Province of

Poland

Poland to have maſtered and given name to the *Prutæni*, *Mazovii*, and other Nations of *Sarmatia Europæa*; as that of *Moſco* hath unto all the Provinces of *Aſiatica*. Thus hath *Sweden* conquered and denominated almoſt all the great Peninſula of *Scandia*; whereof it is but a little parcell: and thus did the *Engliſh Saxons* being the moſt prevailing of the reſt, impoſe the name of *Engliſh* on all the people of the *Heptarchie*.

Et dedit impoſito nomina priſca jugo.

And good reaſon the vanquiſhed ſhould ſubmit themſelves as well unto the appellation, as the laws of the victor. The *French* then are poſſeſſors of ſome parts of old *Gallia*, and maſters of the reſt; poſſeſſors not of their Cities only, but their conditions. A double victory, it ſeemeth, they enjoyed over that people, and took from them at once, both their qualities and their Countries. Certainly whoſoever will pleaſe to peruſe the Commentaries of *Julius Cæſar, de bello Gallico*; he will equally gueſſe him an Hiſtorian and a Prophet; yea he will rather make himſelf believe, that he hath propheciéd the character of the preſent *French*, then delivered one of the antient *Gauls*. And indeed, it is a matter worthy both of wonder and obſervation, that the old *Gaules*, being in a manner all worne out, ſhould yet have moſt of their conditions ſurviving in thoſe men, which now inhabit that region, being of ſo many ſeverall Countries and originals. If we dive into naturall cauſes, we have a ſpeedy recourſe unto the powerfull influence of the heavens; for as thoſe celeſtiall bodies conſidered in the generall, do work upon all ſublunary bodies in the generall, by light, influence and motion; ſo have they a particular operation on particulars. An operation there is wrought by them in a man, as borne at ſuch and ſuch a minute; and again as borne under ſuch and ſuch a Climate. The one derived from the ſetting of the Houſes, and the *Lord* of the *Horoſcope* at the time of his Nativity; the other from that conſtellation which governeth as it were, the Province of his birth, and is the *genius* or *deus tutelaris loci*. *Hinc illa ab antiquâ vitia* (ſaith an Author modern

dern rather in time then judgment) *& patriæ sorte durantia, quæ totæ in historiis gentes aut commendant aut notant.* Two or three Authors by way of parallel, will make it clear in the example, though it appear not obscure in the search of *causes. Primus Gallorum impetus imajor quam virorum, secundus minor quam fœminarum,* saith *Florus* of the *Gaules.* What else is that which Mr. *Dallington* saith of the *French*, when he reporteth that they begin an action like thunder, and end it in a smoak? Their attempts on *Naples* and *Millain* (to omit their present enterprise on *Genoa*) are manifest proofs of it; neither will I now speak of the battail of *Poictiers*, when they were so forward in the onset, and furious in the flight. *Ut sunt Gallorum subita ingenia,* saith *Cæsar*: & I think this people to be as hare-brained as ever were the other. *Juvenal* calleth *Gallia, fæcunda causidicorum*: and among the modern *French* it is related, that there are tryed more law-causes in one year, then have been in *England* since the Conquest. Of the antient *Germans*, the next neighbours and confederates of the *Gaules, Tacitus* hath given us this note, *Diem noctemque continuare potando nulli probrum*; and presently after, *De jungendis affinitatibus, de bello denique & pace, in conviviis consultant.* Since the time of *Tacitus* hath *Germanie* shifted almost all her old inhabitants, and received new Colonies of *Lombards, Sueves, Gothes, Sclavonians, Hunns, Saxons, Vandals,* and divers other Nations not known to that writer. Yet still is that exorbitancy of drinking in fashion; and to this day do the present *Germans* consult of most of their affairs in their cups. If the *English* have borrowed any thing of this humor, it is not to be thought the vice of the Countrey, but the times. To go yet higher and further, the Philosopher *Anacharsis* (and he lived 600 and odd yeers before Christ) noted it in the *Greeks*, that at the beginning of their feasts, they used little goblets, and greater towards the end, when they were now almost drunken. Θαυμάζειν ἔφη πῶς Ἕλληνες ἀρχόμενοι μὲν ἐν μικροῖς πίνειν, πλησθέντες δ᾽ ἐν μεγάλοις, as *Laertius* reporteth it. *George Sandys* in the excellent discourse of his own travailes, relateth the same custome to continue still amongst them; notwithstanding the length of time, and all the changes of state and people which have since hapned. Their Empire indeed they have lost; their valour, learning, and all

other

other graces which set them out in the sight of the World; and no marvell these were not nationall conditions, but personall endowments. I conclude then this digression with the words of *Barklay*, *Hæret itaque in omni gente vis quædam inconcussa, quæ hominibus pro conditione terrarum, in quibus nasci contigerit, sua fata diviserit.*

The present *French* then, is nothing but an old *Gaule* moulded into a new name, as rash he is, and as head-strong, and as hare-brain'd. A nation whom you shall win with a feather, and lose with a straw. Upon the first sight of him you shall have him as familiar as your sleep, or the necessity of breathing. In one houres conference, you may indeer him to you, in the second unbutton him; the third pumps him drie of all his secrets, and he gives them you as faithfully, as if you were his ghostly father, and bound to conceal them *sub sigillo confessionis*: when you have learned this, you may lay him aside, for he is no longer serviceable. If you have an humor of holding him in a further acquaintance, (a favour of which he confesseth, and I believe him, he is unworthy:) himself will make the first separation. He hath said over his lesson to you, and must now finde out some body else to whom to repeat it. Fare him well, he is a garment whom I would be loath to wear above two days together, for in that time he will be thread-bare. *Familiare est homini omnia sibi remittere*, saith *Vellelus* of all; it holdeth most properly in this people. He is very kind-hearted to himself, and thinketh himself as free from wants, as he is full: so much he hath in him of the nature of a *Chinoy's*, that he thinketh all men blind but himself. In this pride of self-conceitednesse he hateth the *Spaniard*, loveth not the *English*, and contemneth the *German*; himself is the only Courtier, and compleat Gentleman; but it is his own glasse which he seeth in, out of this conceit of his own excellency, and partly out of a shallownesse of brain; he is very liable to exceptions. The least distast that can be, draweth his sword, and a minutes pause sheathes it to your hand. If afterwards you beat him into better manners, he shall take it kindly and cry *serviteur*. In this one thing they are wonderfully like the Devill. Meeknesse or submission maketh them insolent, a little resistance putteth

putteth them to their heels, or makes him your Spaniel. In a word (for I have held him too long) he is a walking vanity in a new fashion.

I will now give you a taste of his table, which you shall finde in a measure furnished; (I speak not of the *Paisant*:) but not in so full a manner as with us. Their Beef they cut out in so little chops, that that which goeth there for a laudable dish, would be thought here to be an University commons, new served from the hatch. A loine of Mutton serves amongst them for three roastings, beside the hazard of making pottage with the rump. Fowle also they have in good plenty, especially such as the King found in *Scotland*. To say truth, that which they have is sufficient for nature and a friend, were it not for the Mistresse of the Kitchin-wench. I have heard much fame of *French* Cooks, but their skill lyeth not in the handling of Beef or Mutton. They have (as generally have all this Nation) good fancies, and are speciall fellowes for the making of puffe-pastes, and the ordering of banquets. Their trade is not to feed the belly, but the palat. It is now time you were set down, where the first thing you must do, is to say your own Grace; private Graces are as ordinary there, as private Masses: and from thence I think they learned them. That done, fall to where you like best. They observe no methods in their eating, and if you look for a Carver, you may rise fasting. When you are risen, if you can digest the sluttishnesse of the cookery, (which is most abominable at first sight) I dare trust you in a Garrison. Follow him to Church, and there he will shew himself most irreverent and irreligious; I speak not this of all, but of the generall. At a Masse in the *Cordeliers* Church in *Paris*, I saw two *French Papists*, even when the most sacred mystery of their faith was celebrating, break out into such a blasphemous and Atheisticall laughter, that even an *Ethnick* would have hated it. It was well they were known to be *Catholicks*; otherwise some *French* hot-head or other, would have sent them laughing to *Pluto*.

The *French* language is, indeed, very sweet and delectable. It is cleared of harshnesse, by the cutting off, and leaving out the consonants, which maketh it fall off the tongue very volubly;

lubly; yet in my opinion, it is rather elegant then copious, and therefore is much troubled for want of words to find out periphrases. It expresseth very much of it self in the action. The head, body, and shoulders concurre all in the pronouncing of it; and he that hopeth to speak it with a good grace, must have somewhat in him of the *Mimick.* It is inriched with a full number of significant Proverbs, which is a great help to the *French* humor of scoffing; and very full of courtship, which maketh all the people complementall. The poorest Cobler in the Village hath his Court-cringes, and his *eau benisté de Cour*, his court holy water, as perfectly as the Prince of *Conde*.

In the Passados of their court-ship, they expresse themselves with much variety of gesture, and indeed, it doth not misbecome them. Were it as gratious in the Gentlemen of other Nations as in them, it were worth your patience; but the affectation of it is scurvy and ridiculous. *Quecunque salutationis artificio corpus inflectant, putes nihil ista institutione magis convenire. Vicinæ autem gentes ridiculo errore deceptæ, ejusdem venustatis imitationem ludicram faciunt & ingratam:* as one happily observed at his being amongst them. I have heard of a young Gallant, son to a great Lord of one of the three *Brittish* Kingdoms, that spent some years in *France* to learn fashions. At his return he desired to see the King, and his father procured him an entervenie. When he came within the Presence-chamber, he began to compose his head, and carry it as if he had been ridden with a Martingall: next he fell to draw back his legs and thrust out his shoulders, and that with such a gracelesse apishnesse, that the King asked him if he meant to shoulder him out of his chair, and so left him to act out his complement to the hangings. In their courtship they bestow even the highest titles, upon those of the lowest condition. This is the vice also of their common talk. The bigger begetteth *Monsieurs* and *Madams* to his sons and daughters, as familiarly as the King. Were there no other reason to perswade me, that the *Welch* or *Brituins* were the descendants of the *Gaules*, this only were sufficient, that they would all be Gentlemen.

His discourse runneth commonly upon two wheels, *treason* and *ribaldrie*. I never heard people talke lesse reverently of their Prince, nor more sawcily of his actions. Scarce a day passeth away without some seditious Pamphlet printed and published, in the disgrace of the King, or of some of his Courtiers. These are every mans mony, & he that buyeth them is not coy of the Contents, be they never so scandalous; of all humors the most base and odious. Take him from this (which you can hardly do, till he hath told all) and then he falleth upon his ribaldry. Without these crutches, his discourse would never be able to keep pace with his company. Thus shall you have them relate the stories of their own uncleannesse, with a face as confident, as if they had no accidents to please their hearers more commendable. Thus will they reckon up the severall profanations of pleasure, by which they have dismanned themselves; sometimes not sparing to descend to particulars. A valiant Captain never gloried more in the number of the Cities he had taken, then they do of the severall women they have prostituted.

Egregiam vero laudem & spolia ampla ———

Foolish and most perishing wretches, by whom each severall incontinencie is twice committed; first, in the act; and secondly, in the boast. By themselves they measure others, and think them naturals, or *Simplicians*, which are not so conditioned. I protest, I was fain sometimes to put on a little impudence, that I might avoid the suspicion of a gelding or a sheep-biter. It was St. *Austins* case, as himself testifyeth in the second book of his Confessions, *Fingebam me* (saith that good Father) *fecisse quod non feceram, ne cæteris viderer abjectior*. But he afterwards was sorry for it, and so am I; and yet, indeed, there was no other way to keep in a good opinion, that unmanly and ungoverned people.

Chap. II.

The French Women, their persons, prating and conditions. The immodesty of the French Ladies. Kissing not in use among them; and the sinister opinion conceived of the free use of it in England. The innocence and harmelsnesse of it amongst us. The impostures of French Pandars in London, with the scandall thence arising. The peccancie of an old English Doctor. More of the French Women. Their Marriages, and lives after wedlock, &c. An Elogie to the English Ladies.

I Am come to the *French* Women, and it were great pity they should not immediately follow the discourse of the men, so like they are one to the other, that one would think them to be the same, and that all the difference lay in the apparell. For person, they are generally of an indifferent stature, their bodies straight, and their wastes commonly small: but whether it be so by nature, or by much restraining of these parts, I cannot say. It is said, that an absolute woman should have (amongst other qualities requisite) the parts of a *French* woman from the neck to the girdle; but I believe it holdeth not good, their shoulders and backs being so broad, that they hold no proportion with their midles; yet this may be the vice of their apparell. Their hands are, in mine opinion, the comliest and best ordered part about them, long, white and slender. Were their faces answerable, even an *English* eye would apprehend them lovely: but herein do I finde a *pretty contradictorie*. The hand, as it is the best ornament of the whole structure, so doth it most disgrace it. Whether it be that ill diet be the cause of it, or that hot bloud wrought upon by a hot and scalding aire, must of necessity by such means vent it self, I am not sure of. This I am sure of, that scarce the tithe of all the maids we saw, had her hands and arme-wrists free from scabs, which had over-run them like a leprosie. Their hair is generally black, and indeed, somewhat blacker then a gracious lovelinesse would admit. The Poets commend *Leda* for her black hair, and not unworthily.

Leda fuit nigris conspicienda comis.
                                    As *Ovid* hath it.

Yet was that blacknesse but a darker brown; and not so fearfull as this of the *French* women. Again, the blacknesse of the hair is then accounted for an ornament, when the face about which it hangeth, is of so perfect a complexion and *symmetrie*, that it giveth it a lustre. Then doth the hair set forth the face, as a shadow doth a picture; and the face becometh the haire, as a *field-argent* doth a *sable-bearing*, which kind of Armory the *Heralds* call the most fairest. But in this the *French* women are most unluckie. *Don Quixote* did not so deservedly assume to himself the name of *The Knight of the ill-favoured face*, as may they, that of the *damosels* of it. It was therefore a happy speach of a young *French* gallant that came in our company out of *England*, and had it been spoken amongst the Antients, it might have been registred for an Apophthegme; that the *English* of all the people in the world were only *nati ad voluptates*. You have (saith he) the fairest women, the goodliest horses, and the best breed of dogs, under heaven. For my part, as far as I could in so short a time observe, I dare in this first believe him. *England* not only being (as it is said.) *a paradise for women*, by reason of their priviledges; but also *a paradise of women*, by reason of their unmatchable perfections.

Their *dispositions* hold good intelligence with their faces. You cannot say to them as *Sueton* doth of *Galba*, *Ingenium Galbæ male habitat*. They suit so well one with another, that in my life I never met with a better *decorum*; but you must

must first hear them speak. *Loquere ut te videam*, was the method in old times, and it holdeth now. You cannot gather a better character of a *French* woman, then from her prating, which is so tedious and infinite, that you shall sooner want ears, then she tongue. The *fastidious* pratler which *Horace* mentioneth in his ninth *Satyre*, was but a *puisnè* to her. The writers of these times, call the *Sicilians*, *Gerræ Siculæ*, and not undeservedly; yet were they but the Scholars of the *French*, and learned this faculty of them, before the Vespers. It is manners to give precedency to the Mistresse, and she will have it, if words may carry it. For two things I would have had *Aristotle* acquainted with these Starlings. First, it would have sav'd him a labour in taking such paines about finding out the perpetuall motion. Secondly, it would have freed him from an Heresie with which his Doctrine is now infected, and that is, *Quiquid movetur, ab alio movetur*; their tongues, I am certain move themselves, and make their own occasions of discoursing. When they are going, they are like a watch, you need not winde them up above once in twelve houres, for so long the thread of their tongues will be in spinning. A dame of *Paris* came in Coach with us from *Roven*; fourteen houres we were together, of which time (I'le take my oath upon it) her tongue fretted away eleaven houres and 57 minutes. Such everlasting talkers are they all, that they will sooner want breath then words, and are never silent, but in the grave; which may also be doubted. As they are endlesse in their talk, so also are they regardlesse of the company they speak in. Be you stranger or of their acquaintance, it much matters not; though indeed, no man is to them a stranger. Within an hour of the first sight, you shall have them familiar more then enough, and as merry with you, as if they had known your bearing-clothes. It may be they are chaste, and I perswade my self many of them are; but you will hardly gather it out of their behaviour. *Te tamen & cultus damnat*, as *Ausonius* of an honest woman that carried her self lesse modestly. They are abundantly full of laughter and toying, and are never without variety of lascivious Songs; which they spare not to sing in what company soever. You would think modesty were quite banished the Kingdom; or rather, that it had never been there. — Neither is this the weaknesse of some few. It is an epidemicall disease, Maids and Wives are alike sick of it, though not both so desperately; the gallantry of the maide, being of the two a little more tolerable; that of the women coming hard upon the confines of *shamelesnesse*. As for the Ladies of the Court, (I cannot say this, but upon hear-say) they are as much above them in their lightnesse, as they are in their place; and so much the worse in that they have made their lightnesse impudent. For whereas the daughter of *Pythagoras*, being demanded what most shamed her to discourse of, made answer ταῦτα δ' ἃ γυνὴ κέκληται, *those parts which made her woman*: these French dames will speak of them, even in the hearing of men, as freely, and almost as broadly, as a Midwife, or a Barber-surgeon. Nay, I have heard a Gentleman of good credence relate, that being at a tilting, he saw a Courtier going to remove a boy, which very roguishly look'd under a Ladies clothes: but when her Ladiship perceived his intention, she hindred him with this complement, *Laisse, Monsieur, laisse, les yeuxne sont pas larrens*; the boyes eyes would steal nothing away; a very mercifull and gentle Lady. If that of *Justine* be still true, *Vera mulierum ornamenta pudicitiam esse, non vestes*; that modesty were the best apparell of a woman; I am afraid many of the female sex in *France* would be thinly clad, and the rest go naked.

Being a people thus prone to a suddain familiarity, and so prodigall of their tongue and company, you would scarce imagine them to be coy of their lips. Yet this is their humor. It seemed to me strange at first and uncivill, that a woman should turn away from the proffer of a salutation. Afterward I liked the custome very well, and I have good cause for it, for it saved me from many an unsavory piece of mannerlinesse. This notwithstanding could not but amaze me, that they who in their actions were so light and wanton, should yet think themselves modest, and confine all lasciviousnesse unto a kisse. A woman that is kissed, they account more then half whored, be her other deportment never so becoming; which maketh them very sparing of receiving such kindnesses.

nesses. But this is but a dissembled unwillingnesse, and hath somewhat in it of the *Italian*. For as they had rather murder a man in private, then openly speak ill of him: so it may be thought that these Damosels would hardly refuse a mans bed, though education hath taught them to flie from his lip. Night and the curtains may conceal the one: the other can obtain no pardon in the eye of such as may happen to observe it.

Upon this ground your *French* Traveller, that perhaps may see their Hostesse kissed at *Dover*, and a Gentleman salute a Lady in the streets of *London*; relateth at his coming home, strange *Chimera's* of the *English* modesty. To further this sinister opinion, he will not spare to tell his *Camerades* (for this I have noted to you, to be a part of his humor) what Merchants wives he enjoyed in *London*; and in what familiarity such a Lady entertained him at *Westminster*. Horrible untruths! and yet my poor gallant thinketh he lyeth not. I remember I met in *Paris* with an *English* Doctor and the Master of a Colledge there, who complained much of the lasciviousness of the *English* women: and how infamously every *French* Taylor that came from us, reported of them: withall, he protested, that it did not grieve him much, because he thought it a just judgement of God upon our Nation, that all the married men should be cuckolds. A strange piece of Divinity to me who never before had heard such preaching: but this was the reason of the Doctrine: In the old *English* Masse-book called *Secundum usum Sarum*, the woman at the time of marriage, promiseth her future husband to be *bonny and buxom at bed and at board, till death us depart*, &c. This being too light for the gravity of the action then in hand, and in mine opinion somewhat lesse reverend then a Church duty would require; the reformers of that book thought good to alter: and have put in the place of it, *to love, cherish and obey*. That this was a sufficient assurance of a conjugal faith, he would not grant; because the promise of being *Buxom* in bed was excluded. Besides he accounted the supposed dishonesty of the *English* wives, as a vengeance plucked down upon the heads of the people, for chopping and changing the words of the holy Sacrament: (for such they esteem the form of

Matrimony) though his argument needed no answer, yet this accusation might expect one: and an *English* Gentleman (though not of the *English* Faith) thus laid open the abuse; and seemed to speak it out of knowledge. When the *Monsieurs* come over full pursed to *London*, the *French Pandars*, which lie in wait for such booties, grow into their acquaintance: and promise them the embraces of such a Dame of the City, or such a Lady of the Court; women perchance famed for admirable beauties. But as *Ixion* amongst the Poets expected *Juno*, and enjoyed a cloud: so these beguiled wretches in stead of those eminent persons mentioned to them, take into their bosomes some of the common prostitutes of the Town. Thus are they cousen'd in their desires, thus do they lie in their reports: whilest poor souls, they think themselves guilty of neither imposture.

For the other accusation, which would seem to fasten a note of immodesty upon our *English* womens lips: I should be like enough to confess the crime, were the *English* kisses like unto those of the *French*. As therefore Dr. *Dale* Master of the Requests, said unto *Mendoza* the *Spanish* Ambassador, upon his dislike of the promiscuous sitting of men and women in our Churches; *Turpe quidem id esse apud Hispanos qui etiam in locis sacris cogitarent de explenda libidine, a qua procul aberant Anglorum mentes*: So do I answer to the bill of the complainant. An *Oxford* Doctor upon this text, *Betrayest thou the Son of man with a kisse?* made mention of four manner of kisses, viz. *Osculum charitatis, osculum gratioris familiaritatis, osculum calliditatis,* and *osculum carnalitatis.* Of these I will bestow the last on the *French*, and the third on the *Spaniards*; retaining the two first unto our selves: whereas the one is enjoyned by the precept, and the other warranted by the examples of holy Scripture. For my part, I see nothing in the innocent and harmless salutations of the *English*, which the Doctor calleth *Osculum gratioris familiaritatis*, that may move a *Frenchmans* suspicion; much I confess to stir his envie. Perhaps a want of the like happiness to himself, maketh him dislike it in us: as the Fox that had lost his taile, perswaded all others to cut off theirs; but I have already

ready touched the reason, why that Nation is unworthy of such a favour: their kisses being hot and sulphury, and indeed nothing but the prologue to their lusts. Whereas on the contrary, and I dare be confident in it; the chaste and innocent kisse of the *English* Gentlewomen, is more in heaven, then many of the best of their devotions. It were not amisse to explain in this place a verse of *Ovids*, common in the mouthes of many, but the understanding of few. Thus then saith the Poet:

Oscula qui sumpsit, si non & cetera sumpsit,
Hæc quoque quæ sumpsit perdere dignus erit.

He that doth only kisse, and doth no more,
Deserves to lose the kisses given before.

Which must be understood according to the fashion of *Rome* and *Italy* (and since of *France* and *Spain*); where they were given as pawns of a dishonest contract: and not according to the customes of *England*, where they are only proffer'd in way of a gracious and innocent familiarity; and so accepted.

I return again to the *French* women; and though I may not kisse them (which he that seeth them will swear I have good cause to thank God for) yet they are at liberty to be courted: an office which they admit freely, and return as liberally. An office to which they are so used; that they can hardly distinguish complement from wooing, till the Priest expecteth them at the Church door. That day they set themselves forth with all the variety of riches their credit can extend to. A Scholar of the University never disfurnished so many of his friends, to provide for a journey, as they do neighbours, to adorn their wedding. At my being in *Pontoyse*, I saw Mris. Bride returning from the Church. The day before she had been somewhat of the condition of a Kitchen-wench, but now so tricked up with scarfs, rings, and cross-garters, that you never saw a Whitsun-Lady better rigged. I should much have applauded the fellowes fortune, if he could have married the clothes: but God be mer-

merciful to him) he is chained to the wench. Much joy may they have together most peerless couple!

Hymen, O Hymenæe Hymen, Hymen O Hymenæe.

The match was well knit up between them. I would have a *French* man marry none but a *French* woman.

Being now made mistress of an house, she can give her selfe a dispensation to drink wine: before she had a fling at the bottle by stealth, and could make a shift to play off her whole one in a corner: as St. *Austine* in the ninth book of his Confessions reporteth of his mother *Monica*. Now she hath her draughts like the second edition of a book, augmented and revised: and which is more, published *cum privilegio*. Her house she doth keep as she doth her self. It would puzzle a strong judgement, to resolve which of the two are the more nasty: yet after ten of the clock, you may come nigh her; for by that time she hath not only eaten, but it may be her hall hath had a brushing: if you be not careful of your time, you shall commonly finde her speechless; her mouth being stopped with some of the reliques of last nights supper. To five meals a day she is very constant; and for varieties sake, will make some of them at street-door. She is an exceeding good soul (as *Sancho Panco* said of his wife) and one that will not pine her self, though her heirs smart for it. To her husband she is very servile, seldome sitteth with him at the table, readily executeth all his commands, and is indeed rather a married servant then a wife: or an houshold drudge under the title of a Mistress: yet on the other side she hath freedome enough, and certainly much more then a moderate wisdome would permit her. It is one of her *jura conjugalia* to admit of Courtship, even in the sight of her husband; to walk arm in arm about the streets or into the fields with her *Frisado*, to proffer occasions of familiarity and acquaintance at the first sight of one, whose person she relisheth: and all this *sans scrupsen*, without any the least imputation: a liberty somewhat of the largest, and we may justly fear that having thus wholly in her own power the keyes of the Cabinet, that she sheweth her jewels to more then her husband.

Such

Such are the *French* women; and such lives do they lead both maids and married.

> *Thou happy* England: *thy four seas contain*
> *The pride of beauties: such as may disdain*
> *Rivals on earth. Such at once may move*
> *By a strange power, the envie, and the love*
> *Of all the sex besides. Admit a dame*
> *Of* France *or* Spain, *passe in the breath of fame,*
> *And her thoughts, for fair: yet let her view*
> *The commonst beauty of the* English *crew;*
> *And in despair she'l execrate the day*
> *Which bare her black; and sigh her self away.*
> *So pin'd the* Phrygian *dames and hang'd the head,*
> *When into* Troy, Paris *did* Helen *lead.*
> *But boast not* Paris, England *now enjoyes*
> Helens *enough to sack a world of* Troyes.
> *So doth the vulgar tapers of the skie,*
> *Lose all their lustre when the Moon is nigh.*
> *Yet* English Ladies, *glorious lights, as far*
> *Exceed the Moon; as doth the Moon a star.*
> *So do the common people of the groves*
> *Grow husht, when* Philomel *recounts her loves.*
> *But when our Ladies sing, even she forbears*
> *To use her tongue; and turns her tongue to ears.*
>
> *Nay more; Their beauties should proud* Venus *see,*
> *Shee'd blush her self out of her Deity:*
> *Drop into* Vulcans *forge, her raign now done;*
> *And yeeld to them her Empire, and her son.*
> *Yet this were needless. I can hardly finde*
> *Any of this land stars, but straight my minde*
> *Speaks her a* Venus; *and me thinks I spie*
> *A little* Cupid *sporting in her eye.*
> *Who thence his shafts more powerfully delivers,*
> *Then ere did t'other* Cupid *from his quivers.*

Such in a word they are; you would them guesse
An harmony of all the goddesses;
Or swear that partial Nature at their birth,
Had rob'd the heaven to glorifie the earth.

Such though they are, yet mean these graces bin
Compar'd unto the vertues lodg'd within:
For needs the Jewels must be rich and precious,
When as the Cabinet is so delicious.

Chap. III.

France described. The valley of Montmorancie, and the Dukes of it. Mont-martre. Burials in former times not permitted within the wals. The prosecuting of this discourse by manner of a journal, intermitted for a time. The Town and Church of St. Denis. The Legend of him, and his head. Of Dagobert and the Leper. The reliques to be seen there. Martyrs how esteemed in St. Augustine's time. The Sepulchres of the French Kings, and the treasury there. The Kings house of Madrit. The Queen Mothers house at Ruall, and fine devices in it. St. Germains en lay, another of the Kings houses. The curious painting in it Gorramburie Window: the Garden belonging to it and the excellency of the Water-works. Boys St. Vincent, de Vincennes, and the Castle called Bisester.

I Have now done with the *French*, both men and women, a people much extolled by many of our *English* Travellers for all those graces which may enoble & adorn both sexes. For my part, having observed them as well as I could and traced them in all their several humors: I set up my rest with this proposition, that *there is nothing in them to be envied but their Countrey*. To that indeed I am earnestly, and I think not unworthily affected: here being nothing wanting which may be required, to raise and reward ones liking. If nature was ever prodigal of her blessings, or scattered them with an over-plentiful hand; it was in this Island: into which we were entred, as soon as we passed over the bridge of *Pontoyse*. The first part of it, which lasted for three leagues; was upon the plain of a mountain: but such a mountain, as will hardly yeeld to the best valley in *Europe*, out of *France*. On both sides of us the Vines grew up in a just length, and promised to the husbandman a thriving vintage. The Wines they yeeld are far better then those of *Normandy*, or *Gascoyne*; and indeed the best in the whole Continent, those of *Orleans* excepted: yet what we saw here, was but as a bit to prepare our stomachs; lest we should surfeit in the valley.

Here we beheld nature in her richest vestiments. The fields so interchangeably planted with Wheat and Vines, that had *L. Florus* once beheld it, he would never have given unto *Campania* the title of *Cereris & Bacchi certamen*. These fields were dispersedly here and there, beset with Cherry trees; which considered with the rest, gave unto the eye an excellent object. For the Vines yet green; the Wheat ready for the sithe; and the cherries now fully ripened, and shewing forth their beauties through the vails of the leaves: made such a various and delightsome mixture of colours, that no art could have expressed it self more delectably. if you have ever seen an exquisite Mosaical work, you may the best judge of the beauty of this valley. Add to this, that the River *Seine* being now past *Paris*; either to embrace that flourishing soyle, or out of a wanton desire to play with it self, hath divided it self into sundry lesser channels; besides its several windings and turnings: so that one may very justly, and not irreligiously, conceive it to be an Idea, or representation of the Garden of *Eden*: the river so happily separating it self, to water the ground. This valley is of a very large circuit; and as the *Welch* men say of *Anglesey*.

Mam mam Gymye; id est, Anglesey is the mother of *Wales*: so may we call this the mother of *Paris*. For so abundantly doth it furnish that great and populous City, that when the Dukes of *Berry* and *Burgundy* besieged it with 100000 men; there being at that time 3 or 400000 Citizens and Souldiers within the walls: neither the people within, nor the enemies without, found any want of provision.

It is called the Valley of *Montmorency*, from the Town or Castle of *Montmorency* seated in it: but this town nameth not the Valley only. It giveth name also to the ancient family of Dukes of *Montmorency*, the antientest house of Christendome. He stileth himself *Le primier Christien & plus viel Baron de France*: and it is said that his ancestors received the Faith of Christ by the preaching of St. *Denis*, the first Bishop of *Paris*. Their principal houses are that of *Chantilly*, and *Ecquan*, both seated in the Isle: this last being given unto the present Dukes Father, by King *Henry* 4. to whom it was confiscated by the condemnation of one of his Treasurers. This house also (and so I leave it) hath been observed to have yeelded to *France*, more Constables, Marshals, Admirals, and the like officers of power and command, then any three other in the whole Kingdome. Insomuch that I may say of it, what *Irenicus* doth of the Count *Palatines*, the name of the Countrey only changed: *Non alia Galliæ est familia, cui plus debeat nobilitas*. The now Duke, named *Henry*, is at this present Admiral of *France*.

The most eminent place in all this Isle is *Mont-martre*, eminent I mean by reason of its height; though it hath also enough of antiquity to make it remarkable. It is seated within a mile of *Paris*, high upon a mountain: on which many of the faithfull, during the time that *Gaule* was heathenish, were made Martyrs. Hence the name. Though *Paris* was the place of apprehension and sentence, yet was this Mountain commonly the scaffold of execution: it being the custome of the ancients, neither to put to death, nor to bury within the wals of their Cities. Thus the *Jewes* when they crucified our Saviour, led him out of the City of *Hierusalem* unto Mount *Calvarie*: unto which St. *Paul* is thought to allude, Heb. 13. saying, *Let us therefore go forth to him, &c.* Thus also doth St. *Luke* (to omit other instances) report of St. *Stephen*, Act. 7. *And they cast him out of the city, and stoned him.* So in the state of *Rome*, the Vestall Virgin having committed fornication, was stifled in the *Campus sceleratus*; and other malefactors thrown down the *Tarpeian* rock: both situate without the Town. So also had the *Thessalians* a place of execution, from the præcipice of an hill, which they called the κρεμός, or *Cord*: whence arose the proverb εἰς κρεμός, be hanged. As they permitted not executions of malefactors within their wals: so neither would they suffer the best of their Citizens to be buried within them. This was it which made *Abraham* to buy him a field wherein to bury his dead: and thus we read in the 7. of *Luke*, that the widow of *Naims* son was *carried out to be buried*. This custome also we find amongst the *Athenians, Corinthians,* and other of the *Grecians, Qui in agris suis,* (as saith *Alexander ab Alexandro*) *aut in fundo suburbano, seu in avito & patrio solo corpora humari consuevere.* Amongst the *Romans*, it was the fashion to burn the bodies of the dead, within their City. This continued till the bringing in of the Lawes of *Athens*, commonly called the Lawes of the 12. Tables: one of which Lawes runneth in these words, *In urbe ne sepelito, neve urito.* After this prohibition, their dead corps were first burned in *Campus Martius*; and their urnes covered in sundry places in the fields. The frequent urnes or sepulchral stones, digged up amongst us here in *England*, are sufficient testimonies of this assertion. Besides we may finde in *Appian*, that the chief reason why the rich men in *Rome* would not yeeld to that Law, called *Lex Agraria*, or the Law of dividing the *Roman* possessions equally among the people, was, because they thought it an irreligious thing that the Monuments of their forefathers should be sold unto others. The first that is registred to have been buried in the City, was *Trajan* the Emperour. Afterwards it was granted as an honourary to such as had deserved well of the republick: and when the Christian Religion prevailed, and Church-yards, those dormitories of Saints were consecrated; the liberty of burying within the wals, was to all equally granted.

On this ground it not being lawful to put to death or bury, within the Town of *Paris*; this Mountain was destinate to those purposes. Then was it only a Mountain; now it is enlarged unto a Town: it hath a poor wall, an Abbey of *Benedictine* Monks, and a Chappel called *La Chapelle des Martyrs*; both founded by *Lewis* the 6. called the Grosse. Amongst others, which received here the Crown of Martyrdome, none more famous then St. *Denis* (said to be *Dionysius Areopagita*) the first Bishop of *Paris*; *Rusticus* his Archpriest; and *Eleutherius*, his Deacon. The time when, under the reign of *Domitian*; the person by whose command, *Fescininus* Governor of *Paris*; the crime, for not bowing before the Altar of *Mercury*, and offering sacrifice unto him. Of St. *Denis* being the patron or tutelary Saint of *France*, the Legend reports strange wonders. As namely, when the Executioner had smitten off his head, that he caught it between his armes; and ran with it down the hill as fast as his legs could carry him; half a mile from the place of his execution, he sate down and rested: and so he did nine times in all, even till he came to the place where his Church is now built. There he fell down and died, being three *English* miles from *Mont-martre*: and there he was buried together with *Rusticus*, and *Eleutherius*, who not being able to go as fast as he did, were brought after him by the people. *O impudentiam admirabilem & vere Romanam!* and yet so far was the succeeding age possessed with a belief of this miracle, that in the nine several places where he is said to have rested there are erected so many hansome Crosses of stone; all of a making.

To the memory of this Saint, did *Dagobert* the first build a Temple: and the times ensuing improved it to a Town. Afterwards in honour of St. *Denis*, and because it lay neer *Paris*; some of the following Kings bestowed a wall upon it. A wall it is of a large circuit, and very much unproportionable to the Town, which standeth in it, for all the world like a *Spaniards* little face in his great ruffe, or like a small chop of Mutton in a large dish of portage at the three penny Ordinary. Thus was the Town built (as you see) by natural means: but it was not so with the Temple. Unlesse that be worth a miracle, both in the building, and in the consecrating of it: I will not give a straw for it.

Thus

Thus, then saith the story. *Dagobert* afterwards King of *France*, during the life of *Clotoyre* the second his Father, had cruelly slain *Sadrasegille* his governour. To avoid the fury of his Father, much incensed with that unprincely action; he was compelled to wander up and down *France* hungry and thirsty. And so he went, and he went, (for this tale should be told in the same stile, that wenches tell theirs by the fire side) till he came to the Sepulchre of St. *Denis*, where he laid down and slept: and then there appeared unto him a fine old man, with a staffe in his hand, and he told him that his father was dead, and that he should be King, and he prayed him of all loves, that when he came to be King, he would build a Church there, in the honour of St. *Denis*. He had an hard heart, that could deny so sweet an old man so little a courtesie, for so much good newes, and I trow the King was more kinde then so. And so when the Church was built, the Bishop was sent for in all haste to blesse it. But it chanced that the night before the day wherein the Bishop was to blesse it, there came to the Town an ugly Leper, and the soulest that ever was seen: and this Leper would needs lie in the Church. And when he was there, about twelve a clock at night, our Saviour came into the Church in garments as white as the driven snow, and there came with him the Apostles, and the Angels and the Martyrs, and the sweetest Musick that ever was heard in the world. And then Christ blessed the Church, and said unto the Leper, that he should tell the Bishop that the Church was already blessed, and for a token of it, he gave the Leper his health, who presently became as fine a sweet youth as one should see in a summers day. *Auditum admissi risum teneatis?* you may laugh if you please, but I'le assure you this is the story: neither is it a jot the lesse authentick because of the stile. Such ridiculous stuffe, did the Fryers and Munks of those times invent to please and blinde the people. So prone were our Ancestors to believe as Oracles, what ever was delivered unto them by these Impostors. *Majoribus nostris tam facilis in mendaciis fides fuit, ut temere crediderint etiam monstrosa miracula: & quicquid famæ licet fingere, illis erat libenter laudire.* *Minutius Fælix* spake it of his forefathers

thers being Heathens: we may juſtly affirm it of ours alſo, being Chriſtians.

But (to omit the additions of the Legend) true it is, that *Dagobert* the firſt, was the founder of the Church: which was after rebuilt and beautified by the 25. Abbot of it, called *Sugger*, in the reign of King *Lewis* the ſixth. A reverend and comely fabrick, certainly it is; dark, as the Churches of thoſe times commonly were: and none of the pooreſt. It maintaineth 262 Monks and an Abbot, whoſe ſingle revenue is thought to be worth 10000 Crowns and upwards. The preſent Abbot is *Henry* of *Lorrein*, ſon to the Duke of *Guiſe*, a young Gentleman of ſome 14 years of age, or thereabouts: but of him more hereafter. The Abbot of it, among many other priviledges, hath a full power upon the lives, goods, and honours of his vaſſals: and hath a voice in the *Parliament* of *Paris*, as full and binding as any of the Counſellors there ſitting. As for the Church it ſelf, it is in height 80 foot, 100 in breadth; and in length 300. The high Altar, under which the bodies of St. *Denis* and his two fellow-Martyrs, are ſaid to be buried; is a very rich and excellent work: the Crucifix which ſtandeth over it, being all of pure gold, enchaſed with divers Pearls and precious Stones of great value. Before it hangeth a ſilver Lamp continually burning: and if you look about it, you ſhall ſee the richeſt and the faireſt glaſſe for painting, in all *France*; that of *Amiens* only excepted. One thing further I will note in this Church, before I come to to the Tombes and reliques; which is, how *Henry* 4. in this Church ſaid his firſt Maſſe, after his laſt reconcilement to the Church of *Rome*. And good reaſon I have to ſay his laſt. For having been firſt brought up in the *Romiſh* Faith, he was by his Mother made a Proteſtant. At the maſſacre of *Paris*, fear of death or impriſonment, turned him Papiſt: liberty again made him an Hugonot. In this vein he continued till the year 1595. and then once more re-emboſom'd himſelf into the *Roman* Synagogue; which was the time we now ſpeak of. *Quo teneam nodo mutantem Protea vultum?* The only *Proteus* in matters of faith in our times. Doctor *Perne* was a Diamond to him.

CHAP. III.   *the State of* France.   57

It is now time I should shew you the Reliques; but you must first stay till the Clerk hath put on his Surplice. I have heard of a blinde Priest that could never mumble over his Masse handsomely without his spectacles. This fellow and his Surplice is just like him. I perswaded my self that the Surplice without the Clerk, could marshall the Reliques, as well as the Clerk without the Surplice. As soon as he was sadled for his journey, he putteth himself into his ways; and followed it with a pace so nimble, that there was no keeping of him company: his tongue ran so fast, that the quickest eye there, was fain to give him over in plain ground: the fellow that sheweth the Tombs at *Westminster*, being no more to be compared to him, for the volubility of his chops, then a Capuchin to a Jesuite: yet as we learned afterwards of him (when he was out of his road) they were thus disposed. On the right hand of the Altar, (not the high Altar above mentioned) there are said to be kept one of the Nails which fastned our Saviour to the Crosse. 2. A piece of the Crosse it self. 3. Some of the Virgin *Maries* Milk. 4. The arm of St. *Simeon* set in a case of gold. And 5. The reliques of St. *Lewis* reserved in a little chappel, all of gold also; and built in the fashion of the *Nostre dame in Paris*. On the left, there was shewed us the head of St. *Denis* and a part of his body. But I mistake my self, it was not the head, but the portraiture of it in gold; the head being said to be within it; by his representation he seemeth to have had a very reverend and awfull countenance: though I perswade my self that the rich Crown and Miter which he there weareth (and certainly they are of a high value) never belonged to him in his life. On each side of the head are two Angels supporting it, all of gold also: both which together with the head and ornaments supported, are reported to be the work of one *Eloy, le plus artificiel orfeure de son temps*, the cunningest Goldsmith of his time; who afterwards was made Bishop of *Noyon*, and Sainted.

Concerning Reliques I shall have occasion to speak further, when I come to the holy Chappel in *Paris*; somewhat now of the honour due unto the memory of Martyrs. I am none of those that think the memories of those Heroes of

I   the

the primitive times, not to be honoured in the dust; neither would I assault their *shrines* with an irreverent finger: on the other side, they shall never have my prayers directed to them, nor my devotions; nor can I think it lawfull to give the remnants of them any bodily observance. Though I do and will honour, I dare not worship them. St. *Austin* hath cut out a mid-way between the *Papist* and the *Zelot*, in the 8. Book of his most excellent work *De Civitate dei*, and his path it is best to follow, *Honoramus sane memorias eorum tanquam sanctorum hominum Dei, qui usque ad mortem corporum pro veritate certarunt*: and a little after, he sheweth the end of these memorials, viz. *Ut ea celebritate Deo vere gratias de eorum victoriis agamus, & nos ad imitationem talium coronarum eorum memoriæ renovatione adhortemur.* One relique there is of which this use cannot possibly be made; and what do you think that should be, but the Lanthorn which *Judas* used when he went to apprehend his Master? a pretty one it is (I confesse) richly beset with studdes of Cryftall, through which all the light cometh; the main of it being of a substance not transparent. Had it been shewed me within the first *century* of years after the passion, I might, perhaps, have been fooled into a beliefe; for I am confident it can be no older. Being as it is, I will acknowledge it to be a Lanthorn, though it belonged not to *Judas*.

From the *reliques* of *Martyrs*, proceed we to those of *Kings*; and amongst those there is nothing which will long detain an *English* man. He that hath seen the tombs at *Westminster* will think these to be but trifles, if he consider the workmanship, or the riches and the magnificence. The chief of those many mean ones which are there, are those of *Henry* II. and *Katharine de Medices* his wife, in a little Chappell of their own building; both in their full proportion, and in their royall habilliments, exceeding stately. There is also a neat tomb of the same *Henry*, built all of brasse, and supported by four brasse pillars: his Statua of the same mettle placed on the top of it, and composed as if at his prayers. The rest are more in tale then weight. But the chief beauties of this Church, are in the treasurie, which it was not my happinesse to see. As I am informed, the most remarkable things

CHAP. III.   *the State of* France.   59

things in it are these, The Swords of *Joan* the Virgin, *Charles* the great, *Rowland* his cousen, and that of *Henry* IV. when he was Crowned. His Boots, Crown and Scepter, as those also of his son *Lewis* now reigning. A crosse three foot high, made of pure gold. A Crown, Scepter and golden ball, given by Pope *Adrian* to *Carolus magnus*. A golden Crown of larger sise, bedecked with Adaments and other pretious stones; given by *Charles Martell* after his victories over the *Saracens*. A very fair Chalice all of gold, in which St. *Denis* is reported to have consecrated the Sacramentall wine. The others of lesser note, I purposely omit, for having not seen them. I am loath to go any further upon trust. And so I leave St. *Denis*, a Church so richly furnished, that had I seen all the rarities and glories of it, that only days content had deserved our journey; *sed hæc infelici nimia*.

Not to continue this discourse any longer by way of journall, or *gesta dierum*. Few dayes after we had wearied our selves with the sight of *Paris*, we went to see some of their Majesties houses in the Countrey. And here we passed by *Madrit*, so called of the King of *Spains* house at *Madrit*, after the forme of which it is built. The founder of it was *Francis* the first, who being taken Prisoner at the battail of *Pavie*, ann. dom. 1525. and thence carryed into *Spain*, had no lesse then a twelve months time to draw the platforme. A fine Countrey house it seemed to be; but our journey lay beyond it. One league beyond it lay *Ruall*, a small Town belonging to the Abbey of St. *Denis*. In a corner of this Town the Queen Mother hath a fine summer house, abundantly adorned with retired walks, and a most curious variety of water-works: for besides the formes of divers glasses, pillars, and Geometricall figures, all framed by the water; there were birds of sundry sorts so artificially made, that they both deceived the eye by their motion, and the ear by their melodie. Somewhat higher in the middest of a most delicious Garden, are two Fountains of admirable workmanship: In the first, the portraitures of *Cerberus*, the Bear of *Calydon*, the *Nemean Lyon*; and in the navell of it *Hercules* killing *Hydra*. In the other only a *Crocodile* full of wild and unruly tricks, and sending from his throat musick not much different from Organs. Had your eyes been shut, you would have thought your self in some Cathedrall Church: this melody of the *Crocodile*, and that other of the birds, so exactly counterfeiting the harmonie of a well ordered Quire. And now we are come into the Grove, a place so full of retired walks, so sweetly and delectably contrived, that they would even entice a man to melancholy, because in them even melancholy would prove delightfull. The trees so interchangeably folded one within the other, that they were at once a shelter against winde and sun: yet not so sullenly close, but that they afforded the eye an excellent Lordship over the Vines and verdure of the earth imprisoned within them: it seemed a Grove, an Orchard, and a Vineyard, so variously interwoven and mixt together, as if it had been the purpose of the Artist to make a man fall in love with confusion. In the middle of this Wildernesse was seated the house, environed round about with a Moat of running water. The house pretty, and therefore little; built rather for a banquet, then a feast. It was built and enriched with this variety of pleasures, by Mr. *de Ponte*, Taylor to King *Henry* IV. and was no question the best garment that ever he cut out in his life. Dying, he gave it to Mr. *Landerboyne*, once his servant, and now his son by adoption; of whom the Queen Mother taking a liking to it, bought it; giving him in exchange, an office in the Treasury worth 400000 crowns to be sold.

Two leagues from *Ruall*, is the Kings house of St. *Germain en Olay*, a house seated on the top of a hill just like *Windsore*. The Town of St. *Germain* lyeth all about it, the river *Seine* (of the same breadth as the *Thames* is at the place mentioned) runneth below it; and the house by reason of the site, having a large command upon the Country round about it. The Town is poor and hath nothing in it remarkable but the name, which it took from St. *Germain* Bishop of *Auxerre*, who together with St. *Lupus* Bishop of *Tropes*, sailed into *Britain* to root out *Pelagianism*. The Castle or seat Royall is divided into two parts, the old and the new; the old, which is next unto the Town, is built of Bricks, and for forme it is triangular: founded it was at the first by

Charle

Charles V. since strengthned and beautified by the *English* when it was in their possession: *Francis* I. added to it the upper story and the battlements, and *in memoriam facti*, hath left a Capitall *F* upon every of the chimnies. The new house, distant from the old about a furlong, and to which you descend by a handsome green Court, was built by *Henry* IV. It consisteth of three severall parts, all joyned together, the two outermost quadrangular, that in the middle almost round and in the fashion of a *Jewish Synagogue*. Here we saw the Volatory full of sundry forain birds, and in one of the lower rooms great store of outlandish conies; but these were accessories. The principall was the majesty of the house, which is, indeed, worth the observation. The Palace of the *Loure* so much famed, is not to be named in the same day with it. The rooms are well ordered, and high roofed, gorgeously set out with the curiosities of the Painter. In some of the Chambers they shewed us some Poeticall fictions expressed by the pencill in the windowes and on the wainscot, and seemed to glory much in them. I confesse they might have plentifully possessed my fancy, had I not seen the window of *Gorrambury gallery*, belonging to the Right Honorable *Francis Viscount* St. *Albans*; a window in which all the Fables of *Ovids Metamorphosis*, are so naturally and lively dissembled, that if ever art went beyond it self, it was in that admirable expression.

Let us now take a view of the water-works, and here we shall see in the first water-house, which is a stately large walk vaulted over head, the effigies of a Dragon, just against the entrance; an unquiet beast that vomiteth on all that come nigh it. At the end toward the right hand is the Statua of a Nymph sitting before a paire of Organs. Upon the loosing of one of the pipes, the Nymphs fingers began to manage the keyes, and brought the Instrument to yield such a musick, that if it were not that of an Organ, it was as like it as could be, and not be the same. Unto the division of her fingers, her head kept a porportionable time; jolting from one shoulder to the other, as I have have seen an old fidler at a Wake. In the same proportion were the counterfeits of all sorts of mils, wch before very eagerly discharged their functions; but upon the beginning of this harmony, they suddenly stood still, as if they had had ears to have heard it. At the other end towards the left hand, we saw a shop of Smiths, another of Joiners, and a backside full of Sawyers and Masons, all idle. Upon the first command of the water, they all fell to their Occupations, and plyed them lustily; the birds every where singing, and so saving the Artificers the labour of a whistling. Besides, upon the drawing of a wooden courtain, there appeared unto us, two Tritons riding on their Dolphins, and each of them with a shell in his hand, which interchangeably and in turns served them in stead of trumpets. A very happy *decorum*, and truly Poeticall.

Caruleum Tritona vocal, conchaque sonanti
Inspirare jubet, ———
      As *Ovid* of him.

Afterward followes Neptune himself, sitting in his Chariot, drawn with four Tortoyses, and grasping his *tricuspis* or three forked Scepter in his hand: the water under them representing, all this while, a sea somewhat troubled. 36 steps from the front of the house we descended into this waterhouse; and by 60 more we descended into a second of the same fashion, but not of an equall length with the other. At the right hand of this, is the whole story of *Perseus*, *Andromeda* and the Whale lively acted; the Whale being killed, and the Lady unloosed from the rock very perfectly. But withall, it was so cunningly managed, and that with such a mutuall change of fortune, on the parties of both the combatants, that one who had not known the fable, would have been sore affraid that the Knight would have lost the victory, and the Lady her life. At the other end there was shown unto us,

Orpheus in sylvis positus, sylvæque sequentes.

There appeared unto us the resemblance of *Orpheus*, playing on a treble Viall, the trees moving with the force of the musick,

musick, and the wilde beasts dancing in two rings about him. An invention which could not but cost K. *Henry* a great sum of money; one only string of the sidle being by mischance broken, having cost King *Lewis* his son 1500 Livres. Upon the opening of a double-leaved door, there were exhibited to us divers representations and conceits, which certainly might have been more gracefull, if they had not so much in them of the puppet play. By some steps more we descended into the Garden, and by as many more into a Green, which opened into the water side; in which the goodliest flower and most pleasing to my eyes, was the *statua* of an horse in brasse, of that bignesse, that I and one of my companions could stand in the neck of him. But dismounting from this horse, we mounted our own, and so took our leaves of St. *Germain*.

On the other side of *Paris*, and up the river, we saw another of the Kings houses, called St. *Vincent* or *Vincennes*. It was beautified with a large park by *Philip Augustus*, anno 1185. who also walled the Park, and replenished it with Deer. In this house have dyed many famous personages, as *Philip* the fair, *Lewis Hutin*, and *Charles* the fair; but none so much to be lamented as that of our *Henry* V. cut down in the flower of his age, and middest of his victories: a man most truly valiant, and the *Alexander* of his times. Not far from thence is an old Castle, once strong, but time hath made it now unserviceable. The people call it *Chasteau Bisestre*, corruptly for *Vincestre*; which maketh me believe it was built by the *English* when they were masters of this Isle.

CHAP.

Chap. IV.

Paris, the names and antiquity of it. The situation and greatnesse. The chief strength and Fortifications about it. The streets and buildings. King James his laudable care in beautifying London. King Henry the fourths intent to fortifie the Town. Why not actuated. The Artifices and wealth of the Parisians. The bravery of the Citizens described under the person of a Barber.

Now we are come unto *Paris*, whither, indeed, I should have brought you the same day we came from *Pontoyse*.

It hath had in divers ages, two severall names; the one taken from the people, the other from the situation; the name taken from the people is that of *Paris*. *J. Cæsar* in his *Commentaries* making mention of the Nation of the *Parisii*, and at that time calling this City *Urbem Parisiorum*. *Ammianus Marcellinus* calleth it by the same appellative; for as yet the name of *Paris* was not appropriated unto it. As for these *Parisii*, it is well known that they were a people of *Gallia Celtica*; but why the people were so called, hath been questioned, and that deservedly. Some derive them from a son of *Paris* the son of *Priam*: but the humour of deriving all nationall originations from *Troy*, hath long since been hissed out of the Schoole of Antiquity. The *Berosus* of *John Annius* bringeth them from one *Paris* King of the *Celtæ*; and his authority is alike authenticall. The bastards which this *Annius* imposed upon the Antient writers, are now taught to know their own father. Others deduce it from παρρησία, a Greek word importing boldnesse of speech; which is approved by *William* of *Breton*, in the first book of his *Phillipiades*.

Finibus

Finibus egressi patriis, per Gallica rura
Sedem quærebant, ponendis mænibus aptam,
Et se Parisios dixerunt, nomine Græco,
Quod sonat expositum nostris, audacia, verbis.

Leaving their native soil, they sought through *Gaul*
A place to build a City, and a wall,
And call'd themselves *Parisians*; which in Greek
Doth note a prompt audacity to speak.

It is spoken of those *Gaules*, who coming out of the more Southern parts, here planted themselves. Neither is it improbable, that a *Gallick* nation should assume to it self a Greek name, that language having taken good footing in these parts, long before *Cæsars* time, as himself testifyeth in his *Commentaries*. How well this name agreeth with the *French* nature, I have already manifested in the character of this people, both men and women. But I will not stand to this *etymologie*. The names of great Cities are as obscure as those of their founders; and the conjecturall derivations of them are oftentimes rather plausible then probable; and sometimes neither. As for the antiquity of it, it is said to be built in the time of *Amasia* King of *Judah*; but this also is uncertain: the beginnings of antient Cities, being as dark and hidden, as the reasons of their names. Certain it is, that it is no *puisnè* in the world; it being a strong and opulent Town in the dayes of *Julius Cæsar*.

The other name of this City, which is indeed the antient, and was taken from the situation of it, is *Lutetia*, from *lutum* dirt; as being seated in an exceeding clammy and dirty soil. To this also consenteth the abovenamed *William* of *Breton*, in his said first Book of the *Phillippiades*, saying,

———*Quoniam tunc temporis illam*
Reddebat palus & terræ pinguedo lutosam,
Aptum Parisii posuere Lutetia nomen.

And since the Fens, and clammy soil did make
Their City dirty: for that reasons sake,
The Town, the name *Lutetia* did take.

As for the *Etymologie* of *Munster*, who deriveth the name from *Luens* one of the Kings of the *Celtæ*: it may (for ought I know) deservedly keep company with that of *Berosus*, already recited. This name of *Lutetia* continued till the coming of the *Franks* into these parts: who to endeer the nation of the *Parisii*, and oblige them the more faithfully to do them service, commanded it for ever after to be called *Paris*. But the situation of this Town gave it not only the name; it gave it also (as the custome of Godfathers in *England*) a christning gift, which is the riches of it; and by consequence, the preheminence. In how delicate and flourishing a soil it is situate, I have already told you in my description of the vally of *Montmorencie* where it standeth. If you will believe *Cominés* In the first book of his Histories, he will tell you, that *Cest la cité que jamais ie veisse environneé de meilleux pais et plantureux*; of all the Cities which ever he saw, it is environed with the best and fruitful'st Countrey. The river of *Seine* is also, no question, a great help to the enriching of it; for though it be not Navigable unto the Town, yet it giveth free passage unto boats of an indifferent big burden, into which the ships are unladen, and so their commodities carryed up the water. A profitable entercourse between the Sea and the City for the Merchants. Of these boats there are an infinite company that plie up and down the water, and more indeed, as the said *Cominés* is of opinion, than any man can believe that hath not seen them.

It is in circuite, as *Boterus* is of opinion, 12 miles. Others judge it at 10. For my part, I dare not guesse it to be above 8; and yet I was told by a *French* man, that it was in compasse no lesse then 14 leagues within the wals; an untruth bigger then the Town. For figure it is circular, that being, according to *Geometricians*, of all figures the most capacious. And questionlesse if it be true, that *Urbs non in mœnibus, sed in civibus posita est*; *Paris* may challenge as great a circuit as the most of *Europe*: it being little inferiour to the biggest, for the multitudes of her inhabitants. Joyne the compasse and the populousnesse together, and you shall hear the wisest of the *French* men say, that *Que ce qu' est l' ame a la raison, et la prunelle a l' oeil; cela mesme est Paris a la France.* Add to this the verdict of *Charles* V. who being demanded which he thought to be the biggest City of *France*: answered, *Reven*: and being then asked, what he thought of *Paris*: made answer, *Un pais*; that it was a whole Countrey. The Emperour did well to flatter *Francis* the first, who asked him these questions, and in whose power he then was; otherwise he might have given men good cause to suspect his judgement. The truth is, that *Paris* is a fair and goodly Town; yet withall, it is nothing like the miracle that some men make it. Were the figure of *London* altered, and all the houses of it cast into a Ring; I dare able it a larger and more goodly Town then *Paris*, and that in the comparison, it may give it at the least half a mile oddes.

For matter of strength and resistance, certain it is that this City is exceeding well seated, were it as well fortifyed. It lyeth in a plain flat levell, and hath no hils nigh unto it, from which it can any way be annoyed; and for the casting and making of rowling-trenches, I think the soil is hardly serviceable. If Art were no more wanting to the strength of it then Nature, in mine opinion, it might be made almost impregnable. *Henry* IV. seeing the present weaknesse of it, had once a purpose (as it is said) to have strengthned it according to the modern art of Fortifications. But it went no further then the purpose. He was a great builder, and had many projects of Masonry in his head, which were little for his profit; and this would have proved lesse then any. For besides the infinite sums of mony which would have been employed in so immense a work; what had this been in effect, but *to put a sword into the hand of a mad man?* The mutinies and sedition of this people have made it little inferiour to *Leige* or *Gaunt*, the two most revolting Towns of *Europe*. And again, the *Baricadoes* against the person of King *Henry* III. and the large resistance it made to himself, being weak; were sufficient to instruct him what might be expected from it by his successors, when it should be strengthned and inabled to rebellion.

The present strength of the Town then is not great, the wals being very weak and ruinous; and those other few helps which it hath, being little availeable for defence. The beautifullest part of the whole resistance is the ditch, deep, precipitate and broad; and to say no more of it, an excellent ward, were there any thing else correspondent to it. As for the Fort next unto St. *Antonies* gate, called the *Bastille*; it is in my conceit too little to protect the Town, and too low to command it. When Swords only and Pick-axes were in use, and afterwards in the infancie of guns, it did some service in the nature of a Fortresse: now it serveth principally as a prison for those of the greater sort, who will permit themselves to be taken. It is said to be built by the *English*, when they were Lords of *Paris*, and the vulgar are all of this opinion. Others, of the more learned sort, make it to be the work of one of the Provosts of the City. *Du Chesne* calleth him *Hugues Aubriot*, in the time of *Charles* V. when as yet the *English* had nothing to do here. The word *Bastille* in generall, signifieth a Fortresse; the article *la*, prefixed before it, maketh it a name, and appropriateth it unto this building. There are also two little turrets, just against the gallery of the *Louure*, on both sides of the *Seine*, intended for the defence of the River; though now they are little able to answer that intention: they also are fathered on the *English*, but how true I know not. An other place I marked, designed perhaps for a Rampart, but imployed at this time only by windmils. It is a goodly mount of earth, high and capacious, situate close unto the gate called St. *Martins*; the most defensible part, if wel manned, of all *Paris*. Thus is the strength of this Town (as you see) but small; and if *Henry* IV. lay so long before it with his Army, it was not because he could not take it, but because he would not. He was loath (as *Biron* advised him) to receive the bird naked, which he expected with all its feathers; and this answer he gave the Lord *Willoughbie*, who undertook to force an entry into it.

For

For the *streets*, they are many of them of a lawfull and competent breadth, well pitched under the foot with fair and large peble. This paving of it was the work of *Philip Augustus*, anno 1223. or thereabouts; before which time it could not but be miserably dirty, if not unpassable. As it now is, the least rain maketh it very slippery and troublesome; and as little a continuance of warme weather, stinking and poisonous. But whether this noisomenesse proceed from the nature of the ground, or the sluttishnesse of the people in their houses, or the neglect of the Magistrates in not providing a sufficiency of Scavengers, or all, I am not to determine. This I am confident of, that the nastiest lane in *London*, is Frankincense and Juniper, to the sweetest street in this City. The antient by-word was (and there is good reason for it) *Il deslaint comme la sange de Paris*: had I the power of making proverbs, I would only change *il deslaint* into *il puit*, and make the by-word ten times more Orthodox. I have spoken somewhat already of the Fortifications of this Town, but they are but trifles: the only veneme of the street, is a strength unto it more powerfull then the ditches or the bulwark of St. *Martins*. *Morrison* in his *Itinerarie* relateth how the Citizens of *Prague* in *Bohemia*, were repairing the wals of their Town for fear of the *Turkes*; but with all he addeth, that if the stink of the streets kept him not thence, there was no assurance to be looked for of the wals. I know now not how true it is of that City, I am sure it may be justly verified of this. It was therefore not unjudiciously said of an *English* Gentleman, that he thought *Paris* was the strongest Town in Christendome; for he took (strong) in that sense as we do in *England*, when we say such a man hath a *strong-breath*. These things considered, it could not but be an infinite happinesse granted by nature to our *Henry* V. that he never stopped his nose at any stink, as our Chronicles report of him. Otherwise, in my conscience, he had never been able to keep his Court there. But that which most amazed me, is, that in such a perpetuated constancy of stinks, there should yet be found so large and admirable a variety. A variety so speciall and distinct, that any Chymicall nose (I dare lay my life on it)

after

two or three perambulations, would hunt out blindfold, each severall street by the smell, as perfectly as another by his eye. A Town of a strange composition, one can hardly live in it in the Summer without poisning, in the Winter without miring.

For the *buildings*, they are I confesse very handsomely and uniformely set out to the street-ward; not unseemly in themselves, and very sutable one with another. High and perpendicular, with windowes reaching from the top almost to the bottom. The houses of the new moule in *London*, are just after their fashion: wherein the care and designe of our late Soveraign King *James* is highly to be magnifyed. Time and his good beginnings well seconded, will make that City nothing inferiour for the beauty and excellency of her structures, to the gallantest of *Europe*; insomuch that he might truly have said of his *London*, what *Augustus* did of his *Rome*, τὴν Ρώμην γηΐνην παραβὼν, λιθίνην ὑμῖν ἀντιλείπω, *Urbem quem lateritiam inveni marmoream relinquo*, as *Dion* hath it. But as *London* now is, the houses of it in the inside, are both better contrived, and richlyer furnished by far then those of *Paris*; the inward beauty and ornament most commonly following the estate of the builders, or the owners. Their houses are distinguished by signes as with us and under every sign there is printed in Capitall letters what signe it is; neither is it more then need. The old shift of This is a Cock, and this is a Bull, was never more requisite in the infancy of painting, then in this City. For so hideously and so without resemblance to the thing signified, are most of these pencil-works: that I may withou danger say of them as *Pseudolus* in *Plautus* doth of the letter which was written from *Phœnicium* to his young master *Callidorus*, *An obsecro hercle, habent quoque gallinæ manus? nam hæ quidem gallina scripsit*. If a hen would not scrape better portraitures on a dunghill then they have hanged up before their doors, I would send to my Hostess of *Tostes* to be executed And indeed generally, the Artificers of *Paris* are as slovenly in their trades, as in their houses; yet you may finde nimble dancers, pretty fidlers for a toy, and a Tayler that can trick you up after the best and newest fashion. Their Cutlers make

such

CHAP. IV.　　*the State of France.*　　71

such abominable and fearfull knives, as would grieve a mans heart to see them: and their Glovers, are worse then they; you would imagine by their Gloves, that the hand for which they are made, were cut of by the wrist: yet on the other side they are very perfect at tooth-picks, beard brushes, and (which I hold the most commendable art of them) at the cutting of a seal. Their Mercers are but one degree removed from a Pedler; such as in *England* we call Chapmen, that is a Pedler with a shop. And for Goldsmiths there is little use of them, glasses being there most in request, both because neat, and because cheap. I perswade my self that the two severall ranks of shops in *Cheapside*, can shew more plate, and more variety of Mercery wares, good and rich, then three parts of *Paris*. Merchants they have here, but not many, and they not very wealthy. The river ebbs not, and floweth not nigher then 75 miles or thereabouts, and the boats which thence serve the City, being no bigger then our Western Barges. The principall means by which the people do subsist, are the Court of the King, most times held amongst them; and the great resort of *Advocates* and *Clients* to the chambers of *Parliament*. Without these two crutches the Town would get a vile halting, and perhaps be scarce able to stand. What the estate of some of their wealthyest Citizens may amount to, I cannot say, yet I dare conjecture it, not to be superfluous. The Author of the book entituled *Les estat du monde*, reckoneth it for a great marvell that some of our London Merchants should be worth 100000 crownes, we account that estate among us not to be so wonderfull, and may thence safely conclude, that they who make a prodigie of so little, are not worth so much themselves.

If you believe their apparell, we may, perhaps, be perswaded otherwise; that questionlesse speaketh no lesse then millions, though like it is, that when they are in their best clothes, they are in the midle of their estates. But concerning the ridiculous bravery of the poor *Parisian*, take along with you this story: Upon our first coming into *Paris*, there came to visit a *German Lord*, whom we met a ship-bord, a couple of *French Gallants*, his acquaintance; the one of them (for I

did

did not much observe the other) had a suit of *Turkie grogran* doubled with Taffeta, cut with long slashes, or carbonadoes, after the *French* fashion, and belaied with bugle lace. Through the openings of his doublet appeared his shirt of the purest Holland, and wrought with curious needle-work; the points at his waste and knees, all edged with a silver edging; his garters, roses and hat-band, sutable to his points; a beaver hat, and a pair of silk stockins; his cloke also of *Turkey grogram*, cut upon black Taffeta. This Lord (for who would have dared to guesse him other?) applyed himself to me, and perceiving my ignorance in the *French*, accosted me in *Latine*, which he spake indifferently well. After some discourse, he took notice of mine eyes, which were then sore and sea-sick, and promised me, if I would call on him at his lodging the next morning, to give me a water, which suddenly would restore them to their strength and vigor. I humbly thanked his Lordship for such an ineffable and immerited favour, in the best complement and greatest obeisance I could devise. It was not for nought, thought I, that our *English* extoll so much the humanity of this people; nay I began to accuse the report of envy, as not having published the one half of their graces and affabilities. *Quantillum enim virtutum illarum acceperim*! And thus taking my leave of his Honor, I greedily expected the next morning. The morning come, and the hour of visiting his Lordship almost at hand, I sent a servant to fetch a Barber to come trim me and make me neat, as not knowing what occasion I might have, of seeing his Lady or his daughters. Upon the return of the messenger, presently followeth his Altitude, and bidding me sit down in his chair, he disburdened one of his pockets (*Quis hoc credat, nisi sit pro teste vetustas?*) of a case of instruments, and the other of a bundle of linnen. Thus accommodated, he falleth to work about me, to the earning of a *quardesou*. In my life I had never more adoe to hold in my laughter. And certainly, had not an anger or vexation at my own folly, in casting away so much humble rhetorick the night before upon him, somewhat troubled me; I should either have

laught

laught him out of his fine sute, or have broke my heart in the restraint.

Quid domini facient, audent cum talia fures?

If a Barber may be thus taken in suspicion for a Lord, no doubt but a Mercer may be accused for a Marquesse.

Chap. V.

Paris *divided into four parts. Of the* Fauxbourgs *in generall. Of the Pest-house. The* Fauxbourg *and Abby of St.* Germain. *The Queen Mothers house there. Her purpose never to reside in it. The Provost of Merchants, and his authority. The Armes of the Town. The Town-house. The Grand Chastelet. The Arcenall. The place Royall, &c. The Vicounty of* Paris. *And the Provosts seven daughters.*

They which write of *Lusitania* divide it into three parts, viz. *Ulteriorem,* lying beyond *Duerus,* North; *Citeriorem,* lying from *Tagus,* South; and *Interamnem,* situate betwixt both the rivers. *Paris* is seated just as that Province, and may in a manner admit of the same division; for the River of *Seine,* hath there so dispersed it self, that it hath divided this *French Metropolis* into three parts also, viz. *Citeriorem,* lying on this side the river, which they call *La Ville,* the Town; *Ulteriorem,* lying beyond the further branch of it, which they call *L'Universitie*; and *Interamnem,* situate between both the streams in a little Island; which they call *La Cité.* To these add the Suburbs, or (as they

they call them) the *Fauxbourgs*, and you have in all four parts of *Paris*.

These *Fauxbourgs* are not incorporated unto the Town, or joyned together with it, as the Suburbs of *London* are unto that City. They stand severed from it a pretty distance, and appear to be what indeed they are, a distinct body from it; For the most part the houses in them are old and ruinous: yet the *Fauxburg* of St. *Jacques* is in a pretty good fashion and the least unsightly of them all, except St. *Germains*. The *Fauxbourg* also of St. *Marcell* hath somewhat to commend it, which is that the great Pest-house built by *Henry* IV. is within the Precincts of it: a house built quadrangular wise, very large and capacious; and seemeth to such as stand afar off it (for it is not safe venturing nigh it or within) to be more like the Palace of a King, then the Kings Palace it self. But the principallest of all the Suburbs is that of St. *Germains*, a place lately repaired, full of divers stately houses, and in bignesse little inferior unto *Oxford*. It took name from the Abbey of St. *Germain*, seated within it, built by *Childebert* the son of *Clouis*, anno 542. In the honor of St. *Vincent*. Afterwards it got the name of St. *German* a Bishop of *Paris*, whose body was there buried, and at whose instigation it had formerly been founded. The number of the Monks was enlarged to the number of 120 by *Charles the balde*, (he began his reign anno 841) and so they continue till this day. The present Abbot is *Henry* of *Burbon* Bishop of *Metz*, base son unto *Henry* IV. He is by his place Lord of all this goodly Suburb; hath power of levying Taxes upon his tenants: and to him accrew all the profits of the great Fair holden here every *February*.

The principall house in it is that of the Queen Mother, not yet fully built. The Gallery of it, which possesseth all the right side of the square, is perfectly finished, and said to be a most royall and majesticall peece. The further part also, opposite to the gate, is finished so far forth as concerneth the outside and strength of it; the ornamentall parts and trappings of it being yet not added. When it is absolutely consummate, if it hold proportion with the other sides, both within and without, it will be a Palace for the elegancy and polite-

politenesse of the Fabrick, not fellowed in *Europe*. A Palace answerable to the greatnesse of her mind that built it; yet it is by divers conjectured that her purpose is never to reside there: for which cause the building goeth but slowly forward. For when upon the death of her great Privado, the Marquesse *D' Ancre*, she was removed to *Blois*: those of the opposite faction in the Court got so strongly into the good opinion of the King, that not without great strugglings, by those of her party, and the hazard of two civill wars, she obtained her former neernesse to his Majesty. She may see by this what to trust to, should her absence leave the Kings mind any way prepared for new impressions. Likely therefore it is, that she will rather choose to leave her fine house unhabited further then on occasions for a Banquet, then give the least opportunity to stagger her greatnesse. This house is called *Luxembourg Palace*, as being built in place of an old house belonging to the Duke of that Province. The second house of note in this Suburb is that of the Prince of *Conde*, to whom it was given by the Queen Mother, in the first year of her Regency.

The Town of *Paris*, is that part of it, which lyeth on this side of the hithermost branch of the *Seine* towards *Picardie*. What was spoken before in the generall hath its reference to this particular; whether it concern the sweetnesse of the streets, the manner of the building, the furniture of the artificer, or the like. It containeth in it 13 Parish Churches, viz. St. *German de l' Auxerre*, 2 St. *Eustace*, 3 *Les Saints Innocents*, 4 St. *Savueur*, 4 St. *Nicolas des champs*. 6 *Le Sepulcre*. 7 St. *Iacques de la boucherie*, 8 St. *Josse*, 9 St. *Mercy*, 10 St. *Jean*, 11 St. *Gervase*, and St. *Protasse*, 12 St. *Paul*, and 13 St. *Jean le ronde*. It also hath in it 7 Gates, sc. 1 St. *Anthony* upon the side of the river neerunto the *Arcenall*. 2 *Porte du Temple*. 3 St. *Martin*. 4 St. *Denis*. 5 *Mont martre*. 6 St. *Honore*, and 7 *Porte Neufue*, so called because it was built since the others, which joyneth hard upon the *Tuilleries*, the Garden of the *Louure*.

The principall Governour of *Paris*, as also of the whole Isle of *France*, is the Duke of *Monbazon*, who hath held this office ever since the year 1619. when it was surrendred by

Luines; but he little medleth with the City. The particular Governours of it are the two Provosts, the one called *Le Provost du Paris*, the other *Le Provost des Merchands*. The *Provost* of *Paris* determineth of all causes between Citizen and Citizen, whether they be criminall or civill. The office is for term of life; the place of judgement, the *Grand Chastelet*. The present *Provost* is called Mr. *Seguier*, and is by birth of the Nobility; as all which are honoured with this office must be. He hath as his assistants three *Lieutenants*; the *Lieutenant* criminall, which judgeth in matters of life and death; the *Lieutenant* civill, which decideth causes of debt or trespasse between party and party; and the *Lieutenant* particular, who supplyeth their severall places in their absence. There are also necessarily required to this Court the *Procureur*, and the *Advocate*, or the Kings *Sollicitour*, and *Attorney*, 12 *Counsellours*, and of under-officers more then enough. This Office is said to have been erected in the time of *Lewis* the son of *Charles* the great. In matters criminall there is appeal admitted from hence to the *Tournelle*. In matters civill, if the sum exceed the value of 250 Livres, to the great *Chamber*, or *Le grande Chambre* in the Court of Parliament. The *Provost* of the *Merchants*, and his authority was first instituted by *Philip Augustus*, who began his reign anno 1190. His office is to conserve the liberties and Indulgences, granted to the Merchants and Artificers of the City: to have an eye over the sales of Wine, Corn, Wood, Cole, &c. and to impose taxes on them; to keep the keyes of the Gates, to give watchword in time of war; to grant Past-ports to such as are willing to leave the Town, and the like. There are also four other Officers joyned unto him, *Eschevins* they call them, who also carry a great sway in the City. There are moreover Assistants to them in their proceedings, the Kings *Sollicitour* (or *Procureur*) and 24 *Counsellours*. To compare this Corporation with that of *London*, the *Provost* is as the *Major*, the *Eschevins* as the *Sheriffs*, the 24 *Counsellours* as the *Aldermen*, and the *Procureur* as the *Recorder*. I omit the under-officers, whereof there is no scarcity. The place of their meetings is called *L'hostel de ville*, or the *Guilde-hall*. The present *Provost*, Mr. *de Grieux*, his habit, as also that of the *Eschevins*, and Counsellours,

CHAP. V.   *the State of* France.

colours, half red, half skie coloured, the City livery with a hood of the same.

This *Provost* is as much above the other in power, as men which are loved, commonly are above those which are feared. This *Provost* the people willingly, yea sometimes factiously obey, as the conservator of their liberties; the other they only dread as the Judge of their lives, and the tyrants over their Estates. To shew the power of this *Provost*, both for and with the people against their Princes, you may please to take notice of two Instances. For the people against *Philip de Valois*, anno 1349. when the said King desiring an Impost of one Livre in five Crowns, upon all wares sold in *Paris*, for the better managing of his Wars against the *English*, could obtain it but for one year only; and that not without speciall letters reversall, that it should no way incommodate their priviledges. With the people, anno 1357. when King *John* was Prisoner in *England*, and *Charles* the *Daulphin*, afterwards the fift of that name, laboured his ransome amongst the *Parisians*. For then *Stephen Marcell* the *Provost*, attended by the Vulgar Citizens, not only brake open the *Daulphins* Chamber, but slew *John de Confians* and *Robert* of *Clermount*, two Marschals of *France*, before his face. Nay, to add yet further insolencies to this, he took his party-coloured hood off his head, putting it on the *Daulphins*, and all that day wore the *Daulphins* hat, being a brown black; *Pour signal de sa dictature*, as the token of his Dictatorship. And which is more then all this, he sent the *Daulphin* cloth to make him a Gowne and an Hood of the City livery; and compelled him to avow the massacre of his servants above named, as done by his commandement: Horrible insolencies! *Quam miserum est cum hæc impune facere potuisse?* as *Tully* of *Marcus Antonius*.

The Armes of this Town, as also of the Corporation of the *Provost* and *Eschevins*, are *Gules*, a *Ship Argent*; a *Chief powdred with flower de Lyces, Or*. The seat or place of their assembly, is called (as we said) *L'hostell de ville*, or the *Guild-hall*. It was built or rather finished by *Francis* the first, anno 1533. and since beautifyed and repaired by *Francis Miron*, once *Provost des Merchands*, and afterwards Privie Counseller to the King.

King. It standeth on one side of the *Grene*, which is the publick place of execution, and is built quadrangular wise, all of free and polished stone, evenly and orderly laid together. You ascend by 30 or 40 steps, fair and large, before you come into the *Quadrate*; and thence by severall staires into the severall rooms and Chambers of it, which are very neatly contrived and richly furnished. The *grand Chastelet* is said to have been built by *Julian* the *Apostata*, at such time as he was Governor of *Gaul*. It was afterwards new built by *Philip Augustus*: and since repaired by *Lewis* XII. In which time of reparation, the *Provost* of *Paris* kept his Courts in the Palace of the *Louvre*. To sight it is not very gracious, what it may be within I know not. Certain I am, that it looketh far more like a prison (for which use it also serveth) then a Town-hall or seat of judgment.

In this part of *Paris* called *La ville*, or the Town, is the Kings *Arcenal* or *Magazin* of War; It carryeth not any great face of majesty on the out-side, neither indeed is it necessary; such places are most beautifull without, when they are most terrible within. It was begun by *Henry* II. finished by *Charles* the ninth, and augmented by Mr. *De Rhosny*, great Master of the Artillery. It is said to contain 100 field-pieces and their carriages; as also Armor sufficient for 10000 horse, and 50000 foot. In this part also of *Paris* is that excellent pile of building called the *Place Royall*, built partly at the charges, and partly at the encouragement of *Henry* IV. It is built in forme of a quadrangle, every side of the square being in length 72 fathomes; the materials Brick of divers colours, which makes it very pleasing, though lesse durable. It is cloystered round, just after the fashion of the *Royall Exchange* in *London*, the walks being paved under foot. The houses of it are very fair and large, every one having its Garden and other out-lets. In all they are 36, nine of a side, and seem to be sufficient capable of a great retinue; the Ambassadour for the estate of *Venice*, lying in one of them. It is situate in that place, whereas formerly the solemn Tiltings were performed, a place famous and fatall for the death of *Henry* II. who was here slain with the splinters of a Lance, as he was running with the Earl of *Montgomery*, a *Scottish-man*; a sad and heavie accident.

To conclude this discourse of the *Ville* or Town of *Paris*, I must a little wander out of it; because the power and command of the *Prevost* saith it must be so: for his authoritie is not confined within the Town. He hath seven daughters on which he may exercise it; *Les sept filles de la Prevoste de Paris*, as the *French* call them. These seven daughters are seven Bailiwicks, comprehended within the *Vicountie* of *Paris*, viz. 1 *Poissy*. 2 St. *German en lay*. 3 *Tornan* 4 *Torcie en Brie*. 5 *Corbeil*. 6 *Montlierie*. And 7 *Gunnesi en France*. Over these his jurisdiction is extended, though not as Provost of *Paris*. Here he commandeth and giveth judgement as *Lieutenant civill* to the Duke of *Monbazon*, or the supream Governour of *Paris*, and the *Isle* of *France*, for the time being. Yet this *Lieutenant* being an Office perpetually annexed to the Provostship, is the occasion that the Bailiwicks above named are called *Les sept filles de la Prevostie*.

CHAP.

Chap. VI.

The University of Paris, and Founders of it. Of the Colledges in general. Marriage when permitted to the Rectors of them. The small maintenance allowed to Scholars in the Universities of France. The great Colledge at Tholoza. Of the Colledge of the Sorbonne in particular; That and the House of Parliament, the chief Bulwarks of the French liberty. Of the Polity and Government of the University. The Rector and his precedency; The disordered life of the Scholars there being. An Apologie for Oxford and Cambridge. The priviledges of the Scholars, their degrees, &c.

THat part of *Paris* which lyeth beyond the furthermost branch of the *Seine*, is called the University. It is little inferiour to the Town for bignels, and lesse superior to it in sweetness or opulency. Whatsoever hath been said of the whole in general, was intended to this part also, as well as the others: all the learning in it, being not able to free it from those inconveniences, wherewith it is distressed. It containeth in it only six parish Churches: the paucity whereof is supplyed by the multitude of religious houses, which are within it. These six Churches are called by the names of St. *Nicholas du Chardonuere*, 2. St. *Estienne*, at this time in repairing. 3. St. *Severin*. 4. St. *Bennoist*. 5. St. *Andre*. And 6. St. *Cosme*. It hath also eight Gates, *viz.* 1. *Porte de Nesle*, by the water side over against the Louure. 2. *Porte de Buçi*. 3. St. *Germain*. 4. St. *Michell*. 5. St. *Jacques*. 6. St. *Marcell*. 7. St. *Victer*, and 8. *Porte de la Tornelle*. It was not accounted as a distinct member of *Paris*, or as the third part of it, untill the year 1304.

CHAP. VI.   *the State of* France.   81

1304. at what time the Scholars having lived formerly dispersed about the City, began to settle themselves together in this place: and so to become a peculiar Corporation.

The University was founded by *Charles* the great, anno 791. at the perswasion of *Alcuine* an *Oxford* man, and the Scholar of venerable *Bede*: who brought with him three of his con-disciples to be the first readers there: their names were *Rabanus Maurus*, *John Erigena*, surnamed *Scotus*; & *Claudus*, who was also called *Clement*. To these four doth the University of *Paris* owe its originall and first rudiments: neither was this the first time, that *England* had been the School-mistress unto *France*; we lent them not only their first Doctors in Divinity and Philosophy; but from us also did they receive the mysteries of their Religion, when they were Heathens. *Disciplina in Britannia reperta,* (saith *Julius Cæsar Com. 6.*) *atque inde in Galliam translata esse existimatur.* An authority not to be questioned by any, but by a *Cæsar.* Learning thus new born at *Paris*, continued not long in any full vigour. For almost 300 years it was fallen into a deadly trance: and not here only, but also through the greatest part of *Europe*: anno 1160. or thereabouts *Peter Lombard*, Bishop of *Paris*, the first author of Scholastical Divinity; and by his followers called the Master of the Sentences; revived it here in this Town by the favour and encouragement of *Lewis 7*. In his own house were the Lectures first read: and after as the numbers of Students did encrease, in sundry other parts of the Town; Colledges they had none till the year 1304. The Scholars till then sojourning in the houses of the Citizens, accordingly as they could bargain for their entertainment.

But anno 1304. *Joane*, Queen of *Navarre*, wife to *Philip* the fair, built that Colledge, which then and ever since hath been called the Colledge of *Navarre*: and is at this day the fairest and largest of all the rest. *Non ibi constituunt exempla ubi cœperunt, sed in tenuem accepta tramitem, latissime evagandi viam sibi faciunt:* as *Velleius*. This good example ended not in it self: but incited divers others of the *French* Kings, and people, to the erecting of convenient places of study. So that

M   in

in process of time, *Paris* became enriched with 52 Colledges. So many it still hath, though the odde forty are little serviceable unto learning, for in twelve only of them is there any publick reading, either in Divinity or Philosophy. Those twelve are the Colledges of *Harcourt* 2. *Caillvi*, or the *Petit Sorbonne*. 3. *Lisseux*, or *Lexovium*. 4. *Boncourte*. 5. *Montague*. 6. *Le Marche*. 7. *Navarre*. 8. *De la Cardinal de Moyne*. 9. *Le Plessis*. 10. *De Beavais*. 11. *La Sorbonne*. 12. *De Clermont*, or the Colledge of the Jesuites there are also publique readings in the houses of the four orders of Fryers Mendicants, viz. the *Carmelites*, the *Augustin* the *Franciscans*, or *Cordeliers*, and the *Dominicans*. The other Colledges are destinated to other uses. That of *Arras* converted to an house of *English* fugitives; and there is another of them hard by the Gate of St. *Jacques*, employed for the reception of the *Irish*. In others of them there is lodging allotted out to Students, who for their instruction have resort to some of the 12 Colledges above mentioned.

In each of these Colledges there is a Rector: most whose places yeeld to them but small profit. The greatest commodity which accreweth to them is raised from chamber Rents: their preferments being much of a nature with that of a Principal of an Hall in *Oxford*; or that of a Treasurer in an Inne of Chancery in *London*. At the first erection of their Colledges, they were all prohibited marriage though I see little reason for it. There can hardly come any inconvenience or dammage by it, unto the scholars under their charge, by the assuming of leases into their own hands: for I think few of them have any to be so imbezle Anno 1520. or thereabouts it was permitted unto such them as were Doctors in Physick, that they might marry the Cardinall of *Toute Vile*, Legat in *France*, giving unto them that indulgence. Afterwards in the year 1534. the Doctors of the Lawes petitioned the University for the like priviledge: which in fine was granted to them, and confirmed by the Court of Parliament. The Doctors of Divinity are the only Academicals now barred from it: and that not as Rectors, but as Priests. These Colledges for the buildings are very inelegant, and generally little beholding to the curiosity of the artificer. So confused and so proportioned in respect of our Colledges in *England*, as *Exeter* in *Oxford* was some 12. years since, in comparison of the rest: or as the two Temples in *London* now are, in reference to *Lincolns Inne*. The revenues of them are suitable to the Fabricks, as mean and curtailed. I could not learn of any Colledge, that hath greater allowances then that of *Sorbonne*: and how small a trifle that is, we shall tell you presently. But this is not the poverty of the University of *Paris* only: all *France* is troubled with the same want, the same want of encouragement in learning: neither are the Academies of *Germanie* in any happier state, which occasioned *Erasmus* that great light of his times, having been in *England* and seen *Cambridge*, to write thus to one of his *Dutch* acquaintance, *Unum Collegium Cantabrigiense (confidenter dicam) superat vel decem nostra.* It holdeth good in the neatness and graces of the buildings, in which sense he spake it: but it had been more undeniable had he intended it of the revenues. Yet I was given to understand, that at *Tholoze* there was amongst 20 Colledges, one of an especiall quality: and so indeed it is, if rightly considered. There are said to be in it 20 Students places, (or fellowships as we call them). The Students at their entrance are to lay down *in deposito* 6000. Florens, or Livres; paid unto him after six years, by his successor: *Vendere jure potest, emerat ille prius.* A pretty market.

The Colledge of *Sorbonne*, which is indeed the glory of this University, was built by one *Robert de Sorbonne* of the chamber of *Lewis* the 9. of whom he was very well beloved. It consisteth meerly of Doctors of Divinity: neither can any of another profession, nor any of the same profession not so graduated, be admitted into it. At this time their number is about 70; their allowance, a pint of wine, (their pinte is but a thought lesse then our quart) and a certain quantity of bread daily. Meat they have none allowed them, unless they pay for it: but the pay is not much: for five Sols (which amounteth to six pence *English*) a day, they may challenge a competency of flesh or fish, to be served to them

them at their chambers. These Doctors have the sole power and authority of conferring degrees in Divinity: the Rector and other officers of the University, having nothing to do in it. To them alone belongeth the examination of the students in the faculty, the approbation, and the bestowing of the honour: and to their Lectures do all such assiduously repair, as are that way minded. All of them in their turns discharge this office of reading, and that by sixes in a day: three of them making good the Pulpit in the forenoon; and as many in the afternoon. These Doctors are accounted, together with the Parliament of *Paris*, the principal pillars of the *French* Liberty: whereof indeed they are exceeding jealous, as well in matters Ecclesiastical as Civil. When *Gerson* Chancellor of *Paris* (he died *Anno* 1429.) had published a book in approbation of the Councell of *Constance*; where it was enacted that the authority of the Councell was greater then that of the Pope: the *Sorbonne* Doctors declared that also to be their Doctrine. Afterwards when *Lewis* the 11. to gratifie Pope *Pius* the 2. purposed to abolish the force of the pragmatick sanction; the *Sorbonnists* in behalf of the Church *Gallican*, and the University of *Paris*; *Magnis obsistebant animis*, (saith *Sleidan* in his Commentaries) *& a Papa provocabant ad Concilium*. The Councell unto which they appealed was that of *Basil*; where that sanction was made: so that by this appeal, they verified their former *Thesis*; that the Councell was above the Pope. And not long since, *anno viz.* 1613. casually meeting with a book written by *Becanus*, entituled, *Controversia Anglicana de potestate regis & papæ:* they called an assembly, and condemned it. For though the main of it, was against the power and supremacy of the Kings of *England*: yet did it reflect also on the authority of the Pope over other Christian Kings by the bie, which occasioned the Sentence. So jealous are they of the least circumstances, in which the immunity of their nation may be endangered.

As for the Government of the University, it hath for its chief directour, a Rector: with a Chancellor, four Procurators or Proctors, and as many others, whom they call *Les Intrantes*, to assist him; besides the Regents. Of these the Regents are such Masters of the Arts, who are by the consent of the rest, selected to read the publick Lectures of Logick and Philosophy. Their name they derive *a regendo, eo quod in artibus rexerint.* These are divided into four Nations, *viz.* 1 The *Norman.* 2 The *Picarde.* 3. The *German.* And 4 The *French.* Under the two first are comprehended the students of those several Provinces: under the third, the Students of all forein nations, which repair hither for the attainment of knowledge. It was heretofore cal'ed *natio Anglica*: but the *English* being thought unworthy of the honour, because of their separation from the Church of *Rome*; the name and credit of it was given to the *Germans.* That of the *French* is again subdivided into two parts: that which is immediately within the Diocese of *Paris*; and that which containeth the rest of *Gallia.* These four Nations (for notwithstanding the subdivision above mentioned, the *French* is reckoned but as one) choose yearly four Proctors or Procurators; so called, *quia negotia nationis suæ procurant.* They choose four other officers, whom they call *les Intrantes:* in whose power there remaineth the Delegated authority of their several Nations. And here it is to be observed, that in the *French* Nation, the Procurator, and Intrant, is one year of the Diocese of *Paris*; and the following year of the rest of *France*: the reason why that Nation is subdivided. These four *Intrantes* thus named, have amongst them the election of the Rector: who is their supreme Magistrate.

The present Rector is named Mr. *Tarrienus,* of the Colledge of *Harcourte:* a Master of the Arts, for a Doctor is not capable of the Office. The honour lasteth only three moneths; which time expired, the *Intrantes* proceed to a new election: though oftentimes it hapneth that the same man hath the lease renued. Within the confines of the University, he taketh place next after the Princes of the bloud: and at the publique exercises of learning before the Cardinals, otherwise he giveth them the precedency. But to Bishops or Archbishops he will not grant it upon any occasion. It was not two moneths before my being there, that there hapned a shrewd controversie about it. For their King had then summoned an assembly of 25. Bishops of the Provinces adjoyning, to consult about some Church affairs; and they had chosen the Colledge of *Sorbonne* to be their Senate-house: when the first day of their sitting came, a Doctor of the house being appointed to preach before them: began his oration with *Reverendissime Rector, & vos amplissimi præsules*. Here the Archbishop of *Roven*, a man of an high spirit, interrupted him and commanded him to invert his stile. He obeyed, and presently the Rector riseth up with *Impono tibi silentium*: which is an injunction within the compasse of his power. Upon this the Preacher being tongue-tied, the controversie grew hot between the Bishops and the Rector, both parties very eagerly pleading their own priority. All the morning being almost spent in this altercation, a Cardinal wiser then the rest, desired that the question might for that time be layed aside: and that the Rector would be pleased to permit the Doctor to deliver his Sermon, beginning it without any præludium at all. To which request the Rector yeelded, and so the contention at that time was ended.

But *salus academiæ non vertitur in istis*. It were more for the honour and profit of the University, if the Rector would leave off to be so mindefull of his place, and look a little to his office. For certainly never the eye and utmost diligence of a Magistrate was wanting more, and yet more necessary, then in this place. *Penelopes* suitors never behaved themselves so insolently in the house of *Ulysses*, as the *Academicks* here do in the houses and streets of *Paris*.

Nos numeri sumus, & fruges consumere nati,
Sponsi Penelopes, nebolones Alcinoiq;——

not so becoming the mouth of any as of those. When you hear of their behaviour, you would think you were in *Turkie*: and that these men were the *Janizaries*. For an Angel given amongst them to drink, they will arrest whom you shall appoint them: double the money, and they shall break open his house, and ravish him into the Gaole. I have not heard that they can be hired to a murder: though nothing be more common amongst them then killing, except it be stealing. Witness those many carkasses which are found dead in the morning, whom a desire to secure themselves and make resistance to their pillages; hath only made earth again. Nay, which is most horrible, they have regulated their villanous practises into a Common-wealth: and have their captains and other officers, who command them in their night-walks; and dispose of their purchases. To be a *Gipsie* and a Scholar of *Paris*, are almost *Synonyma*. One of their Captains had in one week (for no longer would the gallowes let him enjoy his honour) stolne no fewer then 80 cloaks. *Num fuit Autolyci tam piceata manus?* For these thefts, being apprehended, he was adjudged to the wheel: but because the Judges were informed that during the time of his reign, he had kept the hands of himself and his company unpolluted with bloud; he had the favour to be hanged. In a word, this ungoverned rable, (whom to call scholars were to profane that title) omit no outrages or turbulent misdemeanors, which possibly can be, or were ever known to be committed in place; which consisteth meerly of priviledge, and nothing of statute.

I would heartily wish that those who are so ill conceited of their own two Universities of *Oxford* and *Cambridge*, and accuse them of dissolutenesse in their behaviour; would either spend some time in the Schools beyond seas: or enquire what newes abroad, of those which have seen them. Then would they doubtless see their own errors, and correct them. Then would they admire the regularity and civility of those places, which before they condemned of debauchednesse. Then would they esteem those places as the seminary of modesty and vertue, which they now account as the nurseries only of an impudent rudenesse. Such an opinion I am sure some of the *Aristarchi* of these daies, have lodged in their breasts, concerning the misgovernment of our *Athens*. Perhaps a kinsman of theirs hath played the unthrift, equally of his time and money: hence their malice to it, and their invectives against it. Thus of old,

———*Pallas*

———————*Pallas exurere classem*
Argivam, atq; ipsis potuit submergere ponto
Unius ob culpam & furias Ajacis Oilei.

An injustice more unpardonable, then the greatest sin of the Universities. But I wrong a good cause with an unnecessary patronage. Yet such is the peccant humour of some, that they know not how to expiate the follies of one but with the calumnie and dispraise of all. An unmanly weaknesse, and yet many possessed with it. I know it unpossible, that in a place of youth and liberty some should not give occasion of offence. The Ark wherein there were eight persons only, was not without one *Cham*, and of the twelve which Christ had chosen, one was a Devill. It were then above a miracle, if amongst so full a cohort of young souldiers, none should forsake the Ensign of his Generall: he notwithstanding that should give the imputation of cowardize to the whole army; cannot but be accounted malitious or peevish. But let all such as have evill will at *Sion*, live unregarded, and die unremembred, for want of some Scholar to write their Epitaph. Certainly a man not wedded to envie, and a spitefull vexation of spirit, upon a due examination of the civility of our *Lycea*, and a comparison of them with those abroad, cannot but say, and that justly, *Non habent Academiæ Anglicanæ pares, nisi seipsas.*

The principal cause of the rudenesse and disorders in *Paris* have been chiefly occasioned by the great priviledges wherewith the Kings of *France* intended the furtherance and security of learning. Having thus let them get the bridle in their own hands, no marvel if they grow sick with an uncontrolled licenciousnesse. Of these priviledges some are, that no Scholars goods can be seized upon, for the payment of his debts: that none of them should be liable to any taxes or impositions (a royall immunity to such as are acquainted with *France*:) that they might carry and recarry their utensils without the least molestation: that they should have the Provost of *Paris* to be the keeper and defender of
their

their liberties, who is therefore stiled, *Le conservateur des privileges royaux de l' Vniversite de Paris, &c.*

One greater priviledge they have yet then all these; which is their soon taking of degrees. Two years seeth them Novices in the Arts, and Masters of them. So that enjoying by their degrees an absolute freedome, before the follies and violences of youth are broke in them: they become so unruly and insolent, as I have told you. These degrees are conferred on them by the Chancellor, who seldome examineth further of them, then his fees. Those payed, he presenteth them to the Rector, and giveth them their Letters Patents sealed with the University Seal: which is the main part of the creation. He also setteth the Seal to the Authenticall Letters (for so they term them) of such whom the *Sorbonnists* have passed for Doctors. The present Chancellor is named *Petrus de Pierre vive*, Doctor of Divinity, and Canon of the Church of *Nostre Dame*: (as also are all they which enjoy that office). He is chosen by the Bishop of *Paris*, and taketh place of any under that dignity. But of this ill-managed University, enough, if not too much.

Chap. VII.

The City of Paris seated in the place of old Lutetia. The Bridges which joyn it to the Town and University. King Henry's Statua. Alexander's injurious policy. The Church and revenues of Nostre dame. The Holy-water there. The original making and vertue of it. The Lamp before the Altar. The heathenishnesse of both customes. Paris best seen from the top of this Church: the great Bell there never rung but in time of Thunder: the baptizing of Bels, the grand Hospital and decency of it. The place Daulphin. The holy Chappel and Reliques there. What the Ancients thought of Reliques. The Exchange. The little Chastelet. A transition to the Parliament.

THE Isle of *Paris,* commonly called *L'Isle du Palais,* seated between the University and the Town: is that part of the whole, which is called *La Cite,* the City, the epitome and abstract of all *France*. It is the sweetest and best ordered part of all *Paris*; and certainly if *Paris* may be thought to be the eye of the Realm; this Island may be equally judged to be the apple of that eye. It is by much the lesser part, and by as much the richer, by as much the decenter: and affordeth more variety of objects, then both the other. It containeth an equall number of Parish Churches, with the Town, and double the number of the University. For it hath in it 13 Churches parochial, viz. *la Magdalene.* 2 St. *Geniveue des ardents.* 3 St. *Christopher.* 4 St. *Pierre aux Boeufs.* 5 St. *Marine.* 6 St. *Lander.* 7 St. *Symphorian.* 8 St. *Denis de la charite.* 9 St. *Bartelemie.* 10 St. *Pierre des d.s Assis.* 11 St. *Croix.* 12 St. *Marciall.* 13 St. *German de vieux.* Seated it is in the middle of the *Seine*, and in that place where stood the old *Lutetia*: *Lablenus cum quatuor legionibus* (saith *Jul. Cæsar* 70 *Comment.*) *Lutetiam proficiscitur: id est opidum Parisiorum positum in medio fluminis Sequanæ.* It is joyned to the main land, and the other parts of this *French* Metropolis, by six Bridges, two of wood, and four of stone: the stone Bridges, are 1 *Le petit pont,* a Bridge which certainly deserveth that name. 2 *Le pont de Nostre dame,* which is all covered with two goodly ranks of houses: and those adorned with portly and antick imagery. 3 *Le pont St. Michell,* so called, because it leadeth towards the Gate of *St. Michell*; hath also on each side a beautifull row of houses: all of the same fashion, so exactly, that but by their severall doors, you would scarce think them to be several houses. they are all new, as being built in the reign of this present King, whose armes is engraven over every door of them.

The fourth and largest Bridge, is that which standeth at the end of the Isle next the *Louvre*; and covereth the waters now united again into one stream. It was begun to be built by *Katharine* of *Medices,* the Queen-Mother, *anno* 1578. her Son King *Henry* the 3. laying the first stone of it. The finishing of it was reserved unto *Henry* 4. who as soon as he had setled his affairs in this Town, presently set the workmen about it. In the end of it where it joyneth to the Town, there is a water-house which by artificiall engines forceth up waters from a fresh spring, rising from under the river: done at the charge of this King also. In the midst of it is the *Statua* of the said *Henry* 4. all in brasse, mounted on his barbed Steed, of the same mettle. They are both of them very unproportionable unto those which they represent: and would shew them big enough, were they placed on the top of *Nostre dame Church.* What minded King *Lewis* to make his father of so gigantive a stature, I cannot tell. *Alexander* at his return from his *Indian* expedition, scattered Armours, Swords, and Horsebits, far bigger then were serviceable: to make future ages admire his greatnesse. Yet some have hence collected, that the acts he performed are not so great as they are reported: because he strived to make them seem greater then they were. It may also chance to happen, that men in the times to come, comparing the atchievements of this King, with his brazen portraiture: may think that the historians have as much belied his valour as the statuary hath his person.

A ponte ad pontifices. From the Bridge, proceed we to the Church, the principal Church of *Paris*: being that *Nostre dame.* A Church very uncertain of its first founder, though some report him to be St. *Savinian*: of whom I can meet with no more then his name. But who ever laid the first foundation, it much matters not: all the glory of the work being now cast on *Philip Augustus*; who pitying the ruines of it, began to build it *anno* 1196. It is a very fair and awfull building, adorned with a very beautifull front, and two towers of especiall height. It is in length 174 paces, and 60 in bredth: and is said to be as many paces high: and that the two towers are 70 yards higher then the rest of the Church. At your first entrance, on the right hand, is the effigies of St. *Christopher*, with our Saviour on his shoulders. A man, the Legend maketh him as well as the Mason, of a gyantlike stature; though of the two, the Mason's workmanship is the more admirable: his being all cut out of one main stone; that of the *Legendary* being patched up of many fabulous and ridiculous shreds: it hath in, lo four ranks of pillars 30 in rank; and 45 little Chappels, or Masse-closets, built between the outermost range of pillars, and the wals. This is the seat of the Archbishop of *Paris*, for such now he is. It was a Bishoprick only till the year 1622. When Pope *Gregory* the 15. at the request of King *Lewis*, raised it to a Metropolitanship. But by this addition of honour, I think the present Incumbent hath got nothing, either in precedency, or profit. He had before a necessary voice in the Court of Parliament, and took place immediately next after the Presidents, he doth no more now. Before he had the priority of all the Bishops, and now he is but the last of all the Archbishops: a preferment rather intellectuall then reall: and perhaps his successors may account it a punishment; for besides that the dignity is too
un-

unweildy for the revenue, which is but 6000 Livres or 600 *l.* *English* yearly: like enough it is, that some may come into that Sea of *Cæsar's* minde, who being in a small village of the *Alps*, thus delivered his ambition to his followers, *Mallem esse hic primus, quam Romæ secundus.* The present possessor of this Chair, is *Francis de Gondi*, by birth a *Florentine:* one, whom I have heard much famed for a Statesman, but little for a Scholar. But had he nothing in him, this alone were sufficient to make him famous to posterity, that he was the first Archbishop, and the last Bishop of the City of *Paris*. There is moreover in this Church a Dean, 7 Dignities, and 50 Canons. The Deans place is valued at 4000 Livres, the Dignities at 3000, and the Canons at 2000; no great intrados: and yet unproportionable to the Archbishoprick.

At *Dieppe* (as I have said) I observed the first Idolatry of the Papists: here I noted their first superstitions; which were the needlesse use of Holy-water, and the burning of Lamps before the Altar. The first is said to have been the invention of Pope *Alexander* the 7. Bishop of *Rome* in their account after *Peter*. I dare not give so much credit unto *Platina*, as to believe it of this antiquity; much lesse unto *Bellarmine*, who deriveth it from the Apostles themselves. In this paradox, he hath enemies enough at home, his own Doctors being all for *Alexander*, yet they also are not in the right. The principall foundation of their opinion, is an Epistle decretory of this *Alexander:* which in it self carrieth its own confutation. The citations of Scripture, on which this Superstition is thought to be grounded, are all taken out of the vulgar Latine translation attributed to St. *Hierome*, whereas neither was there in the time of *Alexander* any publick Translation of the Bible into Latine: neither was St. *Jerome* born within 300 years after him. Holy-water then is not of such a standing in the Church, as the Papists would perswade us: and as yet I have not met with any, that can justly inform me at what time the Church received it; many corruptions they have among them whereof neither they nor we can tell the beginnings.

It consisteth of two ingredients, salt and water: each of
them

them severally consecrated, or rather exorcised; for so the words go: *Exorcizo te creatura salis.* And afterwards, *Exorcizo te creatura aquæ &c.* This done, the salt is sprinkled into the water in form of a crosse, the Priest in the mean time saying, *Commixtio salis & aquæ pariter fiat, in nomine patris, &c.* Being made, it is put into a cistern standing at the entrance of their Church: the people at their coming in, sometimes dipping their fingers into it, and making with it the sign of the crosse on their foreheads: and sometimes being sprinkled with it by one of the Priests, who in course bestow that blessing upon them. Pope *Alexander* who is said to be the father of it, gave it the gift of purifying and sanctifying all which it washed: *Ut cuncti illa aspersi purificentur, & sanctificentur,* saith his Decretall. The *Roman Rituall* published and confirmed by *Paulus* 5. maketh it very soveraign, *ad abigendos dæmones, & spiritus immundos.* *Bellarmine* maintaineth it a principall remedy, *ad remissionem peccatorum venialium,* and saith; that this was the perpetuall doctrine of the Church. *Augustin Steuchus* in his Commentaries on Numbers, leaveth out *venialia,* and pronounceth it to be necessary, *ut ad ejus aspersum delicta nostra deleantur,* so omnipotent is this Holy-water, that the bloud of our Saviour Christ may be in a manner judged unnecessary; but it is not only used in the Churches, the *Rituale Romanum,* of which I spake but now, alloweth any of the faithfull to carry it away with them in their vessels, *ad aspergendos agros, domos, agros, vineas & alia: & ad habendam eam in cubiculis suis.* To which purposes you cannot but think this water to be exceeding serviceable.

The second superstition which this Church shewed me was the continuall burning of a Lamp before the Altar, a ceremony brought into the Churches (as it is likely) by Pope *Innocent* 3. *anno* 1215. at what time he ordained that there should a pix be bought to cover the bread, and that it should be therein reserved over the Altar. This honour one of late times hath communicated also unto the virgin *Mary*: whose image in this Church, hath a lanthorn *ex diametro* before it: and in that a candle perpetually burning. The name of the Donour, I could not learn, only I met on the

the skreen close by the Ladies image this inscription, *Une ave Maria, et un' pater noster, pour l' in qui cela donne*: which was intended on him that bestowed the Lanthorn. No question but Pope *Innocent*, when he ordered this Vestall fire to be kept amongst the Christians, thought he had done God good service in reviving his old Commandement given to *Moses* in *Exod*. 27. 20, 21 if so, the world cannot clear him of *Judaism*; therefore the best way were to say he learned it of the *Gentiles*: For we read that the *Athenians* had *Lychnum inextincti luminis*, before the Statua of their *Pallas*: that the *Persians* also had *Ignem pervigilem* in their Temples: and so also had the *Medians* and *Assyrians*. To omit the everlasting fire of *Vesta*, and come neer home, we meet with it also here in *Britain*; *In Britannia quoque* (saith a good Philosopher) *Minervæ numen colitur, in cujus templo perpetui ignes*, &c. Afterwards the flattery of the Court applying divine honours unto their Kings, this custome of having fire continually burning before them, began to grow in fashion among the *Romans*. *Herodian* amongst other the ensignes of imperiall majesty, is sure not to omit this, and therefore telleth us, that notwithstanding *Commodus* was fallen out with his sister *Lucilla*, he permitteth her her antient seat in the Theatre, καὶ τὸ πῦρ προπομπεύειν αὐτῆς, and that fire should still be carryed before her. The present *Romans* succeed the former, as in their possessions, so in their follies. For calling the Sacrament their *Lord God*, and the *Virgin* their *Lady*, they thought they should rob them of half their honour, should they not have their Lamps and fires also burning before them.

As are their lamps, so is their holy-water, meerly *Heathenish*: *Siquidem in omnibus sacris* (as we read in the fourth Book *Genialium dierum*) *sacerdos cum diis immolat, & rem divinam facit, corporis ablutione purgatur*. The author giveth a reason for it, and I would have no Papist, no not *Bellarmine* himself to give a better; *Aquæ enim aspersione labem tolli, & castimoniam præstari putant*. Neither did the Priest only use it himselfe, but he sprinkled also the people with it;

Spargere

*Spargere rore levi, & ramo fœlicis olivæ,
Lustravitque viros :* ———

As *Virgil* in the *Æneids.*

In which place two things are to be noted: First, *Ramus olivæ*, now called *Aspersorium*, or the sprinkling rod, wherewith the water is sprinkled on the by-standers. And secondly, the term *lustrare*, meerly the name of *Aqua lustralis*, by which they call it. That the laicks also of the *Gentiles*, were clensed of sin by this water, is evident by that of *Homer*, where he maketh *Orestes* having killed his mother, and thereupon grown mad, at once restored to his wits and quiet thoughts, by washing in the water. Perhaps *Pilate* might allude to this custome, when having condemned our Saviour, he washed his hands in the middest of the Congregation. Hereunto also *Ovid* :

*O faciles nimium, qui tristia crimina cædis
Fluminea tolli posse putatis aqua.*

Too facile souls, which think such hainous matters
Can be aboliz'd by the river waters.

Indeed, in the word *fluminea*, the Poet was somewhat out, the waters only of the Sea serving for the expiation of any crime; the reason was, *Cum propter vim igneam magnopere purgationibus consentanea putaretur*; and for this cause questionlesse, do the Popish Priests use salt in the consecration of their holy-water; that it might as nigh as was possible, resemble the waters of the Sea in saltnesse. So willing are they in all circumstances to act the *Heathens.*

But I have kept you too long within the Church, it is now time to go up to the top, and survey the outworks of it. It hath, as we have already said, at the front two Towers of admirable beauty; they are both of an equal height, and are each of them 377 steps in the ascent. From hence we could clearly see the whole circuite of *Paris*, and each severall street of it; such as we have already described, of an orbicular form and neatly

neatly compacted. From hence could we see the whole valley round about it, such as I have also delineated already, though not in such lively colours as it meriteth.

In one of these Towers there is a ring of Bels, in the other two only, but these for worth are equall to all the rest; the bigger of the two is said to be greater then the Bell of *Roven* so much talked of; as being 8 yards and a span in compasse, and two yards and a half in depth; the bowl also of the clapper being one yard and a quarter round: of a great weight it needs must be, and therefore

Multorum manibus grande levatur onus,

there are no lesse then four main ropes, besides their severall tale-ropes, to ring it. By reason of this trouble it is never rung, but in time of thunders, and those no mean ones neither, lesser bels will serve to disperse the lesser tempests; this is used only in the horrider claps, and such as threaten a dissolution of nature. But how well, as well this as the smaller bels discharge that office, experience would tell us were we void of reason; yet so much do the people affiance themselves to this conceit of the power of them, that they suppose it inherent to them continually, after the Bishop hath baptized them; which is done in this manner. The bell being so hanged that it may be washed within and without, in comes the Bishop in his Episcopall robes, attended by one of his Deacons, and sitting by the Bell in his chaire saith with a loud voice the 50, 53, 56, 66, 69, 85, and 12 *Psalmes*, or some of them: then doth he exorcize severally the salt and the water, and having conjured these ingredients into an Holy-water, he washeth with it the Bell, both on the inside and the outside, wiping it dry with a linnen cloth, he readeth the 145, 146, 147, 148, 149, and 150 *Psalms*; he draweth a crosse on it with his right thumb dipped in hallowed oyl, (*Chrisme* they call it) and then prayeth over it. His prayer finished, he wipeth out that crosse, and having said over the 48 *Psalm*, he draweth on it with the same oyl, seven other crosses, saying, *Sanctificetur & consecetur consecretur Domine campana ista, in nomine, &c.* After another prayer, the Bishop taketh the Censour, and putting into it Myrrhe and Frankincense, setteth it on fire, and putteth it under the Bell that it may receive all the fume of it. This done, the 76 *Psalm* read and some other prayers repeated, the Bell hath received his whole and entire Baptisme, and these virtues following, *viz. Ut per illius tactum procul pellantur omnes insidiæ inimici, fragor grandinum, procella turbinum, impetus tempestatum, &c.* For so one of the prayers reckoneth them prescribed in the *Roman Pontificall*, authorized by *Clement* VIII. A strange piece of Religion that a Bell should be Baptized; and so much the stranger, in that these inanimate bodies can be received into the Church, by no other ministry then that of the Bishop; the true Sacrament being permitted to every hedge Priest.

Not farre from the West gate of this Church of *Nostre dame*, is the *Hostel dieu*, or *Le grand Hospital de Paris*; first founded by St. *Lewis, anno* 1258. it hath been since beautifyed and enlarged, *anno* 1535. by Mr. *Anthony Pratt* Chancellour of *France*, who augmented the number of Hospitalers; and gave fair revenues for the maintaining of Chirurgeons, Apothecaries, and Religious men among them. Since that time, the *Provosts* and *Eschevins* of *Paris* have been especiall Benefactors unto it. At the first entrance into it, you come into their Chappell, small, but handsome and well furnished; after, you passe into a long gallery, having four ranks of beds, two close to the two wals, and two in the middle. The beds are all sutable one to the other; their Valence, Curtains and Rugs being all yellow. At the right hand of it, was a gallery more then double the length of this first, so also furnished. At the further end of this a door opened into another Chamber, dedicated only to sick women: and within them another room, wherein women with childe are lightned of their burden, and their children kept till seven years of age, at the charge of the Hospitall. At the middle of the first gallery towards the left hand,

were

were four other ranks of beds, little differing from the rest, but that their furniture was blew; and in them there was no place for any but such as were somewhat wounded, and belonged properly to the Chirurgeon. There are numbred in the whole Hospitall no fewer then 700 beds (besides those of the attendants, Priests, Apothecaries, &c) and in every bed two persons. One would imagine that in such a variety of wounds and diseases, a walke into it, and a view of it, might savour more of curiosity, then discretion, but indeed it is nothing lesse; for besides that no person of an infectious disease is admitted into it: which maketh much for the safety of such as view it; all things are there kept so cleanly, neatly and orderly, that it is sweeter walking there then in the best street of *Paris*, none excepted.

Next unto these succeedeth *La Sancte Chappelle*, situate in the middle of the *Palais*; a Chappell famous for its forme, but more for its Reliques. It was founded by *Lewis* IX. vulgarly called St. *Lewis*, 1248. and is divided into two parts, the upper and the lower, the lower serving for the keeping of the Reliques; and the upper for celebrating the Masse. It is a comely spruce Edifice without, but far more curious within; the glasse of it for the excellency of painting, and the Organs for the richnesse and elaborate workmanship of the case, not giving way to any in *Europe*. I could not learn the number of *Chanoins*, which are maintained in it, though I heard they were places of 300 Crowns revenue. As for their Treasurer, *Le Thresaururier*, so they call their Governour; He hath granted him by especall priviledge licence to wear all the Episcopall habits, except the Crosier-staffe; and to bear himselfe as a Bishop within the liberties of his Chappell. In the top of the upper Chappell (it is built almost in forme of a *Synagogue*) there hangeth the true proportion (as they say) of the Crown of thornes: but of this more when we have gone over the Reliques. I was there divers times to have seen them, but (It seemeth) they were not visible to an *Hugnots* eyes; though me thinketh, they might have considered, that my money was Catholique. They are kept, as I said, in the lower Chappell, and are thus marshalled in a Table, hanging in the upper; know then that you may believe that they can shew you the crown of thornes, the bloud which ran from our Saviours brest, his swadling cloutes, a great part of the Crosse (they also of *Nostre dame* have some of it) the chaine by which the *Jewes* bound him, no small peece of the stone of the Sepulchre, *Sanctam toelam tabulæ insertam*, which I know not how to *English*. Some of the Virgins milke, (for I would not have those of St. *Denis* think, that the Virgin gave no other milk, but to them) the head of the Lance which pierced our Saviour, the purple Robe, the Sponge, a piece of his Shroud, the napkin wherewith he was girted when he washed his Disciples feet, the rod of *Moses*, the heads of St. *Blase*, St. *Clement*, and St. *Simeon*, and part of the head of *John Baptist*. Immediately under this recitall of these Reliques (and venerable ones I durst say they were, could I be perswaded there were no imposture in them) there are set down a *Prayer* and an *Anthem*, both in the same Table; as followeth.

Oratio.

Quæsumus Omnipotens Deus, ut qui sacra sanctissimæ redemptionis nostræ insignia, temporaliter veneramur: per hæc indesinenter muniti, æternitatis gloriam consequamur, per dominum nostrum, &c.

De

De sacrosanctis reliquiis

Antiphona.

Christo plebs dedita, Tot Christi donis prædita
 Jocunderis hodie, Tota sis devota,
Erumpens in jubilum, Depone mentis nubilum;
 Tempus est lætitiæ, Cura sit summota,
Ecce crux et Lancea, ferrum, corona spinea,
 Arma regis gloriæ, Tibi offerantur,
Omnes terræ populi, laudent actorem seculi,
 Per quem tantis gratiæ signis gloriantur. Amen.

Pretty Divinity, if one had time to examine it. These Reliques as the Table informeth us, were given unto St. *Lewis*, *ann.* 1247. by *Baldwin* the II. the last King of the *Latines* in *Constantinople*; to which place the *Christians* of *Palestine* had brought them, during the times that those parts were harryed by the *Turks* and *Saracens*. Certainly, were they the same, which they are given out to be, I see no harme in it, if we should honour them. The very reverence due unto antiquity and a silver head, could not but extract some acknowledgment of respect, even from an *Heathen*. It was therefore commendably done by Pope *Leo*, having received a parcell of the Crosse from the Bishop of *Jerusalem*, that he entertained it with respect; *Particulam dominicæ crucis* (saith he in his 72. Epistle) *cum Eulogiis dilectionis tuæ veneratur accepi.* To adore and worship that or any other Relick whatsoever, with *Prayers* and *Anthems*, as the *Papists* you see do, never came within the minds of the Antients, and therefore St. *Ambrose* calleth it, *Gentilis error, & vanitas impiorum*. This also was St. *Hieroms* Religion, as himself testifieth in his Epistle to *Riparius*, *Nos* (saith he) *non dicas Martyrum reliquias, sed ne Solem quidem & Lunam, non Angelos*, &c. *colimus & adoramus*. Thus were those two fathers minded towards such Reliques, as were known to be no others then what they seemed: Before too many centuries of years had consumed the true ones; and the impostures of the Priests had brought in false, had they lived in our times, and seen the supposed remnants of the Saints, not honoured only, but adored and worshipped by their blind and infatuated people; what would they have said? or rather, what would they not have said? Questionlesse the least they could do, were to take up the complaint of *Vigilantius* (the *Papists* reckon him for an *Heretick*) saying, *Quid necesse est tanto honore non solum honorare, sed etiam adorare, illud nescio quid, quod in vasculo transferendo colis?*

Presently without the Chappell is the Burse, *La Galerie des Merchands*; a rank of shops, in shew, but not in substance, like to those in the *Exchange* in *London*. It reacheth from the Chappell unto the great hall of Parliament; and is the common through-fare between them. On the bottome of the staires and round about the severall houses, consecrated to the execution of Justice, are sundry shops of the same nature, meanly furnished if compared with ours; yet I perswade my self the richest of this kind in *Paris*. I should now go and take a view of the *Parliament house*; but I will step a little out of the way to see the *Place Daulphin*, and the little *Chastelet*; this last serveth now only as the Gaole or Common-prison belonging to the Court of the *Prevost* of *Merchants*, and it deserveth no other imployment. It is seated at the end of the Bridge called *Petit Pont*, and was built by *Hugh Aubriet* once *Prevost* of this Town, to represse the fury and insolencies of the Scholars, whose rudenesse and misdemeanors can no wayes be better
bridled.

bridled. *Omnes eos, qui nomen ipsum Academiæ, vel serio, vel joco nominassent, hereticos pronunciavit,* saith *Platina* of Pope *Paul* the II. I dare say it of this wildernesse, that whosoever will account it as an Academy, is an Heretick to Learning and Civility. The *Place Daulphin,* is a beautifull heap of building, situate nigh unto the new Bridge. It was built at the encouragement of *Henry* IV. and entituled according to the title of his Son. The houses are all of brick, high built, uniforme, and indeed such as deserve and would exact a longer description, were not the Parliament now ready to sit, and my self summoned to make my appearance.

Chap. VIII.

The Parliament of France when begun; of whom it consisted. The dignity and esteem of it abroad, made sedenturie at Paris, appropriated to the long robe. The Palais *by whom built, and converted to seats of Justice. The seven Chambers of Parliament. The great Chamber. The number and dignity of the Presidents. The Duke of* Biron *afraid of them. The Kings seat in it. The sitting of the* Grand Signeur *in the* Divano. *The authority of this Court in causes of all kinds; and over the affaires of the King. This Court the main pillar of the Liberty of* France. La Tournelle, *and the Judges of it. The five Chambers of* Enquestes *severally instituted, and by whom. In what cause it is* decisive. *The forme of admitting Advocates into the Courts of Parliament. The* Chancellour of France *and his Authority. The two Courts of* Requests, *and Masters of them. The vain envy of the* English Clergy *against the Lawyers.*

THe Court of Parliament was at the first instituted by *Charles Martell* Grandfather to *Charlemaine*, at such time as he was *Maire* of the *Palace*, unto the lasie and rechlesse Kings of *France*. In the beginnings of the *French* Empire, their Kings did justice to their people in person: afterwards banishing themselves from all the affaires of State, that burden was cast upon the shoulders of their *Maiors*; an office much of a nature with the *Præfecti prætorio* in the *Roman* Empire. When this office was bestowed upon the said

Charles

Charles Martell, he partly weary of the trouble, partly intent about a businesse of an higher nature, which was, the estating the Crown in his own posterity; but principally to endeer himselfe to the common people, ordained this Court of Parliament, *anno* 720. It consisted in the beginning of 12 *Peers*, the *Prelates* and noble men of the best fashion, together with some of the principallest of the Kings houshold. Other Courts have been called the Parliaments with an addition of place, as of *Paris*, at *Roven*, &c. this only *Tʼoxdy*, the Parliament. It handled as well causes of estate, as those of private persons. For hither did the Ambassadors of neighbour Princes repaire, to have their audience and dispatch; and hither were the Articles agreed on, in the nationall *Synods* of *France* sent to be confirmed and verified; here did the subjects tender in their homages, and Oaths of fidelity to the King; and here were the appeals heard of all such as had complained against the *Comites*, at that time the Governours and Judges in their severall Counties. Being furnished thus with the prime and choycest Nobles of the Land, it grew into great estimation abroad in the world; insomuch that the Kings of *Sicilie*, *Cyprus*, *Scotland*, *Bohemia*, *Portugall*, and *Navarre*, have thought it no disparagement unto them to sit in it; and which is more, when *Frederick* II. had spent so much time in quarrels with Pope *Innocent* IV. he submitted himselfe and the rightnesse of his cause to be examined by this Noble Court of Parliament. At the first institution of this Court, it had no setled place of residence, being sometimes kept at *Tholoza*, sometimes at *Aix la Chappelle*, sometimes in other places, according as the Kings pleasure, and ease of the people did require. During its time of peregrination, it was called *Ambulatoire*, following for the most part the Kings Court, as the lower *spheres* do the motion of the *primum mobile*; but *Philip le bel* (he began his reign *anno* 1286) being to take a journey into *Flanders*, and to stay there a long space of time, for the setling of his affaires in that Countrey, took order that this Court of Parliament should stay behind at *Paris*; where ever since it hath continued.

Now began it to be called *Sedentaire* or setled, and also *peus peu*, by little and little to lose much of its lustre. For the chief Princes and Nobles of the Kings retinue, not able to live out of the aire of the Court, withdrew themselves from the troubles of it; by which means at last it came to be appropriated to them of the Long robe, as they term them, both Bishops and Lawyers. In the year 1463. the Prelates also were removed by the command of *Lewis* XI. an utter enemy to the great ones of his Kingdome, only the Bishop of *Paris*, and Abbot of St. *Denis*, being permitted their place in it: since which time the Professors of the civill law have had all the sway in it, *Et cedunt arma togæ*, as *Tully*.

The place in which this Sedentarie Court of Parliament is now kept, is called the *Palace*, being built by *Philip le bel*, and intended to be his mansion or dwelling house. He began it in the first year of his reign, *anno* 1286. and afterwards assigned a part of it to his Judges of the Parliament: it being not totally and absolutely quitted unto them till the dayes of King *Lewis* XII. In this the *French* Subjects are beholding to the *English*; by whose good example they got the ease of a Sedentarie Court: our Law courts also removing with the King, till the year 1224. when by a Statute in the *Magna Charta* it was appointed to be fixt; and a part of the Kings Palace in *Westminster* allotted for that purpose.

Within the verge of this *Palais* are contained the seven Chambers of the Parliament; that called *La grande Chambre*; five Chambers of Inquisition, *Des Enquestes*; and one other called *La Tournelle*. There are moreover the Chambers, *des aides, des accomptes, de l' edict, des monnoyes*, and one called *La Chambre Royall*; of all which we shall have occasion to speak in their proper places: these not concerning the common government of the people, but only of the Kings revenues. Of these seven Chambers of Parliament, *La grande Chambre* is most famous; and at the building of this house by *Philip le bel*, was intended for the Kings bed. It is no such beautifull piece as the *French* make it, that of *Roven* being far beyond it; although indeed it much excell the
fairest

fairest room of Justice in all *Westminster*; so that it standeth in a middle rank between them, and almost in the same proportions as *Virgil* betwixt *Homer* and *Ovid*.

Quantum Virgilius magno concessit Homero;
Tantum ego Virgilio Naso poeta meo.

It consisteth of seven *Presidents*, 22 *Counsellours*, the Kings *Attorney*; and as many *Advocates* and *Proctours* as the Court will please to give admission to. The *Advocates* have no setled studies within the *Palais*, but at the Barre; but the *Procureurs* or *Attorneys* have their severall pews in the great Hall, which is without this *Grande Chambre*, in such manner as I have before described at *Roven*: a large building it is, fair and high roofed: not long since ruined by a casualty of fire, and not yet fully finished. The names of the Presidents are Mr. *Verdun*, the first President, or by way of excellencie, *Le Président*, the second man of the Long robe in *France*. 2. Mr. *Sequer*, lately dead, and likely to have his son succeed him, as well in his Office, as in his Lands. 3. Mr. *Leiger*. 4. Mr. *Dosembe*. 5. Mr. *Sevin*. 6. Mr. *Bailleure*. And 7. Mr. *Meisme*. None of these, neither Presidents nor Counsellors, can go out of *Paris*, when the Lawes are open, without leave of the Court: it was ordained so by *Lewis* XII. anno 1499. and that with good judgement; Sentences being given with greater awe, and businesses managed with greater majesty when the Bench is full: and it seemeth indeed that they carry with them great terror; for the Duke of *Biron*, a man of as uncontrouled spirit, as any in *France*, being called to answer for himself in this Court, protested, that those scarlet roabs did more amaze him, then all the red cassocks of *Spain*.

At the left hand of this *Grande Chambre*, or *Golden Chambre* as they call it, is a Throne or seat Royall, reserved for the King, when he shall please to come and see the administration of Justice amongst his people; at common times it is naked and plain, but when the King is expected, it is clothed with blew-purple Velvet, semied with *flowers de lys*; on each side of it are two formes or benches, where the Peers

P 2   of

of both habits, both Ecclesiasticall and Secular, use to sit and accompany the King. But this is little to the ease or benefit of the Subject, and as little availeable to try the integrity of the Judges; his presence being alwayes foreknown, and so accordingly they prepared. Far better then is it, in the *Grande Signeur*, where the *Divano*, or Councell of the *Turkish* affairs holden by the *Bassas*, is hard by his bed-chamber which looketh into it: the window which giveth him this entervenue is perpetually hidden with a curtain on the side of the partition, which is towards the *Divano*; so that the *Bassas* and other Judges cannot at any time assure themselves that the Emperor is not listning to their sentences: an action in which nothing is *Turkish* or *Mahometan*.

The authority of this Court extendeth it self unto all causes within the jurisdiction of it, not being meerly ecclesiasticall. It is a law unto it self, following no rule written, in their sentences, but judging according to equity and conscience. In matters criminall of greater consequence, the processe is here immediately examined, without any preparation of it by the inferior Courts; as at the arraignment of the Duke of *Biron*: and divers times also in matters personall. But their power is most eminent in disposing the affaires of State, and of the Kingdome. For such prerogatives have the *French* Kings given hereunto, that they can neither denounce War, nor conclude Peace, without the consent (a formall one at the least) of this Chamber. An alienation of the Lands of the Crown, is not any whit valid, unlesse confirmed by this Court: neither are his Edicts in force, till they are here verified: nor his Letters Patents for the creating of a Peer, till they are here allowed of. Most of these, I confesse, are little more then matters of form, the Kings power and pleasure being become boundlesse; yet sufficient to shew the body of authority which they once had, and the shadow of it, which they still keep; yet of late they have got into their disposing one priviledge belonging formerly to the *Conventus ordinum*, or the Assembly of three Estates, which is the conferring of the regency or protection of their King during his minority. That the Assembly of the three Estates formerly had this priviledge is evident

dent by their stories. Thus we finde them to have made Queen *Blanche* Regent of the Realm, during the nonage of her son St. *Lewis*, 1227. That they declared *Philip de Valois* successor to the Crown, in case that the widow of *Charles le bel*, was not delivered of a son, 1357. As also *Philip* of *Burgogne*, during the Lunacy of *Charles* VI. 1394. with divers other. On the other side we have a late example of the power of the Parliament of *Paris* in this very case. For the same day that *Henry* IV. was slain by *Ravilliac*, the Parliament met, and after a short consultation, declared *Mary de Medices*, Mother to the King, *Regent* in *France*, for the government of the State, during the minority of her son, with all power and authority. Such are the words of the Instrument, Dated the 14 of *May* 1610.

It cannot be said but that this Court deserveth not only this, but also any other indulgence, whereof any one member of the Common-wealth is capable. So watchfull are they over the health of the State, and so tenderly do they take the least danger threatned to the liberty of that Kingdom, that they may not unjustly be called, *patres patriæ*. In the year 1614. they seized upon a discourse written by *Suarez* a Jesuite, Entituled, *Adversus Anglicanæ sectæ errores*: wherein the Popes temporall power over Kings and Princes is averred: which they sentenced to be burnt in the Palace-yard by the publick hangman. The year before they inflicted the same punishment upon a vain and blasphemous discourse penned by *Gasper Sclopplus*, a fellow of a most desperate brain, and a very incendiary. Neither hath *Bellarmine* himself, that great *Atlas* of the *Roman* Church, escaped much better: for writing a book concerning the temporall power of his Holinesse, it had the ill luck to come into *Paris*, where the Parliament finding it to thwart the liberty and royalty of the King and Countrey, gave it over to the Hangman, and he to the fire. Thus it is evident that the titles which the *French* writers give it, as the *true Temple of French Justice*, the *buttresse of equity*, and the *guardian of the rights of France*, and the like, are abundantly deserved of it.

The next Chamber in esteem is the *Tournelle*, which handleth all matters criminall. It is so called from *tourner*, which signifieth to change or alter; because the Judges of the other severall chambers give sentence in this, according to their severall turns; the reason of which institution is said to be, lest a continuall custome of condemning, should make the Judges lesse mercifull, and more prodigall of bloud: an order full of health and providence. It was instituted by the above named *Philip de bel*, at the same time when he made the Parliament *sedentarie* at *Paris*; and besides its peculiar and originall imployments, it receiveth appeals from, and redresseth the errors of the Provost of *Paris*. The other five Chambers are called *Des Enquestes*, or *Cameræ inquisitionum*; the first and antientest of them was erected also by *Philip le bel*, and afterwards divided into two by *Charles* VII. Afterwards the multitude of Processes being greater then could be dispatched in these Courts, there was added a third. *Francis* the first established the fourth for the better raising of a sum of money which then he wanted; every one of the new Counsellors paying right deerly for his place. The fifth and last was founded in the year 1568. In each of these severall Chambers there are two Presidents, and 20 Counsellors, besides Advocates and Proctours *ad placitum*. In the *Tournelle*, which is an aggregation of all the other Courts, there are supposed to be no fewer then 200 officers of all sorts; which is no great number considering the many causes there handled. In the *Tournelle*, the Judges sit on life and death; in the Chamber of *Enquests*, they examine only civill affaires of estate, title, debts, or the like. The pleaders in these Courts are called *Advocates*, and must be at the least *Licentiates* in the study of the Law. At the Parliaments of *Tholoza* and *Bourdeaux*, they admit of none but Doctors. Now the forme of admitting them is this: In an open and frequent Court, one of the aged'st of the Long roab presenteth the party, which desireth admission, to the Kings Attorney generall, saying with a loud voice, *Paise a cour recevoir N. N. licencie* (or *Docteur*) *en droict civil, a la office d' Advocate*; This said, the Kings Attorney biddeth him hold up his hand, and saith to him in Latine, *Tu jurabis observare omnes regias consuetudines;*

CHAP. VIII.   *the State of* France.   111

suetudines; he answereth *Juro*, and departeth. At the Chamber door of the Court, whereof he is now sworn an Advocate, he payeth two crowns; which is forthwith put into the common treasury appointed for the relief of the distressed widows of ruined Advocates and Proctours; *Hanc veniam petimusque damusque*, it may be their own cases, and therefore it is paid willingly. The highest preferment of which these Advocates are capable is that of Chancellor, an office of great power and profit: the present Chancellor is named Mr. *d' Alegre*, by birth of *Chartres*. He hath no settled Court wherein to exercise his authority, but hath in all the Courts of *France* the Supream place whensoever he will vouchsafe to visite them. He is also President of the Councell of Estate by his place; and on him dependeth the making of good and sacred laws, the administration of Justice, the reformation of superfluous, and abrogation of unprofitable Edicts, &c. He hath the keeping of the Kings great seal, and by virtue of that, either passeth or putteth back such Letters patents and Writs as are exhibited to him. He hath under him, immediately for the better dispatch of his affaires, four Masters of the Requests and their Courts. Their office and manner of proceeding, is the same which they also use in *England*; in the persons there is thus much difference, for that in *France*, two of them must be perpetually of the Clergy. One of their Courts is very ancient, and hath in it two Presidents, which are two of the Masters; and 14 Counsellors. The other is of a later erection, as being founded *anno* 1580. and in that, the two other of the Masters and eight Counsellors give sentence.

Thus have I taken a view of the severall Chambers of the Parliament of *Paris*, and of their particular jurisdictions, as far as my information could conduct me. One thing I noted further, and in my mind the fairest ornament of the Palace, which is the neatnesse and decency of the Lawyers in their apparell; for besides the fashion of their habit, which is I assure you, exceeding pleasing and comely, themselves by their own care and love to handsomenesse, add great lustre to their garments, and more to their persons. Richly drest they are, and well may be so, as being the ablest and most powerfull men under the Princes and *la Noblesse*, in all the Countrey; an

happinesse;

happinesse, as I conjecture rather of the calling then the men. It hath been the fate and destinie of the Law to strengthen and inable its professors beyond any other Art or Science: the pleaders in all Common-wealths, both for sway amongst the people, and vogue amongst the military men, having alwayes had the preheminence. Of this rank were *Pericles*, *Phocion*, *Alcibiades*, and *Demosthenes* amongst the *Athenians*, *Antonius*, *Cato*, *Cæsar* and *Tully* at *Rome*; men equally famous for Oratory and the Sword: yet this I can confidently say, that the severall states above mentioned, were more indebted to *Tully* and *Demosthenes*, being both meer gown-men, then to the best of their Captains; the one freeing *Athens* from the armies of *Macedon*, th' other delivering *Rome* from the conspiracy of *Catiline*.

O fortunatam natam te Consule Romam!

It is not then the fate of *France* only, nor of *England*, to see so much power in the hands of the Lawyers: and the case being generall, me thinks the envie should be the lesse: and lesse it is indeed with them then with us. The *English* Clergy, though otherwise the most accomplisht in the world, in this folly deserveth no Apologie; being so strongly ill affected to the pleaders of their Nation, that I fear it may be said of some of them, *Quod invidiam non ad causam, sed personam & ad voluntatem dirigunt*; a weaknesse not more unworthy of them, then prejudiciall to them. For by fostering between both gowns such an unnecessary emulation, they do but exasperate that power which they cannot controul, and betray themselves to much envie and discontentednesse; a disease whose cure is more in my wishes then my hopes.

CHAP.

Chap. IX.

The Kings Palace of the Louure, *by whom built. The unsutablenesse of it. The fine Gallery of the Queen Mother. The long Gallery of* Henry IV. *His magnanimous intent to have built it into a quadrangle.* Henry IV. *a great builder. His infinite project upon the* Mediterranean *and the* Ocean. La Salle des Antiques. *The* French *not studious of Antiquities.* Burbon *house. The* Tuilleries, &c.

WE have discharged the King of one Palace, and must follow him to the other, where we shall finde his residence. It is seated at the West side of the Town or *Ville* of *Paris*, hard by *Portenusue*, and also by the new bridge. A house of great fame, and which the Kings of *France* have long kept their Court in. It was first built by *Philip Augustus, anno* 1214. and by him intended for a Castle: It first serving to imprison the more potent of the Nobles; and to lay up the Kings treasury. For that cause it was well moated, strengthned with wals and drawbridges, very serviceable in those times. It had the name of *Louure, quasi L'oeuure,* or the work, the building, by way of excellency. An etymologie which draweth nigher to the ear, then the understanding, or the eye; and yet the *French* writers would make it a miracle. *Du Chosne* calleth it, *Superbe bastiment, qui n'a son esgal en toute la Christientè;* and you shall hear it called in an other place, *Bestiment qui passe, aujourd hui en excellence et en grandeur, tous les autres.* Brave elogies, if all were gold that glistered. It hath now given up its charge of money and

Q great

great prisoners to the *Eastile*, and at this time serveth only to imprison the Court. In my life, I never saw any thing more abused by a good report, or that more belyeth the rumors that go of it. The ordinary talk of vulgar travellers, and the big words of the *French*, had made me expect at the least some prodigie of architecture; some such Majesticall house as the Sunne *Don Phœbus* is said to have dwelt in, in *Ovid*.

Regia Solis erat sublimibus alta columnis,
Clara micante auro, flamasque imitante pyropo,
Cujus ebur nitidum, &c.

Indeed I thought no fiction in Poetry had bien able to have paralleld it: and made no doubt but it would have put me into such a passion as to have cryed out with the young Gallant in the Comedy, when he had seen his sweet-heart, *Hei mihi qualis erat? talis erat qualem nunquam vidi*; But I was much deceived in that hope, and could finde nothing in it to admire, much lesse to envie. The Fable of the Mountaine which was with childe, and brought forth a mouse; is questionlesse a fable: this house and the large fame it hath in the world, is the morall of it. Never was there an house more unsutable to it selfe in the particular examination of parts, nor more unsutable to the character and esteem of it in the generall Survey of the whole.

You enter into it over two draw bridges, and through three gates, ruinous enough, and abundantly unsightly. In the Quadrangle you meet with three severall fashions of building, of three severall ages, and they so unhappily joyned one to the other, that one would half believe they had been clapped together by an earthquake. The South and West parts of it are new, and indeed Princelike; being the work of *Francis* the first, and his son *Henry*. Had it been all cast into the same mould, I perswade my self that it would be very gracious and lovely. The other two are of an ancient work, and so contemptible, that they disgrace the rest; and of these I suppose the one side
to

to be at the least 100 years older then his partner: such is it without. As for the inside, it is far more gracefull, and would be pleasing at the entrance, were the Guard-chamber reformed. Some *Hugonot* architect, which were not in love with the errours of Antiquity, might make a pretty room of it; a *catholick* Carpenter would never get credit by it: for whereas the provident thrift of our fore-fathers intended it (for the house would else be too narrow for the Kings retinue) both for a room of safety and of pleasure, both for bill-men and dancers; and for that cause made up some six ranks of seats on each side; that sparingnesse in the more curious eyes of this time, is little Kinglike: Countrey wenches might with indifferent stomach abuse a good Galliard in it, or it might perhaps serve with a stage at one end to entertain the *Parisians* at a play, or with a partition in the middle, it might be divided into two prety plausible Cockpits; but to be employed in the nature it now is, either to solace the King and Lords in a dance, or to give any forain Ambassador his welcome in a Maske, is little sutable with the Majesty of a King of *France*. The Chambers of it are well built, but ill furnished; the hangings of them being somewhat below a meannesse; and yet of these there is no small scarcity. For as it is said of the *Gymnosophists* of *India*, that *Una Domus & mansioni sufficit & sepulturæ*: so may we of this Prince, the same Chamber serveth for to lodge him, to feed him, and also to confer and discourse with his Nobility. But like enough it is that this want may proceed from the severall Courts of the King, the *Monsieur*, the Queen Mother and the Q:en Regnant, being all kept within it.

Proceed we now to the two Galleries, whereof the first is that of the Queen Mother, as being beautified and adorned exceedingly by *Katharine de Medices*, mother to *Henry* III. and *Charles* IX. It containeth the pictures of all the Kings of *France*, and the most loved of their Queens, since the time of St. *Lewis*. They stand each King opposite to his Queen, she being that of his wives which either brought him most estate, or his successors. The tables are all of a just length, very fair, and according to my little acquain-

tance

tance with the Painter, of a most excellent workmanship, and which addeth much grace to it, they are in a manner a perfect History of the State and Court of *France* in their severall times. For under each of the Kings pictures, they have drawn the portraitures of most of those Lords whom valor and courage in the field enobled beyond their births. Under each of the Queens the lively shapes of the most principall Ladies, whose beautie and virtue had honored the Court. A dainty invention, and happily expressed. At the further end of it standeth the last King and the present Queen Mother; who fill up the whole room. The succeeding Princes, if they mean to live in their pictures, must either build new places for them, or else make use of the long Gallery built by *Henry* IV. and which openeth into that of the Queen Mother. A Gallery it is of an incredible length, as being above 500 yards long, and of a breadth and height not unporportionable; a room built rather for ostentation then use, and such as hath more in it of the majesty of its founder then the grace. It was said to have been erected purposely to joyn the *Louvre* unto the House and Garden of the *Tuilleries*, an unlikely matter that such a stupendious building should be designed only for a cleanly conveyance into a Summer house: others are of an opinion that he had a resolution to have made the house quadrangular, every side being correspondent to this which should have been the common Gallery to the rest. Which design had it taken effect, this Palace would at once have been the wonder of the world, and the envy of it. For my part, I dare be of this last minde, as well because the second side is in part begun, as also considering how infinitely this King was inclined to building. The *Place Daulphin*, and the *Place Royall*, two of the finest piles in *Paris*, were erected partly by his purse, but principally by his encouragement. The new Bridge in *Paris* was meerly his work; so was also the new Palace, and most admirable waterworks of St. *Germans en lay*. This long Gallery and the new Pest-house oweth it self wholly to him; and the house of *Fountainebleau*, which is the fairest in *France*, is beholding to him for most of its beauty; add to this his Fortifications bestowed on the *Bastile*;

his

his walling of *Arles*; and his purpose to have strengthned *Paris* according to the modern art of Towns: and you will finde the attribute of *Parietaria* or wall flower, which *Constantine* scoffingly gave unto *Trajan* for his great humour of building, to be due unto this King; but seriously and with reverence.

Besides the generall love he had to building, he had also an ambition to go beyond example, which also induceth me further to believe his intent of making that large and admirable quadrangle above spoken of, to have been serious and reall. For to omit others, certain it is, that he had a project of great spirit and difficulty, which was to joyn the *Mediterranean sea* and the *Ocean* together; and to make the Navigation from the one to the other through *France*, and not to passe by the straight of *Gibraltare*. It came into Councell, *anno* 1604, and was resolved to be done by this means: The river *Garond* is Navigable from the *Ocean* almost to *Tholoza*; and the *Mediterranean* openeth it self into the Land by a little River, whose name I know not, as high as *Narbonne*. Betwixt these two places was there a Navigable channell to have been digged, and it proceeded so far towards, being actuated, that a workman had undertaken it, and the price was agreed upon. But there arising some discontents between the Kings of *France* and *Spain*, about the building of the Fort *Fluentes* in the Countrey of the *Grisons*; the King not knowing what use he might have of Treasure in that quarrell, commanded the work not to go forward. However he is to be commended in the attempt, which was indeed Kinglike, and worthy his spirit: praise him in his heroick purpose and designe.

Quem si non tenuit, magnis tamen excidit ausis.

But the principal beauty, if I may judge of this so much admired Palace of the *Louure*, 's a low plain room, paved under foot with bricks, and without any hangings or tapestrie on the sides; yet being the best set out and furnished to my content of any in *France*. It is called, *La Salle des Antiques*, and hath in it five of the antientest and venerablest pieces of all the Kingdome. For this Nation generally is regardlesse of Antiquity, both in the monuments and studie of it, so that you shall hardly find any ancient inscription, or any famous ruine snatched from the hand of time, in the best of their Cities or Churches. In the Church only of *Amiens* could I meet with an ancient character, which also was but a *Gothish Dutch* letter, and expressed nothing but the name and virtue of a Bishop of the Church on whose tomb it was. So little also did I perceive them to be inclined to be Antiquaries, that both neglects considered, *Si verbis audacia detur*, I dare confidently aver, not only that the Earl of *Arundels* Gardens have more antiquities of this kind, then all *France* can boast of; but that one *Cotton* for the Treasury, and one *Seldon* (now Mr. *Camden* is dead) for the study of the like antiquities; are worth all the *French*. As for these five pieces in *La Salle des Antiques*, they are I confesse worthy observation, and respect also, if they be such as our Trudgemen enforme us. At the farther end of it is the Statua of *Diana*, the same, as is said, which was worshipped in the renowned Temple of *Ephesus*; and of which *Demetrius* the Silversmith and his fellow artists, cryed out μεγάλη Ἄρτεμις τῶ Ἐφεσίων, *Great is Diana of the Ephesians*. Of a large and manly proportion she seemeth to be.

Quantum & quale latus, quam invenile femur!
    As *Ovid* of his Mistresse.

She is all naked save her feet, which are huskin'd; and that she hath a skarfe or linnen rowl, which coming over her left shoulder, and meeting about her middle, hung down with both ends of it a little lower. In the first place on the right hand as we descended towards the door, was the Statua of one of the Gods of *Ethiopia*, as black as any of his people, and one that had nothing about him to expresse his particular being. Next to him the Effigies of *Mercury*, naked all except his feet, and with a pipe in his mouth, as when he inchanted *Argus*: *Namque reperta fistula nuper erat*, saith the *Metamorphosis*. Next unto him the portraiture of *Venus* quight, and most immodestly unapparelled; in her hand her
little

little son *Cupid*, as well arraied as his mother, sitting on a *Dolphin*. Last of all *Apollo* also in the same naked truth, but that he had shooes on, he was portraied as lately returned from a combate, perhaps that against the Serpent *Python*.

> *Quem Deus arcitenens & nunquam talibus armis*
> *Ante nisi in damis capreisque fugacibus usus,*
> *Mille gravem telis, (exhausta pene pharetra)*
> *Perdidit effuso per vulnera nigra veneno.*
>   As *Ovid.*

The Archer god, who ere that present tide
Nere us'd those armes, but against the Roes and Deer,
With thousand shafts, the earth made to be died
With Serpents bloud, his quiver emptied cleer.

That I was in the right conjecture, I had these reasons to perswade me, the quiver on the Gods right shoulder almost emptied, his warlike belt hanging about his neck, his garments loosely tumbling upon his left armes, and the slain Monster being a water Serpent, as *Python* is fained to be by the Poets: all of these were on the same side of the wall, the other being altogether destitute of ornaments: and are confidently said to be the Statues of those Gods, in the same formes as they were worshipped in, and taken from their severall Temples. They were bestowed on the King by his Holinesse of *Rome*, and I cannot blame him for it, it was worthy but little thanks, to give unto him the Idols of the *Heathens*, who for his Holinesse satisfaction had given himself to the Idols of the *Romans*. I believe that upon the same termes, the King of *England* might have all the Reliques and ruines of Antiquity which can be found in *Rome*.

Without this room, this *Salle des Antiques* and somewhat on the other side of the *Louvre*, is the house of *Burbon*, an old decayed fabrick, in which nothing was observable, but the Omen, for being built by *Lewis* of *Burbon*, the
third

third Duke of that branch, he caused this motto *ESPERANCE* to be engraven in Capitall Letters over the door, signifying his hope, that from his loins should proceed a King which should joyn both the Houses and the Families, and it is acccordingly hapned. For the *Tuilleries* I having nothing to say of them, but that they were built by *Katharine de Medices* in the year 1564. and that they took name from the many Lime-kils and Tile-pits there being, before the foundation of the House and the Garden, the word *Tuilleries* importing as much in the *French* language, I was not so happy as to see, and will not be indebted to any for the relation.

The End of the Second Book.

A SURVEY OF THE STATE of FRANCE.

La BEAUSE, OR, THE THIRD BOOK.

CHAP. I.

Our Journy towards Orleans, *the Town, Castle, and Battail of* Mont l'hierrie. *Many things imputed to the* English *which they never did.* Lewis *the* 11. *brought not the French Kings out of wardship. The town of* Chartroy, *and the mourning Church there. The Countrey of* La Beause *and people of it.* Estampes. *The dancing there. The new art of begging in the Innes of this Countrey.* Angerville. Tury. *The sawciness of the* French *Fidlers. Three kindes of Musick amongst the Ancients. The* French *Musick.*

Having abundantly stifled our spirits in the stink of *Paris*, on Tuesday being the 12 of *July*, we took our leave of it, and prepared our selves to entertain the sweet Air and Wine of *Orleans*. The day fair and not so much as disposed to a cloud, save that they began to gather together about noon, in the nature of a curtain to defend us from the injury of the Sun. The wind rather sufficient to fan the air, then to disturb it, by qualifying the heat of the Celestial fire, brought the air to an excellent mediocrity of temper: you would have thought it a day meerly framed for the great Princesse Nature to take her pleasure in, and that the birds which cheerfully gave us their voices from the neighbouring bushes, had been the loud musick of her Court. In a word, it was a day solely consecrated to a pleasant journey, and he that did not put it to that use, mis-spent it: having therefore put our selves into our wagon, we took a short farewell of Paris, exceeding joyfull that we yet lived to see the beauty of the fields again, and enjoy the happinesse of a free heaven. The Countrey such as that part of the Isle of France towards Normandy; only that the corn grounds were larger, and more even. On the left hand of us we had a side-glance of the royall house of Boys St. Vincennes, and the Castle of Bisestre; and about some two miles beyond them we had a sight also of a new house lately built by Mr. Sillery Chancellor of the Kingdome, a pretty house it promised to be, having two base Courts on the hither side of it, and beyond it a park; an ornament whereof many great mansions in France are altogether ignorant.

Four leagues from Paris, is the the Town of Montlberrie, now old and ruinous: and hath nothing in it to commend it, but the carkasse of a Castle: without it, it hath to brag of a large and spacious plain; on which was fought that memorable battail between Lewis the 11. and Charles le hardie, Duke of Burgogne, a battail memorable only for the running away of each Army: the field being in a manner emptied of all the forces, and yet neither of the Princes victorious. *Hic spe celer, ille salute,* some ran out of fear to die, and some out of hope to live: that it was hard to say, which of the Souldiers made most use of their heels in the combat. This notwithstanding, the King esteemed himself the conquerour, not that he overcame, but because not vanquisht. He was a Prince of no heart to make a warriour, and therefore resistance

sistance was to him almost hugged as victory. It was *Antonies* case in his war against the *Parthians*: a Captain whose Launce King *Lewis* was not worthy to bear after him. *Crassus* before him had been taken by that people: but *Antonius* made a retreat, though with losse, *Hanc itaq; fugam suam, quia vivus exierat, victoriam vocabat*; as *Paterculus*, one that loved him not, saith of him. Yet was King *Lewis* so puffed up with this conceit of victory, that he ever after slighted his enemies: and at last ruined them, and their cause with them. The war which they undertook against him, they had entituled the war of the Weal publick: because the occasion of their taking armes was for the liberty of their Countrey and people: both whom the King had beyond measure oppressed. True it is, they had also their particular purposes; but this was the main, and failing in the expected event of it, all that they did, was to confirm the bondage of the Realm, by their own overthrow. These Princes once disbanded, and severally broken; none durst ever afterwards enter into the action; for which reason King *Lewis* used to say that he had brought the Kings of *France*, *Hors pupillage*, out of their ward-ship: a speech of more brag then truth. The people I confesse, he brought into such terms of slavery; that they no longer merited the name of subjects, but yet for all his great boast, the Nobles of *France* are to this day the Kings Guardians. I have already shewn you much of their potency. By that you may see that the *French* Kings have not yet sued their livery, as our Lawyers call it. Had he also in some measure broken the powerablenesse of the Princes, he had then been perfectly his words-master; and till that be done, I shall still think his successors to be in their pupillage. That King is but half himself which hath the absolute command only of half his people.

The battail foughten by this Town, the common people impute to the *English*; and so do they also many others which they had no hand in. For hearing their Grandames talk of their wars with our nation, and of their many fields which we gained of them; they no sooner hear of a pitched field; but presently, (as the nature of men in a fright is) is) they attribute it to the *English*; good simple souls, *Qui nos non solum laudibus nostris ornare velint, sed onerare alienis,* as *Tully* in his Philippicks. An humour just like unto that of little children, who being once frighted with the tales of *Robin Goodfellow*, do never after hear any noise in the night, but they straight imagine, that it is he which maketh it; or like the women of the villages neer *Oxford*, who having heard the tragicall story of a duck or an hen killed, and carried to the Univerfity: no sooner misse one of their chickens, but instantly they cry out upon the Scholars. On the same false ground also, hearing that the *English*, whilest they had possessions in this Countrey, were great builders; they bestow on them without any more adoe, the foundation and perfecting of most of the Churches and Castles in the Countrey. Thus are our Ancestors said to have built the Churches of *Roven, Amiens, Bayon*, &c. as also the Castles of *Bels*, St. *Vincennes*, the *Baftile*; the two little forts on the river side by the *Louure*: that of St. *Germans*; and amongst many others, this of *Mont l' Hierrie*, where we now are; and all alike: as for this Castle, it was built during the reign of K. *Robert, anno* 1015. by one of his servants, named *Thibald*: long before the *English* had any possessions in this Continent. It was razed by *Lewis* the Grosse, as being a harbourer of rebels in former times; and by that means, as a strong bridle in the mouth of *Paris*: nothing now standing of it, save an high Tower, which is seen a great distance round about, and serveth for a land-mark.

Two leagues from *Mont l' Hierrie* is the Town of *Caftres*; seated in the farthest angle of *France*, where it confineth to *La Beause*. A Town of an ordinary size, somewhat bigger then for a Market, and lesse then would beseem a City, a wall it hath, and a ditch; but neither serviceable further then to refist the enemy at one gate, whilest the people run away by the other: nothing else remarkable in it, but the habit of the Church, which was mourning: for such is the fashion of *France*, that when any of the Nobles are buried, the Church which entombeth them is painted black within and without, for the breadth of a yard, or thereabouts; and their Coats of Armes drawn on it. To go to the charges of

hang-

hanging it round with cloth is not for their profits: besides, this counterfeit sorrow feareth no theef; and dareth out-brave a tempest: he for whom the Church of *Castres* was thus apparelled, had been Lord of the Town: by name, as I remember, Mr. St. *Benoist*; his Armes were Argent, three Cressants, Or, a Mullet of the same; but whether this Mullet were part of the Coat, or a mark only of difference, I could not learn. The like Funeral Churches, I saw also at *Tostes* in *Normandie*; and in a village of *Picardie*, whose name I minde not, *Nec operæ pretium*. And now we are passed the confines of *France*; a poor river, which for the narrowness of it, you would think to be a ditch; parting it from the Province of *La Beause*.

La Beause hath on the North, *Normandie*; on the East the Isle of *France*; on the South, *Nivernois* and *Berry*; and on the West the Countreys of *Tcureine* and *Lemaine*. It lyeth in the 22 and 23 degree of Longitude; and 48 and 49 of Latitude: taking wholly up the breadth of the two former, and but parts only of each of the later; if you measure it with the best advantage for length, you will finde it to extend from *la ferte Bernard* in the North-west corner of it, to *Gjan*, in the South east; which according to the proportion of degrees, amounteth to 60 miles *English*; and somewhat better: for breadth, it is much after the same reckoning. The antient inhabitants of this Province, and the reason of the name I could not learn amongst the people: neither can I finde any certainty of it in my books with whom I have consulted. If I may be bold to go by conjecture, I should think this Countrey to have been the seat of the *Bellocassi*, a people of *Gaule Celtick* mentioned by *Cæsar* in his Commentaries. Certain it is, that in or neer this tract they were seated; and in likelihood in this Province: the names ancient and modern, being not much different in sense, though in sound; for the *Francks* called that (which in Latine is *Pulcher*, or *Bellus*) by the name of *Bel*, in the Masculine Gender, (*Ben* they pronounce it) and *Beau* if it were feminine; so that the name of *Bello cassi*, is but varied into that of *Beause*; besides, that Province which the *Roman* writers stile *Bellovaci*, the *French* now call *Beauvais*; where

Bello

Bello is also turned into *L'eau*. Add to this that the *Latine* writers do term this Countrey *Belsia*; where the ancient *Bello* is still preserv'd; and my conjecture may be pardoned, if not approved. As for those which have removed this people into *Normandie*; and found them in the City of *Baieux*: I appeal to any understanding man, whether their peremptory sentence, or my submisse opinion, be the more allowable.

> ―――*Hæc si tibi vera videntur,*
> *Dede manus; t au si falsa est, accingere contra.*

The same night, we came to *Estampes*, a Town situate in a very plentiful and fruitful soyl; and watred with a river of the same name, stored with the best crevices. It seemeth to have been a town of principall importance; there being five wals and gates in a length, one before another: so that it appeareth to be rather a continuation of many towns together, then simply one. The streets are of a large breadth; the building for substance are stone; and for fashion, as the rest of *France*. It containeth in it five Churches, whereof the principal, which is a Colledge of *Chanoins*, is that of *Nostre dame*; built by King *Robert*: who is said also to have founded the Castle; which now can scarsely be visited in its ruines. Without the town, they have a fine green medow, daintily seated within the circlings of the water; into which they use to follow their recreations. At my being there, the sport was dancing; an exercise much used by the *French*, who do naturally affect it. And it seemeth this natural inclination, is so strong and deep rooted; that neither age nor the absence of a smiling fortune can prevail against it. For on this dancing green, there assembled not only youth and Gentry, but age also and beggery. Old wives which could not put foot to ground without a Crutch, in the streets; had here taught their feet to hoble; you would have thought by the cleanly conveyance of their bodies that they had been troubled with the *Sciatica*: and yet so eager in the sport, as if their dancing daies should never be done. Some there were so ragged, that a swift Galliard would almost

have

have shaked them into nakedness: and they also most violent to have their carkasses directed in a measure. To have attempted the staying of them at home, or the perswading of them to work, when they had heard the Fiddle, had been a task too unwieldy for *Hercules*. In this mixture of age and condition, did we observe them at their pastime; the rags being so interwoven with the silks, and wrinkled browes so interchangeably mingled with fresh beauties: that you would have thought it, to have been a mummery of fortune. As for those of both sexes, which were altogether past action; they had caused themselves to be carried thither in their chairs, and trod the measure with their eyes. The Inne which we lay in was just like those of *Normandy*; or at the least so like, as was fit for sisters; for such you must think them.

——— *Facies non omnibus una,*
Nec diversa tamen, qualem decet esse sororum.

All the difference between them lay in the morning: and amongst the maid-servants. For here we were not troubled with such an importunate begging as in that other Countrey. These here had learned a more neat and compendious way of getting money; and petitioned not our ears, but our noses. By the rhetorick of a posie, they prevailed upon the purse; and by giving each of us a bundle of dead flowers tacked together, seemed rather to buy our bounties, then to beg them. A sweeter and more generous kinde of Petitioning then the other of *Normandie*; and such as may seem to employ in it some happy contradiction. For what else is it, that a maid should proffer her self to be deflowred without prejudice to her modesty: and raise to her future husband an honest stock, by the usury of a kindness? Refreshed with these favours, we took our leave of *Estampes*, and the dancing miscellany: jogging on through many a beautifull field of corn, till we came unto *Augerville* which is six leagues distant. A Town of which I could not observe, nor hear of any thing memorable; but that it was taken by *Montacute* Earl of *Salisbury*; as he went this way

way to the siege of *Orleans*; and indeed, the taking of it was no great miracle, the wals being so thin, that an arrow would almost as soon make a breach in them as a Canon. The same fortune befell also unto *Toury*, a place not much beyond it in strength or bigness: only that it had more confidence (as *Savage* an *English* Gentleman once said) in the wals of bones, which were within it, then in the wals of stones which were without it. ——— This Town standeth in the middle way betwixt *Estampes* and *Orleans*: and therefore a fit stage to act a dinner on; and to it we went. By that time we had cleared our selves of our pottage, there entred upon us three uncouth fellowes, with hats on their heads like covered dishes. As soon as ever I saw them, I cast one eye on my cloak, and the other on my sword: as not knowing what use I might have of my steel, to maintain my cloth. There was great talk at that time of Mr. *Soubises* being in armes: and I much feared that these might be some stragglers of his Army: and this I suspected by their countenances, which were very theevish and full of insolencies. But when I had made a survey of their apparel, I quickly altered that opinion: and accounted them as the excrement of the next prison: deceived alike in both my jealousies; for these pretty parcels of mans flesh, were neither better nor worse, but even arrant fidlers: and such which in *England* we should not hold worthy of the whipping-post. Our leave not asked, and no reverence on their parts performed, they abused our ears with an harsh lesson: and as if that had not been punishment enough unto us, they must needs add to it one of their songs. By that little *French* which I had gathered, and the limpring of a *fille de j'y* of *Paris* who came along with us; I perceived it was bawdy: and to say the truth, more then could be patiently endured by any but a *French* man. But *quid facerem*, what should I do but endure the misery? for I had not language enough to call them Rogues handsomely; and the villains were inferiour to a beating: and indeed not worthy of mine or any honest mans anger.

Præda canum lepus est, vastos non implet hiatus;
Nec gaudet tenui sanguine tanta sitis.

They were a knot of rascals so infinitely below the severity of a statute, that they would have discredited the stocks; and to have hang'd them, had been to hazard the reputation of the gallowes. In a year you would hardly finde out some vengeance for them, which they would not injure in the suffering: unlesse it be not to hearken to their ribaldry, which is one of their greatest torments. To proceed, after their song ended, one of the company (the Master of them it should seem) draweth a dish out of his pocket, and layeth it before us: into which we were to cast our benevolence: custome hath allowed them a Sol for each man at the table: they expect no more, and they will take no lesse. No large sum, and yet Ile assure you richly worth the Musick: which was meerly *French*, that is, lascivious in the composure; and *French* also, that is unskilfully handled in the playing.

Among the Ancients I have met with three kindes of Musick, *viz.* first that which the Greeks call Ἀσμορίαν, which consisteth altogether of long notes, or *spondæus*. This was the gravest and saddest of the rest; called by *Aristotle* in the last chapter of his Politicks, ἠθική, or morall; because it setled the affections. *Boetius* whom we account the Classical author in this faculty, calleth it *Lydian*, because in much use with those of that Nation, at this day we may call it *Italian*, as being generally a peculiar musick to that people. This is the musick which *Elisha* called for, to invite into him the spirit of Prophesie, 1 King. 3. 15. and this is it which is yet sung in our Churches. A practice which we derive from the ancients, however some of late have opposed it: and which is much commended by S. *Austin*; this being the use of it; *Ut per oblectamenta aurium, infirmior animus in pietatis affectum assurgat.* The second kinde the artists call ἰαμβική, which consisteth of a mixture of long and and short notes, or of the *Dactylus*. The philosopher termeth it πρακτική or active, because it raised up the affections. *Boetius* termeth it the *Dorian*, because it had been in much esteem amongst the *Dores* a *Greek* nation: we may now call it *English*; and is that musick which cheereth the spirits, and is so soveraign an antidote to a minde afflicted; and

S   which

which as the Poet hath it, doth *saxa movere sono*. The third sort is that which the Greeks call χεῦμα, consisting altogether of short notes, or *Tribrachys*. *Aristotle* calleth it Ἐνθυσιαστικὸν, or ravishing; because it unhinged the affections, and stirred them to lasciviousnesse. *Boetius* termeth it *Phrygian*, as being the strain of the wanton and luxuriant people. In these times we may call it *French*, as most delighted in, by the stirring spirits, and lightnesse of this nation. A note of musick forbidden unto youth by *Aristotle* and *Plato*; and not countenanced by any of them but on the common theatres, to satisfie the rude manners and desires of the vulgar; ϗ τοῖς παιδίοις πρὸς ἀνάπαυσιν, and to give them also content in their recreations: yet is this musick altogether in use in this Countrey, no lesson amongst their profest Musitians that I could hear, which had any gravity or solid art shewed in the composition. They are pretty fellowes I confess for the setting of a Maske, or a Caranto; but beyond this, nothing: which maketh the musick in their Churches so base and unpleasing. So that the glory of perfect musick, at this time lyeth between the *English*, and *Italian*: that of *France* being as trivial as their behaviour, of which, indeed, it is concomitant: *Mutata musica, mutantur mores*, saith *Tully*: and therefore he giveth us this lesson, *Curandum itaq; est ut musica quam gravissima & sedatissima retineatur*: a good Item for the *French*.

CHAP

CHAP. II.

The Country and site of Orleans *like that of* Worcester. *The Wine of* Orleans. *Præsidial Towns in* France, *what they are. The sale of Offices in* France. *The fine walk and pastime of the* Palle Malle. *The Church of St.* Croix *founded by Superstition and a miracle. Defaced by the* Hugonots. *Some things hated only for their name. The Bishop of* Orleans, *and his priviledge. The Chappel and Pilgrims of St.* Jacques. *The form of Masse in St.* Croix. *Censing an Heathenish custome. The great siege of* Orleans, *raised by* Joane *the Virgin. The valour of that woman: that she was no witch. An Elogie on her.*

WEE are now come into the Countrey of *Orleans,* which though within the limits of *La Beause,* will not yet be an entire County of it self. It is a dainty and pleasing Region, very even and large in the fields of it, insomuch that we could not see an hill, or swelling of the ground within eye-sight. It consisteth in an indifferent measure of Corn, but most plentifully of Vines; and hath of all other fruits a very liberall portion; neither is it meanly beholding to the *Loyre,* for the benefits it receiveth by that river: on which the City of *Orleans* it self is sweetly seated. Of all places in *England, Worcestershire,* in mine opinion, cometh most nigh it; as well in respect of the Countrey, as the situation of the Town. For certainly that Countrey may be called the Epitome of *England*; as this of *France.* To the richest of the corn-fields of *Orleanoys* we may compare the Vale of *Evesham*: neither will it yeeld for the choice and variety of fruits, the Vine only excepted. The hedges in that Countrey are prodigall and lavish of those

S 2   trees

trees which would become the fairest Orchards of the rest; and in a manner recompenseth the want of Wine, by its plenty of Perry and Sider. In a word, what a good writer hath said of one, we may say of both; *Cœlum & solum adeo propitium habent, ut salubritate & ubertate vicinis non concedant.* But the resemblance betwixt the Towns, is more happy. Both seated on the second river of note in their several Countreys; and which are not much unlike in their several courses. *Severne* washing the wals of *Glocester*, and passing nigh unto *Bristol*, seated on a little riveret and its homager, divideth the Antients *Britains* from the rest of the *English*. The *Loyre*, gliding by the City of *Tours*, and passing nigh to *Augeire*, seated also up the land, on a little river, and one of its tributories, separateth the modern *Bretagnes* from the rest of the French. *Posita est in loco modico acclivi ad flumen, quod turrigero ponte conjungitur, & muro satis firmo munita*, saith Mr. *Camden* of *Worcester*: *Orleans* is seated on the like declivity of an hill; hath its bridge well fortified with turrets, and its wals of an equall ability of resistance. *Sed decus est ab incolis, qui sunt numerosi & humani: ab edificiorum nitore, a templorum numero, & maxime a sede episcopali*; saith he of ours in general; we shall see it fitly applyed to this in each particular.

The people of this town are not of the fewest: no Town in *France*, the capacity of it considered, being more populous; for standing in so delicate an air, and on so commodious a river, it inviteth the Gentry or Nobles of the Countrey about it, to inhabit there: and they accept it. Concerning their behaviour and humanity, certainly they much exceed the *Parisians*. I was about to say all the *French* men; and indeed, I need not grudge them that Elogie which *Cæsar* giveth unto those of *Kent*: and verifie, that they are *omnium incolarum longe humanissimi*; my self here observing more courtesie and affability in one day, then I could meet withall in *Paris*, during all my abode. The buildings of it are very suitable to themselves, and the rest of *France*; the streets large and well kept: not yeelding the least offence to the most curious nosethrill. Parish Churches it hath in it 26 of different and unequall being: as it useth to be in other places. Besides these, it contains the Episcopal Church

Church of St. *Croix*, and divers other houses of religious persons; amongst which St. *Jacques*: of both which I shall speak in their due order. Thus much for the resemblance of the Towns: the difference betwixt them is this. That *Orleans* is the bigger, and *Worcester* the richer; *Orleans* consisteth much of the Nobles, and of sojourners; *Worcester* of Citizens only, and home dwellers. And for the manner of life in them; so it is, that *Worcester* hath the handsomer women in it; *Orleans* the finer (and in mine opinion the lovelieft of all *France:*) *Worcester* thriveth much on Clothing; *Orleans* on their Vine-presses.

And questionless the Vine of *Orleans* is the greatest riches not of the Town only, but of the Countrey also about it. For this cause *Andre du Chesne* calleth it the prime cellar of *Paris*. *Est une pais* (saith he) *si heureuse & si fecunde sur tout en vine, qui en la dire l' un de premiers celiers de Paris.* These Vines wherein he maketh it to be so happy, deserve no less a commendation then he hath given them: as yeelding the best wines in all the Kingdome. Such as it much griev'd me to mingle with water; they being so delicious to the palat, and the epicurism of the taste. I have heard of a *Dutch* Gentleman, who being in *Italy*, was brought acquainted with a kinde of Wine, which they there call *Lachrymæ Christi*. No sooner had he tasted it, but he fell into a deep melancholy: and after some seven sighs, besides the addition of two grones, he brake out into this pathetical ejaculation: *Dii boni, quare non Christus lachrymatus esset in nostris regionibus!* This *Dutch* man and I, were for a time of one minde: insomuch that I could almost have picked a quarell with nature, for giving us none of this liquor in *England*: at last we grew friends again, when I had perceived how offensive it was to the brain, (if not well qualified) for which cause it is said, that King *Lewis* hath banished his Cellar: no doubt to the great grief of his drinking Courtiers, who may therefore say with *Martial*,

Quid tantum fecere boni tibi pessima vina?
Aut quid fecerunt optima vina mali?

This Town called *Genabum* by *Cæsar*, was reedified by *Aurelian* the Emperour, *anno 276*. and called by his name *Aurelianum*; which it still retaineth amongst the *Latines*. It hath been famous heretofore for four Councels here celebrated; and for being the siege royal of the Kings of *Orleans*, though as now I could not hear any thing of the ruines of the Palace. The fame of it at this time consisteth in the University, and its seat of justice: this Town being one of them which they call *Seiges presidiaux*. Now these *Seiges Presidiaux*, Seats or Courts of Justice were established in diverse Cities of the Realm, for the ease of the people; *anno* 1551, or thereabouts. In them all civil causes not exceeding 250 livres in money, or 10 livres in rents; are heard and determined soveraignly and without appeal. If the sum exceed those proportions, the appeal holdeth good, and shall be examined in that Court of Parliament under whose jurisdiction they are. This Court here consisteth of a Bailly whose name is Mr. *Digion*, of 12 Counsellors, two Lieutenants, one civil and the other criminal; and a publick notary. When Mr. *Le Comte de* St. *Paul*, who is Governor or Lieutenant Generall of the Province, cometh into their Court, he giveth precedency to the Bailly: in other places he receiveth it. This institution of these Presidentiall Courts, was at first a very profitable ordinance, and much eased the people: but now it is grown burthensome: the reason is, that the offices are made salable, and purchased by them with a great deal of money, which afterwards they wrest again out of the purses of the pesants: the sale of offices drawing necessarily after it, the sale of justice; a mischief which is spread so far, that there is not the poorest under-officer in all the Realm, who may not safely say with the Captain in the 22. of the *Acts* and the 28. vers. Ἐγὼ πολλῦ κεφαλαίω τὲν πολιτείαν τάυτην ἐκτησάμων, with a great sum of money obtained I this freedome. Twenty years purchase is said to be no extraordinary rate: and I have read, that only by the sale of offices, one of the Kings had raised in 20 years 139 millions: which amounteth to the proportion of seven millions yearly, or thereabouts: of all waies to thrift and treasure the most unkingly. In the year 1614 the King
mo-

motioned the abolishing of the sales of this market, but it was upon a condition more prejudicial to the people then the mischief: for he desired in lieu of it, to have a greater imposition laid upon Salt and on the Aides: which those who were Commissioners for the Commonalty would not admit of; because then a common misery had been bought out of the State to make their particular misery the greater, and so the corruption remaineth unaltered.

This Town, as it is sweetly seated in respect of the air: so is it finely convenienced with walks: of which the chief are that next unto *Paris* Gate, having the wall on one hand, and a rank of palm-trees on the other; the second that near unto the Bridge, having the water pleasingly running on both sides: and a third, which is indeed the principal, on the east side of the City. It is called the *Pall: Maile*, from an exercise of that name, much used in this Kingdome: a very Gentleman-like sport, not over violent; and such as affordeth good opportunity of discourse, as they walk from one mark to the other. Into this walk, which is of a wonderful length and beauty, you shall have a clear evening empty all the Town: the aged people borrowing legs to carry them; and the younger, armes to guide them. If any young Dame or Monsieur, walk thither single, they will quickly finde some or other to link with them: though perhaps such with whom they have no familiarity. Thus do they measure and re-measure the length of the *Palle Maile*, not minding the shutting in of the day, till darkness hath taken away the sense of blushing. At all hours of the night, be it warm and dry, you shall be sure to finde them there, thus coupled: and if at the years end, there be found more children then fathers in the Town; this walk and the night are suspected shrewdly to be accessaries. A greater inconvenience in my opinion then an *English* kisse.

There is yet a fourth walk in this Town called *L' Estapp*, a walk principally frequented by Merchants: who here meet to conferre of their occasions. It lyeth before the house of Mr. *Le Comte de St. Paul* the Governour, and reacheth up to the Cloyster of *St. Croix*: of the building of which Church, I could never yet hear or read of any thing, but that which
is

is meerly fabulous, for the Citizens report, that long since, time out of minde, there appeared a vision to an holy Monk, which lived thereabouts, and bad him dig deep in such a place, where he should finde a piece of the holy Crosse, charging him to preserve that blessed relique in great honour, and to cause a Church to be built in that place where it had been buried: upon this warning the Church was founded, but at whose charges they could not enform me: so that all which I could learn concerning the foundation of this Church, is that it was erected only by Superstition and a lie. The Superstition is apparent in their worshipping of such rotten sticks, as they imagine to be remnants of the Crosse; their calling of it holy, and dedicating of this Church unto it. Nay they have consecrated unto it two holy daies, one in *May*, and the other in *September*: and are bound to salute it as often as they see it in the streets or the high-waies, with these words, *Ave salus totius seculi arbor salutifera*. Horrible blasphemy, and never heard but under Antichrist! *Cruces subeundas esse non adorandas*, being the lesson of the Ancients. As for the miracle, I account it as others of the same stamp: equally false and ridiculous. This Church in the year 1562. was defaced and ruined by the *Hugonots*, who had entred the Town under the conduct of the Prince of *Conde*. An action little savouring of humanity, and lesse of Religion: the very Heathens themselves never demolishing any of the Churches, of those Towns which they had taken. But in this action, the *Hugonots* consulted only with rashnesse, and a zealous fury, thinking no title so glorious as to be called the Scourge of Papists, and the overthrowers of Popish Churches.

Quid facerent hostes capta crudelius urbe?

The most barbarous enemy in the world could not more have exercised their malice on the vanquished; and this I perswade my self had been the fate of most of our Churches, if that faction had got the upper hand of us. But this Church notwithstanding, is likely now to survive their madnesse. King *Henry* the 4. began the repairing of it, and

his

his Son *Lewis* hath since continued: so that the quire is now quite finished, and the workmen are in hand with the rest. What should move the *Hugonots* to this execution, I cannot say: unlesse it were a hate which they bare unto the name; and perhaps that not unlikely. We read how the *Romans* having expelled their Kings, banished also *Collatinus* their Consul: a man in whom they could finde no fault but this, that his surname was *Tarquin*; *tantum ob nomen & genus regium*, saith *Florus*: afterwards, *quam invisum regis nomen*, is very frequent in the stories of those times. Amongst those which had been of the conspiracy against *Julius Cæsar*, there was one named *Cinna*, a name so odious amongst the people, that meeting by chance with one of *Cæsar's* chief friends, and hearing that his name was *Cinna*, they presently murthered him in the place, for which cause one *Casca*, which was also the name of one of the Conspirators, published a writing of his name and per' gree: shewing therein, that he neither was the traytor, nor any kin to him. The reason of his action *Dion* giveth us ὅτι κίννα ὁμωνυμίας ἀπώλετο, *Quod Cinna nominis causa occideretur*. With a like hate it may be were the *French* Protestants possessed against the name of the Crosse: for they not only ruined this temple but beat down also all those little crossets, betwixt *Mont Martre*, and St. *Denis*, though now King *Lewis* hath caused them to be re-edified. And what troubles the *French* party here in *England* have raised, because of that harmlesse ceremony of the crosse; *Notius est quam ut stilo egeat*, and therefore I omit it. This Church is the seat of a Bishop, who acknowledgeth the Archbishop of *Sens*, for his Metropolitan. The present Bishop is named *Franciscus d' Aubespine*, said to be a worthy Scholar, and a sound Politician; though he were never graduated further then the arts. Of his revenue I could learn nothing, but of his priviledge this: namely, that at the first entrance of every new Bishop into this Church, he hath the liberty of setting free any of the prisoners of the Gaole: though their crime be never so mortall. For, the original of this indulgence: we are beholding to St. *Aignan*, once Bishop here, and who defended the City against *Attila* the *Hunne*. At his first entrance

trance into the town, (saith the story) after he was invested Bishop, he besought *Agrippinus* the Governour, that for his sake he would let loose all his prisoners, *ut omnes quos pro variis criminibus pœnalis carcer detinebat inclusos, in sui intritus gratiam redderet absolutos*; when the Governour had heard his request, he denied it: and presently a stone falleth upon his head, no man knew from whence: wounded and terrified with this, the Governor granteth his desire, recovereth her health: and ever since the custome hath continued. For the truth of this story, I intend to be no Champion: for I hold it ridiculous and savouring too much of the Legend: but this I am certain of, that every new Bishop maketh a very solemn and majestick entry into the City; and at his entry, releaseth a prisoner.

Let us follow the Bishop into his Church, and there we shall finde him entertained with an high Masse; the ceremonies whereof are very pretty and absurd. To go over them all, would require a volume, I will therefore mention those only wherein they differ from other Masses: and they are two: the one fantastical, the other heathenish. For as soon as the priest at the altar hath read a certain lesson, but what, his voice was not audible enough to tell me: out marcheth the Dean, or in his absence, the senior Canon, out of the Church. Before him two or three torches, and a long crosse silvered over, after him all those of the Church, and lastly the lay people, both men and women: so that there is none left to keep possession, but the Priest and the Altar; and such strangers as come thither for curiosity, they go out at one door, and having first circuited the quire, and afterwards the body of the Church; they return to their places: and the Priest proceedeth. I have seen many a dumb shew in a play just like it. This only is the difference, that here we had no interpreter nor Chorus afforded us to shew us the mysterie of this silent gesticulation. The other addition which I observed here at the Masse (though I have since been told that it is ordinary at high Masses, in the Cathedral Churches) was the censing of the people: which was performed in this manner. Whilest the Priest was busie at the Altar, there entred into the quire at a side door, two boyes in

their

their Surplices, bearing wax-tapers in their hands: and immediately after them the foresaid fellow with the Crosse, in the rere there came two of the Priests in their copes, and other stately vestiments: between both a young lad with the incense-pot, made full of holes to let out the fume; which he swingeth on all sides of him, with a chain, to which it was fastned: having thus marched through the Church and censed the people, he ascendeth unto the Altar, and there censeth the crosse, the relicks, the bread, the wine, the chalice, the images: and I know not what not. A custome very much used amongst the Heathen. *Omnibus viris factæ sunt statuæ & ad eas thus & cerei*, saith *Tully*: and, *Jane tibi primum thura merumq; fero*, saith *Ovid* in his *de Fastis*. So have we in *Martiall*, *Te primum pia thura rogent*: and the like in divers other writers of antient. At what time it crept into the Churches of the Christians, I cannot tell. Sure I am it was not used in the primitive times, nor in the third age after our Saviour: save only in their burials, *Sciant Sabæi* (saith *Tertullian*, who at that time lived) *pluris & caricres merces suas, Christianis sepeliendis profligari, quam fumigantibus*. *Arnobius* also in the 7 book *adversus gentes*, disclaimeth the use of it: and yet the Councell of *Trent* in the 22. Session, defineth it to be as boldly, *ex Apostolica institutione & traditione*, as if the Apostles themselves had told them so. I know they had rather seem to derive it from the 30 chap. and 7. vers. of *Exodus*: and so Bishop *Durand* is of opinion in his *Rationale divinorum*: but this will not help them. *Aaron* there is commanded only to burn incense on the Altar: and not to cense men and images, crosses and relicks, &c. as the Papists do. So that will they, nill they, they must be counted followers of the Heathen: though I envie them not the honour of being Jewes.

From the history and view of the Church, proceed we to that of the Town: where nothing occurreth more memorable then the great siege laid before it by the *English*. A siege of great importance to both parties. *France* having been totally won unto King *Henry*, if this Town had yeelded, and once so nigh it was to submit it self, that the people proffer'd to yeeld themselves to *Philip* Duke of *Burgundie*, then a great confederate of our Nation: who had not been present in the Camp. But this the *English* Generall would not consent to; and it was the resolution of *Antigonus* in long time before us. *Negavit Antigonus* (faith *Justine*) *se in ejus belli prædam socios admittere, in cujus periculum solus descenderat.* On this determinate sentence of the General (he was *Montacute* Earl of *Salisbury*) the Town purposed to hold out a little longer, and was at the last relieved by *Jane D' Arc*, a maid of *Vaucoleur* in *Lorrein*: whom they called *La Pusille*: how that excellent souldier the Generall was slain, and the siege raised, I need not relate. It is extant in all our Chronicles. This only now, that ever since that time the people of *Orleans* keep a solemn procession on every eighth day of *May*: on which day *anno* 1427. their City was delivered from its enemies.

But the atchievements of this brave *Virago* stayed not here, she thinks it not enough to repulse her enemies unlesse she also vanquish them: arm'd therefore, Cap a pe, she went to seek occasion of battail: and was alwaies formost, and in the head of her troops.

Ducit Amazonidum lunatis agmina bellis
Penthiselea furens: mediisq; in millibus ardet.

For her first service she taketh *Jargeau*, discomfiteth the *English*, which were within it, and maketh the Earl of *Suffolk* prisoner. Soon after followed the battail of *Patay*: in which the *English* were driven out of the field, and the great *Talbot* taken. This done, she accompanieth *Charles* the 7. whose Angel Guardian she was, through all *Campagne* unto *Rhemes*: where she saw him solemnly crowned all the Towns of those Countreys yeelding upon the approach of her, and the Kings Army. Finally, after many acts performed above the nature of her sexe, which will not stand here to particulate, she was taken prisoner at the siege of *Campeigne*: delivered over unto the Duke of *Bedford*, by him sent unto *Roven*, and there burnt for a Witch on the 6. of *July, anno* 1431. There was also another crime objected against her, as namely that sh had abused the nature of her sexe, marching up and down in the habit of a man, *Et nihil muliebre præter corpus gerens.* Of all accusations the most impotent, for in what other habit could she dresse her self, undertaking, the actions of a Generall? and besides, to have worn her womans weeds in time of battail, had been to have betrayed her safety; and to have made her self the mark of every arrow. It was therefore requisite that she should array her self in compleat harnesse; and in that habit of complete armour, have those of *Orleans* erected her Statua all in brasse, upon the middle of their bridge.

As for that other imputation of being a Witch, saving the credit of those which condemn'd her, and theirs also who in their writings have so reported her: I dare be of the contrary opinion, for dividing her actions into two parts, those which preceded her coming unto *Orleans*, and those which followed it: I finde much in it of cunning, somewhat perhaps of valour: but nothing that is devillish. Her relieving of *Orleans*, and courage shewn at the battails of *Patay* and *Gergeau*, with her conducting of the King unto *Rhemes*: are not such prodigies, that they need to be ascribed unto witchcraft. She was not the first woman whom the world knew famed in armes, there being no Nation almost of the earth, who have not had a Champion of this sexe, to defend their Liberties: to omit the whole Nation of *Amazons*. To the Jewes in the time of their afflictions, the Lord raised up salvation by means of two women, *Deborah* and *Judith*: and God is not the God of the *Jewes* only, but also of the *Gentiles*; amongst the *Syrians Zenobia* Queen of *Palmira* is very famous; the *Romans* whom she often foyled, never mentioning her without honour. The like commendable testimony they give of *Velleda*, a Queen amongst the *Germans*: a woman that much hindred their affairs in that Countrey. Thus had the *Gothes* their *Amalasunta*: the *Assyrians* their *Semiramis*, the *Scythians* their *Tomyris*, the *Romans* their *Fulvia*: all brave Captains, and such as posterity hath admired without envie. To come home unto our selves, the writers of the *Romans* mention the revolt of *Britain*, and the slaughter of 70000 *Roman* Confederates under the conduct of *Voadilia*: and she in the beginning of her incouragements to the action, telleth the people this, *Solitum quidem Britannis fœminarum ductu bellare*. Of all these heroical Ladies, I read no accusation of witchcraft: invasive courage and a sense of injury, being the armes they fought withall; neither can I see why the *Romans* should exceed us in modesty; or that we need envie unto the *French* this one female warriour, when it is a fortune which hath befaln most Nations. As for her atchievements, they are not so much beyond a common being: but that they may be imputed to natural means: for had she been a Witch, it is likely she would have prevented the disgrace which her valour suffered, in the ditches of *Paris*, though she could not avoid those of *Compeigne*, who took her prisoner: the Devill at such an exigent only being accustomed to forsake those which he hath entangled. So that she enjoyed not such a perpetuity of felicity, as to entitle her to the Devils assistance, she being sometimes conqueror, sometimes overthrown, and at last imprisoned. *Communia fortunæ ludibria*, the ordinary sports of fortune. Her actions before her march to *Orleans*, have somewhat in them of cunning, and perhaps of imposture, as the vision which she reported to have incited her to these attempts, her finding out of the King disguised in the habit of a countrey man; and her appointing to her self an old Sword hanging in St. *Katharines* Church in *Tours*. The *French* were at this time meerly crest-faln: not to be raised but by miracle. This therefore is invented, and so that which of all the rest must prove her a sorceresse, will only prove her an impostor. *Gerrard, Seigneur du Hailan*, one of the best writers of *France*, is of opinion that all that plot of her coming to the King, was contriv'd by three Lords of the Court; to hearten the people; as if God now miraculously intended the restauration of the Kingdome. Add to this, that she never commanded in any battail, without the assistance of the best Captains of the *French* Nation: and amongst whom was the Bastard of *Orleans*, who is thought to have put this device into her head. The Lord of *Bellay* in his discourse of *arte militarie*, proceedeth further, and maketh her a man: only thus habited, *pour faire revenir le courage aux Francois*: which,

had

had it been so, would have been discovered at the time of her burning. Others of the later *French* writers (for those of the former age favour too much of the Legend) make her to be a lusty Lasse of *Lorrein*, trained up by the Bastard of *Orleans*, and the Seigneur of *Baudricourte*; only for this service. And that she might carry with her the reputation of a Prophetesse, and an Ambassadresse from heaven; admit this, and farewell witchcraft. And for the sentence of her condemnation, and the confirmation of it by the Divines and University of *Paris*; it is with me of no moment: being composed only to humour the Victor. If this could sway me, I had more reason to incline to the other party; for when *Charles* had setled his estate, the same men, who had condemned her of sorcery, absolved her: and there was also added in defence of her innocency, a Decree from the Court of *Rome*. *Joane* then with me shall inherit the title of *La pucille d' Orleans*: with me she shall be ranked amongst the famous Captains of her times; and be placed in the same throne, equall with the valiantest of all her sexe, in time before her. Let those whom partiality hath wrested aside from the path of truth, proclaim her for a sorceresse, for my part I will not flatter my best fortunes of my Countrey to the prejudice of a truth: neither will I ever be enduced to think of this female warrier, otherwise then of a noble Captain.

———— Audetq; viris concurrere virgo.

Penthesilea *did it. Why not she*
Without the stain of spels and sorcerie?
Why should those acts in her be counted sin,
Which in the other have commended bin?

Nor is it fit that France should be deni'd
This female souldier, since all Realms beside,
Have had the honour of one: and relate
How much that sexe hath re-enforc'd the state
Of their decaying strengths. Let Scythia spare
To speak of Tomyris, *th' Assyrians care*

Shall

Shall be no more to hear the deeds recited
Of Ninus *wife. Nor are the* Dutch *delighted*
To hear their Valleda *extoll'd: the name*
Of this French *warrier hath eclips'd their fame:*
And silenc'd their atchievements. Let the praise,
That's due to vertue, wait upon her. Raise
An obelisque unto her, you of Gaule,
And let her acts live in the mouthes of all
Speak boldly of her, and of her alone,
That never Lady was as good as Jone.

She died a virgin: 'twas because the earth
Held not a man, whose vertues, or whose birth
Might merit such a blessing. But above,
The gods provided her a fitting love:
And gave her to St. Denis, *shee with him*
Protects the Lillies and their Diadem.
You then about whose armies she doth watch,
Give her the honour due unto her match.
And when in field your standards you advance,
Cry loud, St. Denis *and* St. Jone *for* France.

CHA

Chap. III.

The study of the Civill Law revived in Europe. The dead time of learning. The Schools of Law in Orleans. The œconomie of them. The Chancellour of Oxford antiently appointed by the Diocesan. Their methode here, and prodigality in bestowing degrees. Orleans a great conflux of strangers. The language there. The Corporation of Germans there. Their house and priviledges. Dutch and Latine. The difference between an Academie and an University.

I Have now done with the Town and City of *Orleans*, and am come unto the University or Schools of Law which are in it; this being one of the first places in which the study of the Civill Lawes was revived in *Europe*. For immediately after the death of *Justinian*, who out of no lesse then 2000 volumes of law-writers had collected that bodie of the Imperiall Lawes, which we now call the *Digests*, or the *Pandects*: the study of them grew neglected in these Western parts, nor did any for a long time professe or read them, the reason was, because *Italy*, *France*, *Spain*, *England* and *Germany*, having received new Lords over them; as the *Franks*, *Lombards*, *Saxons*, *Saracens*, and others were fain to submit themselves to their Laws. It happened afterwards that *Lotharius Saxo* the Emperour, who began his reign, *anno* 1126. (being 560 years after the death of *Justinian*) having taken the City of *Melphy* in *Naples*, found there an old copy of the *Pandects*. This he gave to the *Pisans* his confederates, as a most reverend relick of Learning and Antiquity; whence it is called

U *Littera*

Littera Pisana. Moreover he founded the University of *Bologne* or *Bononia,* ordering the Civill Law to be profest there: one *Wirner* being the first Professor; upon whose advice the said Emperor ordained that *Bononia* should be *Legum & juris Schola una & sola:* and here was the first time and place of that study in the Western Empire. But it was not the fate only of the Civill Laws, to be thus neglected. All other parts of learning, both Arts and languages, were in the same desperate estates; the Poets exclamation of *O seclum insipiens & infacetum,* never being so applyable as in those times. For it is with the knowledge of good letters, as it was with the effects of nature; they have times of groweth alike, of perfection and of death. Like the sea, it hath its ebbs as well as its flouds; and like the earth, it hath its Winter, wherein the seeds of it are deaded and bound up, as weil as a Spring wherein it reflourisheth. Thus the learning of the *Greeks* lay forgotten, and lost in *Europe* for 700 years, even untill *Emanuel Chrysolaras* taught it at *Venice,* being driven out of his Countrey by the *Turks.* Thus the Philosophy of *Aristotle* lay hidden in the moath of dust and libraries, *Et nominabatur potius quad legebatur,* as *Ludovicus Vives* observeth in his notes upon St. *Austine,* untill the time of *Alexander Aphrodiseus.* And thus also lay the elegancies of the *Roman* tongue obscured, till that *Erasmus, More* and *Reuchlyn,* in the severall Kingdomes of *Germany, England,* and *France,* endeavoured the restauration of it.

But to return to the Civill Law. After the foundation of the University of *Bologne,* it pleased *Philip le bel* King of *France* to found another here at *Orleans,* for the same purpose, *anno* 1312. which was the first School of that profession on this side the mountains. This is evident by the Bull of *Clement* V. dated at *Lyons* in the year 1367. where he giveth it this title, *Fructiferum universitatis Aurelianensis intra cætera ciltramontana studia; prius solennius, antiquius, tam civilis, quam Canonicæ facultatis studium.* At the first there were instituted eight Professors, now they are reduced to four only; the reason of this decrease, being the increase of Universities. The place in which they read

their

their Lectures, is called *Les grand escoles*, and part of the City, *La Universite*; neither of which attributes it can any way remit. Colledge they have none, either to lodge the students, or entertain the Professors, the former sojourning in divers places of the Town, these last in their severall houses. As for their place of reading which they call *Les grans escoles*, it is only an old barn converted into a School, by the addition of five ranks of formes, and a pew in the middle, you never saw a thing so mock its own name: *Lucus* not being more properly called so *a non lucendo*, then this ruinous house is a great School, because it is little. The present professors are Mr. *Furner*, the *Rector* at my being there; Mr. *Tuil'erie*, and Mr. *Grand*. The fourth of them named Mr. *Augrand*, was newly dead, and his place like a dead pay among Souldiers not supplyed; in which estate was the function of Mr. *Bredee*, whose office it was to read the Book of Institutions, unto such as come newly to the Town. They read each of them an hour, in their turns, every morning in the week, unlesse Holydayes and Thursdayes, their hearers taking their Lectures in their tables. Their principall office is that of the *Rector*, which every three months descends down unto the next, so that once in a year, every one of the professors hath his turn of being *Rector*. The next in dignity unto him is the *Chancellour*, whose office is during life, and in whose name all degrees are given, and the Letters Authenticall, as they term them, granted. The present *Chancellour* is named Mr. *Bouchier* Dr. of Divinity and of both the Laws, and *Prebend* also of St. *Croix*; his place is in the gift of the Bishop of *Orleans*; and so are the *Chancellors* places in all *France* at the bestowing of the *Diocesan*. Antiently it was thus also with us at *Oxford*; the Bishop of *Lincolne* nominating to us our *Chancellors*, till the year 1370. *William* of *Remington* being the first *Chancellour* elected by the University.

In the bestowing of their degrees here, they are very liberall, and deny no man that is able to pay his fees. *Legem ponere* is with them more powerfull then *legem dicere*, and he that hath but his gold ready, shall have a sooner dispatch, then the best Scholar upon ticket.

Ipse licet venias Musis comitatus Homere,
Si nihil attuleris, ibis Homere foras.

It is the money wch disputeth best with them, τὰ χρήματα ἀνήρ, *money makes th: man;* said the *Greek*, and *English* proverb. The exercise which is to be performed, before the degree taken, is very little, and as trivially performed. When you have chosen the Law which you mean to defend, they conduct you into an old ruinous chamber. They call it their Library; for my part, I should have thought it to have been the warehouse of some second hand Bookseller. Those few books which were there, were as old as Printing; and could hardly make amongst them one cover, to resist the violence of a rat. They stood not up endlong, but lay one upon the other, and were joyned together with cobwebs in stead of strings. He that would ever guesse them to have been looked into since the long reign of ignorance, might justly have condemned his own charity; for my part, I was prone to believe that the three last centuries of years had never seen the inside of them; or that the poor paper had been troubled with the disease called *N li me tangere.* In this unluckie roome do they hold their disputations, unlesse they be solemn and full of expectation, and after two or three arguments urged, commend the sufficiency of the *Re'pondent,* and pronounce him worthy of his degree. That done, they cause his Authenticall Letters to be sealed; and in them they tell the Reader with what diligence and pains they sifted the *Candidati*; that it is necessary to the Commonwealth of learning, that industry should be honoured; and that on that ground they have thought it fitting *post angustias solamen, post vigilias requietem, post dolorem gaudia,* (for so as I remember goeth the form) *to recompense the labours of N.N. with the degree of Doctor or Licentiate;* with a great deal of the like formall foolery, *Et ad hunc modum fiunt Doctores.*

From the study of the Law, proceed we unto that of the Language, which is said to be better spoken here, then in any part of *France*, and certainly the people hereof speak it
more

more distinctly then the rest; I cannot say more elegantly. Yet partly for this reason, partly because of the study of the Law, and partly because of the sweetnesse of the aire; the Town is never without abundance of strangers of all Nations which are in correspondency with the *French*. But in the greatest measure it is replenished with those of *Germany* who have here a corporation, and indeed do make amongst themselves a better University, then the University. This Corporation consisteth of a *Procurator*, a *Questor*, an *Assessor*, two *Bibliothecarii*, & 12 *Counsellors*. They have all of them their distinct jurisdiction, and are solemnly elected by the rest of the company every third moneth. The *Consulship* of *Rome* was never so welcome to *Cicero*, as the office of *Procurator* is to a *Dutch* Gentleman; he for the time of his command ordering the affaires of all his Nation; and to say truth, being much respected by those of the Town. It is his office to admit of the young comers, to receive the moneys due at their admission, and to receive an account of the dispending of it of the *Questor* at the expiring of his charge. The office of *Assessor* is like that of a Clerk of the Councels, and the Secretary mixt. For he registreth the Acts of their Councels, writeth Letters in the name of the House to each of the *French* Kings, at their new coming to the Crown; and if any prime or extraordinary Ambassador cometh to the Town, he entertaineth him with a speach. The *Bibliothecarii* looke to the Library, in which they are bound to remain three houres in a day in their severall turns. A prety room it is, very plentifully furnished with choise books, and that at small charge; for it is here the custome, that every one of the Nation at his departure, must leave with them one book, of what kind or price it best pleaseth him. Besides, each of the officers at the resigning up of his charge, giveth unto the new *Questor* a piece of gold about the value of a Pistolet, to be expended according as the necessitie of the state requires; which most an end is bestowed upon the increase of their Library.

Next unto this *cité des Lettres* (as one of the *French* writers calleth *Paris*) is their Councell house; an handsome square Chamber, and well furnished. In this they hold their Consultations,

sultations, and in this preserve their Records and Priviledges, the keeping of the one, and summoning the other, being meerly in the hands of the *Procurator*. About the Table they have five chairs for the five principall Officers; those of the Councell sitting round the Chamber on stools, the armes of the Empire being placed directly over every of the seats. If it happen that any of them die there, they all accompany him to his grave, in a manner mixt so orderly of grief and state, that you would think the obsequies of some great Potentate were solemnized. And to say truth of them, they are a hearty and a loving Nation, not to one another only, but to strangers, and especially to us of *England*. Only I would wish that in their speech and complement, they would not use the *Latine* tongue, or else speak it more congruously. You shall hardly finde a man amongst them, which cannot make a shift to expresse himself in that language; nor one amongst a hundred that can do it Latinly. *Galleriam, Compagniam, Gardinum*, and the like, are as usuall in their common discourse, as to drink at three of the clock; and as familiar as their sleep. Had they bent their studies that way, I perswade my self they would have been excellent good at the Common Lawes; their tongues so naturally falling upon those words which are necessary to a Declaration. But amongst the rest, I took notice of one Mr. *Gebeur*, a man of that various mixture of words, that you would have thought his tongue to have been a very *Amsterdam* of languages. *Cras main oὐ̓ ϑιϛ̃ nous irons ad magnam Galleriam*, was one of his most remarkable speeches, when we were at *Paris*; but here at *Orleans* we had them of him thick and threefold. If ever he should chance to die in a strange place where his Countrey could not be known, but by his tongue, it could not possible be, but that more Nations would strive for him, then ever did for *Homer*. I had before read of the confusion of *Babel*; in him I came acquainted with it, yet this use might be made of him and his hotch-pot of languages, that a good Chymicall Physitian would make an excellent medicine of it against the stone. In a word, to go no more upon the particular, I never knew a people that spake more words, and lesse Latine.

Of thesee ingredients is the University of *Orleans*, compounded, if at the least it be lawfull to call it an University, as I think it be not. The name of *Academie* would beseem it better, *and God grant* (as *Sancto Pancto* said of his wife) *it be able to discharge that calling*. I know that those names are indifferently used, but not properly. For an *Academie* (the name is derived from a place neer *Athens*, called *Academia*, where *Plato* first taught Philosophy) in its strict and proper sense, is such a study, where some one or two Arts are professed; as Law at *Orleans* and *Bononia*, and Physick at *Montpelier* and *Padua*; an University is so called; *Quod Universæ ibi traduntur disciplinæ*, as the name importeth; where learning is professed in the generality, and in the whole Ἐγκυκλοπαιδία of it; the first the *Germans* call *Schola illustris*; the latter *Generale ludium*; very opposite titles, and in which there is little of a *German*.

Chap. IV.

Orleans not an University till the coming of the Jesuites. Their Colledge there by whom built. The Jesuites no singers. Their laudable and exact method of teaching. Their policies in it. Received not without great difficulty into Paris. Their houses in that University. Their strictness unto the rules of their order. Much maliced by the other Priests and Fryers. Why not sent into England with the Queen; and of what order they were that came with her. Our returne to Paris.

THe difference between an University and an Academie standing thus, Those which lived in our Fathers dayes could hardly have called *Orleans* an University; a School of Law being the name most fit for it. At this time since the coming of the Jesuites, that appellation may not misbecome it, they having brought with them those parts of learning, which before were wanting in it: but this hath not been of any long standing, their Colledge being not yet fully finished. By an inscription over the gate, it seemeth to be the work of Mr. *Gagliery*, one of the Advocates in the Parliament of *Paris*, a man of large practise, and by consequence, of great possessions; and who having no childe but this Colledge, is said to intend the fastning of his estate upon it. In this house do those of this order apply themselves to the study of good Letters, in the pursuit whereof, as the rest of this fraternity are, they are good proficients, and much exceed all other sorts of Fryers, as having better teachers and

more

more leasure to learn. That time which the other spent at high Masses, and at their Canonicall hours, these men bestowed upon their books: they being exempted from these duties by their order. Upon this ground they trouble not their heads with the crotchets of Musick, nor spend their moneths upon the chanting out of their services. They have other matters to imploy their brains upon, such as are the ruin of Kingdoms, and desolation of Countries. It was the saying of *Themistocles*, being requested to play a lesson on the Lute, *That he could not fidle, but he could tell how to make a little Town a great City*. The like we may say of the Jesuites; They are no great singers, but are well skilled in making little Cities great, and great ones little. And certain it is, that they are so far from any ability or desire this way, that upon any of their solemn Festivals, when their Statutes require musick, they are faine to hire the singing men of the next *Cathedrall*. As here upon the feast of their Patron St. *Ignatius*, being the 21 of *July*, they were compelled to make use of the voyces of the Church of St. *Croix*.

To this advantage of leasure is added the exact method of their teaching, which is indeed so excellent, that the Protestants themselves in some places send their sons to their Schools; upon desire to have them prove exquisite in those arts they teach. To them resort the children of the rich as well as of the poor, and that in such abundance, that wheresoever they settle, other houses become in a manner desolate, or frequented only by those of the more heavie and phlegmatick constitutions. Into their Schooles when they have received them, they place them in that forum or Classis into wch they are best fitted to enter. Of these Classes, the lowest is for Grammar: the second for Composition, or the making of Theames, as we call it: the third for Poetry: the fourth for Oratory: the fifth for Greek Grammar and compositions: the sixt for the Poesie and Rhetorick of that language: the seventh for Logick: and the eight and last for Philosophy. In each of these Schooles there is a severall Reader or Institutor, who only mindeth that art, and the perfection of it, which for that year he teacheth.

teacheth. That year ended, he removeth both himself and Scholars with him, into the Classis or Schooles next beyond him, till he hath brought them through the whole studies of humanity. In this last forme, which is that of Philosophy he continueth two years, which once expired, his Scholars are made perfect in the University of learning, and themselves manumitted from their labours, and permitted their private studies. Nor do they only teach their Scholars an exactnesse in those severall parts of Learning which they handle, but they also endevour to breed in them an obstinacy of mind, and a sturdy eagernesse of spirit to make them thereby hot prosecutors of their own opinions, and impatient of any contrary consideration. This is it which maketh all those of their education, to affect victory in all the controversies of wit or knowledge, with such a violence, that even in their very Grammaticall disputations, you shall find little boyes maintaine arguments with such a fierie impatience, that you would think it above the nature of their years. And all this they performe freely and for nothing; the poor Paisants son being by them equally instructed, with that of the Noblest.

By this meanes they get unto their Society, great honour and great strength; honour in furnishing their Schooles with so many persons of excellent quality or Nobility, of whom afterwards they make their best advantages for their strength also. As for those of the poorer sort, they have also their ends upon them; for by this free and liberall education of their children, the common people do infinitely affect them: besides that, out of that ranke of their Scholars they assume such into their fraternity, whom they finde to be of a rare wit and excellent spirit, or any other way fitted for their profession. Thus do they make their own purposes out of all conditions, and refuse no fish which either they can draw into their nets, or which will offer it self unto them. *Si locuples quis est, avari sunt, si pauper, ambitiosi, quos non oriens, non occidens satiaverit, soli omnium opes, atque in piam part affectu concupiscunt*: *Galgacus* a Brittish Captain, spake it of the Souldiers of the *Romans* Empire: we may as justly verifie it of these Souldiers of the *Romish* Church, they being the men whom
neither

CHAP. IV.   *the State of* France.   155

neither the *West* nor *East-Indies* can satisfie; and who with a like fervencie desire the education of the needy and the wealthy. Moreover, by this method of teaching they do not only strengthen themselves in the affections of men abroad, but also fortifie themselves within their own wals at home; for by this means, there is not one of their society, who hath not only perfectly concocted in his head the whole 'Εγκυκλοπαιδεία of knowledge, but hath gained unto himself the true art of speaking, and a readinesse of expressing what he knoweth; without the least demurre or hæsitancie: the greatest happinesse of a Scholar. To conclude then and say no more of them, and their rare abilities (for *virtus & in hoste probatur*) it is thought by men of wisdome and judgement, that the planting of a Colledge of Jesuites in any place, is the onely sure way to reestablish that Religion which they professe, and in time to eate out the contrary.

This notwithstanding, they were at the first institution of them mightily opposed, and no where more violently then in the University of *Paris*. An University that standeth much upon its liberty and priviledges; to which this order was imagined to be an hindrance: it being lawfull for them to take any degree in their own houses, without reference to any publick exercise or examination. In the year 1554. at what time they first began to set foot in *France*, the Colledge of the *Sorbonists* made a long decree against them, in the end whereof are these words, and they are worth the reading, *Videtur hæc societas in negotio fidei periculosa, pacis Ecclesiæ perturbativa, monasticæ religionis eversiva & magis ad destructionem, quam ad edificationem*; a censure too full of vineger and bitternesse. Afterwards in the year 1564. they preferred a Petition to the University, that the Colledge which the Bishop of *Clermont* had built for them, might be incorporated into the University, and enjoy the immunities of it. Upon the Universities deniall of their desire, there arose a suit between them and the University in the high Court of Parliament; *Peter Versoris* pleading for the Jesuits, and *Stephen Pasquier* for the other party.

X 2   In

In the end they were admitted, though upon terms of wondrous strictnesse. *Anno* 1594. *John Castell* a novice of this order, having wounded King *Henry* IV. in the mouth, occasioned the banishment of this Society out of all *France*, into which they were not again received till the year 1624. and then also upon limitations more strict then ever. Into *Paris* they were not readmitted untill *anno* 1606. neither had the liberty of reading Lectures and instructing the youth confirmed unto them till *anno* 1611. which also was compassed not without great trouble and vexation.

Per varios casus & tot discrimina rerum,

As *Aeneas* and his companions came into *Latium.*

In this University they have at this instant three houses, one of the Novices, a second of Institutors, which they call the Colledge; and a third of professed Jesuites, which they style their Monastery, or the professed house of St. *Lewis*. In their house of Novices they train up all those whom they have culled out of their Schooles to be of their order, and therein initiate them in the arts of Jesuitism, and their mysteries of iniquity. They there teach them not Grammaticall constructions or composition, but instruct them in the paths of virtue, courage and obedience, according to such examples as their Authors afford them. This they say of themselves and their friends for them. But he that made the funerall Oration for *Henry* IV. *anno* 1610. reporteth it otherwise, *Latini sermonis obtentu* (saith he) *impurissime Gallicæ juventutis mores ingenuos fœdant. Bonarum litterarum prætextu, pessimas edocent artes. Dum ingenia excolunt, animas perdunt,* &c. In their Colledge they have the same method of teaching which the others of their company use in *Orleans*. A Colledge first given unto them by Mr. *William Pratt*. Bishop of *Clermount*, whose house it was; but much beautifyed by themselves after his decease. For with the mony which he gave unto them by his will, which amounted (as it was thought) to

60000

60000 crowns; they added to it the Court called *De Langres*, in St. *James street, anno* 1582. Their Monastery or house of profession is that unto which they retire themselves after they have discharged their duties in the Colledge, by reading and studying publickly in their severall Classes. When they are here, their studies both for time and quality is *ad placitum*; though generally their only studie in it is Policy, and the advantage of their cause. And indeed out of this *Trojan* horse it is, that those firebrands and incendiaries are let out to disturb and set in combustion the affaires of Christendom, out of this forge come all those stratagems and tricks of *Machiavilianism*, which tend to the ruine of the Protestants, and the desolation of their Countries. I speak not this of their house of Profession here in *Paris*, either only or principally: wheresoever they settle, they have a house of this nature, out of which they issue to overthrow the Gospell. Being sent once by their Superiors, a necessity is layed upon them of obedience, be the imployment never so dangerous. And certainly this Nation doth most strictly obey the rules of their order, of any whatsoever, not excepting the *Capouchins* nor the *Carthusians* This I am witnesse to, that whereas the Divinity Lecture is to end at the tilling of a Bell; one of the Society in the Colledge of *Clermont*, reading about the fall of the Angels, ended his Lecture with these words, *Denique in quibuscunque*: for then was the warning given, and he durst not so far trespasse upon his rule, as to speak out his sentence.

But it is not the fate of these Jesuits to have great persons only, and Universities only to oppose their fortunes: they have also the most accomplisht malice, that either the secular Priests or Fryers amongst whom they live, can fasten upon them. Some envie them for the greatnesse of their possessions, some because of the excellency of their learning; some hate them for their power, some for the shrewdnesse of their brains; all together making good that saying of *Paterculus*, that *Semper eminentis fortunæ comes est invidia*. True indeed it is, that the Jesuits have in a manner deserved all this clamor and stomach by their own insolencies; for they have not only drawn into their own hands all the principall affairs of Court and State; but upon occasions cast all the scorn and contempt they can, upon those of the other Orders. The Janizaries of the *Turke* never more neglectfully speak of the *Afapi*, then those doe of the rest of the Clergy. A great crime in those men, who desire to be accounted such excellent Masters of their own affections. Neither is the affection born to them abroad, greater then that at home; amongst those I mean of the opposite party; who being so often troubled and crumped by them, have little cause to afford them a liking, and much lesse a welcome. Upon this reason they were not sent into *England* with the Queen, although at first they were destinate to that service. It was well known how odious that name was amongst us, and what little countenance the Court or Countrey would have afforded them. They therefore who had the Governance of that businesse, sent hither in their places the *Oratorians*, or the *Fratres congregationis Oratorii*; a race of men never as yet offensive to the *English*, further then the generall defence of the *Romish* cause, and so lesse subject to envie and exception. They were first instituted by *Philip Nerius*, not long after the Jesuits, and advanced and dignified by *Pope Sixtus* V. principally to this end, that by their incessant Sermons to the people, of the lives of Saints, and other Ecclesiasticall Antiquities, they might get a new reputation; and so divert a little the torrent of the peoples affections from the Jesuites. *Baronius*, that great and excellent Historian, and *Bozius* that deadly enemie to the Soveraignity of Princes, were of the first foundation of this Order.

I have now done with *Orleans* and the Jesuits, and must prepare for my return to *Paris*. Which journey I begun the 23 of *July*, and ended the day following. We went back the same way that we came, though we were not so fortunate as to enjoy the same company we came in, for in stead of the good and acceptable society of one of the *French* Nobles, some Gentlemen of *Germany*, and two Fryers of the Order of St. *Austin*; we had the perpetuall vexation of four tradesmen of *Paris*, two *filles de joye*, and an old woman; the Artizans so slovenly attired

red and greasie in their apparell, that a most modest apprehension could have conceived no better of them, then that they had been newly raked out of the scullery. One of them by an Inkehorne that hung at his girdle, would have made us believe that he had been a *Notarie*; but by the thread of his discourse, we found out that he was a *Sumner*: so full of ribaldrie was it, and so rankly did it favour of the *French* bawdie-courts. The rest of them talked according to their skill, concerning the price of commodities; and who was the most likely man of all the City, to be made one of the next years *Eschevins*. Of the two wenches, one so extreamly impudent, that even any immodest ear would have abhorred her language, and of such a shamelesse deportment, that her very behaviour would have frighted lust out of the most incontinent man living. Since I first knew mankinde and the world, I never observed so much impudence in the generall, as I did then in her particular, and I hope shall never be so miserable, as to suffer two dayes more the torment and hell of her conversation. In a word, she was a wench born to shame all the Fryers with whom she had traficked, for she would not be *casta*, and could not be *cauta*, and so I leave her; a creature extreamly bold, because extreamly faulty. And yet having no good property to redeem both these, and other unlovely qualities; but (as Sir *Philip Sydney* said of the Strumpet *Baccha* in the *Arcadia*) a little counterfeit beauty disgraced with wandring eyes, and unwayed speeches. The other of the younger females (for as yet I am doubtfull whether I may call any of them women) was of the same profession also, but not half so rampant as her companion.

Hæc habitu casto cum non sit, casta videtur,

as *Ausonius* giveth it one of the two wanton sisters. By her carriage a charitable stranger would have thought her honest; and to that favourable opinion had my self been inclinable, if a *French Monsieur* had not given me her character

racter at *Orleans*: besides there was an odd twinkling of her eye, which spoyled the composedness of her countenance; otherwise she might have passed for currant. So that I may safely say of her, in respect of her fellow Harlot, what *Tacitus* doth of *Pompey*, in reference to *Cæsar*, viz. *Secretior Pompeius, Cæsare non melior*. They were both equally guilty of the sin; though this last had the more cunning to dissemble it, and avoid the infamie and censure due unto it. And so I come to the old woman, which was the last of our goodly companions. A woman so old, that I am not at this day fully resolved whether she were ever young or no. 'Twas well I had read the Scriptures, otherwise I might have been very prone to have thought her one of the first pieces of the creation, and that by some mischance or other, she had escaped the flood; her face was for all the world like unto that of *Sibylla Erythrea* in an old print, or that of *Solomons* two harlots in the painted cloth; you could not at the least but have imagined her one of the Relicks of the first age after the building of *Babel*; for her very complexion was a confusion more dreadfull then that of languages. As yet I am uncertain whether the Poem of our arch-poet *Spencer*, entituled, *The Ruines of time*, was not purposely intended on her; sure I am it is very applyable in the title. But I might have saved all this labour: *Ovid* in his description of *Fames*, hath most exactly given us her portraicture; and out of him, and the eight book of his *Metamorphosis*, you may take this view of her.

> *Nullus erat crinis, cava lumina, pallor in ore,*
> *Labra incana situ, scabri rubigine dentes,*
> *Dura cutis, per quam spectari viscera possent;*
> *Ventris erat pro ventre locus: pendere putares*
> *Pectus, et a spinæ tantummodo crate teneri.*

> Unhair'd, pale-fac'd, her eyes sunk in her head,
> Lips hoary-white, and teeth most rustie-red,

Through

Through her courſe skin, her guts you might eſpie,
In what eſtate and poſture they did lie.
Belly ſhe had none, only there was ſeen
The place whereas her belly ſhould have been.
And with her hips her body did agree,
As if 'twas faſtned by Geometrie.

But of this our companion, as alſo of the reſt of the Coachfull, Sunday-night, and our arrivall at *Paris*, hath at the laſt delivered us. A bleſſing for which I can never be ſufficiently thankfull; and thus

———*Dedit Deus his quoque finem.*

The End of the Third Book.

A SURVEY

OF THE
STATE of FRANCE.

PICARDIE:

OR,

THE FOURTH BOOK.

CHAP. I.

Our return towards England. More of the Hugonots hate unto Crosses. The town of Luzarch, and St. Loupx The Country of Picardie and people. The Picts of Britain not of this Country. Mr. Lee Dignicoes Governo of Picardie. The office of Constable what it is in France By whom the place supplyed in England. The marbl table in France, and causes there handled. Clermount and the Castle there. The war raised up by the Prince against D'Ancre. What his designes might tend to, &c

July the 27. having dispatched that businesse which brought us into *France*, and surveyed as much of the Countrey, as that opportunity would permit, we began our journey towards *England* in a Coach of *Amiens* Bette

Better accompaned we were then when we came from *Orleans*, for here we had Gentlemen of the choicest fashion, very ingenious, and in my opinion of finer condition then any I had met withall in all my acquaintance with that Nation. We had no vexation with us in the shape of a *French* woman, which appeared unto me somewhat miraculous, to torment our ears with her discourse, or punish our eyes with her complexion. Thus associated we began to jog towards St. *Loup*, where that night we were to be lodged. The Countrey such as already I have described it in the Isle of *France*, save that beyond St. *Denis* it began to be somewhat more hilly. By the way I observed those little crossets erected in the memorie of St. *Denis*, as being vainly supposed to be his resting places, when he ran from *Mont-martre* with his head in his hand, which the zealous madnesse of the *Hugonots* had thrown down, and were now reedified by King *Lewis*. It could not but call to mind the hate of that Nation unto that harmelesse monument of Chrifts sufferings, the Crosse; which is grown it seemeth so exorbitant, that the Papists make use of it to discover an *Hugonot*. I remember as I passed by water from *Amiens* to *Abbeville*, we met in the boat with a levie of *French* Gentlewomen; to one of them, with that *French* as I had, I applyed my self, and she perceiving me to be *English*, questioned my Religion. I answered (as I safely might) that I was a *Catholick*: and she for her better satisfaction proffered me the little crosse which was on the top of her beads to kisse, (and rather should I desire to kisse it then many of their lips) whereupon the rest of the company gave of me this verdit, that I was *Un vrai Chriftien, & ne point un Hugonot*. But to proceed in our journall. The same day we parted from *Paris*, we passed through the Town of *Luzarch*, and came to that of St. *Loup*. The first famous only in its owner, which is the Count of *Soissons*. The second in an Abbey there situate built in memory of St. *Lupus* Bishop of *Trios* in *Champagne*. These Townes passed, we were entred into *Picardie*.

Picardie is divided into the higher, which containeth the Countries of *Calice* and *Boulogne*, with the Town *Monstrevill*: and the lower, in which are the goodly Cities of *Amiens*, *Abbeville*, and many other places of principall note. The higher which is the lesser, and more Northern part is bounded North and West with the *English* Ocean; and on the East with *Flanders* and *Artoys*. The lower, which is the larger, the richer and the more Southern, hath on the East the little Country of *Veromandys*; on the West *Normandy*; and on the South the Countrey of *Champagne*. In length it comprehendeth all the 51 degree of Latitude, and three parts of the 50; extending from *Calice* in the North, to *Clermont* in the South. In breadth it is of a great inequality For the higher *Picardie* is like *Linea* amongst the *Legitians*, which they define to be *longitudo sine latitudine*. It being indeed nothing in a manner, but a meer border The lower is of a larger breadth, and containeth in it the whole 24 degree of longitude, and a fourth part of the 23; so that by the proportion of degrees, this Province is 105 miles long, and 25 broad.

Concerning the name of *Picardie*, it is a difficulty beyond my reading and my conjecture. All I can do is to overthrow the lesse probable opinions of other writers, and make my self subject to that scoffe which *Lactantius* bestoweth on *Aristotle*, *Rede hic sustulit aliorum disciplinas, sed non recte fundavit suam*. Some then derive it from *Piquon*, one forsooth of *Alexander* the greats Captains, whom they fain to have built *Amiens* and *Piquigni*; an absurdity not to be honoured with a confutation: some from the Town of *Piquigni* it self, of which mind is *Mercator*; but that Town never was of such note as to name a Province: others derive it from *Picardus* a fanaticall Heretick of these parts, about the year 1300 and after; but the appellation is far older then the man: others fetch it from the *Picts* of *Britain*, whom they would have to flie hither after the discomfiture of their Empire and Nation, by the *Scots*; transmigration of which all Histories are silent: this being the verdict of the best Antiquary ever was nursed up in *Britain*. *Picti itaque funestissimo praelio debellati, aut penitus fuerunt extincti, aut paulatim in Scotorum nomen & nationem concesserint*.

Lastly,

CHAP. I. *the State of France.* 165

Lastly, some others derive the name from *Pique*, which signifieth a Lance or a Pike, the Inventors of which warlike weapon, the fathers of this device would fain make them. In like manner some of *Germany* have laboured to prove that the *Saxons* had that name given them from the short swords which they used to wear, called in their language *Seaxon*; but neither truely. For my part I have consulted *Ptolemie* for all the Nations; and the *Itinerarium* of *Ant.nius* for all the Towns in this tract, but can find none on which I may fasten any probable Etymologie. All therefore that I can say, is, that which *Robert* Bishop of *Auranches* in *Normandy* hath said before me, and that only in the generall, *Quos itaque ætas nostra Picardos appellat veræ Belgæ dicendi sunt: qui postmodum in Picardorum nomen transmigrarunt.*

This Countrey is very plentifull of Corne and other grain, with which it abundantly furnisheth *Paris*; and hath in it more store of pasture and medow grounds, then I else saw in any part of *France*. In Vines only it is defective, and that (as it is thought) more by the want of industry in the people, then any inhability in the soil. For indeed they are a people that will not labour more then they needs must, standing much upon their state and distance, and in the carriage of their bodies savouring a little of the *Spaniard*; whence *Picarder*, to play the *Picard*, is usually said of those who are lofty in their looks, or gluttonous at their tables: this last being also one of the symptomes of a *Picard*. The Governor of this Province is the Duke of *Les Diguieres*, into which office he succeeded Mr. *Luynes* as also he did into that of the Constable. Two preferments which he purchased at a deer rate, having sold or abandoned that religion to compasse them, which he had professed more then 60 years together; an apostasie most unworthy of the man, who having for so many years supported the cause of religion, hath now forsaken it; and thereby made himself gilty of the cowardise of M. *Antonius, Qui cum in desertores sævire debuerat, desertor sui exercitus factus est.* But I fear an heavier censure waiteth upon him; the crown of immortality not being promised to all those which run, but to those only which hold out till the end. For the present indeed he hath augmented his honours by this office,

Y 3 which

which is the principall of all *France*. He hath place and command before and over all the Peers and Princes of the bloud; and at the Coronation of the *French* Kings, ministreth the oath: when he entreth a City in state, or upon the rediction of it, he goeth before with the Sword naked; and when the King sitteth in an assembly of the three estates, he is placed at the Kings right hand. He hath command over all his Majesties forces; and he that killeth him is guilty of high treason. He sitteth also as chief Judge at the Table of marble upon all suits, actions, persons, and complaints whatsoever concerning the wars.

This Table *de Marbre* was wont to be continually in the great hall of the *Palais* at *Paris*; from whence upon the burning of that hall, it was removed to the *Louure*. At this table doth the Admirall of *France* hold his Sessions, to judge of trafick, prizes, letters of marts, piracy, and businesse of the like nature. At this table judgeth also *Le grand Maistre des eaues et forrests*; we may call him the Justice in Eire of all his Majesties Forrests and waters. The actions here handled, are Thefts, and abuses committed in the Kings Forrests, Rivers, Parks, Fishponds, and the like. In the absence of the *grand Maistre*, the power of sentence resteth in the *Les grand Maistres Enquesteurs, et generaux reformateurs*, who have under their command no fewer then 300 subordinate officers. Here also sit the Marshals of *France*, which are ten in number, sometimes in their own power, and sometimes as Assistants to the Constable, under whose direction they are. With us in *England* the Marshalship is more entire, as that which besides its own jurisdiction, hath now incorporated into it self most of the authority, anciently belonging to the Constables, which office ended in the death of *Edward* Lord Duke of *Buckingham*, the last hereditary and proprietary Constable of *England*. This office of Constable, to note unto you by the way so much, was first instituted by *Lewis* the grosse, who began his reign, *anno* 1110. and conferred on Mr. *Les Diguieres* on the 24 of *July*, 1622. in the Cathedrall Church of *Grenoble*, where he first heard Masse, and where he was installed Knight of both Orders. And so I leave the Constable to take a view of his Province, a man at this time beloved of neither parties:
hated

hated by the Protestants as an Apostata, and suspected by the Papists not to be entire.

To proceed, *July* the 28. we came unto *Clermont*, the first Town of any note that we met with in *Picardie*: a prety neat Town, and finely seated on the rising of an hill. For the defence of it, it hath on the upper side of it, an indifferent large Castle, and such which were the situation of it somewhat helped by the strength of Art, might be brought to do good service. Towards the Town, it is of an easie accesse, to the fieldwards more difficult, as being built on the perpendicular fall of a rock. In the year 1615, it was made good by Mr. *Harancourt* with a Regiment of eight Companies, who kept it in the name of the Prince of *Conde*, and the rest of that confederacy; but it held not long, for at the Marshall *D' Ancres* coming before it with his Army, and Artillery, it was presently yeelded. This war, which was the second civill war which had happened in the reign of King *Lewis*, was undertaken by the Princes, chiefly to thwart the designes of the Queen mother, and crush the powerfulnesse of her grand favourite, the Marshall. The pretence (as in such cases it commonly is) was the good of the Common-wealth: the occasion, the crosse marriages then consummated by the Marshall, between the Kings of *France* and *Spain*; for by those marriages they seemed to fear the augmentation of the *Spaniards* greatnesse; the alienation of the affections of their anient allies; and by consequence the ruine of the *French* Empire. But it was not the fate of *D' Anire*, as yet to perish. Two years more of command and insolencies, his destinies llow'd him, and then he tumbled. This opportunity of his eath ending the third civill war, each of which his faulty reatnesse had occasioned.

What the ambition of his designes did tend to, I dare not bsolutely determine; though like enough it is, that they imed further then at a private, or a personall potencie; for aving under the favour and countenance of the Queen mo- er made himself master of the Kings ear, and of his Coun- ll; he made a shift to get into his own hands an authority lmost as unlimited, as that of the old *Mayre* of the Palace. For e had suppressed the liberty of the generall estates, and of the

sove-

soveraign Courts; removed all the officers and Counsellors of the last King; ravish'd one of the Presidents of the great Chamber, by name Mr. *le Jay*, out of the Parliament into the prison, and planted Garrisons of his own in most of the good Towns of *Normandy*, of which Province he was Governour. Add to this, that he had caused the Prince of *Conde*, being acknowledged the first Prince of the bloud, to be imprisoned in the *Bastile*, and had searched into the continuance of the lives of the King and his brother, by the help of Sorcery and Witchcraft. Besides, he was suspected to have had secret intelligence with some forain Princes, ill willers to the State; and had disgraced some and neglected others of the Kings old confederates. Certainly these actions seem to import some project beyond a private and obedient greatnesse, though I can hardly believe that he durst be ambitious of the Crown; for being a fellow of a low birth, his heart could not but be too narrow for such an hope, and having no party amongst the Nobility, and being lesse gracious with the people, he was altogether destitute of means to compasse it. I therefore am of an opinion, that the *Spanish* gold had corrupted him to some project concerning the enlargement of that Empire, upon the *French* dominion; which the crosse marriages, whereof he was the contriver, and which seemed so full of danger to all the best Patriots of *France*, may seem to demonstrate. And again, at that time when he had put the Realm into his third combustion, the King of *Spain* had an Army on foot against the Duke of *Savoy*, and another in the Countries of *Cleve* and *Jullers*; which had not the timely fall of this Monster, and the peace ensuing prevented it, might both perhaps have met together in the midst of *France*. But this only conjecturall.

CHAP.

Chap. II.

The fair City of Amiens; *and greatnesse of it. The* English *feasted within it; and the error of that action; the Town how built, seated and fortified. The Citadell of it, thought to be impregnable. Not permitted to be viewed. The overmuch opennesse of the* English *in discovering their strength. The watch and form of Government in the Town.* Amiens *a Visdamate: to whom it pertaineth. What that honour is in* France. *And how many there enjoy it, &c.*

THat night we went from *Clermont* to a Town called *Breteaul*, where we were harboured: being from *Clermont* 6 *French* leagues; and from *Paris* 20. Our entertainment there such as in other places: as sluttish, as inconvenient. The next day being the 29, about ten of the clock, we had a sight of the goodly City of *Amiens*. A City of some four *English* miles circuit within the wals, which is all the greatnesse of it: for without the wals it hath houses few or none. A City very capacious, and for that cause hath been many times honoured with the persons and trains of many great Princes: besides that once it entertained almost an whole Army of the *English*. For King *Lewis* the 11. having made an advantagious peace with our *Edward* 4. and perceiving how ungratefull it was amongst the military men, he intended also to give them some manner of satisfaction: He sent therefore unto them 300 carts loaden with the best Wines: and seeing how acceptable a present that had proved, he intended also to feast them in *Amiens*, within half a league of which their Camp was lodged. This entertainment lasted four daies,
each

each street having in it two long tables: and each table being furnished with very plentiful provision. Neither were they denied entrance into any of the Taverns, and Victualling houses, or therein stinted either in meats, or drinks; whatsoever was called for, being defrayed by King *Lewis*. An action wherein, if mine opinion might carry it, there was little of the politician. For there were permitted to enter into the Town so many at once of the *English* men, that had they been but so minded, they might easily have made themselves Masters both of the place, and of the Kings person. Nine thousand are reckoned by *Comines* to have been within it together, and most of them armed: so that they might very easily have surprised the Gates, and let in the rest of the Army. Those of the *French* Kings Counsell much feared it, and therefore enformed both Princes of the danger, the one of his Town, the other of his Honour. But this jealousie was but a *French* distrust, and might well have been spared: the *English* being of that Generals minde, who scorned to steal a victory, and of that generous disposition, that they would not betray their credits. *Nunquam illis adet ulla opportuna visa est victoriæ occasio, quam damno pensarent fides:* as the Historian of *Tiberius*. If this City then escaped a sack or a surprisal, it cannot be imputed to the wisdome of the *French*, but to the modesty and fair dealing of the *English*. But this was not the only solœcism in point of state, committed by that great politick of his time, King *Lewis*: there never being man so famed for his brain, that more grosly over-reached himself, then that Prince, though perhaps more frequently.

The buildings of this Town are of diverse materials, some built of stone, others of wood, and some again of both. The streets very sweet and clean, and the air not giving place to any for a lively pureness. Of their buildings the principal are their Churches, whereof there are twelve only in number: Churches I mean parochial, and besides those belonging to Religious houses. Next unto them the work of most especial note, is a great and large Hospital; in method and the disposing of the beds much like unto the *Hostel Dieu* in *Paris*, but in number much inferiour; *Et me tamen*

tamen rapuerant, and yet the decency of them did delight me. The sweetnesse and neatnesse of the Town, proceeded partly as I said from the air, and partly from the conveniency of the River of *Some*, on which it is seated. For the river running in one entire bank at the further end of the Town, is there divided into six channels, which almost at an equall distance run through the severall parts of it. Those channels thus divided, receive into them all the ordure and filth, with which the Town otherwise might be pester'd: and affordeth the people a plentifull measure of water wherewith to purge the lanes, and blie corners of it, as often as them listeth. But this is not all the benefit of these Channels: they bestow upon the City matter also of commodity, which is the infinite number of Grist-mils, that are built upon them. At the other end of the Town the Channels are again united into one stream: both those places, as well of the division, as of the union of the Channels being exceeding well fortified with chains and piles, and also with bulwarks and outworks.

Neither is the Town well fortified and strengthned at those passages only: the other parts of it having enough of strength to inable them to a long resistance. The ditch round about it, save where it meeteth with the Citadell, is exceeding deep, and steeple: the wals of a good height, broad, and composed of earth and stone equally: the one making up the outside of them, and the other the inside. The Gates are very large and strong, as well in the sinewie composition of themselves, as in the addition of the Drawbridge. Suburbs this City hath none, because a Town of war: nor any liberal circuit of territory, because a frontier. Yet the people are indifferently wealthy, and have amongst them good trading; besides the benefit of the Garrison, and the Cathedral. The Garrison consisteth of 250 men, (500 in all they should be) who are continually in pay to guard the Citadel, their pay eight Sols daily. The Governor of them is the Duke of *Chaune*, who is also the Lieutenant or Deputy Governour of the whole Province under the Constable: their Captain Mr. *Le Noyre*, said to be a man of good experience, and worthy his place. This Citadel was built by *Henry* 4. as soon as he had recovered the Town from the *Spaniards*, anno 1597. It is seated on the lower part of the City, though somewhat on the advantage of an hill, and seemeth in mine opinion, better situate to command the Town, then to defend it; or rather to recover the Town being taken, then to save it from taking. They who have seen it, and know the arts of fortification, report it to be impregnable.

———— Quod nec Jovis ira,nec ignis,
Nec poterit ferrum,nec edax abolere vetustas.

Nor am I able to contradict it. For besides that it is a skill beyond my profession, we were not permitted to come within it, or to take a survey of it, but at a distance. As soon as we approached nigh unto it, one of the Garrison proffer'd us the Musket: a sufficient warning not to be too venturous. So that all which I could observe was this: that they had within themselves good plenty of earth to make their Gabions, and repair their breaches. With the same jealousie also, are the rest of the Forts and Towns of Importance guarded in this and other Countreys: no people that ever I heard being so open in shewing their places of strength and safety unto strangers, as the *English*. For a dozen of Ale a foreiner may pace over the curtain of *Portsmouth*, and measure every stone and bulwark of it. For a shilling more he shall see their provision of powder and other munition. And when that is done, if he will, he shall walk the round too. A *French* crown fathometh the wals of *Dover* Castle: and for a pinte of wine one may see the nakednesse of the blockhouses at *Gravesend*. A negligence which may one day cost us dearly: though we now think it not. For what else do we in it, but commit that prodigall folly, for which *Plutarch* condemned *Pericles*: that is, to break open all the pales and inclosures of our land, to the end that every man might come in freely, and take away our fruit at his pleasure. Jealousie, though a vice in a man towards his wife, is yet one of the safest vertues in a Governor towards

wards his fortresse: and therefore I could with that an *Eng-lishman*, would in this particular borrow a little of the *Italian*.

Besides these souldiers which are continually in garrison for the defence of the Citadell, there are also 300 which keep watch every night for the defence of the City. The watchmen receive no pay of the King, but discharge that duty amongst themselves, and in turns, every house finding one for that service, twelve nights in the year. The weapons which they use, are pikes only, and muskets: there being not one piece of Ordinance all about the Town, or on the walls of it. The Governor of this Town, as it hath reference to the King, is a *Bailly*, who hath belonging to him all the authority which belongeth to a siege Presidial. Under him he hath a Lieutenant generall, and particular; seven Counsellors, a publick Notary, and other inferior Officers and Magistrates. As it is a Corporation, the chief Governor of it is a Maior, and next to him the *Eschevins*, or Sheriffs, as protectors of the inhabitants and their liberties: besides those of the Common-councell.

Another circumstance there is, which ennobleth this Town of *Amiens*, which is, that it is a *Visdamate*: or that it giveth honour to one of the Nobility, who is called the *Visdame* of *Amiens*. This title at this time belongeth to the Duke of *Chaune*, Governor of the Citadell, together with the Lordship of *Piquigni*: both which he obtained by marrying the daughter and heir of the last *Visdame* of *Amiens*, and Lord of *Piquigni*, anno 1619. A marriage which much advanced his fortunes, and which was compassed for him by the Constable *Luynes* his brother, who also obtained for him of the King, the title of Duke: his highest attribute before being that of Mr. *de Cadinet*, by which name he was known here in *England*, at such time when he was sent extraordinary Embassador to King *James*. This honour of *Visdame*, is for ought I could ever see, used only in *France*. True it is that in some old *English* Charters we meet with this title of *Vice-dominus*. As in the Charter of King *Edred* to the Abbey of *Crowland* in *Lincolnshire*, dated in the year 948. there is there subscribed *Ego Ingulph Vice-dominus*: but with us, and at those

those times, this title was only used to denote a subordination to some superior Lord, and not as an honorary attribute, in which sense it is now used in *France*. Besides that, with us it was frequently, though falsly used for *Vice-comes*. Between which two offices of a Vicount and a Visdame, there are found no small resemblances. For as they which did *gerere vicem Comitis*, were called *Vicecomites* or Vicounts: so were they also called Vidames or *Vicedomini, qui domini episcopi vices gerebant in temporalibus*. And as Vicounts from officers of the Earls became honorary: so did the Vidames disclaim their relation to the Bishop, and became Signieural or honorary also.

The Vidames then according to their first institution were the substitutes of the greater Bishops, in matter of secular administration: for which cause, though they have altered their tenure, they take all of them their denomination from the chief town of some Bishoprick. Neither is there any of them, who holdeth not of some Bishoprick or other. Concerning the number of them that are thus dignified I cannot determine. Mr. *Glover*, otherwise called *Somerset Herald*, in his Discourse of Nobility, published by Mr. *Milles* of *Canterbury*, putteth it down for absolute, that here are four only, viz. of *Amiens*, of *Chartres*, of *Chalons*, and of *Gerberoy* in *Beauvais*; but in this he hath deceived both himself and his readers, there being, besides those divers others, as of *Rheimes*, *Mans*, and the like. But the particular and exact number of them, together with the place denominating, I leave to the *French* Heralds: unto whose profession it principally belongeth.

CHAP.

CHAP. III.

The Church of Noſtre Dame *in* Amiens. *The principal Churches in moſt Cities called by her name. More honour performed to her then to her Saviour. The ſurpaſſing beauty of this Church on the outſide. The front of it. King Henry the ſevenths Chappel at* Weſtminſter. *The curiouſneſſe of this Church within. By what means it became to be ſo. The ſumptuous masking cloſets in it. The excellency of perſpective works. Indulgences by whom firſt founded. The eſtate of the Biſhoprick.*

THere is yet one thing which addeth more luſtre to the City of *Amiens*, then either the Vidamite or the Citadel, which is the Church of *Noſtre Dame*. A name by which moſt of the principal Churches are known in *France*. There have we the *Noſtre Dame* in *Roven*, a ſecond in *Paris*, a third in this City, a fourth in *Bouligne*, all Cathedrall: ſo alſo a *Noſtre Dame* in *Abbeville* and another in *Eſtampes*: the principal Church in thoſe Towns alſo: had I ſeen more of their Towns, I had met with more of her Temples: for of ſo many I have heard of, that if there be more then two Churches in a Town, one ſhall be ſure to be dedicated unto her, and that one of the faireſt: of any temples conſecrated to the name and memory of our Saviour, *ne gry quidem*: there was not ſo much as a word ſtirring, neither could I marvail at it, conſidering the honours done to her, and thoſe to her ſon; betwixt which there is ſo great a diſproportion, that you would have imagined that *Mary*, and not *Jeſus* had been our Saviour. For one *Pater noſter* the people are enjoyned ten *Ave Maries*, and to recompenſe one pilgrimage to Chriſts Sepulchre at *Hieruſalem*

salem, you shall hear 200 undertaken to our Lady of *Loretto*: and whereas in their Kalendar they have dedicated only four festivals to our Saviour, which are those of his birth, circumcision, resurrection, and ascension, (all which the *English* Church also observeth) for the Virgins sake they have more then doubled the number. Thus do they solemnize the feasts of her purification, and annuntiation, at the times which we also do: of her visitation of *Elizabeth*, in *July*; of her dedication and assumption in *August*: of her nativity in *September*: of her presentation, in *November*: and of her conception in the womb of her mother, in *December*. To her have they appropriated set formes of Prayers prescribed in the two books called, one *Officium*, and the other *Rosarium beatæ Mariæ virginis*, whereas her son must be contented with those orations which are in the common Masse-book. Her shrines and images are more glorious and magnificent, then those of her son. And in her Chappel are more vowes paid, then before the Crucifix. But I cannot blame the vulgar, when the great masters of their souls are thus also besotted. The *Officium* before mentioned, published by the command of *Pius* 2. saith thus of her. *Gaude Maria virgo; tu sola interemisti hæreses in universo mundo*. *Catharinus* in the Councel of *Trent*, calleth her *fidelissimam dei sociam*: and he was modest if compared with others. In one of their Councels, Christs name is quite forgotten, and the name of our Lady put in the place of it. For thus it beginneth: *Autoritate Dei patris, & beatæ virginis, & omnium sanctorum*: but most horrible is that of one of their writers (I am loth to say it was *Bernard*) *Beata virgo monstra te esse matrem, jube filium*: which *Harding* in his confutation of the apologie, endeavouring to make good; would needs have it to be only an excesse of minde, or a spirituall sport and dalliance. But from all such sports and dalliances, no lesse then from the plague, pestilence and famine, Good Lord deliver us.

Leaving our Lady, let us go to see her Church, which questionlesse is one of the most glorious piles of building under the heavens. What *Velleius* saith of *Augustus*, that he was *eum qui omnibus omnium gentium viris illaturus erat caliginem*:

Or

or what *Suetonius* spake of *Titus*, when he called him *Delitiæ humani generis*; both those attributes and more too, may I most fitly fasten on this most magnificent Structure. The whole body of it is of most curious and polisht stone, every where born up by buttresses of that excellent composure, that they seem to add more of beauty to it then of strength. The Quire of it, as in great Churches commonly it is, is of a fairer fabrick then the body, thick set with dainty pillars, and most of them reaching to the top of it, in the fashion of an arch. I am not well able to judge, whether this Quire, or the Chappell of King *Henry* VII. at *Westminster*, be the more exquisite piece of Architecture; though I am not ignorant that *Leland* calleth that of our King *Miraculum orbis*. I perswade my self, that a most discerning eye could find out but little difference between them, and that difference more subtile then sound: for if such perfection may receive the word of *more*, it might be said, that there were more majesty in this of *Amiens*, and more of lovelinesse in that of *Westminster*; yet so that the ones majesty did exceed in lovelinesse, and the others lovelinesse exceed in majesty.

Tam bene conveniunt, & in una sede morantur
Majestas & amor.

But now we are come unto the divinity of the workmanship; the front, which presenteth it self unto us with two Towers, and three gates, that in the midst being the principall. The front of *Welles* or *Peterborough*, which we so much fame in *England*, deserve not to be named in the same myriad of years with this of *Amiens*; for here have you almost all the sacred stories engraven so lively, that you would no longer think the story of *Pygmalions* image to be a fable; and indeed at the first sight, you would confidently believe that the histories there presented were not carved, but acted. To say no more of it (for all my abilities will but disgrace it in the description) that of *Zeuxis* may most fitly be inscribed upon it, *Invisurum facilius aliquem, quam imitaturum*; so infinitely it is above the ambition of imitation.

A a   The

The outside of the Church being admirable, you would have thought that art and treasure had left nothing of themselves to bestow within it: yet herein would such thoughts deceive you; for although the beauty of the *Nostre dames* in *Paris* and *Roven* lay most without, yet here it serveth but as a maske to hide and conceal those most admirable graces which are within. As soon as entred you will suppose that the materials of it are all of gold; such a lustre doth it cast upon the eyes of all those that look upon it. The glory of *Solomons* Temple, next unto the description of it in the Scriptures, is best read in this Church, of which it seemeth to have been the pattern. *Jupiters* house in heaven described by the Poets, was never half so gorgeous as this on the earth; that therefore which *Ovid* Poetically spake concerning that imaginary Palace of the false God, we may positively verifie of this reall mantion of the true God.

Hic locus est, quem, si verbis audacia detur,
Haud timeam magni dixisse palatia regis.

To instance in particulars; the partition between the Quire and the body, is so overlaid with gold, that the acutest sight could apprehend no other substance of it; and yet the art of the workman so fully expressed its power on it, that the cost was much inferiour to the workmanship; so curiously was it adorned with excellent Imagery, and what else the hand of man could fashion into portraiture: on the top of it was the Statua of our Lady in the just height and proportion of a woman, all either of gold or gilded; her child in her armes, of the same making. She was there expressed as standing in a round circle, unto every point of which she darted out rayes and beams of gold; just as the Sun doth seem to do, when the Painter hath drawn him in his full lustre. The glasse of the Church generally, and particularly that about the Quire, and the Virgins Chappell, is the fullest of life and beauty, of any that I ever yet set eye upon. As much as that of St. *Denis* exceedeth ours at *Canterbury*, so much doth this St. *Denis*. But the largest measure of perfection in it is that of the Pillars, which though full of
majesty

majesty in their height and compasse, have yet an ornament added to them, more majesticall then the majesty, for upon each of them (there are four ranks of them in all) are fastned four Tables, which take up their whole circle, every Table being in length two yards or thereabout. In every of these, are the pictures of sundry men and women of the better quality, so exactly limmed, that neither a curious eye could desire, nor a cunning hand discharge it better. These Tables are the Monuments and Tombs of the Burgers of the City, or of the noblest of the Countrey nigh unto it; who in them have caused their pictures to be drawn with as great art and state as cost could procure them, and in a subscription of golden letters, have eternized their names and that act to all succeeding posterity. So that we may justly say of the sumptuousnesse of this Church, what the Historian doth of the Temple of *Delphos*, *Multa igitur ibi, & opulenta regum populorumque cisuntur munera; quæque magnificentia sui, reddentium voto gratam voluntatem manifestant.* Neither have these Sepulchrall ornaments been of any great standing; the antientest of them which I could observe having been erected since the year 1570. Add to these the curious works which the ingraver hath cut in the main wals, and then you perhaps will fall into the same extasie that I did, and pick a quarell with nature and the heavens, that they had not made you all into an eye.

In this Church, as in others also of this party, besides the high Altar in the middest of the Quire, there are divers others in the private Closets, which are destinate to the mumbling of their low Masses. Of these there are in number 24. all of them seated between the two outermost rankes of pillars and the wals; prety neat places, and it is pity they should be abused to such Idolatries. Of three of them I took especiall notice, they being indeed the chiefest of the rest, either for furniture or use.

The first of them was that of the Virgin, which was divided from the rest of the Church by a sphere made of wood, which reached unto the tops of the parti-

Aa 2   tion.

tition. On the outside the Planets, Starres, and Constellations were most artificially set down in their proper orbes, with the times of absolving their severall courses. On the inside, those spaces were filled up with a pack of Verses in commendation of our Lady. The Altar there, was for matter and making, the most glorious that ever I yet looked upon; that on the other side in the Quire, and over which is the image of our Saviour, being more despicable then were fit for the credit of a Village. Over this Altar was the Virgins Statua, all gilt, and of a full and womanly proportion; two Angels of the same materials attending on her. Finally, this Chappell considering the richnesse and glory of it, may be styled the *Epitome of the Church*; that attribute of *Immensæ opulentiæ Templum*, being no more deservedly applyable to *Solomons* Temple, of which *Tacitus* spake it, then to this.

The second of them, stood as I remember, at the further end of the Church behind the Quire; not directed for ought I could perceive to any particular Saint, yet not to be passed over without a due remembrance. It was separated from the rest of the Church by two ranks of brasse pillars; one rank above the other. The pillars all curiously casted, and such as would not shame the workman. In this Massing Closet over the Altar there was hanged a tablet, which by the many lines and shadowes drawn in it, seemed to represent some piece of building. Moving my hand towards mine eye in the nature and kind of a Perspective glasse, I perceived it to be the representation of that Church in which I stood to see it; and it was done with that cunning, that it would almost have perswaded a man out of himself, and made him believe, that he had been in the Church yard. So perfectly did it shew the majesty of the Front, the beauty of the Iles, the number of the Pillars, and the glory of the Quire. A kinde of work, in mine opinion of all others the most excellent, and such as would infinitely delight an optick. Had not

such

such pieces been vulgar to me, it had more affected me; but in the Gallery of Mr. *Crane* of *Cambridge*, once belonging to that humorous Physitian Mr. *Butler*; and in that of Sir *Noel Caron*, late Leiger for the States, at *Lambeth*, I had seen divers of them, whereof some perfecter.

The third of these Missing closets was that of St. *Peter*, not so gorgeous as the rest, unto the eyes of them that saw it; but more usefull to the souls of those, who had a minde to take the benefit of it. For therein hung an Indulgence granted by Pope *Gregory* the fifteenth unto that Church; Dated the 27 of *July*, anno 1622. and of his Popedome the second. The contents of it were in absolute exemption from the paines and place of Purgatory to those, who upon the Feast of *All-soules* (*Festum commemorationis defunctorum*, the brief calleth it) and the Octaves of it; would come to pay their devotions and moneyes, in that Temple. Had the extent of it been generall, it would quickly have emptied the Popes Treasury; and in time have put an end to Purgatory. His Holinesse therefore did wisely restrain it in his Bull, to the natives of that Diocesse. The Author and first founder of this granting of Indulgences (if it be lawfull to note so much by the way) was Pope *Urban* the second, who began his Popedome *anno* 1088. who conferred them upon all such as would goe unto the warres for the recovering of *Jerusalem*; next they began to be conferred on those, who would side with the Pope, in his unlawfull warres against the Emperours. And lastly, about the time of *Clement* the fifth (he began his reign *anno* 1306) they began to be merchantable; for to him that gainfull invention of the Church Treasury, consisting of the merits of our Saviour and the Saints imputed. But I return againe to the Church of *Amiens*.

This glorious Church is the seat of a Bishop, who acknowledgeth for his Metropolitan, the Archbishop of

Rhemes,

Rhemes, Primate of all *France*; the first Bishop of it was one *Firminus*, a native of *Pampelune* in the Kingdom of *Navarre*, who suffered Martyrdome under the Emperour *Diocletian*. To him succeeded another *Firminus*, to whom the first foundation of the Church is attributed. The present *Diocesan* is named *Franciscus Faber*, his intrade about 6000 crownes a year. *Chansins* there are in the Church to the number of forty, of whose revenue I could not learn any thing; neither could I be so happy as to see the head of St. *John Baptist*, whis is said to be here entire; though it cannot be denied that a piece of it is in the holy Chappell at *Paris*, besides those fractions of it which are in other places.

CHAP.

Chap. IV.

Our Journey down the Some, *and Company. The Town and Castle of* Piquigni, *for what famous. Comines censure of the* English *in matter of Prophecies. A farewell to the Church of* Amiens. *The Town and Castle of* Pont D' Armie. Abbeville *how seated; and the Garrison there. No Governour in it but the* Maior *or* Provost. *The Authors imprudent curiosity; and the curtesie of the* Provost *to him. The French Post-horses how base and tired. My preferment to the Trunke-horse. The horse of* Philip de Comines. *The Town and strength of* Monstreville. *The importance of these three Towns to the* French *border,* &c.

July the 30. we took boat to go down to *Abbeville*, by the river of *Some*; a river of no great breadth, but deep and full; the boat which carryed us was much of the making of those Lighters which live upon the Thames, but that is was made more wieldie and fit for speed. There were in it of us in all, to the number of 30 persons or thereabouts: people of all conditions, and such with whom a man of any humor might have found a companion. Under the tilt we espied a bevie of Lasses, mixt with some young Gentlemen. To them we applyed our selves, and they taking a delight to hear our broken *French*, made much of our company; for in that little time of our abode there we had learned only so much of the *French*, as a little child after a years practise hath of his mothers tongue; *Linguis dimidiata adhuc verba tentantibus; & loquela ipsi offensanti linguæ fragmine dulciori.* The Gentlewomen next those of *Orleans*, were the handsomest that I had seen in *France*, very pleasant and affable; one of them being she which put my Religion to the touchstone of kissing the crosse of her beads. Thus associated, we passed merrily down the streame, though slowly; the delight which our language gave the companie, and the content which their liberal humanity afforded to us, beguiling the tediousnesse of the way.

The first thing we met with observable, was the Town and Castle of *Piquigni*. The Town poor and beggerly, and so unlikely to have named the Province, as *Mercator* would have it; besides the disproportion and dissimilitude of the names. The Castle situate on the top of the hill, is now a place of more pleasure then strength, as having command over an open and goodly Countrey, which lyeth below it. It belongeth as we have said, to the *Vidamiate* of *Amiens*; and so doth the Town also. This Town is famous among the *French* for a Tradition and a truth, the Tradition is of a famous defeat given unto the *English* near unto it; but in whose reign, and under whose conduct, they could not tell us. Being thus routed, they fled to this Town, into which their enemies followed with them, intending to put them all to the sword: but at last their fury being allaied, they proposed that mercy to them, which those of *Gilead* did unto those of *Ephraim* in the Scriptures: life and liberty being promised to all them which could pronounce this word *Piquigni*. It seemeth it was not in those dayes a word possible for an *English* mouth; for the *English* saying all of them *Pequenie* in stead of *Piquigni*, were all of them put to the sword: thus far the Tradition. The Truth of story, by which this Town is famous in the writers of both Nations, is an enterview here given betwixt our *Edward* IV. and their *Lewis* XI. upon the concluding of their nine years truce. A circumstance of no great moment of it self, had not *Philip de Comines* made it such by one of his own observations. Upon this meeting the Chancellor of *England*, being Bishop of *Ely*, made an oration to both Kings, beginning

ning with a prophesie; which said, that in this place of *Piquigni*, an honourable peace should be concluded between the two Kingdoms: on this ground, which himself also is the only man that relateth, he hath built two observations; the one (I have not the originall by me) *That the English men are never unfurnished with Prophesies*; the other, *That they ground every thing they speak upon Prophesies*. How far those times were guilty of that humor, I cannot say; though sure I am, that we are not the only men that were so affected. *Paulus Jovius* in some place of his Histories (I remember not the particular) hath vindicated that quarrell for us, and fastned the same imputation on the *French*. So true is that of the *Tragedian*, *Quod quisque fecit patitur, authorem scelus repetit.* And now being past *Piquigni*, I have lost the sight of the Church of *Amiens*.

The fairest Fabrick, and most rich to see
That ere was guilty of mortalitie.
No present Structure like it, nor can fame
In all its bed-rols boast an equall name.
Let then the barbarous Egyptians *cease*
So to extoll their huge Pyramides;
Let them grow silent of their Pharus, *and*
Conceale the other triumph of their Land.
And let the Carians *henceforth leave to raise*
Their Mausolæa with such endlesse praise.
This Church alone doth them as much excell,
As they the lowest Cottages, where do dwell
The least of men: as they those urnes which keep
The smallest ashes which are laid to sleep.

Nor be thou vext thou glorious Queen of night,
Nor let a cloud of darknesse mask thy light.
That renownd Temple which the Greeks *did call*
The worlds seventh wonder, and the fair'st of all:
That pile so famous, that the world did see
Two only great and high, thy fame and thee:
Is neither burnt and perisht, Ephesus
Survives the follies of Eroftratus,

Bb *Only*

> On'y thy name in Europe to advance,
> It was transported to the Realm of France.
> And here it stands, not robb'd of any grace
> Which there it had, nor altred, save in place.
> Cast thy brains on it, and t'will soon be prov'd
> Thy Temple was not ruin'd but remov'd.
> Nor are thy rites so chang'd; but thou'lt aver
> This Christian is thy old Idolater.
>
> But oh good God! how long shall thy decree
> Permit this Temple to Idolatrie?
> How long shall they profane this Church, and make
> Those sacred wals and pavements to partake
> Of their loud sins: and here that Doctrine teach,
> 'Gainst which the very stones do seem to preach?
> Reduce them Lord unto thee; make them see
> How ill this building and their rites agree:
> Or make them know, though they be still the same,
> This house was purpos'd only to thy name.

The next place of note that the water conveied us to, was the Town and Castle of *Pont d' Arme*: a place now scarce visible in the ruines, and belonging to one Mr. *Quercy*. It took name, as they say, from a bridge here built for the transportation of an Army; but this I cannot justifie. Three leagues down the river is the Town of *Abbeville*; a Town conveniently seated on the *Some*, which runneth through it. It is of greater circuite within the wals, then the City of *Amiens*, and hath four Parish Churches more then it; but is not so beautifull, nor so populous. For the houses here are of an older stampe, and there is within the Town no scarcity of wast ground. I went round about the wals, and observed the thinness of the houses, & the largeness of the fields, which are of that capacity and extent, that for ought I could apprehend, the Town need never fear to be compelled by famine, if those fields were husbanded to the best advantages. The wals are of earth within and stone without, of an unequall breadth, and in some places ruinous. A Castle it once had, of which there is now scarce any thing remaining. In stead of which, and in places more convenient, they built out

three

CHAP. IV.   *the State of* France.   187

three Baſtions, very large and capacious; and ſuch well manned need not yeeld upon a ſummons. There are alſo a couple of mounts raiſed nigh unto the wall, at that place where the Countrey is moſt plain, upon which good Ordinance would have good command; but at this time there were none upon it. Without the wals it is diverſly ſtrengthned, having in ſome places a deep ditch without water, in ſome a ſhallower ditch but well filled by the benefit of the river, in others only a mooriſh and fennie levell, more dangerous to the enemie, and ſecure to the Town, then either of the reſt, and therefore never guarded by the Souldiers of the Garriſon. But the chief ſtrength of it, is five Companies of *Swiſs*, 100 in a company, proper tall fellowes in appearance, and ſuch as one would imagine fit for the ſervice. It was my chance to ſee them begin their watch; to which imployment they advanced with ſo good order, and ſuch a ſhew of ſtomach, as if they had not gone to guard a Town, but poſſeſſe one. Their watch was at *Porte de Bryes*, and *Porte St. Valery*; the firſt lying near unto *Heſdin* a frontier Town of *Artoys*; the other five leagues only from the Sea and Haven of St. *Valery*. From thoſe places moſt danger was feared, and therefore there kept moſt of their Souldiers, and all their Ordinance. Their Captain is named Mr. *Aillè* a *Griſon* by birth, and reported for a good Souldier. Beſides him they have no Military Commander; the Maior of the Town, contrary to the nature of Towns of war, being there in higheſt authority. A priviledge granted unto the Maiors hereof, not long ſince, as a reward due to one of their integrities, who underſtanding that the Governour of the Town held intelligence with the *Arch-duke*; apprehended him and ſent him to the Court, where he received his puniſhment. This *Abbeville* (and ſo I leave it, and in it my bevie of *French* laſſes) is ſo called *quaſi Abbatis Villa*, as formerly belonging to the Abbot of it.

And yet before I leave this Town, I muſt needs take notice of an Adventure, which might have proved prejudiciall to me, if my good fortune had not overcome all contrary accidents. My companions had no ſooner landed out of the boat which brought us from *Amiens*, but preſently

Bb 2   they

they betook themselves to the Post-house without the Town, that they might be ready for *Bologne* the next morning. But I who did not think that I was to make such a gollopping journey thorow *France*, as the foolish traveller affirmed he had made thorow *Venice*, resolved to satisfie my self in all those particulars which I found capable of note and observation. Which having done, and thinking I had still day enough for my curiosities, I betook my self to the *Corps du guard*, where being soon known to be a Gentleman of *England*, I easily obtained leave to walk round about the works of the Town, and to observe the situation, strength, and defences of it. But so it hapned that before I came to the gate which led towards the Post-house, I found it newly locked up by the Captain of the watch for that night, and thought I might have found passage at the next gate, had I hastned towards it; yet I was so taken up with the orderly march of the Guards, being all proper fellowes and well appointed, that before I came to that gate, it was locked up also: which being the two only gates on that side of the River, deprived me of all ordinary means to come that night to my Companions, who were resolved to be on horse-back the next morning by the break of day. I had now liberty enough to traverse and consult the streets, within which I seemed to be imprisoned, but could meet none that could informe me how to free my self out of that restraint; at last I met with an old Burger of a comely presence, who I thought promised better satisfaction then the rest had given me; who being acquainted with my desire of uniting my self with my companions, and the difficulty which my curiosity had brought upon me, directed me to the house of the Provost, who, as he told me, had the keeping of a Water gate under one of the Arches of the wall by which the River passed thorow the Town, by which I might finde a way out of it, if I could wooe him to make use of his priviledge in that point, which he thought hard, if not impossible to be effected. Well, to the Provosts house I went, whom I found at home, acquainted him that I came with Letters from

the

the Court of *England*, that I was returning thither with my dispatches, that my companions being lesse curious then my self, had presently betook themselves to their lodgings without the Town, that it would be a great reproach to me, if I should not be in *England* as soon as they, and therefore humbly did beseech him (in as good *French* as I could) that he would be my means to set me on the other side of the River without the Town, which I understood to be in his power. To this request he yeelded with a great deal of chearfulnesse, assuring me that he thought himself exceeding happy in having opportunity of doing any acceptable service to an *English* Gentleman: which said, he presently dispatched a servant for his *Bayliffe dell eaw*, or Water Bailiffe (being a sworn officer of the Town) to attend upon him, and in the mean time entertained himself with such discourses as I was able to make him of the Queens reception. News being brought that the Water Bailiffe was coming forwards, he conducted me into a low Parlor very handsomely furnished, where I found a Banquet or Collation provided for me, consisting of cold bake-meats, choise Marmelets, and most excellent Wines, and (which I looked upon as the greater favour) his Wife and Daughters ready for my entertainment. We had scarce ended this refreshment, when the Bailiff brought word that he had made a boat ready to carry me to the Water-gate; whereupon having had the honor to kisse the hands of the women, I made accompt to take my leave of the Provost also, who on the other side was resolved to accompany me to the water side, and not to leave me till he saw me passed thorow the gate (whether out of civility to me, or compliance with the trust reposed In him, I determine not) which was done accordingly; one of his servants waiting on me till he had brought me to the Inne where I was to lodge.

July the last, we took Post-horse for *Bologne*; If at the least we may call those Post-horses, which we rid on. As lean they were, as Envie is in the Poet; *Macies in corpore toto*, being most true of them. Neither were they only lean enough to have their ribs numbred, but the very spur-gals had made such casements through their skins, that it had been no great difficulty to have surveyed their entrails. A strange kind of Cattell in my mine opinion, and such as had neither flesh on their bones, nor skin on their flesh, nor hair on their skin; sure I am they were not so dusty as the horses of the Sun in *Ovid*; neither could we say of them *Fammiseris implent hinnitibus auras*. All the neighing we could hear from the proudest of them, was only an old dry cough, which I'le assure you did much comfort me, for by that noise I first learned there was life in them. Upon such Anatomies of horses, or to speak more properly, upon such severall heaps of bones, when I and my Companion mounted; and when we expected, however they seemed outwardly, to see somewhat of the Post in them, my beast began to move after an *Aldermans* pace, or like Envie in *Ovid*,

Surgit humi pigre, passuque incedit inerti.

Out of this gravity no perswasion could work them; the dull Jades being grown unsensible of the spur, and to hearten them with wands would in short time have disforested the Country. Now was the Cart of *Dieppe* thought a speedy conveyance; and those that had the happinesse of a Waggon were esteemed too blessed, yea though it came with the hazard of the old woman and the wenches. If good nature, or a sight of their journeyes end, did chance to put any of them into a pace like unto a gallop, we were sure to have them tire in the middle way, and so the remainder of the Stage was to be measured by our own feet. Being weary of this trade, I made bold to dismount the Postilion, and ascended the trunk-horse, where I sat in such a magnificent posture, that the best Carrier in *Paris* might envie my felicity. Behind me I had a good large Trunk and a Port-mantle; before me a bundle of cloaks, a cloak-bag, and a parcell of boots; sure I was if my stirrups could poise me equally on both sides, that I could not likely fall backwards nor forwards. Thus preferred, I encouraged my companions, who cast many an envious eye upon my prosperity. And certainly, there was not

any

any of them, who might not more justly have said of me, *Tuas un meilleur temps que le Pape*, then poor *Lazarello's* master did when he allowed him an Onion only for four dayes. This circumstance I confesse might have well been omitted, had I not great example for it. *Philip de Comines* in the midst of his grave and serious relation of the Battail of *Mont l'Hierrie*, hath a note much about this nature, which gave me encouragement, which is, *That himself had an old horse halfe tired (and this was just my case) who by chance thrust his head into a pale of wine and dranke it off, which made him lustier and fresher that day, then ever before*: but in that, his horse had better luck then I had.

On the right hand of us, and almost in the middle way betwixt *Abbeville* and *Bologne*, we left the Town of *Monstrueil*, which we had not leasure to see. It seemeth daintily seated for command and resistance, as being built upon the top and declivity of a hill. It is well strengthned with Bastions and Ramparts on the outside, & hath within it a Garrison of five Companies of Souldiers; their Governour (as I learned of one of the Paisants) being called *Lannay* And indeed it concerneth the King of *France* to look wel to the Town of *Monstrueil*, as being a border Town, within two miles of *Artoys*; and especially considering that the taking of it, would cut off all entercourse between the Countries of *Bologne* and *Calais*, with the rest of *France* Of the like importance also are the Towns of *Ableville* and *Amiens*; and that the *French* Kings are not ignorant of. Insomuch that those two only, together with that of St. *Quintain*, being put into the hands of *Philip* D. of *Burgundy*, to draw him from the party of the *English*; were redeemed again by *Lewis* XI. for 450000 crownes, an infinite sum of money, according to the standard of those times; and yet it seemeth the King of *France* had no bad bargain of it. For upon an hope only of regaining these Towns, *Charles* Earl of *Charaloys* son to D. *Philip* undertook that war against King *Lewis*, by which at the last, he lost his life, and hazarded his estate.

CHAP.

Chap. V.

The County of Boulonnois, *and Town of* Boulogne *by whom Enfranchized. The present of Salt-butter.* Boulogne *divided into two Towns. Procession in the lower Town to divert the Plague. The forme of it. Procession and the Letany by whom brought into the Church. The high Town Garrisoned. The old man of* Boulogne ; *and the desperate visit which the Author bestowed upon him. The neglect of the* English *in leaving open the Havens. The fraternity* De la Charite, *and inconvenience of it. The costly Journey of* Henry VIII. *to* Boulogne. Sir Walt. Raleghs *censure of that Prince condemned. The discourtesie of* Charles V. *towards our* Edward VI. *The defence of the house of* Burgundy *how chargeable to the Kings of* England. Boulogne *yeilded back to the* French; *and on what conditions. The curtesie and cunning of my Host of* Bovillow.

WE are now come to the County of *Boulonnois*, which though a part of *Picardie*, disdaineth yet to be so accounted, but will be reckoned as a County of it self. It comprehendeth in it the Town of *Boulogne*, *Estaples*, and *Neuf-Chastell*, besides divers Villages; and consisteth much of Hils and Vallies, much after the nature of *England*; the soil being indifferent fruitfull of Corne, and yielding more Grasse then any other part of *France* (which we saw) for the quantity. Neither is it only a County of it self, but it is in a manner also a free County, it being holden immediately of the Virgin *Mary*, who is, no question, a very gracious Landladie. For when King *Lewis* XI. after the decease of *Charles* of *Burgundy*, had taken in *Boulogne*, anno 1477. as new Lord of the Town (thus *John de Serres* relateth it) he did homage without Sword or Spurs, bare-headed and on his knee, before the *Virgin Mary*, offering unto her Image an heart of massie gold, weighing 2000 crowns. He added also this, that he and his successors Kings after him, should hold the County of *Boulogne* of the said Virgin, and do homage unto her image in the great Church of the higher Town dedicated to her name, paying at every change of a Vassall an heart of pure gold of the same weight. Since that time, the *Boulonnois* being the Tenants of our Lady, have enjoyed a perpetuall exemption from many of those Tributes and Taxes, under which the rest of *France* is miserably afflicted. Amongst others they have been alwayes freed from the Gabell of Salt; by reason whereof, and by the goodnesse of their Pastures, they have there the best butter in all the Kingdome. I said partly by reason of their salt, because having it at a low rate, they do liberally season all their Butter with it; whereas they which buy their Salt at the Kings price, cannot afford it any of that deer commodity: upon this ground it is the custome of these of *Boulonnois* to send unto their friends of *France* and *Paris*, a barrell of Butter seasoned according to their fashion; a present no lesse ordinary and acceptable, then Turkies, Capons, and the like, are from our Countrey Gentlemen to those of *London*.

As for the Town of *Boulogne*, it is divided into two parts, *La haute Ville*, and *La basse Ville*, or the high Town, and the low Town, distant one from the other above an hundred paces, and upwards. The high Town is seated upon the top of an hill; the low Town upon the declivity of it, and towards the Haven. Or else we may divide it into other parts, viz. the Town, and the City; the Town that towards the water, and the City that which lyeth above it. It was made a City in the reign of *Henry* II. anno 1553. at which time the City of *Terovenne* was totally ruined by the Imperials, and the Bishops seat was removed hither; the Church

Cc   of

of *Nostre Dame* being made the Cathedrall. There came along hither, upon the remove of the Bishop, 20 Canons, which number is here still retained, their revenue being about 1000 Livres yearly. As for the present Bishop, his name is *Pierre d' Armé*, his intrado 2000 Livres, his *Metropolitan* he of *Rhemes*. The Town, or as they call it, the low Town, is bigger then the City, and better built, the streets larger, and the people richer, most of the Merchants living in it, because it lyeth upon the Haven.

But that which made this low Town most pleasing to me, was a solemn procession that passed through the streets of it, intending to pacifie Gods anger, and divert the plague, which at that time was in the City. In the first front there was carried the Crosse, and after that the holy or sanctified Banner; next unto it followed all the Priests of the Town bare-headed, and in their Surplices, singing as they went the Services destinate to that occasion. After them followed the men, and next to them the women of the Town, by two and two, it being so ordered by the *Roman Rituall*, *Ut laici à clericis, fœminæ à viris prosequantur se paratæ*. On the other side of the street went the Brethren *De la Charité*, every one of them holding in his hand a little triangular Banner, or a Pennon; after them the boyes and wenches. In this method did they measure solemnly every lane and angle of the Town; the Priests singing, and all the people answering them in the same note. At the Church they began it with prayers; and having visited all the Town, they returned again thither to end it with the same devotion. An action very grave and solemn, and such as I could well allow of, were it not only for one prayer which is alwayes said at the time of this performance, and the addition of the Banners. The Prayer is this: *Exaudi nos Deus salutaris noster, & intercedente beata & gloriosa Virgine, & beato Sebastiano Martyre tuo* (this *Sebastian* is their *Æsculapius* or tutelary Saint against the Sicknesse) *& omnibus Sanctis; populum tuum ab iracundiæ tuæ terroribus libera, & misericordiæ tuæ fac largitate securum, Amen*. This only excepted, there is nothing in all the liturgie of it, which can be offensive to any conscience, not idlely scrupulous. ——— These Processions were

were first instituted by Pope *Stephanus* II. who began his Popedome *anno* 752. the intent of them, as *Platina* reporteth it, *Ad placandam Dei iram.* The first place that ever they went to in procession, was the Church of our Lady in the Shambles; or *Ad sanctam Dei genitricem ad præsepe*, as the Historiian calleth them. As for the Letany, which is a principall part of it, it was first compiled by *Mamercus* Bishop of *Vienna* in *Daulphine*, in the time of Pope *Leo* the first, which was 308 years before the time of *Stephanus*. The motive of it, was the often danger to which *France* was subject, by reason of the frequency of Earth-quakes. Since those beginnings, which were fair and commendable, the *Romish* Church hath added much to them of magnificence, and somewhat of impiety, and profaneness. As for the Brethren *De la Charitè*, I could not learn any thing of their originall, but much of their Office; for they are bound to visit all such as are infected with the Plague, to minister unto them all things necessary, and if they die, to shrowde them and carry them to their graves. These duties they performe very willingly, as being possessed with this fancie, that they are priviledged from contagion, by virtue of their Order. And to say the truth, they are most of them old, and so lesse subject to it; and indeed such saplesse, thin, unbodied fellowes, that one would think almost no disease could catch them. Yet hath their prerogative not always held to them; of 33 of them in *Calice*, three only surviving the disease, about four yeers since. But were the danger to which themselves are liable, all the inconveniency of it, I should not much disallow it. There is a greater mischief waiteth upon it, and that is, the infecting of others; they immediately after their return from the Pest-house, mixing themselves with any of their neighbours. A most speedy means to spread the Pestilence, where it is once begun; though neither they nor the people will be perswaded to it.

The City or the high Town, standeth, as we have said, on the top of the hill, environed with deep ditches, a strong wall, and closed with a treble gate and two draw-bridges. A little small Town it is, not much above a flights shot thwart, where it is widest; and hath in it but one Church besides that of *Nostre Dame*, which is Cathedrall. The streets not many, and those narrow, unlesse it be in the Market-place, where the *Corpus du Guarde* is kept. What the outworks are, or whether it have any or no, I cannot say. Even in this time of League and Peace, their jealousie will not permit an *English* man to walke their wals, either within or without the Town. A Castle they said that it hath; but such a one as serveth more for a dwelling then a Fort. The Garrison of this Town consisteth of five Companies, 60 in a Company, which amount in all to 300: their Governour being Mr. *D' Aumont*, son to the Marshall *D' Aumont*; who so faithfully adhered to *Henry* IV. in the beginning of his troubles. The cause why this Town being so small, is so strongly Garrisoned, is the safe keeping of the Haven which is under it, and the command of the passage from the Haven up into the Countrey. The first of the services it can hardly performe, without much injury to the low Town, which standeth between them: but for the ready discharge of the last, it is daintily seated, for though to spare the low Town, they should permit an enemie to land; yet as soon as he is in his march up into the higher Countrey, their Ordinance will tear him into pieces.

But for the immediate security of the Haven, their Ancestors did use to fortifie the old Tower, standing on the top of the hill, called *La tour d' ordre*. It is said to have been built by *Julius Cæsar*, at the time of his second expedition into *Britaine*; this Haven being then named *Portus Gessoriacus*. This Tower which we now see, seemeth to be but the remainder of a greater work; and by the height and situation of it, one would guesse it to have been the *Keepe* or *Watch-tower* unto the rest. It is built of rude and vulgar stone, but strongly cemented together, the figure of it is six square, every square of it being nine paces in length. A compasse too little for a Fortresse, and therefore it is long since it was put to that use; it now serving only as a Sea-marke by day, and a *Pharos* by night; *Ubi accensæ noctu faces navigantium cursum dirigunt.* The *English* man calleth it, *The old man*

man of *Boulogne*, and not improperly, for it hath all the signes of age upon it. The Sea by undermining it, hath taken from it all the earth about two squares of the bottom of it; the stones begin to drop out from the top, and upon the least rising of the wind, you would think it were troubled with the Palsie. In a word, two hard Winters, seconded with a violent tempest, maketh it rubbish; what therefore is wanting of present strength to the Haven in this ruine of a Tower, the wisdome of this age hath made good in the Garrison. And here me thinks I might justly accuse the impolitick thrift of our former Kings of *England* in not laying out some money upon the strength and safety of our Haven Towns: not one of them, *Portesm uth* only excepted, being Garrisoned. True it is, that *Henry* VIII. did erect Block-houses in many of them; but what bables they are, and how unable to resist a Fleet royally appointed, is known to every one. I know, indeed, we were sufficiently garrisoned by our Navy, could it either keep a watch on all particular places, or had it not sometimes occasion to be absent I hope our Kings are not of *Darius* mind in the story, *Qui gloriosius ratus est hostem repellere quam non admittere*; neither will I take upon me, to give counsell; only I could wish that we were not inferior to our neighbours, in the greatnesse of our care; since we are equall to the best of them in the goodnesse of our Countrey.

But though the old man was too old to performe this service, or to contribute any thing toward the defence of the Town and Haven, yet I conceived my self obliged to give him a visite; partly out of the reverent esteem which I had of *Antiquity*, but principally that I might from hence take a full view of my dearest *England*, from which for want of winde and Company, I was then restrained. With these desires I made a boy of the Inne acquainted, who told me that there was no way but by the Pest-houses from the Town to the Tower, and that if we were noted to walke that way, we should both be presently shut up as infected persons, or committed to the custody of the *Brethren of Charity*, the worst condition of the two. But finding the impatience of my desires not so easily satisfied, and the temptation of a *Quart escue*, not to be resisted; he told me that if I would venture to climb up the Rocks, as he and other boyes of the Town used to do sometimes, he would undertake to bring me thither. This offer I readily accepted, and as soon as the tide was low enough for us; we began our walke upon the *Beach* till we came to the bottom of the Rocks where the old man dwelt, and presently we began to mount, as if we meant to take the Fortresse by Scalado. I found the way more troublesome and dangerous then I had conceived, and my self before I came halfe way towards the top, which seemed still to be farther of then it was at the first, so vexed and bruised, that I began to be amazed at my own fool-hardinesse, and was many times in a minde to descend again; and questionlesse I had done accordingly, if a resolution of not giving over any enterprise which I was engaged in, and a fear least the boy would laugh at me when we came to the Town, had not pushed me on. Having breathed our selves a while, we advanced again. The old *cripple* who is fabled to have stolen *Pauls* weather-cock, used not more pains and cunning in climbing to the top of that lofty steeple, then we in mounting to the top of these mighty Rocks; which when we had attained at last, me thought I was much of the same humor with old *Tom o Odcombe* on the top of the *Alpes*, of whom the Poet hath informed us:

> *That to the top at last being got,*
> *With very much adoe god wot;*
>   *He eagerly desired,*
> *That mighty Jove would take the pains*
> *To dash out their unworthy brains,*
>   *Who offered to be tired.*

No sooner had my eyes got above the height of the Cliffes, but the first sight I met with was a row of Pest house houses not far distant, and some old women drying the infected cloathes on a bank adjoyning; the sight whereof had almost made me recoil backward with more hast then speed. But having overcome the danger of that apprehension, I first saluted the old man, taking full notice of his great stature, old age, and many infirmities. That done, I turned my face toward *England*, which afforded me a most pleasing object; the course thereof lying within my view at so great a length, that one might easily discerne from *Dover* Castle Eastward, to the West of *Sussex*: an object of so rich contentment and so full of ravishing contemplations, that I was almost of his mind who said *Bonum est nobis esse hic*; and certainly I had dwelt there longer, if the boy had not put me in mind that the flood was coming back amain (as indeed it was) and that if we made not speed to recover the Town before it was got near the foot of the Rocks, we must of necessity be fain to abide there the greatest part of the night till the ebb ensuing. On this advertisement, there was no need to bid me hasten: but then a new humor seized upon me, when I beheld those dreadfull precipices, which I was to descend, together with the infinite distance of the Beach from the top of the Rocks, the danger of being shut up by the sea, if we made not hast, and of tumbling into it if we did. But as curiosity had carryed me up, so necessity brought me down again, with greater safety, I confesse, then I had deserved. This adventure being like some of those actions of *Alexander* the great, whereof *Curtius* telleth us that they were, *magis ad temeritatis quam ad gloriæ famam*.

This Town of *Boulogne*, and the Countrey about it, was taken by *Henry* VIII. of *England*, *anno* 1545. himself being in person at the siege; a very costly and chargeable victory. The whole list of his Forces did amount to 44000 Foot, and 3000 Horse; Field pieces he drew after him above 100 besides those of smaller making: and for the conveyance of their Ordinance, Baggage and other provision, there were transported into the Continent,

above

above 25000 horses. True it is, that his designes had a further aime, had not *Charles* the Emperor, with whom he was to joyne, left the field and made peace without him. So that, judging only by the successe of the expedition, we cannot but say, that the winning of *Boulogne* was a deer purchase. And Indeed in this one particular Sir *Walter Raleigh* in the Preface to his most excellent History saith not amisse of him; namely, *That in his vain and fruitlesse expeditions abroad, he consumed more treasure, then all the rest of our Victorious Kings before him did in their severall Conquests.* The other part of his censure concerning that Prince, I know not well what to think of, as meerly composed of gall and bitternesse. Onely I cannot but much marvell, that a man of his wisdome, being raised from almost nothing by the daughter, could be so severely invective against the Father; certainly a most charitable Judge cannot but condemne him of want of true affection and duty to his Queen: seeing that it is as his late Majesty hath excellently noted in his ΒΑΣΙΛΙΚΟΝ ΔΩΡΟΝ, *A thing monstrous to see a man love the childe, and hate the Parents*; and therefore he earnestly enjoyneth his son *Henry*, *To represse the insolence of such as under pretence to taxe a vice in the person seek craftily to stain the race.*

Presently after this taking of *Boulogne*, the *French* again endevoured their gaining of it, even during the life of the Conquerour; but he was strong enough to keep his gettings. After his death, the *English* being engaged in a war against the *Scots*, and *Ket* having raised a rebellion in *Norfolke*, they began to hope a Conquest of it, and that more violently then ever. Upon news of their preparations, an Embassador was dispatched to *Charles* the fifth, to desire succor of him, and to lay before him the infancy and severall necessities of the young King, who was then about the age of ten years. This desire when the Emperour had refused to hearken to, they besought him, that he would at the least be pleased to take into his hands and keeping, the Town of of *Boulogne*; and that for no longer time, then untill King *Edward* could make an end of the troubles of his Subjects at home. An easie request. Yet did he not only deny to satisfie the King in this, except he would restore the Catholick religion; but he also expresly commanded that neither his men or munition, should go to the assistance of the *English*. An ingratitude, for which I cannot finde a fitting epithite; considering what fast friends the Kings of *England* had alwayes been to the united houses of *Burgundie* and *Austria*; what moneys they have helped them with, and what sundry Warres they have made for them, both in *Belgium* to maintain their Authority, and in *France* to augment their potencie.

From the marriage of *Maximilian* of the family of *Austria*, with the Lady *Mary* of *Burgundy*, which happened in the yeere 1478. unto the death of *Henry* the eighth, which fell in the yeere 1548. are just 70 yeeres. In which time only it is thought by men of knowledge and experience, that it cost the Kings of *England*, at the least six millions of pounds, in the meer quarrels and defence of the Princes of those houses. An expence, which might seem to have earned a greater requitall, then that now demanded. Upon this deniall of the unmindfull Emperour, a Treaty followed betwixt *England* and *France*. The effect of it was, that *Boulogne*, and all the Countrey of it should be restored to the *French*, they paying unto the *English*, at two dayes of payment 800000 Crownes. Other Articles there were, but this the principall. And so the fortune of young *Edward* in his beginning, was like that of *Julius Cæsar* towards his end, *Dum clementiam, quam præstiterat, expectat, incautus ab ingratis occupatus est.*

I am now at the point of leaving *Boulogne*, but must first reckon with mine Host, to whom we were growne into arrears since our first coming thither. Our stock was grown so low, when we came from *Paris*, that had not a *French* Gentleman whom we met at *Amiens* disbursed for us, it would not have brought us to this Town, so that our Host was fain to furnish us with some monies to make even with him. After which staying there from Sunday noon to Wednesday morning, and being then fain to make use of his credit also to provide of a Boat for *England* (which alone stood us in three pound) our engagements grew greater then he had any just reason to adventure on us. But being an ingenuous man, and seeing that we fared well, spent freely, and for the most part entertained him and his family at our table, he was the lesse diffident of payment, as he told me afterwards. Having stayed three dayes for Company, and none appearing, we were fain to hire a boat expresse for my companion and my self to passe over in. In order whereunto, I told him of our present condition, assured him that we had friends in *Dover* who would supply us with all things necessary (as indeed we had) that having summed up what we owed him, and what he had contracted for our passage over, he should have a note under our hands for the payment of it, and that one of us should remain prisoner in the Boat till the other raised money to redeem him. To which he answered, that we had carryed our selves like Gentlemen, which gave him no distrust of a reall payment; that he would take if we pleased a Bill of our hands for the money to be paid in *Dover*; and desired that we would give him leave to send over a servant in our Boat with a basket of poultery, who should receive the money of us and give back our Bond. This being agreed upon, the next morning we took boat for *England*, the Mariners knowing nothing else, but that the servant went over only to sell his Poultery (that being an opportunity frequently indulged by them unto those of the Town) though we knew well enough he went on another errand; and as we could not but commend my Host for his courtesie and his care taken of our credit, so we had reason to esteem our selves in a kinde of custody in that he would not let us stir without a Keeper. Nor did my Host lose any thing by his kindnesse to us. For we not only paid him honestly,

honestly all his just demands, but bestowed a reward upon his servant and sent a present of Gloves and Knives (commodities much prized in *France*) to his Wife and Daughters; that he might see we knew as well how to requite as receive a curtesie. Which said, I must step back into *France* again, that having taken a brief view already of the Principall Provinces; I may render some accompt of the Government also in reference to the Court, the Church and the Civill State.

The End of the Fourth Book.

A SURVEY OF THE STATE of FRANCE.

FRANCE GENERAL:
OR,
THE FIFTH BOOK.

Describing the Government of the Kingdom generally, in reference to the Court, the Church and the Civill Sate.

CHAP. I.

A transition to the Government of France in generall. The person, age and marriage of King Lewis XIII. Conjecturall reasons of his being issuelesse. Iaqueline Countesse of Holland kept from issue by the house of Burgundy. The Kings Sisters all married; and his alliances by them. His naturall Brethren, and their preferments. His lawfull brother. The title of Monsieur in France. Monsieur as yet unmarried; not like to marry Montpensiers daughter. That Lady a fit wife for the Earl of Soissons. The difference between him and the Prince of Conde for the Crown, in case the line of Navarre fall. How the Lords stand affected in the cause. Whether a child may be born in the 11 moneth. King Henry IV. a great lover of fair Ladies. Monsieur Barradas the Kings favorite, his birth and offices. The omniregency of the Queen Mother; and the Cardinall of Richileiu. The Queen mother a wise and prudent woman.

Having thus taken a survey of these four Provinces, which we may call the Abstract and Epitome of the Realm of *France*; and having seen in them the temper, humors and conditions of the people of it: We will

next

next take a generall view of the Governors and Government thereof, with reference to the Court, the Church and the Civill State.

First for the Court, we must in reason in the first place begin with the person of the King, without whose influence and presence, the Court is but a dead carkasse, void of life and Majesty. For person he is of the middle stature, and rather well proportioned then large, his face knoweth little yet of a beard, but that which is black and swarty, his complexion also much of the same hew, carrying in it a certain boisterousnesse, and that in a farther measure then what a gracefull majesty can admit of, so that one can hardly say of him, without a spice of Courtship, which *Paterculus* did of *Tiberius*, *Quod risus prætulerit principem*, that his countenance proclaimed him a King. But questionlesse his greatest defect is want of utterance, which is very unpleasing, by reason of a desperate and uncurable stammering; which defect is likely more and more to grow upon him. At this time he is aged 24 years and as much as since the 27 day of last *September*, which was his birth day; an age which he beareth not very plausible; want of beard, and the swarthinesse of his complexion, making him seem older. At the age of 11 years he was affianced to the Lady *Anna* Infanta of *Spain*, by whom as yet he hath no children. It is thought by many, and covertly spoken by divers in *France*, that the principall cause of the Queens barrennesse proceedeth from *Spain*; that people being loath to fall under the *French* obedience, which may very well happen; she being the eldest Sister of the King. For this cause in the seventh Article of the marriage, there is a clause, that neither the said *Infanta* nor the children born by her (to the King) shall be capable to inherit any of the Estates of the King of *Spain*. And in the eight Article she is bound to make an Act of Renunciation, under her own handwriting, as soon as she cometh to be 12 years old, which was accordingly performed. But this being not sufficient to secure their fears, it is thought, that she was some way or other disabled from conception before ever she came into the Kings imbraces. A great crime, I confesse, if true; yet I cannot say with *Tully* in his defence of *Ligarius*, *Novum Crimen*

Crimen caje Cæsar, & ullis hoc tempus inauditum. Jaqueline Countesse of *Holland*, was Cousen to *Philip* Duke of *Burgundy*, her fruitfulnesse would have debarred him from those Estates of *Holland, Z-aland* and *West Frielzland*; therefore though she had three husbands, there was order taken she should never have childe: with her first two husbands the Duke would never suffer her to live; and when she had stolen a wedding with *Frane* of *Borselle* one of her servants, the Dukes Physicians gave him such a potion, that she might have as well marryed an Eunuch; upon this injury, the poor Lady dyed, and the Duke succeeded in those Countries: which by his Grand-childe *Mary*, were conveyed over into the house of *Austria*, together with the rest of his estates. I dare not say that that Family hath inherited his practises with his Lands; and yet I have heard, that the *Infanta Isabella* had the like or worse measure afforded her before she was bedded by the Arch-Duke *Albertus*. A Diabolicall trick which the prostitutes of the Heathen used in the beginning of the Gospell, and before; of whom *Octavius* complaineth, *Quod originem futuri hominis extinguant, & paricidium faciunt, antequam pariunt,* —— Better luck then the King hath his Sister beyond the Mountains, I mean his eldest Sister Madam *Elizabeth*, marryed to the King of *Spain* now living, as being (or having been) the mother of two children. His second Sister Madam *Christian*, is marryed unto *Amadeo Victor principe major*, or heir apparent to the Duke of *Savoy*; to whom as yet she hath born no issue. The youngest Madam *Henrietta Maria* is newly marryed to his most Excellent Majesty of *England*, to whom may she prove of a most happy and fruitfull womb, *Et pulcra faciat te prole parentem*. Of these Alliances, the first were very profitable to both Princes, could there be made a marriage between the Kingdoms, as well as the Kings. But it is well known that the affections of each people are divided with more unconquerable mountains, then their Dominions. The *French* extreamly hating the proud humor and ambition of the *Spaniard*, and the *Spaniard* as much loathing the vain and unconstant lightnesse of the *French*; we may therefore account each of them, in these Inter-marriages, to have rather intended the perpetuity of their particular houses, then

the

the strength of their Empires; and that they more desired a noble stock wherein to graft posterity, then power. The Alliance with *Savoy* is more advantagious, though lesse powerfull, then that of *Spain*: for if the King of *France* can keep this Prince on his party, he need not fear the greatnesse of the other, or of any of his faction. The continuall siding of this house with that of *Austria*, having given great and many impediments to the fortune of the *French*. It standeth so fitly to countenance the affaires of either King in *Italy* or *Germany*, to which it shall encline, that it is just of the same nature with the state of *Florence* between *Millaine* and *Venice*, of which *Guicciardine* saith, that *Mantennera le cose d' Italia bilanciate*. On this reason *Henry* IV. earnestly desired to match one of his children into this Countrey, and left this desire as a Legacy with his Councell. But the Alliance of most use to the State of *France*, is that of *England*, as being the nighest and most able of all his neighbours; an alliance which will make his estate invincible, and encompassed about as it were with a wall of brasse.

As for the Kings bastard Brethren, they are four in number, and born of three severall beds. The elder is *Alexander*, made Knight of the Order of St. *John* or of *Malta*, in the life time of his Father. He is now Grand Prior of *France*, and it is much laboured and hoped by the *French*, that he shall be the next Master of the Order; a place of great credit and command. The second and most loved of his father, whose lively image and character he is said to be, is Mr. *Cesar* made Duke of *Vendosme* by his father, and at this time Governour of *Britain*, a man of a brave spirit, and one who swayeth much in the affairs of state; his father took a great care for his advancement before his death, and therefore marryed him to the daughter and heir of the Duke of *Mercuer*, a man of great possessions in *Britain*. It is thought that the inheritance of this Lady, both by her Fathers side, and also by the Mothers, who was of the family of *Martiques*, being a stock of the old Ducall tree, is no lesse then 200000 crownes yearly: both these were borne unto the King by Madam *Gabriele*, for her excellent beauty surnamed *La belle*,

Dutchesse

Dutchesse of *Beauforte*; a Lady whom the King entirely affected even to her last gaspe, and one who never abused her power with him. So that one may truly say of her, what *Velleius* flatteringly spake of *Livia* the wife of *Augustus*, *Ejus potentiam nemo sensit, nisi aut levatione periculi, aut accessione dignitatis.* The third of the Kings naturall brethren, is Mr. *Henry* now Bishop of *Metz* in *Lorreine*, and Abbot of St. *Germans* in *Paris*; as Abbot he is Lord of the goodly *Fauxbourg* of St. *Germans*, and hath the profit of the great Fair there holden, which make a large revenue. His Bishoprick yeeldeth him the profits of 20000 Crowns and upwards, which is the remainder of 6000, the rest being pauned unto the Duke of *Lorreine* by the last Bishop hereof, who was of that Family. The mother of this Mr. *Henry*, is the Marchionesse of *Verneville*, who before the death of the King, fell out of his favour into the Prison, and was not restored to her liberty, till the beginning of this Queen mothers Regency. The fourth and youngest is Mr. *Antonie*, born unto the King by the Countesse of *Marret*, who is Abbot of the Churches of *Marseilles* and *Cane*, and hath as yet not fully out 6000 *l*. a year, when his mother dyeth he will be richer.

The Kings lawfull Brother is named *John Baptist Gaston*, born the 25 of *April*, *anno* 1608; a Prince of a brave and manlike aspect; likely to inherit as large a part of his Fathers spirit, as the King doth of his Crown. He is intituled Duke of *Anjou*, as being the third Son of *France*; but his next elder Brother the Duke of *Orleans* being dead in his childhood, he is vulgarly and properly called *Monsieur*. This title is different from that of *Daulphin*, in that that title only is appropriated to the Heir Apparent, being the Kings eldest Son living; this limited to the Heir Apparent being the Kings eldest Brother surviving; if there be neither Son nor Brother, then the next Heir Apparent is styled only *Le premier Prince du sang*, the first Prince of the bloud. This title of *Monsieur* answereth unto that of *Despote* in the *Greek* Empire; and in imitation of that is thought to have been instituted. Others of the *French* Princes are called *Monsieurs* also, but with some addition of place or honour. The Kings eldest Brother only is called *Monsieur sans queue*, as the *French* use to say; that is, simply *Monsieur*. This young Prince is as yet unmarryed, but destinate to the bed of the young Dutchesse of *Montpensier*, whose Father dyed in the time of *Henry* IV. Had the Duke of *Orleans* lived, he had espoused her long ere this; but it is generally believed, that this Prince is not so affected; he seeth his elder Brother as yet childlesse, himself the next heir to the Crown, and it is likely he will look on a while, and expect the issue of his fortune. ——— Some that speak of the affairs of the Court, holdeth her a fitter match for the young Count of *Soissons*, a Prince of the bloud, and a Gentleman of a fine temper; the Lady her self is said not to be averse from the match; neither will the King not be inclinable unto him, as hoping therein to give him some satisfaction, for not performing a Court promise made unto him, as some say, about marrying the young Madam now Queen of *England*. As for the Count it cannot but be advantagious to him divers wayes, partly to joyne together the two families of *Montpensier* and *Soissons*, both issuing from the house of *Burbon*; partly to enrich himself by adding to his inheritance so fair an Estate; and partly by gaining all the friends and allies of that Ladies kindred to his, the better to enable his opposition against the Prince of *Conde*; the difference between them standeth thus, *Lewis* the first Prince of *Conde*, had by two wives, amongst other children two Sons, by his first wife *Henry* Prince of *Conde*; by the second *Charles* Count of *Soissons*. *Henry* Prince of *Conde* had to his first wife *Mary* of *Cleve* daughter to the Duke of *Nevers*, by whom he had no children. To his second wife he took the Lady *Katharine* of *Tremoville*, sister to the Duke of *Thovars*, anno 1586. Two years after his marriage, he dyed of an old grief took from a poisoned cup, which was given him, anno 1552. and partly with a blow given him with a Lance at the battail of *Contras*, anno 1587. In the 11 moneth after his decease, his young Princesse was brought to bed with a young Son, which is the now Prince of *Conde*. *Charles* Count of *Soissons* in the reign of *Henry* IV. began to question the Princes Legitimation; whereupon the King dealt with the Parliament of *Paris* to declare the place of the first Prince of the Bloud, to belong to the Prince of *Conde*.

Ee And

And for the clearer and more evident proof of the title, 24 Phylitians of good faith and skill, made an open protestation upon oath in the Court, that it was not only possible, but common for women to be delivered in the 11 moneth. On this it was awarded to the Prince. ——— This Decree of Parliament notwithstanding, if ever the King and his Brother should die issueleſſe, it is said, that the young Count of *Soiſſons* (his father died *anno* 1614) will not so give over his title. He is Steward of the Kings houſe, as his Father also was before, a place of good credit, and in which he hath demeaned himſelf very plauſibly. In caſe it ſhould come to a tryall, *quod uu' χευτο*, which God prohibit, he is like to make a great party, both within the Realm, and without it. Without it, by means of the houſe of *Savoy*, having matched his eldeſt Siſter unto *Don Thomazo* the ſecond ſon of that Dukedome now living, a brave man of armes, and indeed the faireſt fruit that ever grew on that tree; next heir of his father after the death of *Don Amadeo* yet childleſſe. Within the Realm, the Lords have already declared themſelves, which hapned on this occaſion. In the year 1620, the month of *March*, the King being to waſh, the Prince of *Conde* laid hold of the towell, challenging that honour as firſt Prince of the bloud; and on the other ſide, the Count of *Soiſſons* ſeized on it, as appertaining to his office of Steward, and Prince of the bloud alſo. The King to decide the controverſie for the preſent, commanded it to be given *Monſieur* his Brother; yet did not this ſatiſfie, for on the morning, the friends of both Princes came to offer their ſervice in the cauſe. To the Count came in generall all the oppoſites of the Prince of *Conde*, and of the Duke of *Luynes*, and *Guiſe*; in particular the Duke of *Maien*, the Duke of *Vendoſme*, the Dukes of *Longueville*, *Eſpernon*, *Nemours*, the Grand Prior, the Dukes of *Thovars*, *Retz*, and *Rohan*, the Viſcount of *Aubeterre*, &c. who all withdrew themſelves from the Court, made themſelves maſters of the beſt places in their governments, and were united preſently to an open faction, of which the Queen Mother declared herſelf head. As for the Commons, without whom the Nobility may quarrel, but never fight; they are more zealous in behalf of the Count, as being brought

up

up alwayes a Papist and born of a *Catholick* kindred, whereas the Prince, though at this instant a *Catholick*, yet *non fuit sic ab initio*; he was born, they say, and brought up an *Hugonot*; and perhaps the alteration is but dissembled.

Concerning the Prince of *Conde*, he hath a sentence of Parliament on his side, and a verdict of Physitians, both weak helpes to a Soveraincy, unlesse well backed by the sword. And for the verdict of the Physitians, thus the case is stated by the Doctors of that faculty; *Laurentius* a professour of *Montpellier* in *Languedoc*, in his excellent Treatise of *Anatomie*, maketh three terms of a womans delivery: *primus, intermedius* and *ultimus*. The first is the seventh moneth after conception, in each of which the childe is vitall, and may live if it be borne. To this also consenteth the Doctor of their chaire *Hippocrates*, saying, παιδίον ἑπταμηνον γόνιμον γιγνεται ζῆν, that a child born in the seventh moneth, if it be well looked to, may live. We read also how in *Spain*, the women are oftentimes lightned in the end of the seventh moneth, and commonly in the end of the eight. And further, that *Sempronius* and *Corbulo*, both *Roman* Consuls, were born in the seventh moneth, *Pliny* in his Naturall History reporteth it as a truth; though perchance the women which told him, either misreskoned their time, or else dissembled it to conceal their honesties. The middle time (*terminus Intermedius*) is in the ninth and tenth moneths, at which time children do seldome miscarry. In the former two moneths, they had gathered life; in these latter, they only consummate strength, so said the Physitians generally. *Non enim in duobus sequentibus mensibus* (they speak it of the *intermedii*) *additur aliquod ad perfectionem partium, sed perfectionem roboris*. The last time (*terminus ultimus*) in the common account of this profession, is the eleventh moneth, which some of them hold neither unlikely, nor rare. *Massurius* recordeth *Papirius* a *Roman* Prætor, to have recovered his inheritance in open Court, though his Mother confessed him to be borne in the thirteenth moneth. And *Avicen* a *Moore* of *Corduba* relateth (as he is cited in *Laurentius*) that he had seen a a childe born after the fourteenth. But these are but the

impostures

impostures of women: and yet, indeed, the modern Doctors are more charitable, and refer it to supernaturall causes, *Et extraordinariam artis considerationem.* On the other side, *Hippocrates* giveth it out definitively, ἐν δίκα μησὶ γίνεται ταῦτα τὸ μακρότατον, that in ten moneths at the furthest (understand ten moneths compleat) the childe is borne. And *Ulpian*, the great Civilian of his times, in the title of the *Digests de Testamentis*, is of opinion, that a childe born after the tenth moneth (compleat) is not to be admitted to the inheritance of his pretended father. As for the Common Law of *England*, as I remember (I have read it in a book written of Wils and Testaments) it taketh a middle course between the charity of nature, and the severity of the Law; leaving it meerly to the conscience and circumstance of the Judge.

But all this must be conceived (as it was afterwards alleaged by the party of the Earl of *Soissons*, taking it in the most favourable construction) of the time after the conception of the mother, and by no means after the death of the Father: and so no way to advantage the Prince of *Conde*. His Father had been extremely sick no small time before his death, for the particular, and supposed since his poison taken *anno* 1552. to be little prone to women in the generall. They therefore who would have him set besides the Cushion, have cunningly, but maliciously, caused it to be whisppered abroad, that he was one of the by-blowes of King *Henry* IV. and to make the matter more suspiciously probable, they have cast out these conjectures for it; but being but conjectures only, and prosecuted for the carrying on of so great a project, they were not thought to be convincing, or of any considerable weight or moment amongst sober and impartiall men. They therefore argued it,

First, From the Kings care of his education, assigning him for his Tutor *Nicholas de Febure*, whom he also designed for his Son King *Lewis*.

Secondly, From his care to work the Prince, then young, *Mollis et aptius agi*, to become a Catholick.

Thirdly,

Thirdly, The infirmity of *Henry* of *Conde*, and the privacy of this King with his Lady, being then King of *Navarre*, in the prime of his strength, and in discontent with the Lady *Marguerite* of *Valoys* his first wife; add to this that Kings love to fair Ladies in the generall, and then conclude this probability to be no miracle. For besides the Dutchesse of *Beauforte*, the Marchionesse of *Verneville*, and the Countesse of *Morret* already mentioned; he is believed to have been the Father of Mr. *Luynes* the great favourite of King *Lewis*. And certain it is, that the very year before his death, when he was even in the winter of his days, he took such an amorous liking to the Prince of *Condes* wife, a very beautifull Lady, and daughter to the Constable, Duke of *Montmorencie*; that the Prince to save his honour was compelled to flie, together with his Princesse, into the Arch-Dukes Countrey; whence he returned not, till long after the death of King *Henry*. If *Mary de Medices* in her husbands life time, had found her self agrieved it, I cannot blame her, she only made good that of *Quintilian*, *Et uxor mariti exemplo incitata, aut imitari se putat aut vindicare.* And yet perhaps a consciousnesse of some injuries, not only mooved her to back the Count of *Soissons* and his faction against the Prince and his; but also to resolve upon him for the husband of her daughter —— From the Princes of the bloud, descend we to the Princes of the Court; and there in the first place we meet with Mr. *Barradas*, the Kings present favourite; a young Gentleman of a fresh and lively hew, little bearded and one whom as yet the people cannot accuse for any oppression or misgovernment. Honours, the King hath conferred none upon him, but only pensions and offices; he is the Governour of the Kings children of honour, (Pages we call them in *England*) a place of more trouble then wealth or credite. He is also the Master of the horse, or *Le grand Esquire*, the esteem of which place recompenseth the emptinesse of the other; for by vertue of this office, he carryeth the Kings sword sheathed before him at his entrances into *Paris*. The cloth of estate carryed over the King by the *Provost* and *Escheuins*, is his fee. No man can be the Kings spurmaker, his Smith, or have any place in the Kings Stables, but from him, and the like. This place (to note so much by the way) was

taken

taken out of the Constables office, (*Comes stabuli* is the true name) to whom it properly belonged, in the time of *Charles* VII. Besides this, he hath a Pension of 50000 Crowns yearly; and had an office given him, which he sold for 100000 Crowns in ready money. A good fortune for one, who the other day was but the Kings Page.

And to say truth, he is as yet but a little better, being only removed from his servant to be his play-fellow. With the affairs of State he intermedleth not, if he should, he might expect the Queen mother should say to him, what *Apollo* in *Ovid* did to *Cupid*:

> ——— *Tibi quid cum fortibus armis*
> *Mi puer? ista decent humeros gestamina nostros.*

For indeed first during her Sons minority, and after since her reintegration with him, she hath made her self so absolute a mistresse of his mind, that he hath intrusted to her the entire conduct of all his most weighty affaires. For her assistant in the managing of her greatest businesse, she hath peeced her self to the strongest side of the State, the Church; having principally (since the death of the Marshal *D'Ancre*, I mean) assumed to her counsels the Cardinall of *Richileiu*, a man of no great birth, were Nobility the greatest parentage; but otherwise to be ranked amongst the noblest. Of a sound reach he is, and a close brain; one exceedingly well mixt of a lay understanding, and a Church habit; one that is compleatly skilled in the art of men, and a perfect master of his own mind and affections; him the Queen useth as her Counsellour, to keep out frailty; and the Kings name as her countenance to keep off envie. She is of a *Florentine* wit, and hath in her all the virtues of *Katharine de Medices*, her Ancestor in her Regency, and some also of her vices; only her designes tend not to the ruine of the Kingdome and her children. *Joan de Seirres* telleth us in his *Inventaire* of *France*, how the Queen *Katharine* suffered her son *Henry* III. a devout and a supple Prince, to spend his most dangerous times, even uncontrouled upon his beads; whilest in the mean time, she usurped the Government of the Realm. Like it is that Queen *Mary* hath learned

so

so much of her Kinswoman, as to permit this son of hers to spend his time also amongst his play-fellowes and the birds, that she may the more securely manage the State at her discretion. And to say nothing of her untrue or misbecoming her vertue, she hath notably well discharged her ambition; the Realm of *France*, being never more quietly and evenly governed, then first during her Regencie, and now during the time of her favour with the King. For during his minority she carryed her self so fairly between the factions of the Court, that she was of all sides honoured; the time of this Marquesse D'*Ancre* only excepted; and for the differences in Religion, her most earnest desire was not to oppresse the Protestants, insomuch that the war raised against them, during the command of Mr. *Luynes*, was presently after his death, and her restoring into grace ended. An heroicall Lady, and worthy the report of posterity; the frailties and weaknesse of her, as a woman, not being accounted hers, but her sexes.

CHAP.

Chap. II.

Two Religions strugling in France, like the two twins in the womb of Rebecca. The comparison between them two, and those in the generall. A more particular survey of the Papists Church in France; in Policie, Priviledge and Revenue. The complaint of the Clergy to the King. The acknowledgment of the French Church to the Pope meerly titular. The pragmatick sanction, Maxima tua fatuitas, and Conventui Tridentino, severally written to the Pope and Trent Councell. The tedious quarrell about Investitures. Four things propounded by the Parliament to the Jesuites. The French Bishops not to medle with Fryers, their lives and land. The ignorance of the French Priests. The Chanoins Latine in Orleans. The French not hard to be converted, if plausibly humoured, &c.

FRom the Court of the King of *France*, I cannot better provide for my self then to have recourse to the King of heaven; and though the Poet meant not *Exeat aula qui vult esse pius*, in that sense, yet will it be no treason for me to apply it so. And even in this, the Church, which should be like the Coat of its Redeemer, without seam; do I finde rents and factions: and of the two, these in the Church more dangerous then those in the *Louure*. I know the story of *Rebecca*, and of the children strugling in her, is generally applyed to the births and contentions of the Law and

the

the Gospel; in particular we may make use of it in expressing the State of the Church and Religions of *France*: for certain it is, that here were divers pangs in the womb of the *French* Church before it was delivered. And first she was delivered of *Esau*, the *Popish* faith being first after the strugling countenanced by authority; *And he came out red all over like an hairy garment,* saith the text, which very appositely expresseth the bloudy and rough condition of the *French* Papists at the birth of the Reformation, before experience and long acquaintance had bred a liking between them. *And after came his Brother out, which laid hold on Esaus heel, and his name was called Jacob*; wherein is described the quality of the Protestant party, which though confirmed by publick Edict after the other, yet hath it divers times endevoured, and will perhaps one day effect, the tripping up of the others heels. *And Esau* (saith *Moses*) *was a cunning hunter, a man of the field; and Jacob a plain man, dwelling in tents*: in which words the comparison is made exact. *A cunning hunter,* in the Scripture signifieth, *a man of art and power mingled*; as when *Nimrod* in *Genesis* 10. is termed *a mighty hunter.* Such is the Papist, a side of greater strength and subtility, a side of war and of the field; on the other side the Protestants are a plain race of men, simple in their actions, without craft and fraudulent behaviours, and dwelling in tents, that is, having no certain abiding place, no Province which they can call theirs; but living dispersed and scattered over the Countrey; which in the phrase of the Scripture is *dwelling in tents.* As for the other words differencing the two brethren, *and the elder shall serve the younger,* they are rather to be accounted a Prophesie then a Character; we must therefore leave the analogie it holds with this *Rebecca* of *France* and her two children, to the event and to prayer.

For a more particular insight into the strength and subtilty of this *Esau*, we must consider it in the three main particular strengths of it; its Polity, Priviledges and Revenue. For the first, so it is that the Popish Church in *France* is governed like those of the first and purest times, by *Archbishops* and *Bishops*. *Archbishops* it comprehendeth 12, and of *Bishops* 104; of these the Metropolitan is he of *Rheimes,* who

Ff useth

useth to anoint the Kings, which office and preheminence hath been annexed unto this seat ever since the times of St. *Remigius* Bishop hereof, who converted *Clovis* King of the *Franks* unto the Gospell. The present Primate is son unto the Duke of *Guise*, by name *Henry de Lorrain*, of the age of 14 years or thereabouts, a burden too unweildie for his shoulders.

———*Et quæ non viribus istis*
Munera conveniunt, nec tam puerilibus annis.

For the better government therefore of a charge so weighty, they have appointed him a Coadjutor to discharge that great function till he come to age to take orders. His name is *Gifford* an *English* fugitive, said to be a man worthy of a great fortune, and able to bear it. The revenues of this Archbishoprick are somewhat of the meanest, not amounting yearly to above 10000 Crowns, whereof Dr. *Gifford* receiveth only 2000, the remainder going to the *Cadet* of *Lorreine*. This trick the *French* learn of the Protestants in *Germany*, where the Princes after the Reformation began by *Luther*, took in the power and Lordships of the Bishops, which together with their functions, they divided into two parts. The lands they bestowed upon some of their younger sons or kinsmen, with the title of *Administrator*; the office and pains of it they conferred with some annuall pension, on one of their Chaplaines, whom they styled the *Superintendent* of the Bishoprick. This Archbishop together with the rest of the Bishops have under them their severall Chancellours, Commissaries, Archdeacons, and other officers attending in their Courts; in which their power is not so generall as with us in *England*. Matters of testament never trouble them, as belonging to the Court of Parliament; who also have wrested to their own hands almost all the businesse of importance; sure I am, all the causes of profit originally belonging to the Church, the affairs meerly Episcopall and spirituall are left unto them, as granting Licence for Marriages, punishing whoredome by way of penance and the like; to go beyond this were *ultra crepidam*, and they should be sure to have a *prohibition* from the Parliaments. Of their priviledges the chiefest of the Clergy men is, the little or no dependence upon the Pope, and the little profits they pay unto their King; of the Pope anon; to the King they pay only their Dismes, or Tithes according to the old rate; a small sum if compared unto the payments of their neighbours; it being thought that the King of *Spain* receiveth yearly one half of the living of the Churches; but this I mean of their livings only, for otherwise they pay the usuall gabels and customes, that are paid by the rest of the Kings liege people. In the generall assembly of the three Estates the Clergy hath authority to elect a set number of Commissioners, to undertake for them and the Church; which Commissioners do make up the first of the three Estates, and do first exhibit their grievances and Petitions to the King. In a word, the *French* Church is the freest of any in Christendome, that have not yet quitted their subjection to the Pope, as alwayes protesting against the Inquisitions, not submitting themselves to the Councell of *Trent*, and paying very little to his Holinesse, of the plentifull revenue, wherewith God and good men have blessed it.

The number of those which the Church Land maintaineth in *France* is *tantum non* infinite, therefore the Intrado and Revenue of it must needs be uncountable. There are numbred in it, as we said before, 12 Archbishops, 104 Bishopricks; to these add 540 Archpriories, 1450 Abbies, 12320 Priories, 567 Nunneries, 700 Covents of Fryers, 259 Commendames of the order of *Malta*, and 130000 Parish Priests. Yet this is not all, this reckoning was made in the year 1598. Since which time the Jesuits have divers Colledges founded for them, and they are known to be none of the poorest. To maintain this large wildernesse of men, the Statistes of *France*, who have proportioned the Countrey; do allow unto the Clergy almost a fourth part of the whole. For supposing *France* to contain 200 millions of Arpens (a measure somewhat bigger then our Acre) they have allotted to the Church for its temporall revenue, 47 of them. In particular of the Archbishops, Bishops, Abbots and Parish Priests, they of *Aux, Alby, Cluniac* and St. Esti-

St. *Eftiennes* in *Paris*, are said to be the wealthyest; the Archbishoprick of *Aux* in *Gascoine* is valued at 400000 Livres or 40000 l. *English* yearly. The Bishop of *Alby* in *Languedoc*, is prized at 10000 Florens, which is a fourth part of it; a great part of this revenue rising out of Saffron. The Abbot of *Cluniac* in the Dutchie of *Burgundy*, is said to be worth 50000 Crowns yearly; the present Abbot being *Henry* of *Lorreine*, Archbishop of *Rheimes*, and Abbot of St. *Dennis*. The Parish Priest of St. *Estiennes*, is judged to receive yearly no fewer then 8000 Crowns, a good Intrado. As for the vulgar Clergy they have little Tithe and lesse Glebe, most part of the revenue being appropriated unto *Abbeys* and other Religious houses; the greatest part of their means is the *Baisse-maine*, which is the Church-offerings of the people at Christnings, Marriages, Burials, Dirges, Indulgences, and the like; which is thought to amount to almost as much as the temporall estate of the Church, an income able to maintain them in good abundance, were it not for the greatnesse of their number; for reckoning that there are (as we have said) in *France* 130000 Parish Priests, and that there are only 27400 Parishes; it must of necessity be, that every Parish one with another must have more then four Priests; too many to be rich.

But this were one of the least injuries offered to the *French* thrist, and would little hinder them from rising, if it were not that the goodliest of their preferments were before their faces given unto boyes and children. An affront which not only despoileth them of the honors due unto their calling, but disheartneth them in their studies and by consequence draweth them unto debauched and slanderous courses.

————*Quis enim virtutem exquireret ipsam,*
Præmia si tollas?————

The Clergy therefore *anno* 1617. being assembled at the house of *Austin Fryers* in *Paris* (as every two years they use to do) being to take their leaves of the King, elected the Bishop of *Aire* to be their spokesman; and to certifie his Majesty

Majesty of their grievances. In performing which businesse, the principall thing of which he spake was to this purpose; That whereas his Majesty was bound to give them fathers, he gave them children; that the name of Abbot signifieth a Father; and the function of a Bishop is full of fatherly authority: that France notwithstanding was now filled with Bishops and Abbots, which are yet in their Nurses armes, or else under their Regents in Colledges; nay more, that the abuse goeth before their being; Children being commonly designed to Bishopricks and Abbacies, before they were born. He made also another complaint, that the Soveraign Courts by their decrees, had attempted upon the authority which was committed to the Clergy, even in that which meerly concerned Ecclesiasticall discipline and government of the Church. To these complaints he gave them, indeed, a very gracious hearing, but it was no further then an hearing, being never followed by redresse. The Court of Parliament knew too well the strength of their own authority, and the King was loath to take from himself those excellent advantages of binding to himself his Nobility, by the speedy preferring of their children; and so the clergie departed with a great deal of envy, and a little satisfaction. Like enough it were, that the Pope would in part redresse this injury, especially in the point of jurisdiction, if he were able. But 'his wings are shrewdly clipped in this Countrey, neither can he fly at all, but as far as they please to suffer him. For his temporall power they never could be induced to acknowledge it, as we see in their stories, *anno* 1610. he Divines of *Paris* in a Declaration of theirs rendred to he Queen Mother, affirmed the *supremacie* of the *Pope*, to be in *Erroneous Doctrine*, and the ground of that *hellish position* of *deposing and killing of Kings*. *Anno* 1517. when the Councell of *Lateran* had determined the Pope to be the head of he Church In causes also temporall: the University of Paris testifieth against it in an Apology of theirs, Dated the 2 of *March* the same year; *Leo decimus* (saith the Apology) *in quodam cœtu, non tamen in Spiritu Domini congregato, contra fidem Catholicam*, &c. *Sacrum Basilienfe concilium damnavit.* In which Councell of *Basil*, the Supremacy of the Pope was condemned

ned. Neither did the Kings of *France* forget to maintain their own authority. And therefore when as Pope *Boniface* VIII had in a peremptory Letter, written to *Philip le Bel* King of *France*, styled himself *Dominus totius mundi tam in temporalibus quam in spiritualibus:* the King returned him an answer with an Epithite sutable to his arrogancy, *Sciat maxima tua fatuitas nos in temporalibus alicui non subesse*, &c. The like answer, though in modester termes, was sent to another of the Popes, by St. *Lewis*, a man of a most milde and sweet disposition, yet unwilling to forgoe his royalties.

His spirituall power is alwayes as little in substance, though more in shew; for whereas the Councell of *Trent* hath been an especiall authorizer of the Popes spirituall supremacy; the *French* Church would never receive it. By this means the Bishops keep in their hands, their own full authority; whereof an obedience to the decrees of that Councell would deprive them. It was truely said by St. *Gregory*, and they well knew it, *Lib.* 7. *Epist.* 70. *Si unus universalis est, restat ut vos Episcopi non sitis.* Further the University of *Paris* in their Declaration, *anno* 1610 above mentioned, plainly affirme, that it is directly opposite to the Doctrine of the Church which the University of *Paris* alwayes maintained, that the Pope hath the power of a Monarch in the spirituall government of the Church. To look upon higher times, when the Councell of *Constance* had submitted the authority of the Pope unto that of a Councell; *John Gerson, Theologus Parisiensis magni nominis*, as one calleth him, defended that decree: and intitulethhem, *Perniciosos admodum esse adulatores qui tyrannidem istam in Ecclesiam invexere, quasi nullis legum teneatur vinculis, quasi neque parere debeat concilio Pontifex, nec ab eo judicari queat* The Kings themselves also befriend their Clergy in this cause; and therefore not only protested against the Councell of *Trent*, wherein this spirituall tyranny was generally consented to by the Catholick faction. But *Henry* II. also would not acknowledge them to be a Councell, calling them by another name then *Conventus Tridentinus*. An indignity which the Fathers took very offensively.

But

But the principall thing in which it behoveth them not to acknowledge his spirituall Supremacy, is the collation of Benefices and Bishopricks, and the Annats and first fruits thence arising. The first and greatest controversie between the Pope and Princes of Christendome, was about the bestowing the livings of the Church, and giving the investure unto Bishops; the Popes had long thirsted after that authority, as being a great means to advance their followers, and establish their own greatnesse: for which cause in divers petty Councels, the receiving of any Ecclesiasticall preferment of a Lay man was enacted to be *Simony*. But this did little edifie with such patrons as had good livings. As soon as ever *Hildebrande*, in the Catalogue of the Popes called *Gregory* VII. came to the Throne of *Rome*, he set himself entirely to effect this businesse as well in *Germany*, now he was Pope, as he had done in *France* whilest he was Legat; he commandeth therefore *Henry* III. Emperour, *Ne deinceps Episcopatus & beneficia* (they are *Platinas* own words) *per cupiditatem Simonaicam committat; aliter se usurum in ipsum censuris Ecclesiasticis*. To this injustice, when the Emperour would not yeeld, he called a solemn Councell at the *Lateran*; wherein the Emperour was pronounced to be *Simoniacall*, and afterwards Excommunicated; neither would this Tyrant ever leave persecuting of him, till he had laid him in his grave. After this there followed great struggling for this matter, between the Popes and the Emperours; but in the end the Popes got the victory. In *England* here, he that first beckoned about it was *William Rufus*; the controversie being, whether he or Pope *Urban* should invest *Anselme* Archbishop of *Canterbury*. *Anselme* would receive his investure from none but the Pope, whereupon the King banished him the Realm, into which he was not admitted till the Reign of *Henry* II. He to endeer himself with his Clergy, relinquished his right to the Pope, but afterwards repenting himselfe of it, he revoked his grant; neither did the *English* Kings wholly lose it, till the reign of that unfortunate prince King *John*. *Edward* the first again recovered it, and his successors kept it.

The

The Popes having with much violence and opposition wrested into their hands, this priviledge of nominating P.iests and investing Bishops, they spared not to lay on what taxes they pleased; as on the Benefices, first fruits, pensions, subsidies, fifteenths, tenths; and on the Bishopricks for palles, miters, croliers, rings, and I know not what bables. By these means the Churches were so impoverished, that upon complaint made to the Councell of *Basil*, all these cheating tricks, these *aucupia & expilandi rationes*, were abolished. This decree was called *Pragmatica sanctio*, and was confirmed in *France* by *Charles* VII. *anno* 1438. An act of singular improvement to the Church and Kingdome of *France*; which yearly before, as the Court of Parliament manifested to *Lewis* XI. had drained the State of a million of Crowns; since which time the Kings of *France* have sometimes omitted the rigor of this sanction, and sometimes also exacted it, according as their affairs with the Pope stood; for which cause it was called *Frænum pontificum*. At last King *Francis* I. having conquered *Millaine*, fell into this composition with his Holinesse; namely, that upon the falling of any Abbacy or Bishoprick, the King should have 6 months time allowed him to present a fit man unto him, whom the Pope should legally invest. If the King neglected his time limited, the Pope might take the benefit of the relapse, and institute whom he pleased. So is it also with the inferior Benefices, between the Pope and the Patrons; insomuch that any or every Lay-patron, and Bishop together in *England*, hath for ought I see (at the least in this particular) as great a Spirituall Supremacy, as the Pope in *France*.

Nay to proceed further, and shew how meerly titular both his supremacies are, as well the spirituall as the temporall, you may plainly see in the case of the Jesuites, which was thus: In the year 1609 the Jesuites had obtained of King *Henry* IV. licence to read again in their Colledges of *Paris*; but when their Letters patents came to be verified in the Court of Parliament, the Rector and University opposed them, on the 17 of *December*, 1611. both parties came to have an hearing, and the University got the day, unlesse the Jesuites would subscribe unto these four points. *viz.*

1. That a Councell was above the Pope.

2. That

2. That the Pope had no temporall power over Kings, and could not by Excommunication deprive them of their Realm and Estates.

3. That Clergy men having heard of any attempt or conspiracy against the King or his Realm, or any matter of treason in confession, he was bound to reveal it.

And 4. That Clergy men were subject to the secular Prince or politick Magistrate. It appeared by our former discourse, what little or no power they had left the Pope over the Estates and preferments of the *French*.

By these Propositions (to which the Jesuites in the end subscribed, I know not with what mentall reservation) it is more then evident, that they have left him no command neither over their consciences, nor their persons; so that all things considered, we may justly say of the Papall power in *France*, what the Papists said falsly of *Erasmus*, namely that it is *Nomen sine rebus*.

In one thing only his authority here is intire, which is his immediate protection of all the orders of Fryers, and also a superintendency or supreme eye over the Monks, who acknowledge very small obedience, if any at all, to the *French* Bishops: for though at the beginning every part and member of the Diocesse, was directly under the care and command of the Bishop; yet it so happened that at the building of Monasteries in the Western Church, the Abbots being men of good parts and a sincere life, grew much into the envie of their Diocesan. For this cause, as also to be more at their own command, they made suit to the Pope that they might be free from that subjection, *Utque in tutelam divi Petri admitterentur*; a proposition very plausible to his Holinesse ambition, which by this means might the sooner be raised to its height; and therefore without difficulty granted. This gap opened, first the severall orders of Fryers; and after even the Deans and Chapters, purchased to themselves the like exemptions. In this the Popes power was wonderfully strengthned, as having such able, and so main props to uphold his authority; It being a true Maxime in State, *Quod qui privilegia obtinent, ad eadem conservanda tenentur authoritatem concedentis tueri*. This continued till the Councell of *Trent*

Gg un-

unquestioned. Where the Bishops much complained of their want of authority, and imputed all the Schismes and Vices in the Church, unto this, that their hands were tyed; hereupon the Popes Legats thought it fit to restore their jurisdiction, their Deans and Chapters. At that of the Monks and Monasteries, there was more sticking, till at the last *Sebastian Pighinus*, one of the Popes officers, found out for them this satisfaction; that they should have an eye and inspection into the lives of the Monks, not by any authority of their own, *Sed tanquam a sede Apostolica delegati*. But as for the Orders of Fryers, the Pope would not by any means give way to it. They are his *Janizaries*, and the strongest bulwarke of his Empire, and are therefore called in a good Author, *Egregia Romanæ curiæ instrumenta*. So that with them the Diocesan hath nothing to do, each severall religious house being as a Court of *Peculiars*, subjects only to the great Metropolitan of *Rome*.

This meer dependence on his Holinesse, maketh this generation a great deal more regardlesse of their behaviour, then otherwise it would be: though since the growth of the Reformation, shame and fear hath much reformed them, they have still howsoever, a spice of their former wantonnesse, and on occasions will permit themselves a little good fellowship; and to say truth of them, I think them to be the best companions in *France* for a journey, but not for acquaintance. They live very merrily, and keep a competent table, more I suppose then can stand with their vow; and yet far short of that affluency whereof many of our books accuse them. It was my chance to be in a house of the *Franciscans* in *Paris*, where one of the Fryers upon the intreaty of our friends, had us into the hall, it being then the time of their *refectory*; a favour not vulgar; there saw we the Brothers sitting all of a side, and every one a pretty distance from the other, their severall commons being a dish of pottage, a chop of Mutton, a dish of cherries, and a large glasse of water: this provision together with a liberall allowance of ease, and a little of study keepeth them exceeding plump and in a good liking, and maketh them, having little to take thought for, as I said before, passing good company. As I travailed towards *Orleans* we had in our Coach with us three of these mortified sinners, two of the Order of St. *Austin*, and one *Franciscan*; the merryest crickets that ever chirped, nothing in them but mad tales and complements; and for musick, they would sing like hawkes. When we came to a vein of good wine they would cheer up themselves and their neighbours with this comfortable Doctrine, *Vivamus ut bibamus, & bibamus ut vivamus*. And for courtship and toying with the wenches, you would easily believe that it had been a trade with which they had not been a little acquainted; of all men, when I am marryed, God keep my wife from them, till then, my neighbours.

On the other side, the common Priests of *France*, are so dull and blockish, that you shal hardly meet with a more contemptible people. The meanest of our Curates in *England*, for spirit and discourse, are very Popes to them; for learning they may safely say with *Socrates*, *Hoc tantum scimus quod nescimus*; but you must not look they should say it in Latine: Tongues they have none but that of their Mother and the Masse book: of which last they can make no use except the book be open, and then also the book is fain to read it self. For in the last *Romanum Missale*, established by *Pius* V. and recognized by *Clement* VIII. *anno* 1600. every syllable is diversly marked, whether it be sounded long or short; just as the versifying examples are in the end of the Grammar. When I had lost my self in the streets of *Paris*, and wanted *French* to enquire homeward, I used to apply my self to some of these reverend habit. But *O. scelum Insipiens & infacetum!* you might as easily have wrung water out of the flint, as a word of Latine out of their mouths. Nor is this the disease of the vulgar Masse-mumbler only, it hath also infected the right Worshipfull of the Clergy. In *Orleans* I had businesse with a Chanoin of the Church of St. *Croix*, a fellow that wore his Surplice (it was made of Lawn and lace) with as good a credit, as ever I saw any, and for the comlinesse and capacity of his Cap, he might have been a Metropolitan: perceiving me to speak to him in a strange tongue, for it was Latine, he very readily asked me this question, *Num potestis loqui Gallia?* which when I had denyed, at last he broke out into another interrogatory, *viz. Quam diu fuistis in Gallice?* To conclude, having read over my Letter, with two or three deadly pangs, and six times rubbing of his temples, he dismissed me with this cordiall, and truly it was very comfortable to my humour, *Ego negotias vestras curabo*. A strange beast, and one of the greatest prodigies of ignorance, that I ever met with in mans apparrell.

Such being the *Remish* Priests, it is no marvel that the *French* Papist be no more setled and resolute in their Religion. If the eye be blinde, the body cannot choose but be darkned. And certainly there is nothing that hath prepared many of this Realm more to imbrace the Reformation, then the blockishnesse of their own Clergy. An excellent advantage to the Protestant Ministers, could they but well humor it, and likely to be a fair enlargement to their party, if well husbanded. Besides this, the *French Catholicks* are not over earnest in the cause, and so lie open to the assaults of any politick enemy. To deal with them by main force of argument, and in the fervent spirit of zeal, as the Protestants too often do, is not the way; men uncapable of opposition, as this people generally are, and furious if once thwarted; must be tamed as *Alexander* did his horse *Bucephalus*; those which came to back him with the tyranny of the spur and cudgell, he quickly threw down and mischiefed. *Alexander* came otherwise prepared, for turning the horse towards the sun that he might not see the impatience of his own shadow, he spake kindly to him, and gently clapped him on the back, till he had left his flinging and wildnesse, he lightly leapt into the saddle, the horse never making resistance: *Plutarch* in his life relateth the story, and this is the morall of it.

CHAP.

Chap. III.

The correspondency between the French *King and the Pope. This Pope an Omen of the Marriages of* France *with* England. *An* English *Catholicks conceit of it. His Holiness Nuncio in* Paris. *A learned Argument to prove the Popes universality. A continuation of the allegory between* Jacob *and* Esau. *The Protestants compelled to leave their Forts and Towns. Their present estate and strength. The last War against them justly undertaken; not fairly managed. Their insolencies and disobedience to the Kings command. Their purpose to have themselves a free estate. The war not a war of Religion. King* James *in justice could not assist them more then he did. First forsaken by their own party. Their happinesse before the war. The Court of the edict. A view of them in their Churches. The commendation which the* French *Papists give to the Church of* England. *Their Discipline and Ministeries,* &c.

WE have seen the strength and subtility, as also somewhat of his poverties at home: Let us now see the alliance which this *French Esau* hath abroad in the world; in what credit and opinion he standeth in the eye of *Beeri* the *Romish Hittite*, the daughter of whose abominations he hath marryed. And here I find him to hold good correspondency, as being the eldest son of the Church, and an equall poise to ballance the affaires of *Italy* against the Potency of *Spain*. On this ground the present Pope hath alwayes shewn himselt very favourable to the *French* side; well knowing into what perils an unnecessary and impolitick dependance on the *Spanish* party only; would one day bring the State Ecclesiastick. As in the generall, so also in many particulars hath he expressed much affection unto him. As

1. By taking into his hands the *Valtolin*, till his Sonne of *France* might settle himself in some course to recover it.

2. His not stirring in the behalf of the *Spaniard*, during the last wars in *Italy*. And

3. His speedy and willing grant of the dispensation for Madams marriage, notwithstanding the *Spaniard* so earnestly laboured the deniall, or at least the delay of it.

To speak by conjectures, I am of opinion, that his Genius prompted him to see the speedy consummation of this marriage, of which his Papacy was so large an Omen, so far a prognostick.

Est Deus in nobis, agitante calescimus illo.

The *Lar* or angell guardian of his thoughts hastned him in it; in whose time there was so plausible a Presage, that it must be accomplished. For thus it standeth: *Malachi* now a Saint, then one of the first Apostles of the *Irish*, one much reverenced in his memory unto this day by that Nation; left behind him by way of Prophesie a certain number of Mottoes in Latine, telling those that there should follow that certain number of Popes only, whose conditions successively should be lively expressed in those Mottos, according to that order which he had placed them. *Messingham* an *Irish* Priest, and Master of the Colledge of *Irish* fugitives in *Paris*, collected together the lives of all the *Irish* Saints; which book himself shewed me. In that Volume, and the life of this Saint, are the severall Mottos and severall Popes set down Column wise one against the other: I compared the lives of them with the Mottos, as far as my memory would carry me, and found many of them very answerable.

As

CHAP. III.   *the State of* France.   231

As I remember there are 36 Mottos yet to come, and when just so many Popes are joyned to them, they are of opinion (for so *Malachie* foretold) that either the world should end, or the Popedom be ruined. Amongst the others, the Motto of the present Pope was most remarkable, and sutable to the action likely to happen in his time: being this, *Lilium & Rosa*, which they interpret, and in my mind not unhappily, to be intended to the conjunction of the *French Lilly* and *English Rose*. To take from me any suspicion of Imposture, he shewed an old book, printed almost 200 years agoe, written by one *Wion a Flemming*, and comparing the number of the Mottos with the Catalogue of the Popes; I found the name of *Urban* (the now Pope) to answer it. On this ground an *English* Catholick, whose acquaintance I gained in *France*, made a copy of Verses in *French*, and presented them to the *English* Ambassadours, the Earls of *Carlile* and *Holland*. Because he is my friend, and the conceit is not to be despised, I begged them of him, and these are they.

Lilia juncta Rosis.

Emblème de bon presage de l' Alliance de la France, avec l' Angle terre.

Ce grand dieu qui d'un oeil voit tout ce que les ans,
Soubs leurs voiles sacrez vont a nous yeux cachans.
Decouvre quelque fois, ainsi qu' bon lui semble,
Et les maux a venir, et les biens tout ensemble,
Ainsi fit-il jades a celui, qui primier.
Dans l' Ireland porta de la froy le laurier;
Malachie son nom qu' au tymon de l'eglise
On verra seoir un jour, cil qui pour sa devise.

Aura

Aura les lys chenus ioints aux plus belles fleures,
Qui dorent le prin-temps, de leurs doubles colours.
CHARLES est le fleuron de la Rose pourpree;
Heuritte est le Lys, que la plus belle pree
De la France nourrit: pour estre quelque jour
Et la Reina des fleurs, et des roses l' amour.
Adorable banquet, b.en heureuse couronne,
Que la bonte du ciel e parrage nous donne;
Heureuse ma partie, heureuse mille fois,
Celle qui te sera restorier en les roys.

With these Verses I take my leave of his Holinesse, wishing none of his successors would presage worse luck unto *England*. I go now to see his *Nuncio*, to whose house the same *English Catholick* brought me, but he was not at home; his name is *Bernardino d' Espada*: a man, as he informed me, able to discharge the trust reposed in him by his Master, and one that very well affected the *English* Nation. He hath the fairest house, and keepeth the largest retinue of any ordinary Ambassador in the Realm; and maketh good his Masters Supremacies, by his own precedency. To honour him against he was to take his charge, his Holinesse created him Bishop of *Damiata* in *Egypt*; a place which I am certain never any of them saw but in a map, and for the profits he receiveth thence, they will never be able to pay for his Crozier. But this is one of his Holinesse usuall policies, to satisfie his followers with empty titles. So he made Bishop, whom he sent to govern for him in *England*, Bishop of *Chalcedon* in *Asia*; and *Smith* also who is come over about the same businesse, with the Queen, Bishop of *Archidala* a City of *Thrace*. An old *English* Doctor used it, as an especiall argument to prove the universality of power in the Pope, because he could ordain Bishops over al Cities in Christendom; if he could as easily give them also the revenue, this reason (I confesse) would much sway me, till then I am sorry that men should still be boyes, and play with bubbles. By the same authority he might do well to make all his Courtiers Kings,

Kings, and then he were sure to have a most royall and beggerly Court of it.

To proceed a little further in the Allegory, so it is that when *Jacob* saw *Esau* to have incurred his fathers and mothers anger, for his heathenish marriage, he set himself to bereave his elder brother of his blessing. Prayers, and the sweet smell of his Venison, the sweet smelling of his sacrifices, obtained of his Lord and Father a blessing for him: for indeed the Lord hath given unto this his *French Jacob*, as it is in the text, *the dew of heaven, and the fatnesse of the earth, and plenty of corne and wine*, Gen. 27. 28. It followeth in the 41. verse of the *Chapter. And Esau hated Jacob, because of the blessing wherewith his father had blessed him; and Esau said in his heart, The days of mourning for my father are at hand, then will I slay my brother Jacob.* The event of which his bloudy resolution was, that *Jacob* was fain to relinquish all that he had, and flie unto his Uncle. This last part of the story, expresseth very much of the present estate of the *French* Church. The Papists hated the Protestants to see them thrive and increase so much amongst them. This hatred moved them to a war, by which they hoped to root them out altogether; and this war compelled the Protestants to abandon their good Towns, their strong holds, and all their possessions, and to flie to their friends wheresoever they could finde them. And indeed, the present estate of the Protestants is not much better then that of *Jacob* in *Mesopotamia*, nor much different. The blessing which they expect lyeth more in the seed then the harvest. For their strength it consisteth principally in their prayers to God: and secondly, in their obedience to their Kings. Within these two fortresses, if they can keep themselves, they need fear none ill; because they shall deserve none. The only outward strengths they have left them, are the two Towns of *Montaban* and *Rochell*, the one deemed invincible, the other threatned a speedy destruction. The Duke of *Espernon* (at my being there) lay round about it, and it was said, that the Town was in very bad terms: all the neighbouring Towns, to whose opposition they much trusted, having yeelded at the first sight of the Canon. *Rochell*, it is thought, cannot be forced

Hh by

by assault, nor compelled by a famine. Some Protestants are glad of, and hope to see the *French* Church restored to its former powerfulnesse, by the resistance of that Town meerly. I rather think, that the perverse and stubborn condition of it, will at last, drive the young King into a fury, and incite him to revenge their contradiction, on their innocent friends, now disarmed and disabled. Then will they see at last the issue of their own peremptory resolutions, and begin to believe, that the Heathen Historian was of the two the better Christian, when he gave us this note, *Non turpe est ab eo vinci, quem vincere esset nefas, neque illi inhoneste etiam submitti, quem fortuna super omnes extulisset.* This weaknesse and misery which hath now befallen the Protestants, was an effect, I confesse, of the ill-will which the other party bare them; but that they bare them ill will, was a fruit of their own graffing. In this circumstance, they were nothing like *Jacob*, who in the hatred which his brother *Esau* had to him, was simply passive; they being active also in the birth of it. And indeed that lamentable and bloudy war, which fell upon them, they not only endevoured not to avoid, but invited, during the reign of *Henry* IV. who would not see it, and the troublesome minority of *Lewis* XIII. who could not molest them, they had made themselves masters of 99 Towns, well fortifyed and enabled for a siege: a strength too great for any one faction to keep together, under a King which desires to be himself, and rule his people. In the opinion of this their potency, they call Assemblies, Parliaments as it were, when and as often as they pleased. There they consulted of the common affairs of Religion, made new Laws of government, removed and rechanged their generall officers; the Kings leave all this while never so much as formally demanded. Had they only been guilty of too much power, that crime alone had been sufficient to have raised a war against them, it not standing with the safety and honour of a King, not to be the absolute commander of his own Subjects. But in this their licentious calling of Assemblies, they abused their power into a neglect, and not dissolving them at his Majesties commandment, they increased

their

CHAP. III.   *the State of* France.   235

their neglect into into a disobedience. The Assembly which principally occasioned the war and their ruine, was that of *Rochell*, called by the Protestants presently upon the Kings journey into *Bearn*. This generall meeting the King prohibited by his especiall Edicts, declaring all them to be guilty of treason; which notwithstanding they would not hearken to, but very undutifully went on in their purposes. It was said by a Gentleman of their party, and one that had been imployed in many of their affairs, *That the fiery zeal of some who had the guiding of their consciences, had thrust them into those desperate courses*; and I believe him;

Tantum relligio potuit suadere malorum.

Being assembled, they sent the King a *Remonstrance* of their grievances, to which the Duke *Lesdiguiers*, in a Letter to them written, gave them a very fair and plausible answer, wherein also he intreateth them to obey the Kings Edict, and break up the Assembly. Upon the receipt of this Letter, those of the Assembly published a Declaration, wherein they verified their meeting to be lawfull, and their purpose not to dismisse themselves, till their desires were granted. This affront done to the King, made him gather together his Forces; yet at the Duke of *Lesdiguiers* request, he allowed them 24 dayes of respite; before his Armies should march towards them, he offered them also very fair and reasonable conditions, such also as their Deputies had solicited, but far better then those which they were glad to accept, when all their Towns were taken from them. *Profecto ineluctabilis fatorum vis, cujus fortunam mutare constituit, ejus corrumpit consilia.* It held very rightly in this people, who turned a deaf eare to all good advice, and were resolved it seemeth, *Not to hear the voice of the Charmer, charmed he never so sweetly.* In their Assemblie therefore they make Lawes and Orders to regulate their disobedience, as, That no peace should be made without the consent of the generall Convocation, about paying of Souldiers wages, for the detaining of the Revenues of the King and Clergy, and the like. They also there divided *France* into seven circles or parts, assigning over every circle severall Generals and Lieutenants, and prescribed Orders how those Generals should proceed in the wars.

Thus we see the Kings Army leavied upon no slight ground, his Regall authority was neglected, his especiall Edicts violated, his gracious profers slighted, and his Revenues forbidden him, and his Realm divided before his face, and allotted unto officers not of his own election. Had the prosecution of his action been as fair, as the cause was, just and legall, the Protestants had only deserved the infamy; but *hinc illæ lachrymæ*. The King so behaved himself in it, that he suffered the sword to walk at randome; as if his main design had been, not to correct his people, but to ruine them. I will instance onely in that tyrannicall slaughter, which he permitted at the taking of *Nigrepelisse*, a Town of *Quercu*; wherein indeed, the Souldiers shewed the very rigour of severity, which either a barbarous victor could inflict, or a vanquished people suffer, *Nec ullum sævitiæ genus emisit ira & victoria*, as *Tacitus* of the angred *Romans*. For they spared neither man, nor woman, nor childe, all equally subject to the cruelty of the sword and the Conquerour. The streets paved with dead carkasses, the channels running with the bloud of Christians; no noise in the streets, but o such as were welcoming death, or suing for life. Their Churches, which the *Goths* spared at the sack of *Rome*, were at this place made the Theatres of lust and bloud; neither priviledge of Sanctuary, nor fear of God, in whose holy house they were, qualifying their outrage; this in the common places.

At domus interior gemitu, miseroque tumultu
Miscetur; penitusque cavæ plangoribus ædes
Fæmineis ululant. ———

As *Virgil* in the ruine of *Troy*

But the calamities which befell the men, were mercifull an sparing, if compared to those which the women suffered when the Souldiers had made them the objects of their lust they made them also the subjects of their fury, in that onl

pitifu

CHAP. III.   *the State of* France.   237

pittifull to that poor and diftreffed fex that they did not let them furvive their honours. Such of them who out of fear and faintneſs had made but little refiſtance, had the favour to be ſtabbed; but thoſe whoſe virtue and courage maintained their bodies valiantly from the rapes of thoſe villains, had the ſecrets of nature (*procul hinc eſte caſtæ & miſericordes aures*) filled with gun-powder; and ſo blown into aſhes. Whither, O you divine powers! is humanity fled when it is not to be found in Chriſtians? or where ſhall we look for the effects of a pitifull nature, when men are become ſo unnaturall? It is ſaid that the King was ignorant of this barbarouſneſſe, and offended at it. Offended I perſwade my ſelf he could not but be, unleſſe he had totally put off himſelf, and degenerated into a Tyger. But for his ignorance I dare not conceive it to be any other then that of *Nero*, an ignorance rather in his eye then underſtanding: *Subduxit oculos Nero* (ſaith *Tacitus*) *juſſitque ſcelera, non ſpectavit* ——— Though the Proteſtants deſerved affliction for their diſobedience; yet this was an execution above the nature of a puniſhment, a miſery beyond the condition of the crime. True it is, and I ſhall never acquit them of it, that in the time of their proſperity, they had done the King many affronts, and committed many acts of diſobedience and inſolency, which juſtly occaſioned the war againſt them; for beſides thoſe already recited, they themſelves firſt broke thoſe Edicts, the due execution whereof ſeemed to have been their only petition. The King by his Edict of pacification, had licenced the free exerciſe of both Religions, and thereupon permitted the Prieſts and Jeſuits to preach in the Towns of *Caution*, being then in the hands of the Proteſtants. On the other ſide, the Proteſtants aſſembled at *London*, ſtrictly commanded all their Governors, Majors and Sheriffs, not to ſuffer any Jeſuits, nor any of any other Order to preach in their Towns, although licenced by the Biſhop of the Dioceſe. When upon diſlike of their proceedings in that Aſſembly the King had declared their meeting to be unlawfull, and contrary to his peace; and this Declaration was verified againſt them by the Parliament:

ment; they notwithstanding would not separate themselves, but stood still upon terms of capitulation, and the justifiableness of their action again. Whereas it hapned, that the Lord of *Pilou*, a Town full of those of the Religion, dyed in the year 1620. and left his daughter and heir in the bed and marriage of the Viscount of *Cheylane*, a Catholick: this new Lord according to law and right, in his own Town changed the former Garrison, putting his own servants and dependants in their places. Upon this the Protestants of the Town and Countrey round about it, draw themselves in troops, surprise many of the Towns about it, and at last compelled the young Gentleman to flie from his inheritance; an action, which jumping even with the time of the Assembly at *Rochel*, made the King more doubtfull of their sincerity. I could add to these divers others of their undutifull practises, being the effects of too much felicitie, and of a fortune which they could not govern.

Atqui animus meminisse horret, luctuque refugit.

These their insolencies and unruly acts of disobedience, made the King and his Counsell suspect, that their designes tended further then Religion, and that their purpose might be to make themselves a free State, after the example of *Geneva*, and the Low-countreymen. The late power which they had taken of calling their own Synods and Convocations, was a strong argument of their purpose; so also was the intelligence which they held with those of their own faith. At the Synod of *Gappe*, called by the permission of *Henry* the fourth, on the first of *October*, anno 1603. they not only gave audience to Ambassadours, and received Letters from forain Princes; but also importuned his Majesty to have a generall liberty of going into any other Countries, and assisting at their Councels: a matter of especiall importance: and therefore the King upon a foresight of the dangers, wisely prohibited them to goe to any
Assemblies

Assemblies without a particular Licence, upon pain to be declared Traytors. Since that time growing into greater strength, whensoever they had occasion of businesse with King *Lewis*, they would never treat with him, but by their Ambassadours, and upon especiall Articles.

An ambition above the quality of those that professe themselves Subjects, and the only way, as *Du Serres* noteth, *To make an Estate in the State*. But the answers made unto the King by those of *Clerac* and *Montauban*, are pregnant proofs of their intent and meaning in this kinde; the first being summoned by the King and his Army the 25 of *July*, *Anno* 1621. returned thus, *That the King should suffer them to enjoy their Liberties, and leave their Fortifications as they were, for the safety of their lives, and so they would declare themselves to be his Subjects*. They of *Montauban*, made a fuller expression of the generall designe and disobedience, which was, *That they were resolved to live and die in the union of the Churches*, had they said for the service of the King, it had been spoken bravely, but now rebelliously.

This Union and Confederacy of theirs, King *Lewis* used to call *the Common-wealth of Rochell*; for the overthrow of which, he alwayes protested, that he had only taken armes, and if we compare circumstances, we shall finde it to be no other.

In the second of *Aprill*, before he had as yet advanced into the field, he published a Declaration in favour of all those of the Religion, which would contain themselves within duty and obedience. And whereas some of *Tours*, at the beginning of the wars, had tumultuously molested the Protestants, at the buriall of one of their dead; five of them, by the Kings commandement, were openly executed. When the war was hottest abroad, those of the Religion in *Paris* lived as securely as ever, and had their accustomed meetings at *Charenton*; so had also those of other places. Moreover, when tidings came to *Paris* of the Duke of *Mayens* death, flain before *Montauban*, the rascall *French*, according to their hot headed dispositions, breathed out nothing but ruine to the *Huguaits*. The Duke of *Monbazon* governour of the City commanded their houses and the streets to be safely guarded. After, when this rabble had burnt down their Temple at *Chareaton*, the Court of Parliament on the day following ordained, that it should be built up again in a more beautifull manner, and that at the Kings charge. Add to this, that since the ending of the wars, and the reduction of almost all their Towns, we have not seen the least alteration of Religion. Besides that, they have been permitted to hold a Nationall Synod at *Charenton* for establishing the truth of their Doctrine, against the errours of *Arminius* professour of *Leiden* in *Holland*.

All things thus considered in their true being, I cannot see for what cause our late Soveraign should suffer so much censure as he then did, for not giving them assistance. I cannot but say, that my self have too often condemned his remissenesse in that cause, which upon better consideration I cannot tell how he should have dealt in. Had he been a medler in it further then he was, he had not so much preserved Religion, as supported Rebellion; besides the consequence of the example. He had Subjects of his own more then enough, which were subject to discontent, and prone to an apostasie from their alleagiance. To have assisted the disobedient *French* under the colour of the liberty of conscience, had been only to have taught that King a way into *England* upon the same pretence; and to have trod the path of his own hazard. He had not long before denied succour to his own children, when he might have given them on a better ground, and for a fairer purpose; and could not now in honour countenance the like action in another. For that other, deniall of his helping hand, I much doubt how far posterity will acquit him, though certainly he was a good Prince, and had been an happy instrument of the peace of Christendome, had not the
latter

CHAP. III.   *the State of* France.   241

latter part of his reign hapned in a time so full of troubles. So that betwixt the quietnesse of his nature, and the turbulency of his latter dayes, he fell into that miserable exigent mentioned in the Historian, *Miserrimum est cum aliud, aut natura sua extendenda est, aut minuenda dignitas.* Add to this, that the *French* had been first abandoned at home by their own friends, of seven Generals which they had appointed for the seven circles into which they divided all *France*, four of them never giving them incouragement. The three which accepted of those unordinate Governments, were the Duke of *Roban*, his brother M. *Soubise*, and the Marquesse of *Laffares*; the four others being the Duke of *Tremoüille*, the Earl of *Challillon*, the Duke of *Lesdisguier*, and the Duke of *Bouillon*, who should have commanded in chief. So that the *French* Protestants cannot say that he was first wanting for them, but they to themselves.

If we demand what should move the *French* Protestants to this Rebellious contradiction of his Majesties commandements. We must answer, that it was too much happinesse: *Causa hujus belli eadem quæ omnium, nimia felicitas,* as *Florus* of the Civill wars between *Cæsar* and *Pompey.* Before the year 1620 when they fell first into the Kings disfavour, they were possessed of almost 100 good Towns, well fortified for their safety; besides beautifull houses and ample possessions in the Villages, they slept every man under his own Vine and his own Fig-tree; neither fearing, nor needing to fear the least disturbance: with those of the Catholick party, they were grown so intimate and entire, by reason of their inter marriages, that a very few years would have them incorporated, if not into one faith, yet into one family. For their better satisfaction in matters of Justice, it pleased King *Henry* the fourth, to erect a Chamber in the Court of the Parliament of *Paris*, purposely for them. It consisteth of one President and 16 Counsellours; their office to take knowledge of all the Causes and Suits of them of the reformed Religion, as well within the jurisdiction of the Parliament of *Paris*, as also in *Normandy* and *Britain*, till there should be a Chamber erected in either of them. There were appointed also two Chambers in the Parliaments of *Burdeaux* and *Grenoble*, and one at the *Chastres* for the Parliament of *Tholoza*. These Chambers were called *Les Chambre de l' Edict*, because they were established by especiall Edict, at the Towns of *Nantes* in *Britain*, *Aprill* the 8. *anno* 1598. In a word, they lived so secure and happy, that one would have thought their felicities had been immortall.

O faciles dare summa deos, eademque tueri
Difficiles ———

And yet they are not brought so low, but that they may live happily, if they can be content to live obediently; that which is taken from them, being matter of strength only, and not priviledge.

Let us now look upon them in their Churches, which we shall finde as empty of magnificence as ceremony. To talke amongst them of Common-prayers, were to fright them with the second coming of the Masse; and to mention Prayers at the buriall of the dead, were to perswade them of a Purgatory. Painted glasse in a Church window, is accounted for the flag and ensigne of Antichrist; and for Organs, no question but they are deemed to be the Devils bag-pipes. Shew them a Surplice, and they cry out, a rag of the Whore of *Babylon*; yet a sheet on a woman, when she is in child-bed, is a greater abomination then the other. A strange people, that could never think the Masse book sufficiently reformed, till they had taken away, Prayers; nor that their Churches could ever be handsome, untill they were ragged. This foolish opposition of their first Reformers, hath drawn the Protestants of these parts into a world of dislike and envie, and been no small disadvantage to the side. Whereas the Church of *England*, though it dissent as much from the Papists in point of Doctrine, is yet not uncharitably thought on by the Modern Catholicks, by reason it retained such an excellency of Discipline. When the *Liturgie*
of

of our Church was translated into Latine by Dr. *Morket*, once Warden of *All-Souls* Colledge in *Oxford*, it was with great approofe and applause received here in *France*, by those whom they call the Catholicks royall; as marvelling to see such order and regular devotion in them, whom they were taught to condemn for Hereticall. An allowance, which with some little help, might have been raised higher, from the practice of our Church, to some points of our judgement, and it is very worthy of our observation, that which the Marquesse of *Rhosny* spake of *Canterbury*, when he came as extraordinary Ambassadour from King *Henry* IV. to welcome King *James* into *England*. For upon the view of our solemn Service and ceremonies, he openly said unto his followers, *That if the reformed Churches in France, had kept the same orders amongst them which we have, he was assured that there would have been many thousands more of Protestants there, then now are.* But the Marquesse of *Rhosny* was not the last that said so, I have heard divers *French* Papists, who were at the Queens coming over, and ventured so far upon an excommunication, as to be present at our Church solemn Services, extoll them and us for their sakes, even almost unto hyperboles. So graciously is our temper entertained amongst them.

As are their Churches, such is their Discipline, naked of all Antiquity, and almost as modern as the men which imbrace it. The power and calling of *Bishops*, they abrogated with the Masse, upon no other cause then that *Geneva* had done it. As if that excellent man Mr. *Calvin* had been the *Pythagoras* of our age, and his αὐτὸς ἔφη, his *ipse dixit*, had stood for Oracles. The *Hierarchie* of Bishops thus cast out, they have brought in their places the Lay-Elders, a kind of Monster never heard of in the Scriptures, or first times of the Gospell. These men leap from the stall to the bench, and there partly sleeping, and partly stroaking of their beards; enact laws of Government for the Church, so that we may justly take up the complaint of the Satyrist, saying, *Surgunt nobis e sterquilinio Magistratus, nec dum lotis manibus publica tractant negotia*; yet to these very men, composed equally of ignorance and a trade, are the most weighty matters of the Church committed. In them is the power of ordaining Priests, of conferring places of charge, and even of the severest censure of the Church, Excommunication. When any businesse which concerneth the good of the Congregation is befallen, they must be called to councell, and you shall finde them there as soon as ever they can put off their Aprons; having blurted out there a little Classicall non-sense, and passed their consents rather by nodding of their heads, then any other sensible articulation, they hasten to their shops, as *Quintius* the Dictator in *Florus* did to his plough, *Ut ad quatriduum festinasse videatur*. Such a plat-form, though it be, that needeth no further confutation then to know it, yet had it been tolerable if the contrivers of it had not endevoured to impose it on all the Reformation. By which means what great troubles have been raised by the great zelots here in *England*, there is none so young, but hath heard some Tragicall relations. God be magnified, and our late King praised, by whom this weed hath been snatched up out of the garden of this our *Israel*.

As for their Ministery, it is indeed very learned in their studies, and exceeding painfull in their calling. By the first they confute the Ignorance of the *Roman* Clergy; by the second their lazinesse. And questionlesse it behoveth them so to be, for living in a Countrey full of opposition, they are enforced to a necessity of book-learning, to maintain the cause, and being continually as it were beset with spies, they do the oftner frequent the Pulpits, to hold up their credits. The maintenance which is allotted to them, scarce amounteth to a competency, though by that name they please to call it. With receiving of tithes they never meddle, and therefore in their Schismaticall tracts of Divinity, they do hardly allow of the paying of them. Some of them hold that they were *Jewish*, and abrogated with the Law. Others think them to be meerly *jure humano*, and yet that they may lawfully be accepted, where they are tendred. It is well known yet that there are some amongst them, which will commend grapes, though they cannot reach them. This competence may come unto 40 or 50 *l.* yearly, or a little more. *Beza* that great and famous
Preacher

Preacher of *Geneva*, had but 80 *l.* a year; and about that rate was *Peter de Moulins* pension, when he Preached at *Charenton*. These stipends are partly payed by the King, and partly raised by way of Collection. So the Ministers of these Churches, are much of the nature with the *English* Lecturers.

As for the Tithes, they belong to the severall Parish Priests in whose Precincts they are due; and they, I'le warrant you, according to the little learning which they have, will maintain them to be *jure divino*. The Sermons of the *French* are very plain and home-spun, little in them of the Fathers, and lesse of humane learning; it being concluded in the Synod of *Gappe*, that only the Scriptures should be used in their Pulpits. They consist much of Exhortation and Use, and of nothing in a manner which concerneth knowledge; a ready way to raise up and edifie the Will and Affections, but withal to starve the understanding. For the education of them being children, they have private Schools; when they are better grown, they may have free recourse unto any of the *French* Academies; besides the new University of *Saumur*, which is wholly theirs, and is the chiefe place of their study.

Chap. IV.

The connexion between the Church and Commonwealth in generall. A transition to the particular of France. *The Government there meerly regall. A mixt forme of Government most commendable. The Kings Patents for Offices. Monopolies above the censure of Parliament. The strange office intended to Mr.* Luynes. *The Kings gifts and expences. The Chamber of Accounts.* France *divided into three sorts of people. The* Conventus Ordinum *nothing but a title. The inequality of the Nobles and Commons in* France. *The Kings power how much respected by the Princes. The powerablenesse of that rank. The formall execution done on them. The multitude and confusion of Nobility. King* James *defended. A censure of the* French Heralds. *The command of the* French Nobles *over their Tenants. Their priviledges, gibbets and other* Regalia. *They conspire with the King to undoe the Commons.*

Having thus spoken of the Churches; I must now treat a little of the Common-wealth. Religion is as the soul of a State, Policy as the body; we can hardly discourse of the one, without a relation to the other; If we do, we commit a wilfull murder, in thus destroying a republick. The Common-wealth without the Church, is but a carkasse, a thing inanimate. The Church without the Common-wealth is as it were *anima separata,*

the

the joyning of them together maketh of both one flourishing and permanent body; and therefore as they are in nature, so in my relation, *Connubio jungam stabili*. Moreover, such a secret sympathy there is between them, such a necessary dependance of one upon the other, that we may say of them, what *Tully* doth of two twins in his book *De fato*, *Eodem tempore, eorum morbus gravescit, & eodem levatur*. They grow sick and well at the same time, and commonly run out their races at the same instant. There is besides the general respect of each to other, a more particular band betwixt them here in *France*, which is a likenesse and resemblance. In the Church of *France* we have found an head and a body; this body again divided into two parts, the Catholick and the Protestant: the head is in his own opinion, and the minds of many others, of a power unlimited; yet the Catholick party hath strongly curbed it. And of the two parts of the body, we see the Papists flourishing and in triumph, whilest that of the Protestant is in misery and affliction. Thus is it also in the body Politick. The King in his own conceit boundlesse and omnipotent, is yet affronted by his Nobles; which Nobles enjoy all the freedome of riches and happinesse; the poor Paisants in the mean time living in drudgery and bondage.

For the government of the King is meerly, indeed, regal, or to give it the true name *despoticall*; though the Countrey be his wife, and all the people are his children, yet doth he neither govern as an husband or a father; he accounteth of them all as of his servants, and therefore commandeth them as a Master. In his Edicts which he over frequently sendeth about, he never mentioneth the good will of his Subjects, nor the approbation of his Councell, but concludeth all of them in this forme, *Car tell est nostre plaisir*, *Sic volo sic jubeo*. A forme of government very prone to degenerate into a tyranny, if the Princes had not oftentimes strength and will to make resistance. But this is not the vice of the entire and Soveraign Monarchy alone; which the Greek call παμβασιλεία; the other two good formes of regiment, being subject also to the same frailty. Thus in the reading of Histories have we observed an *Aristocracie*, to have been frequently

quently corrupted into an *Oligarchie*; and a πολιτεία (or Common-wealth properly so called) into a *Democratie*. For as in the body naturall, the purest complexions are lesse lasting, but easily broken and subject to alteration; so is it in the body Civill, the pure and unmixt formes of Government, though perfect and absolute in their kinds, are yet of little continuance, and very subject to change into its opposite. They therefore which have written of Republicks do most applaud and commend the mixt manner of rule, which is equally compounded of the Kingdome and the *Politeia*; because in these the Kings have all the power belonging to their title, without prejudice to the populacie. In these there is referred to the King, absolute Majesty; to the Nobles, convenient authority; to the People, an incorrupted liberty: all in a just and equall proportion. Every one of these is like the Empire of *Rome*, as it was moderated by *Nerva*, *Qui res olim dissociabiles miscuerat, principatum & libertatem*; wherein the Soveraignty of one endamaged not the freedome of all. A rare mixture of Government, and such at this time is the Kingdome of *England*, a Kingdome of a perfect and happy composition; wherein the King hath his full Prerogative, the Nobles all due respects, and the People, amongst other blessings perfect in this, that they are masters of their own purposes, and have a strong hand in the making of their own Lawes.

On the otherside, in the Regall government of *France*, the Subject frameth his life meerly as the Kings variable Edicts shall please to enjoyn him; is ravished of his money as the Kings taske-masters think fit; and suffereth many other oppressions, which in their proper place shall be specified. This *Aristotle* in the third book of his *Politicks* calleth, Ἀρχὴ δεσποτική, or the command of a Master, and defineth it to be Αὐτη δ' ἐςὶ καθ' ἥν, ἄρχει πάντων κ⁑ τὴν ἑαυτῦ βούλησιν, ὁ βασιλεύς, Such an Empire by which a Prince may command, and do whatsoever shall seem good in his own eyes. One of the Prerogatives Royall of the *French* Kings. For though the Court of Parliament doth seem to challenge a perusall of his Edicts, before they passe for Laws; yet is

that

that but a meer formality. It is the *cartel ost nostre p'aisir*, which maketh them currant; which it seemeth these Princes learned of the *Roman Emperors*. *Justinian* in the book of *Institutions*, maketh five grounds of the Civill Laws, *viz.* *Lex*, (he meaneth the law of the 12 Tables) *Plebiscita, Senatusconsulta, Prudentum Responsa, & Principum placita*; to this last he addeth this generall strength, *Quod principi placuerit, legis habet vigorem*; the very foundation of the *French* Kings powerfulnesse. True it is, that the Courts of Parliament do use to demur sometimes upon his Patents and Decrees, and to petition him for a reversall of them; but their answer commonly is, *Stat pro ratione voluntas*. He knoweth his own power, and granteth his Letters patents for new Offices and Monopolies abundantly. If a monied man can make a friend in Court, he may have an office found for him, of six pence upon every Sword made in *France*; a Livre, upon the selling of every head of Cattell; a brace of Sols, for every paire of boots, and the like. It is the only study of some men to finde out such devices of enriching themselves, and undoing the people. The Patent for Innes granted to Sr. *Giles Mompesson*, was just one of the *French* offices.

As for Monopolies, they are here so common, that the Subject taketh no notice of it; not a scurvey petty book being Printed, but it hath its priviledge affixed, *Ad imprimendum solum*. These being granted by the King, are carryed to the Parliament, by them formally perused, and finally verified; after which, they are in force and virtue against all opposition. It is said in *France* that Mr. *Luynes* had obtained a Patent of the King, for a *quart d' escu* to be paid unto him upon the Christning of every child thoughout all the Kingdome. A very unjust and unconscionable extortion. Had he lived to have presented it to the Court, I much doubt of their deniall, though the only cause of bringing before them such Patents, is onely intended that they should discusse the justice and convenience of them.

As the Parliament hath a formality of power left in them, of verifying the Kings Edicts, his grants of Offices and Monopolies. So hath the *Chamber of Accounts*, a superficiall survey also of his gifts and expences. For his expences, they are thought to be as great now as ever, by reason of the severall retinues of himself, his Mother, his Queen, and the *Monsieur*; neither are his gifts lessened. The late Wars which he managed against the Protestants cost him deer, he being fain to bind unto him most of his Princes by money and pensions. As the expenses of the King are brought unto this Court to be examined, so are also the Gifts and Pensions by him granted to be ratified. The titulary power given unto this Chamber, is to cut off all those of the Kings grants which have no good ground and foundation; the officers being solemnly (at the least formally) sworn, not to suffer any thing to passe them, to the detriment of the Kingdome, whatsoever Letters of command thay have to the contrary. But this Oath they oftentimes dispense with. To this Court also belongeth the *Enfranchisement* or *Naturalization of Aliens*, anciently certain Lords, officers of the Crown, and of the prime counsell were appointed to look unto the accounts. Now it is made an ordinary and soveraigne Court, consisting of two Presidents and divers Auditors, and other under Officers. The *Chamber* wherein it is kept, called *La Chambre des comptes*, is the beautifullest peece of the whole *Palais*; the great Chamber it self, not being worthy to be named in the same day with it. It was built by *Charles* VIII. anno 1485. afterwards adorned and beautified by *Lewis* XII. whose Statua is there standing in his royall robes, and the Scepter in his hand. He is accompanied by the four Cardinall vertues expressed by way of *Hieroglyphicks*, very properly and cunningly; each of them having its particular Motto, to declare its being. The Kings portraiture also as if he were the fifth virtue, had its word under written, and contained in a couple of Verses, which let all that love the Muses skip them in the reading, and are these:

Quatuor has comites foveo, Cælestia dona,
Innocuæ pacis prospera sceptra gerens.

From

From the King descend we to the Subjects, *ab equis (quod aiunt) ad asinos*, and the phrase is not much improper; the *French* commonalty being called *the Kings asses*. These are divided into three ranks or Classes, the Clergy, the Nobles, the Paisants; out of which certain delegates or Committees, chosen upon occasion, and sent to the King, did anciently concur to the making of the Supreme Court for Justice in *France*. It was called the Assembly of the three Estates, or the *Conventus ordinum*; and was just like the Parliament of *England*. But these meetings are now forgotten, or out of use; neither, indeed, as this time goeth, can they any way advantage the State; for whereas there are three principall, if not sole causes of these conventions, which are, the desposing of the Regency during the nonage or sicknesse of a King; the granting Aides and Subsidies; and the redressing of Grievances: there is now another course taken in them. The Parliament of *Paris*, which speaketh, as it is prompted by power and greatnesse, appointeth the Regent; the Kings themselves with their officers determine of the Taxes; and as concerning their Grievances, the Kings eare is open to private Petitions.

Thus is that little of a Common-wealth which went to the making up of this Monarchie, escheated, or rather devoured by the King, that name alone containing in it both Clergy, Princes and People. So that some of the *French* Counsellors, may say with *Tully* in his Oration for *Marcellus* unto *Cæsar*, *Doleoque cum respub. immortalis esse debeat, eam unius mortalis anima consistere*. Yet I cannot withall but affirme, that the Princes and Nobles of *France*, do, for as much as concerneth themselves, upon all advantages flie off from the Kings obedience; but all this while the poor Paisant is ruined; let the poor Tenant starve, or eat the bread of carefulnesse, it matters not, so they may have their pleasure, and be counted firme zelots of the common liberty. And certainly this is the issue of it, the former liveth the life of a slave to maintain his Lord in pride and lazinesse; the Lord liveth the life of a King to oppresse his Tenant by fines and exactions. An equality little answering to the old platformes of Republicks. *Aristotle*, *Genius ille naturæ*, as a

learned

learned man calleth him, in his fourth book of Politicks hath an excellent discourse concerning this disproportion. In that Chapter, his project is, to have a correspondency so far between Subjects under the King or people of the same City, that neither the one might be over rich, nor the other too miserably poor. They, saith he, which are too happy, strong, or rich, or greatly favoured, and the like, can not nor will not obey, with which evill they are infected from their infancy. The other through want of these things are too abjectly minded and base; so that the one cannot but command, nor the other but serve. And this he calleth δέλων ἢ διατότων πόλιν, a City inhabited onely by Slaves and Tyrants. That questionlesse is the most perfect and compleat forme of Government, *Ubi veneratur protentem humilis, non timet; antecedit, non contemnit humiliorem potens*, as *Velleius*. But this is an unhappinesse of which *France* is not capable; their Lords being Kings, and their Commons Villains.

And not to say lesse of them then indeed they are, the Princes of this Countrey, are but little inferiour in matter of Royalty, to any King abroad; and by consequence little respective, in matter of obedience, to their own King at home. Upon the least discontent, they withdraw themselves from the Court, or put themselves into armes; and of all other comforts are ever sure of this, that they shall never want partizans. Neither do they use to stand off from him fearfully, and at distance, but justifie their revolt by publick Declaration, and think the King much indebted to them, if upon fair terms and an honourable reconcilement, they will please to put themselves again into his obedience. *Henry* IV. was a Prince of as undaunted and uncontroulable a spirit, as ever any of his predecessors, and one that loved to be obeyed; yet was he also very frequently baffled by these Roytelets, and at the last dyed in an affront. The Prince of *Conde* perceiving the Kings affection to his new Lady, began to grow jealous of him, for which reason he retired unto *Bruxells*: the King offended at his retreat, sent after him, and commanded him home. The Prince returned answer, that he was the Kings most humble

ble Subject and servant; but into *France* he would not come unlesse he might have a Town for his assurance; withall he protested in publick writing a nullity of any thing that should be done to his prejudice in his absence. A stomach-full resolution, and misbecoming a Subject; yet in this opposition he persisted, his humor of disobedience out-living the King whom he had thus affronted. But these tricks are ordinary here, otherwise a man might have construed this action, by the term of Rebellion. The chief means whereby these Princes become so head strong, are an immunity given them by their Kings, and a liberty which they have taken to themselves. By their Kings they have been absolutely exempted from all Tributes, Tolles, Taxes, Customes, Impositions and Subsidies. By them also they have been estated in whole entire Provinces, with a power of *haute ard main Justice* (as the Lawyers term it) passed over to them; the Kings having scarce an homage or acknowledgment of them. To this they have added much for their strength and security, by the insconcing and fortifying of their houses, which both often moveth, and afterwards inableth them to contemn his Majesty. An example we have of this in the Castle of *Rochfort* belonging to the Duke of *Tremoville*, which in the long Civill wars endured a siege of 5000 shot, and yet was not taken. A very impolitick course (in my conceit) of the *French*, to bestow honours and immunities upon those, *Qui* (as the Historian noteth) *ea suo arbitrio aut repositus, aut retenturi videantur; quique modum habent in sua voluntate.* For upon a knowledge of this strength in themselves, the Princes have been always prone to Civill wars, as having sufficient means for safety and resistance. On this ground also they slight the Kings authority, and disobey his Justice. In so much that the greater sort of Nobles in this Kingdome, can seldome be arraigned or executed in person; and therefore the Lawes condemn them in their images, and hang them in their pictures. A pretty device to mock Justice. If by chance, or some handsome sleight, any of them are apprehended, they are put under a sure guard, and not done to death without great fear of tumult and unquietnesse.

Neither is it *unus & alter*, only some two or three, that

thus stand upon their distance with the King, but even all the Nobility of the Realm, a rout so disordered, unconfined, and numberlesse, that even *Fabius* himselfe would be out of breath in making the reckoning. I speak not here of those that are styled *La Nobleſſe*, but of *Titulados*, men only of titular Nobility, or the degree of Baron and above. Of these there is in this Countrey a number almost innumerable. *Quot Cælum Stellas*; take quantity for quantity, and I dare be of the opinion, that heaven hath not more Stars, then *France* Nobles. You shall meet with them so thick in the Kings Court especially, that you would think it almost impossible the Countrey should bear any other fruit. This, I think, I may safely affirme, and without Hyperbole, that they have there as many Princes, as we in *England* have Dukes; as many Dukes, as we Earls; as many Earls, as we Barons; and as many Barons as we have Knights; a jolly company, and such as know their own strength too. I cannot therefore but much marvell, that these Kings should be so prodigall in conferring honours; considering this, that every Noble man he createth, is so great a weakning to his power.

On the other side, I cannot but as much wonder at some of our Nation, who have murmured against our late Soveraign, and accused him of an unpardonable unthriftinesse, in bestowing the dignities of his Realm, with so full and liberall a hand. Certainly, could there any danger have arisen by it unto the State, I could have been as impatient of it as another. But with us, titles and ennoblings in this kind, are only either the Kings favour, or the parties merit, and maketh whomsoever he be that receiveth them, rather reverenced then powerfull. *Raro eorum honoribus invidetur, quorum is non timetur*, was a good Aphorisme in the dayes of *Paterculus*; and may for ought I know be as good still. Why should I envie any man that honour, which taketh not from my safety; or repine at my Soveraign for raising any of his Servants into an higher degree of eminency, when that favour cannot make them exorbitant? Besides it concerneth the improvement of the Exchequer, at the occasions of Subsidies, and the glory of the Kingdome, when the

Prince

Prince is not attended by men meerly of the vulgar. Add to this, the few Noble men of any title weh he found at his happy cominge in amongst us, and the additions of power which his comming brought unto us; and we shall finde it proportionable, that he should enlarge our Nobility, with our Empire: neither yet have we, indeed, a number to be talked of, comparing us with our neighbour Nations. We may see all of the three first ranks in the books of *Miller*, *Brooke*, and *Vincent*; and we are promised also a Catalogue of the Creations and successions of all our Barons. Then we should see that as yet we have not surfeited. Were this care taken by the Heralds in *France*, perhaps the Nobility there would not seem so numberlesse; sure I am not so confused. But this is the main vice of that profession, of six Heralds which they have amongst them, viz. *Montjoy*, *Normandy*, *Guyenne*, *Valys*, *Bretagne*, and *Burgogne*, not one of them is reported to be a *Genealogist*; neither were their Predecessors better affected to this study. *Paradine* the only man that ever was amongst them, hath drawn down the Genealogies of 24 of the chief families, all ancient and of the bloud, in which he hath excellently well discharged himself. But what a small pittance is that compared to the present multitude?

The Nobles being so populous, it cannot be but the *Noblesse*, as they call them; that is, the Gentry, must needs be thick set and only not innumerable. Of these Nobles there are some which hold their estates immediately of the Crown, and they have the like immunities with the Princes. Some hold their Feifes (or *feuda*) of some other of the Lords, and he hath only *Basse Justice* permitted to him, as to mulct and amerce his Tenants, to imprison them, or give them any other correction under death. All of them have power to raise and inhance up their Rents, to Tax his Subjects on occasion, and to prohibit them such pleasures, as they think fit to be reserved for themselves. By *Breteuil* in *Picardy*, I saw a post fastned in the ground, like a race-post with us, and therein an inscription; I presently made to it, as hoping to have heard of some memorable battell there foughten; but when I came at it, I found it to be nothing;
but

but a Declaration of the Prince of *Condes* pleasure, that no man should hunt in those quarters; afterwards I observed them to be very frequent. But not to wander through all particulars, I will in some few of them only give instance of their power here. The first is *Proist de bailliage*, power to keep Assize, or to have under him a *Bailli*, and a Superiour seat of Justice, for the decision of such causes as fall under the compasse of ordinary jurisdiction. In this Court there is notice taken of Treasons, Robberies, Murders, Protections, Pardons, Faires, Markets, and other matters of priviledge. Next they have a Court of ordinary jurisdiction, and therein a Judge whom they call *Le guarde de Justice*, for the decision of smaller businesse, as Debts, Trespasses, breach of the Kings peace, and the like In this the purse is only emptied, the other extendeth to the taking of life also; for which cause every one which hath *Haute Justice* annexed to his Feise, hath also his peculiar Gibbet; nay which is wonderfully methodicall, by the criticisme of the Gibbet, you may judge at the quality of him that owneth it. For the Gibbet of one of the Nobles hath but two pillars, that of the Chastellan three, the Barons four, the Earls six, the Dukes eight; and yet this difference is rather precise then generall. The last of their *jura regalia*, which I will here speak of, is the command they have upon their people, to follow them unto the wars; a command not so advantagious to the Lord, as dangerous to the Kingdom.

Thus live the *French* Princes, thus the Nobles. Those sheep which God and the Lawes hath brought under them, they do not sheer but fleece; and which is worse then this, having themselves taken away the Wooll, they give up the naked carkasse to the King. *Tondi tres meas velis, non deglubi*, was accounted one of the golden sayings of *Tiberius*; but it is not currant here in *France*. Here the Lords and the King, though otherwise at oddes amongst themselves, will be sure to agree in this, the undoing and oppressing of the poor Paisant; *Ephraim* against *Manasseh*, and *Manasseh* against *Ephraim*, but both against *Judah*, saith the Scripture.

The

The reason why they thus defire the poverty of the Commons, is, as they pretend, the fafety of the State, and their owne particulars. Were the people once warmed with the feeling of eafe and their' own riches, they would prefently be hearkning after the warres; and if no imployment were proffered abroad, they would make fome at home. Hiftories and experience hath taught us enough of their humour in this kind; it being impoffible for this hot-headed, and hare-brained people, not to be doing. *Si extraneus deeft, domi hoftem querunt,* as *Juftin* hath obferved of the Ancient *Spaniards*; a prety quality, and for which they have often fmarted.

Chap. V.

The base and low estate of the French Paisant. The misery of them under their Lord. The bed of Procrustes. The suppressing of the Subject prejudiciall to a State. The wisdome of Henry VII. The French forces all in the Cavallerie. The cruell impositions laid upon the people by the King. No Demaine in France. Why the tryall by twelve men can be used only in England. The Gabell of Salt. The Popes licence for wenching. The Gabell of whom refused, and why. The Gascoines impatient of Taxes. The taille, and taillion. The Pancarke or Aides. The vain resistance of those of Paris. The Court of Aides. The manner of gathering the Kings moneys. The Kings revenue. The corruption of the French publicans. King Lewis why called the just. The monies currant in France. The gold of Spain more Catholick then the King. The happinesse of the English Subjects. A congratulation unto England. The conclusion of the first Journey.

BY that which hath been spoken already of the Nobles, we may partly guesse at the poor estate of the Paisant, or Countreymen; of whom we will not now speak, as subjects to their Lords, and how far they are under their commandment; but how miserable and wretched they are in their Apparell and their Houses. For their Apparell it is well they can allow themselves

Canvasse,

Canvasse, or an outside of that nature. As for Cloth, it is above their purse equally, and their ambition; if they can aspire unto Fustian, they are as happy as their wishes, and he that is so arrayed, will not spare to aime at the best place in the Parish, even unto that of the Church-warden. When they go to plough or to the Church, they have shooes and stockins; at other times they make bold with nature, and wear their skins. Hats they will not want, though their bellies pinch for it; and that you may be sure they have them, they will alwayes keep them on their heads: the most impudent custome of a beggerly fortune, that ever I met with, and which already hath had my blessing. As for the women, they know in what degree nature hath created them, and therefore dare not be so fine as their Husbands; some of them never had above one pair of stockins in all their lives, which they wear every day, for indeed they are very durable. The goodnesse of their faces tell us, that they have no need of a band, therefore they use none. And as concerning Petticoats, so it is, that all of them have such a garment, but most of them so short, that you would imagine them to be cut off at the placket. When the Parents have sufficiently worn these vestures, and that commonly is till the rottennesse of them will save the labour of undressing, they are a new-cut-out and fitted to the children. Search into their houses, and you shall finde them very wretched, destitute as well of furniture as provision. No Butter salted up against Winter, no powdring tub, no Pullein in the Rick-barten, no flesh in the pot or at the spit, and which is worst, no money to buy them. The description of the poor aged couple *Philemon* and *Baucis* in the eight book of the *Metamorphosis*, is a perfect character of the *French* Paisant, in his house-keeping; though I cannot affirme, that if *Jupiter* and *Mercury* did come amongst them, they should have so hearty an entertainment; for thus *Ovid* marshalleth the dishes:

Penitur hic bicolor sincera bacca Minervæ,
Intybaque, & radix, & lactis massa coacti,
Ovaque non acri leviter versata favilla,
Prunaque, & in patulis redolentia mala canistris.
Hic nux, hic mixta est rugosis carica palmis,
Et de purpureis collectæ vitibus uvæ;
Omnia fictilibus nitide. ———

They on the table set *Minerva's* fruit,
The double-colour'd Olive, Endive-root;
Radish and Cheese: and to the board there came
A dish of Egges, rear-roasted by the flame.
Next they had Nuts, course Dates and Lenten-figs,
And Apples from a basket made of twigs,
And Plums, and Graps cut newly from the tree:
All serv'd in earthen dishes, Housewifely.

But you must not look for this cheer often. At Wakes or Feasts dayes, you may perchance be so happy as to see this plenty; but at other times, *Olus omne patella*, the best provision they can shew you is a piece of Bacon wherewith they fatten their pottage; and now and then the inwards of Beasts killed for the Gentlemen. But of all miseries, this me thinketh is the greatest, that sowing so many acres of excellent wheat in an year, and gathering in such a plentifull Vintage as they do, they should not yet be so fortunate, as to eat white bread, or drink wine; for such infinite rents do they pay to their Lords, and such innumerable taxes to the King, that the profits arising out of those commodities, are only sufficient to pay their duties, and keep them from the extremities of cold and famine. The bread then which they eat, is of the coursest flowre, and so black, that it cannot admit the name of brown. And as for their drink, they have recourse to the next Fountain. A people of any, the most unfortunate, not permitted to enjoy the fruit of their labours; and such as above all

others

others are subject to that *Sarcasme* in the Gospell, *This man planted a Vineyard, and doth not drink of the fruit thereof.*

Nec prosunt domino, quæ prosunt omnibus, artes.

Yet were their case not altogether so deplorable, if there were but hopes left to them of a better, if they could but compasse certainty, that a painfull drudging and a thrifty saving, would one day bring them out of this hell of bondage. In this, questionlesse, they are intirely miserable, in that they are sensible of the wretchednesse of their present fortunes, and dare not labour nor expect an alteration. If industry and a sparing hand hath raised any of this afflicted people so high, that he is but 40 s. or 5 l. richer then his neighbour, his Lord immediately enhaunceth his Rents, and enformeth the Kings task-masters of his riches, by which means he is within two or three years brought again to equall poverty with the rest. A strange course, and much different from that of *England*, where the Gentry take a delight in having their Tenants thrive under them, and hold it no crime in any that hold of them to be wealthy. On the other side, those of *France* can abide no body to gain or grow rich upon their farmes; and therefore thus upon occasions rack their poor Tenants. In which they are like the Tyrant *Procrustes*, who laying hands upon all he met, cast them upon his bed; if they were shorter then it, he racked their joynts till he had made them even to it, if they were longer, he cut as much of their bodies from them, as did hang over; so keeping all that fell into his power in an equality. All the *French* Lords are like that Tyrant.

How much this course doth depresse the military power of this Kingdome is apparent by the true principles of war, and the examples of other Countries. For it hath been held by the generall opinion of the best judgements in matters of war, that the main Buttresse and Pillar of an Army is the foot, or (as the Martialists term it) the *Infantry*. Now to make a good Infantery, it requireth that men be brought up not in a flavish and needy fashion of life, but in some free and liberall manner. Therefore It is well observed by the Vicount St. *Albans* in his History of *Henry* VII. that if a State run most to Nobles and Gentry, and that the Husbandmen be but as their meer drudges, or else simply Cottagers, that that State may have a good Cavallery, but never good stable bands of foot. Like to Coppice woods, in which if you let them grow too thick in the stadles, they run to bushes or bryers, and have little clean under-wood. Neither is this in *France* only, but in *Italy* also, and some other parts abroad; in so much, that they are enforced to imploy mercenary Souldiers for their battalions of foot: whereby it cometh to passe, that in those Countries they have much people, and few men. On this consideration King *Henry* VII. one of the wisest of our Princes took a course so cunning and wholesome, for the increase of the military power of his Realm; that though it be much lesse in territory, yet it should have infinitely more Souldiers of its native forces, then its neighbour Nations. For in the fourth year of his Reign, there passed an Act of Parliament pretensively against the depopulation of Villages, and decay of tillage, but purposedly to inable his subjects for the wars. The Act was, *That all houses of husbandry which had been used with twenty acres of ground and upwards, should be maintained and kept up for, together with a competent proportion of Land, to be used and occupied with them,* &c. By this meanes, the houses being kept up, did of necessity enforce a dweller, and that dweller, because of the proportion of Land, not to be a begger, but a man of some substance, able to keep Hinds and Servants, and to set the plough a going. An order which did wonderfully concerne the might and manhood of the Kingdome; these Farmes being sufficient to maintaine an able body out of penury; and by consequence to prepare them for service, and encourage them to higher honours, for

Haud facile emergent, quorum virtutibus obstat
Res angusta domi. ———

As the Poet hath it.

But

But this Ordinance is not thought of such use in *France*, where all the hopes of their Armies consist in the Cavallery or the horse; which perhaps is the cause why our Ancestors have won so many battailes upon them. As for the *French* foot, they are quite out of all reputation, and are accounted to be the basest and unworthyest company in the world.

Besides, should the *French* people be enfranchised, as it were, from the tyranny of their Lords, and estated in freeholds and other tenures, after the manner of *England*, it would much trouble the Councell of *France*, to find out a new way of raising his revenues, which are now meerly sucked out of the bloud and sweat of the Subject. Antiently the Kings of *France* had rich and plentifull demeans, such as was sufficient to maintain their greatnesse and Majesty, without being burdensome unto the Countrey. Pride in matters of sumptuousnesse, and the tedious Civill wars, which have lasted in this Countrey, almost ever since the death of *Henry* II. have been the occasion that most of the Crown lands have been sold and morgaged; in so much that the people are now become the *Demaine*, and the Subject only is the Revenue of the Crown. By the sweat of their browes is the Court fed, and the Souldier paid; and by their labours are the Princes maintained in idlenesse. What impositions soever it pleaseth the King to put upon them, It is almost a point of treason not only to deny, but to question. *Apud illos vere regnatur, nefasque quantum regi liceat, dubitare*; as one of them. The Kings hand lyeth hard upon them, and hath almost thrust them into an *Egyptian* bondage, the poor Paisant being constrained to make up dayly his full-tale of bricks, and yet have no straw allowed them. Upon a sight of the miseries and poverties of this people, Sir *John Fortescue*, Chancellour of *England*, in his book intituled, *De Laudibus legum Angliæ*, concludeth them to be unfit men for Jurors or Judges, should the custome of the Countrey admit of such tryals. For having proved there unto the Prince, (he was son to *Henry* VI.) that the manner of tryall according to the Common Law, by 12 Jurates, was more commendable then the practise of the Civill or

Emperiall

Emperiall Lawes, by the deposition only of two witnesses, or the forced confession of the persons, arraigned, the Prince seemed to marvell, *Cur ea lex Angliæ quæ tam frugi & optabilis est, non sit toti mundo communis.* To this he maketh answer, by shewing the free condition of the *English* Subjects, who alone are used at these indictments; men of a fair and large estate, such as dwell nigh the place of the deed committed, men that are of ingenuous education, such as scorn to be suborned or corrupted, and afraid of infamie. Then he sheweth how in other places all things are contrary, the Husbandman an absolute begger; easie to be bribed by reason of his poverty; the Gentlemen living far asunder, and so taking no notice of the fact; the Paisant also neither fearing infamie, nor the losse of goods, if he be found faulty, because he hath them not. In the end he concludeth thus, *Ne mireris igitur princeps, si lex per quam in Anglia veritas inquiritur, alias non pervagetur nationes, ipsæ namque ut Anglia nequerunt facere sufficientes consimilesque Juratas.* The last part of the latine, favoureth somewhat of the Lawyer, the word *Juratas* being put thereto to signifie a *Jury.*

To go over all those impositions, which this miserable people are afflicted withal, were almost as wretched as the payment of them; I will therefore speak only of the principall. And here I meet in the first place, with the Gabell or Imposition on Salt. This *Gabelle de sel*, this Impost on Salt was first begun by *Philip* the *Long*, who took for it a double (which is half a Sol) upon the pound. After whom *Philip* of *Valoys*, anno 1328. doubled that. *Charles* the VII. raised it unto three doubles; and *Lewis* the XI. unto six. Since that time it hath been altered from so much upon the pound to a certain rate on the Mine, which containeth some 30 bushels *English*; the rates rising and falling at the Kings pleasure. This one commodity were very advantagious to the Exchequer, were it all in the Kings hands; but at this time a great part of it is morgaged. It is thought to be worth unto the King three millions of Crowns yearly; that only of *Paris* and the Provosts seven Daughters, being farmed at 1700000 Crowns the year. The late Kings since *anno* 1581. being intangled in wars, have been constrained to
let

CHAP. V.   *the State of* France.   265

let it out to others; in so much that about *anno* 1599. the King lost above 800000 Crowns yearly: and no longer agone then *anno* 1621. the King taking up 600000 pounds, of the Provost of Merchands and the Eschevines, gave unto them a rent charge of 40000 *l.* yearly, to be issuing out of his Customes of Salt, till their money were repaid them. This Gabell is, indeed, a Monopoly, and that one of the unjustest and unreasonablest in the World. For no man in the Kingdom (those Countries hereafter mentioned excepted) can eat any Salt, but he must buy of the King and at his price, which is most unconscionable; that being sold at *Paris* and elsewhere for five Livres, which in the exempted places is sold for one. Therefore that the Kings profits might not be diminished, there is diligent watch and ward, that no forain Salt be brought into the Land, upon pain of forfeiture and imprisoment. A search which is made so strictly, that we had much ado at *Dieppe* to be pardoned the searching of our trunks and port-mantles, and that not, but upon solemn protestation, that we had none of that commodity. This Salt is of a brown colour, being only such as we in *England* call Bay-salt; and imposed on the Subjects by the Kings Officers with great rigour, for though they have some of their last provision in the house, or perchance would be content (through poverty) to eat meat without it, yet will these cruell villaines enforce them to take such a quantity of them; or howsoever they will have of them so much money.

But this Tyranny is not generall, the *Normans* and *Picards* enduring most of it, and the other Paisant the rest. Much like unto which was the Licence which the Popes and Bishops of old granted in matter of keeping Concubines. For when such as had the charge of gathering the Popes Rents happened upon a Priest which had no Concubine, and for that cause made deniall of the Tributes; the Collectours would return them this answer, that notwithstanding this, they should pay the money, because they might have the keeping of a wench if they would.

This Gabell, as it sitteth hard on some, so are there some also which are never troubled with it. Of this sort are the Princes in the generall released, and many of the Nobless in particular; in so much that it was proved unto King *Lewis*, anno 1614. that for every Gentleman which took of his Majesties Salt, there were 2000 of the Commons. There are also some intire Provinces which refuse to eat of this Salt, as *Bretagne*, *Gascoine*, *Poictou*, *Quercu*, *Xaintogne*, and the County of *Boulonnois*. Of these the County of *Boulonnois* pretendeth a peculiar exemption, as belonging immediately to the patrimony of our Lady (*Nostre Dame*); of which we shall learn more when we are in *Bovillon*. The *Bretagnes* came united to the Crown by a fair marriage, and had strength enough to make their own capitulations, when they first entred into the *French* subjection. Besides, here are yet divers of the Ducall family living in that Countrey, who would much trouble the peace of the Kingdome, should the people be oppressed with this bondage, and they take the protection of them. *Poictou* and *Quercu* have compounded for it with the former Kings, and pay a certain rent yearly, which is called the *Equivalent*. *Xaintogne* is under the command of *Rochell*, of whom it receiveth sufficient at a better rate. And as for the *Gascoynes*, the King dareth not impose it upon them for fear of Rebellion. They are a stuborne and churlish people, very impatient of a rigorous yoak, and such which inherit a full measure of the *Biscanes* liberty and spirit, from whom they are descended. *Le droitt de fouage*, the priviledge of levying a certain piece of money upon every chimney in an house that smoketh, was in times not long since one of the *jura regalia* of the *French* Lords, and the people paid it without grumbling; yet when *Edward* the black Prince returned from his unhappy journey into *Spain*, for the paying of his Souldiers to whom he was indebted, laid this *Fouage* upon this people, being then *English*, they all presently revolted to the *French*, and brought great prejudice to our affairs in those quarters.

Next to the Gabell of Salt, we may place the Taille or Taillon, which are much of a nature with the Subsidies in *England*, as being levied both on Goods and Lands. In this again they differ, the Subsidies of *England* being granted by the people, and the sum of it certain; but this of *France* being at the pleasure of the King, and in what manner he shall please to impose them. Anciently the Tailles were only levyed by way of extraordinary Subsidie, and that but upon four occasions, which were, the Knighting of the King Son, the marriage of his Daughters, a Voyage of the Kings beyond sea, and his Ransome in case he were taken Prisoner; *Les Tailles ne sont point devis de voir ordinaire* (saith *Ragueau*) *ains ont este accordees durant la necessite des affaires seulement*. Afterwards they were continnally levyed in times of war; and at length *Charles* the VII. made them ordinary. Were it extended equally on all, it would amount to a very fair Revenue. For supposing this, that the Kingdome of *France* containeth 200 millions of Acres (as it doth) and that from every acre there were raised to the King two Sols yearly, which is little in respect of what the Taxes impose upon them: That income alone, besides that which is levyed on Goods personall, would amount to two millions of pounds in a year. But this payment also lyeth on the Paisant; the greater Towns, the officers of the Kings house, the Officers of War, the President, Counsellors and Officers of the Courts of Parliament, the Nobility, the Clergy, and the Scholars of the University being freed from it.

That which they call the Taillon, was intended for the ease of the Countrey, though now it prove one of the greatest burdens unto it. In former times the Kings Souldiers lay all upon the charge of the Villages, the poor people being fain to finde them diet, lodging, and all necessaries, for themselves, their horses, and the harlots which they brought with them. If they were not well pleased with their entertainment, they used commonly to beat their Host, abuse his family, and rob him of that small provision, which he had laid up for his children; and all this *Cum privilegio*. Thus did they move from one Village to another, and at the last again returned to them from whence they came; *Ita ut non sit ibi villula una expers cala-*

mitatis

miteriis istius; quæ non semel aut bis in anno, bac nefanda pressura depilatur, as Sir *John Fortescue* observed in his time. To redresse this mischief, King *Henry* II. *anno* 1549. raised this imposition called the Taillon.

The *Pancarte* comprehendeth in it divers particular Imposts, but especially the Sol upon the Livre; that is, the twentieth penny of all things bought or sold, Corne, Sallets, and the like only excepted. Upon wine, besides the Sol upon the Livre, he hath his severall Customes of the entrance of it into any of his Cities, passages by Land, Sea or Rivers. To these *Charles* the IX. *anno* 1461. added a Tax of five Sols upon every Muye (which is the third part of a Tun) and yet when all this is done, the poor Vintner payeth unto the King the eight penny he takes for that Wine which he selleth. In this *Pancarte* is also contained the *Haut passage*, which are the Tolles paid unto the King for passage of Men and Cattell over his bridges, and his City gates, as also for all such commodities as they bring with them: a good round sum considering the largenesse of the Kingdome; the through-fare of *Lyons* being farmed yearly of the King for 100000 Crowns. Hereunto belong also the *Aides*, which are a Tax of the Sol also in the Livre, upon all sorts of Fruits, Provision, Wares, and Merchandise, granted first unto *Charles* Duke of *Normandy*, when *John* his father was Prisoner in *England*, and since made perpetuall. For such is the lamentable fate of this Countrey, that their kindnesses are made duty; and those moneys which they once grant out of love, are always after exacted of them, and payed out of necessity. The *Bedroll* of all these Impositions and Taxes, is called the *Pancarte*, because it was hanged in a frame, like as the Officers fees are in our Diocesan Courts; the word *Pan* signifying a frame or a pane of Wainscot. These Impositions time and custome hath now made tolerable, though at first they seemed very burdensome, and moved many Cities to murmuring, some to rebellion; amongst others, the City of *Paris*, proud of her ancient liberties and immunities, refused to admit of it. This indignity so incensed *Charles* the VI. their King, then young and in hot bloud, that he seized into his hands all
their

their priviledges, took from them their *Prævôst des Merchands*, and the *Eschevins*, as also the Keyes of their gates, and the Chaines of their streets, and making through the whole Town such a face of mourning, that one might justly have said,

Hic fuciet Troje, cum caperetur, erat.

This hapned in the year 1383. and was for five years together continued, which time being expired, and other Cities warned by that example, the Imposition was established, and the priviledges restored. For the better regulating of the Profits arising from these Imposts, the *French* King erected a Court called, *Le Cour des Aides*; It consisted at the first of the Generals of the Aides, and of any four of the Lords of the Councell, whom they would call to their assistance. Afterwards *Charles* the V. *anno* 1390 or thereabouts setled it in *Paris*, and caused it to be numbred as one of the Soveraign Courts. *Lewis* the XI. dissolved it, and committed the managing of his Aids to his houshold servants, as loath to have any publick officers take notice how he fleeced his people. *Anno* 1464. It was restored again. And finally, *Henry* II. *anno* 1551. added to it a second Chamber composed of two Presidents and eight Counsellours; one of which Presidents, named Mr. *Chevalier*, is said to be the best monied man of all *France*. There are also others of these Courts in the Countrey, as one at *Roven*, one at *Montferrant* in *Avergne*, one at *Burdeaux*, and another at *Monpellier*, established by *Charles* VII *anno* 1437.

For the levying and gathering up of these Taxes, you must know that the whole Countrey of *France* is divided into 21 *Generalities*, or Counties as it were, and those again into divers *Esteélisnes*, which are much like our Hundreds. In every of the *Generalities*, there are 10 or 12 Treasurers, 9 Receivers for the generalty, and as many Comptrollers; and in the particular *Esteélisnes*, eight Receivers and as many Comptrollers, besides all under-officers, which are thought to amount in all to 30000 men.

When then the King levyeth his Taxes, he sendeth his Letters Patents to the principall Officers of every Generalty, whom they call *Les Generaux des Aides*, and they dispatch their Warrant to the *Esleus* or Commissioners. These taxing every one of the Parishes and Villages within their severall divisions at a certaine rate, send their receivers to collect it, who give account for it to their Comptrollers. By them it ascendeth to the *Esleus*, from him to the Receiver generall of that Generalty, next to the Comptroller, then to the Treasurer, afterwards to the *Generall des Aides*; and so

> *Per varios casus & tot discrimina rerum*
> *Tendimus ad Latium.* ————

By all these hands it is at last conveyed into the Kings purse; in which severall passages, *Necesse est ut aliquid hæreat*, it cannot be but that it must have many a shrewd snatch. In so much that I was told by a Gentleman of good credence in *France*, that there could not be gathered by the severall exactions above specified, and other devises of prowling, which I have omitted, lesse then 85 millions a year, whereof the King receiveth 15 only. A report not altogether to be slighted, considering the President of the Court of Accomptes made it evident to the Assembly at *Bloys*, in the time of King *Henry* IV. that by the time that every one of the Officers had his share of it, there came not to the Kings Coffers one *teston* (which is 1 s. 2 d.) of a Crown; so that by reckoning 5 *testons* to a Crown or *Escu* (as it is but 2 d. over) these Officers must collect five times the money which they pay the King, which amounteth to 75 millions, and is not much short of that proportion which before I spake of. The Kings Revenues then, notwithstanding this infinite oppression of his people, amounteth to 15 millions (some would have it 18.) which is a good improvement in respect of what they were in times afore. *Lewis* the XI. as good a husband of his Crown, as ever any was in *France*, gathering but one and a half only. But as you reckon the flood, so also if you may reckon the ebb of his Treasures, you will finde much wanting of a full sea in his Coffers; it being

ing generally known, that the fees of officers, pensions, garrisons, and the men of armes, draw from him yearly no fewer then 6 of his 15 millions.

True it is, that his Treasure hath many good helps by way of Eschear, and that most frequently, when he cometh to take an accompt of his Treasurers and other Officers. A Nation so abominably full of base and unmanly villainies in their severall charges, that the *Publicans* of *Old-Rome*, were milke and white broath to them. For so miserably do they abuse the poor *Paisant*, that if he hath in all the world but eight Sols, it shall go hard, but he will extort from him five of them.

Non missura cutem nisi plena cruoris hirundo.

He is just of the nature of the Horse-leech, when he hath once gotten hold of you, he will never let you go till he be filled. And which is most strange, he thinks it a greater clemency that he hath left the poor man some of his money, then the Injury was in wresting from him the rest. Nay they will brag of it, when they have taken but five of the eight Sols, that they have given him three, and expect thanks for it. A kindnesse of a very theevish nature, it being the condition of Robbers, as *Tully* hath observed, *Ut commemorent illis se dediisse vitam, quibus non ademerint.* Were the people but so happy, as to have a certain rate set upon their miseries, it could not but be a greater ease to them, and would well defend them from the tyrany of these Theeves. But (which is not the least part of their wretchednesse) their Taxings and Assessements are left arbitrary, and are exacted accordingly as these Publicans will give out of the Kings necessities; so that the Countryman hath no other remedy, then to give *Cerberus* a crust, as the saying is, to kisse his rod and hug his punishment. By this means the Questors thrive abundantly, it being commonly said of them, *Hert kewrler aviourdhui chevalier,* to day a Swine-heard, to morrow a Gentleman; and certainly they grow into great riches. Mr. *Beaumaichels* one of the Treasurers (Mr. *De Vitroy,* who slew the Marquesse *D' Ancre,* marryed his only Daughter)

Daughter) having raked unto himself, by the villanous abuse of his place, no lesse then 22 millions of Livres, as it was commonly reported. But he is not like to carry it to his grave, the King having seized upon a good part of it, and himself being condemned to the gallowes by the grand *Chambre* of Parliament, though as yet he cannot be apprehended and advanced to the Ladder. And this hath been the end of many of them, since the reign of this present King, whom (it may be) for this cause, they call *Lewis* the *just*. This fashion of affixing Epithites to the names of their Kings was in great use heretofore with this Nation. *Carolus* the son of *Pipin*, was by them sur-named *Le Magne*: *Lewis* his son *Debonaire*, and so of the rest. Since the time of *Charles* VI. who was by them surnamed the *Beloved*, it was discontinued; and now revived again in the persons of King *Henry* IV. and his son King *Lewis*. But this by the way. It may be also he is called the *Just* by way of negation, because he hath yet committed no notable act of Injustice, (for I wink at his cruell and unjust slaughter at *Nigrepelisse*) it may be also to keep him continually in mind of his duty, that he may make himself worthy of that attribute;

Vere Imperator sui nominis, ———

As one said of *Severus.*

Let us add one more misery to the State and commonalty of *France*, and that is, the base and corrupt money in it. For besides the *Sol*, which is made of Tinne, they have the *Double* made of Brasse, whereof six make a *Sol*, and the *Denier*, whereof two make a *Double*; a coyne so vile and small of value, that 120 of them go to an *English* shilling. These are the common coynes of the Countrey; silver and gold not being to be seen but upon holydayes. As for their silver, it is most of it of their own coyning, but all exceeding clipt and shaven; their gold being most of it *Spanish*. In my little being in the Countrey, though I casually saw much gold, I could only see two pieces of *French* stampe, the rest coming all from *Spain*, as *Pistolets*, *Demi-pistolets* and *Double-pistolets*. Neither is *France* alone furnished thus with *Castilian* coyn, it is the happinesse also of other Countries, as *Italy*, *Barbary*, *Brabant*, and elsewhere; and indeed it is kindly done of him, that being the sole Monopolist of the mines, he will yet let other nations have a share in the mettle. Were the King as Catholick as his money, I think I should be in some fear of him, till then we may lawfully take that ambitious title from the King, and bestow it upon his pictures. The Soveraignty of the *Spanish* gold is more universally embraced, and more seriously acknowledged in most parts of Christendome, then that of him which stampt it. To this he which entituleth himself Catholick is but a prisoner, and never saw half those Provinces, in which this more powerfull Monarch hath been heartily welcomed. Yet if he will needs be King, let him grow somewhat more jealous of his Queen, and confesse that his gold doth royally deserve his Imbraces, whom before the extent of his dominion, the Ancient Poets styled *Regina pecunia*. True it is, that by the figure and shape of this Emperesse, you would little think her to be lovely, and lesse worthy of your imbracement. The stones which little boyes break into Quoits, are a great deal better proportioned; if a *Geometrician* were to take the angles of it, I think it would quite put him besides his *Euclide*; neither can I tell to what thing in the world fitter to resemble it, then a *French* Cheese; for it is neither long, nor square, nor round, nor thin, nor thick, nor any one of these, but yet all, and yet none of them. No question, but it was the Kings desires, by this unsightly dressing of his Lady, to make men out of love with her, that so he might keep her to himself. But in this his hopes have consened him; for as in other Cuckoldries, so in this, some men will be bold to keep his wife from him, be it only in spight.

These circumstances thus laid together and considered, we may the clearer and the better see our own felicities, which to expresse generally and in a word, is to say only this, *That the English Subject is in no circumstance a Frenchman.*

Nn   Here

Here have we our money made of the best and purest, that only excepted, which a charitable consideration hath coyned into farthings. Here have we our Kings royally, and to the envie of the world, magnificently provided for, without the sweat and bloud of the people, no Pillages, no Impositions upon our private wares, no Gabels upon our commodities; *Nullum in tam ingenti regno vectigal, non in urbibus pontiumve discriminibus, Publicanorum stationes*; as one truely hath observed of us. The monies which the King wanteth to supply his necessities, are here freely given him. He doth not here compell our bounties, but accept them. The Laws by which we are governed, we in part are makers of, each Paisant of the Countrey hath a free voice in the enacting of them; If not in his person, yet in his proxie. We are not here subject to the lusts and tyranny of our Lords, and may therefore say safely, what the *Jews* spake factiously, *That we have no King but Cæsar*. The greatest Prince here is subject with us to the same Law, and when we stand before the tribunall of the Judge, we acknowledge no difference. Here do we inhabite our own houses, plough our own Lands, enjoy the fruits of our labour, comfort our selves with the wives of our youth, and see our selves grow up in those children, which shall Inherit after us the same felicities. But I forget my self. To endevour the numbring of Gods blessings, may perhaps deserve as great a punishment as *Davids* numbring the people. I conclude with the Poet,

O fortunati nimium, bona si sua norint
Agricolæ nostri.————

And so I take my leave of *France*, and prepare for *England*, towards which (having stayed 3 dayes for winde and company) we set forwards on Wednesday the 3 of *August*, the day exceeding fair, the Sea as quiet, and the winde so still that the Mariners were fain to take down their Sails, and betake themselves unto their Oares. Yet at the last with much endevour on their side, and no lesse patience on ours

ours, we were brought into the midst of the channell, when suddainly———

>*But soft, what white is that which I espie,*
>*Which with its lustre doth ec'lipse mine eyes;*
>*That which doth Neptunes fury so disdain,*
>*And beates the Billow back into the main?*
>*Is it some dreadfull Scylla softned there,*
>*To shake the Sailer into prayer and fear?*
>*Or is 't some Island floating on the wave,*
>*Of which in writers we the story have?*
>*'Tis England, ha! tis so! clap, clap your hands,*
>*That the full noise may strike the neighbouring Lands*
>*Into a Palsie. Doth not that lov'd name*
>*Move you to extasie? O were the same*
>*As dear to you as me, that very word*
>*Would make you dance and caper over board.*
>*Dull shipmen! how they move not, how their houses*
>*Grow to the planks; yet stay, here's sport enough.*
>*For see, the sea Nymphs foot it, and the fish*
>*Leap their high measures equall to my wish.*
>*Triton doth sound his shell, and to delight me*
>*Old Nereus bobleth with his Amphitrite.*
>*Excellent triumphs! But (curs'd fates!) the main*
>*Quickly divides and takes them in againe;*
>*And leaves me dying, till I come to land,*
>*And kisse my dearest Mother in her sand.*

>*Hail happy England! hail thou sweetest Isle,*
>*Within whose bounds, no Pagan rites defile*
>*The purer faith: Christ is by Saints not mated,*
>*And he alone is worship'd that created.*
>*In thee the labouring man enjoyes his wealth,*
>*Not subject to his Lords rape, or the stealth*
>*Of hungry Publicans. In thee thy King*
>*Feares not the power of any underling;*
>*But is himself, and by his awfull word,*
>*Commands not more the begger then the Lord.*

In thee those heavenly beauties live, would make
Most of the Gods turn mortals for their sake.
Such as outgo report, and make fame see
They stand above her big'st Hyperbole.
And yet to strangers will not grutch the blisse
Of salutation, and an harmlesse kisse.

Hail then sweet England! may I breath my last,
In thy lov'd armes, and when my dayes are past,
And to the silence of the grave I must;
All I desire is, thou would'st keep my dust.

The End of the Fifth Book and the first Journey.

THE

THE SECOND JOURNEY:

CONTAINING
A SURVEY of the ESTATE
of the two ILANDS

Guernzey and Jarsey,

With the ISLES appending.

According to their Politie,
and Formes of Government, both
Ecclesiasticall and *Civill*.

THE SIXTH BOOK.

LONDON,

Printed by *E. Cotes* for *Henry Seile* over against
St. *Dunstans* Church in *Fleetstreet*, 1656.

A SURVEY of the ESTATE OF Guernzey and Jarsey, &c.

The Entrance.

(1) *The occasion of*, &c. (2) *Introduction to this Work.* (3) *The Dedication,* (4) *and Method of the whole. The beginning, continuance of our Voyage; with the most remarkable passages which hapned in it. The mercenary falsnesse of the Dutch exemplified in the dealing of a man of warre.*

When first I undertook to attend upon my Lord of *Danby* to the Islands of *Guernzey* and *Jarsey*; besides the purpose which I had of doing service to his Lordship, I resolved also to do somewhat for my self: and, if possible, unto the places. For my self, in bettering,

what

what I could my understanding, if peradventure the persons or the place might add unto me the knowledge of any one thing, to which I was a stranger. At the least I was in hope to satisfy my curiosity, as being not a little emulous of this kind of living, *Multorum mores hominum qui vidit & urbes*; which had seen so much of men and of their manners. It was also not the last part of mine intention, to do something in the honour of the Island, by committing to memory their Antiquities, by reporting to posterity their Arts of Government, by representing, as in a Tablet, the choycest of their beauties; and in a word, by reducing these and the Achievements of their people, as far as the light of Authors could direct me, into the body of an History. But when I had a little made my self acquainted with the place and people, I found nothing in them which might put me to that trouble. The Churches naked of all Monuments, and not so much as the blazon of an Armes permitted in a window, for fear, as I conjecture, of Idolatry. No actions of importance to be heard of in their Legends, in their remembrancers; whereby to ennoble them in time to come, unlesse perhaps some slight allarmes from *France*, may occasion speech of them in our common Chronicles. The Countrey, indeed, exceeding pleasant and delightsome, but yet so small in the extent and circuit, that to speak much of them, were to put the shooe of *Hercules* upon the foot of an Infant. For being in themselves, an abridgement only of the greater works of nature, how could the character and description of them be improved into a Volume? Having thus failed in the most of my designes, I applyed my self to make enquirie after their form of Government, in which, I must needs confesse, I met with much which did exceedingly afflict me. Their Lawes, little beholding in the composition of them, to *Justinian*; and of no great affinity with the laws of *England*, which we call Municipall or common. The grand Customarie of *Normandy*, is of most credit with them; and that indeed the only rule by which they are directed, save that in some few passages it hath been altered by our Prince, for the conveniency of this people.

Sed

Sed quid hoc ad Iphycli boves? But what had I, a Priest of the Church of *England*, to do with the Laws and Customes of the *Normans?* Had I gone forward in my purpose, I deny not, but I had mingled that knowledge which I have gotten of their Laws, amongst other my Collections; but failing in the main of my intent, I must only make such use of them, as shall be necessary for this present argument. An Argument not so much as in my thoughts, when first I resolved upon the Journey; as little dreaming that any alterations had lately hapned in the Churches of those Islands, or that those alterations could afford one such variety. An Argument more sutable to my profession, as having had the honour to be reputed with the Clergy; and such as in it self may justly be intituled to your Lordships patronage. God and the King have raised you above your brethren to be a Master in our *Israel*, a principall pillar in the glorious structure of the Church. An advancement which doth call upon you for the establishment and supportation of the meanest Oratory dependant on the Church of *England*; your most indulgent, and in you most happy mother. No marvail therefore, if those little Chappels, even those two Tribes and a half, which are on the other side of the flood, most humbly cast themselves at your Lordships feet, and by me lay open their estate unto you.

Which that I may the better do, in discharge of the trust reposed in me, and for your Lordships more ample satisfaction I shall proceed in this order following.

First, I shall lay before your Lordship, the full successe and course of our Navigation, till we were setled in those Islands; that so the rest of this discourse being more materiall, may receive no interruption in the processe of it.

Next, I shall briefly, as in a map, present your Lordship with the situation, quality and story of the Islands; with somewhat also of their Customes, of their Government; but this (as the great Cardinall acknowledgeth the Popes power in temporall affaires) *in ordin. tantum ad spiritualia*: the better to acquaint you with the occurrents of their Churches.

That done, I shall draw down the successe of their affairs from the beginning of the Reformation in matters of Religion, to the accomplishment of that Innovation which they had made in point of discipline; and therein, the full platforme or discipline it self, according as by *Snape* and *Cartwright* it was established in their Synods.

In the third place, I shall shew your Lordship, by what degrees and means the Ministers and Church of *Jarsey*, were perswaded to conforme unto the discipline of *England*; together with a copy of those Canons and constitutions Ecclesiasticall, whereby the Church and Ministery of that Island is now governed.

Last of all, I shall commence a suit unto your Lordship in the name of those of *Guernzey* for their *little sister which hath no breasts*; that by your Lordships place and power the one Island may conforme unto the other, and both to *England*. In which I shall exhibit unto your Lordship a just survey of such motives, which may have most sway with you in the furthering of a work so commendable; and shall adventure also upon such particulars, as may conduce to the advancing of the businesse. Not that therein I shall presume positively to advise your Lordship, or to direct you in the readiest way for the accomplishment of this designe; but that by this propounding of mine own conceits, I may excite your Lordship to have recourse unto the excellent treasures of your own mind, and thence to fashion such particulars for this purpose, as may be most agreeable to your Lordships wisdome.

In order whereunto your Lordship may be pleased to call to mind that on provocation given unto the *French* at the Isle of *Rhe*, the King received advertisement of some reciprocall affront intended by the *French* on the Isles of *Jarsey* and *Guernzey*, with others thereupon appendant, the only remainders of the Dukedome of *Normandy* in the power of the *English*; and that for the preventing of such inconveniences as might follow on it, it was thought good to send the Earl of *Danby* (then Governour of the Isle of *Guernzey*) with a considerable supp'y of Men, and Armes, and Ammunition to make good those Islands, by fortifying and assuring them

against

against all invasions. This order signified to his Lordship about the beginning of *December*, anno 1628. he chearfully embraced the service, and prepared accordingly. But being deserted by his own Chaplaines in regard of the extremity of the season, and the visible danger of the enterprise, he proposed the businesse of that attendance unto me (not otherwise relating to him then as to an honourable friend) in whom he found as great a readinesse and resolution, as he found coldnesse in the other. According to his Lordships summons, I attended him in his Majesties house of St. *James*, a little before the Feast of *Christmas*; but neither the Ships, money, nor other necessaries being at that time brought together, I was dismissed again at the end of the Holydayes, untill a further intimation of his Lordships pleasure. Toward the latter end of *February* I received a positive command to attend his Lordship on Friday the 20 of that month, at the house of Mr. *Arthur Brumfeild*, in the Parish of *Tichfeild* near the Sea, situate between *Portsmouth* and *Southampton*; whither accordingly I went, and where I found a very chearfull entertainment. It was a full week after that, before we heard of his Lordships coming, and yet his Lordship was fain to tarry two or three dayes before he had any advertisement that his Ships, Men and Ammunition (which he thought to have found there in readinesse) were Anchored in the road of *Portsmouth*. News whereof being brought unto us on the Monday morning, we spent the remainder of that day in preparations for our Journey, and taking leave of those good friends by whom we were so kindly entertained and welcomed.

On Tuesday *March* the 3. about ten in the morning, we went aboard his Majesties Ship called the *Assurance*, being a Ship of 800 tun, furnished with 42 pieces of Ordinance, and very well manned with valiant and expert Sailors; welcomed aboard (after the fashion of the Sea) with all the thunder and lightning which the whole Navy could afford from their severall Ships. Our whole Navy consisted of five Vessels, that is to say, the *Assurance* spoken of before, two of his Majesties *Pinnaces* called the *Whelps*, a *Catch* of his Majesties called the *Minikin*, and a Merchants ship called

Oo 2 the

the *Charles*, which carryed the Armes and Ammunition for the use of the Islands. Aboard the Ships were stowed about 400 foot with their severall Officers, two Companies whereof under the command of Collonell *Piperrell* (if I remember his name aright) and Lieutenant Collonell *Francis Connisby* were intended for the Isle of *Guernzey*; the other two under the command of Lieutenant Collonell *Francis Rainsford*, and Captain *William Kilegre* for the Isle of *Jarsey*. The Admirall of our Navy (but in subordination to his Lordship when he was at Sea) was Sir *Henry Palmer* one of the Admirals of the Narrow-seas. All of them men of note in their severall wayes, and most of them of as much gallantry and ingenuity, as either their own birth or education in the Schoole of war could invest them with. The Sea was very calme and quiet, and the little breath of winde we had, made us move so slowly, that the afternoon was almost spent before we had passed through the Needles, a dangerous passage at all times, except to such only who being well skilled in these sharpe points, and those dreadfull fragments of the Rocks, which so intituled them, could steer a steady course between them: *Scylla* and *Charybdis* in old times, nothing more terrible to the unskilled Mariners of those dayes, then those Rocks to ours. Being got beyond them at the last, though we had got more Sea roome, we had little more winde, which made us move as slowly as before we did, so that we spent the greatest part of the night with no swifter motion, then what was given us by the tide. About 3 of the clock in the morning we had winde enough, but we had it directly in our teeth, which would have quickly brought us to the place we had parted from, if a great Miste arising together with the Sun, had not induced our Mariners to keep themselves aloofe in the open Sea for fear of falling on those Rocks wherewith the Southside of the *Wight* is made unaccessable. About 2 of the clock in the afternoon, the winds turning somewhat Eastward, we made on again, but with so little speed, and to so little purpose, that all that night we were fain to lie at *Hull* (as the Mariners phrase it) without any sensible moving either backward or forward, but so uneasily withall, that it must be a very great tempest indeed,

which

which gives a passenger a more sickly and unpleasing motion. For my part I had found my self good Sea-proof in my Voyage to *France*, and was not much troubled with those disturbances to which the greatest part of our Land-men were so sensibly subject. On Thursday morning about day-break being within sight of *Portland*, and the winde serving very fitly, we made again for the Islands. At 11 of the clock we discovered the main Land of *Normandy*, called by the Mariners *Le Hagge*. About 2 in the afternoon, we fell even with *Aldernie* or *Aurnie*; and about 3 discerned the Isle of *Jarzey* to which we were bound, at which we aimed, and to which we might have come much sooner then we did had we not found a speciall entertainment by the way to retard our haste. For we were hardly got within sight of *Jarsey* but we descried a sail of *French* consisting of ten barks laden with very good *Gascoygne* Wines, and good choyce of Linen (as they told us afterwards) bound from St. *Maloes* to *New-Haven* for the trade of *Paris*, and convoyed by a *Holland-man of war*, for their safer passage. These being looked on as good prize, our two *Whelpes* and the *Catch* gave chace unto them, a great shot being first made from our Admirals Ship to call them in. The second shot brought in the *Holland-man of war*, who very sordidly and basely betrayed his charge before he came within reach of danger; the rest for the greatest part of the afternoon, spun before the winde, sometimes so neer to their pursuers, that we thought them ours, but presently tacking about, when our *Whelpes* were ready to seaze on them, and the *Catch* to lay fast hold upon them, they gained more way then our light Vessels could recover in a long time after. Never did Duck by frequent diving so escape the Spaniell, or Hare by often turning so avoid the Hounds, as these poor Barks did quit themselves by their dexterity in sailing from the present danger. For my part I may justly say that I never spent an afternoon with greater pleasure, the greater in regard that I knew his Lordships resolution to deal favourably with those poor men if they chanced to fall into his power. Certain I am, that the description made by *Ovid* of the Hare and Hound, was here fully veryfied, but farre more excellently in the application then the first originall; of which thus the Poet:

Ut canis in vacuo leporem cum Gallicus arvo
Vidit, & hic prædam pedibus petit, ille salutem;
Alter inhæsuro similis jam jamque tenere
Sperat, & obtento stringit vestigia collo;
Alter in ambiguo est, an sit compressus, & ipsis
Morsibus eripitur, tangentiaque ora relinquit.

Which I finde thus *Englished* by G. *Sandis*.

As when the Hare the speedy Gray-hound spies;
His feet for prey, she hers for safety plies.
Now beares he up, now, now he hopes to fetch her;
And with his snowt extended strains to catch her.
Not knowing whether caught or no, she slips
Out of his wide-stretcht-jawes and touching lips.

But at the last a little before the close of the evening, three of them being borded and brought under Lee of our Admirall, the rest were put to a necessity of yeelding, or venturing themselves between our two great ships and the shoar of *Jarsey*, to which we were now come as near as we could with safety. Resolved upon the last course and favoured with a strong leading gale, they passed by us with such speed and so good successe, (the duskinesse of the evening contributing not a little to a fair escape) that though we gave them 30 shot, yet we were not able to affirme that they received any hurt or dammage by that encounter; with as much joy unto my self (I dare boldly say) as to any of those poor men who were so much in-

terested

terested in it. This Chase being over, and our whole Fleet come together, we Anchored that night in the Port of St. *Oen*, one of the principall Ports of that Island; the Inhabitants whereof (but those especially which dwelled in the inland parts) standing all night upon their guard, conceiving by the thunder of so many great shot, that the whole powers of *France* and the Devill to boot were now falling upon them; not fully satisfied in their fears, till by the next rising of the Sun they descried our colours.

On Friday *March* the 6. about nine in the morning (having first landed our foot in the long boats) we went aboard his Majesties *Catch* called the *Minikin*, and doubling the points of *Le Corbiere* and of *Normont*, we went on shoar in the Bay of St. *Helliers*, neer unto *Mount St. Albin* in the Parish of *St. Peter*. The greatest part of which day we spent in accommodations and refreshments, and receiving the visits of the Gentry which came in very frequently to attend his Lordship. You need not think, but that sleep and a good bed were welcome to us, after so long and ill a passage; so that it was very near high noon before his Lordship was capable to receive our services, or we to give him our attendance; after dinner his Lordship went to view the Fort *Elizabeth* (the chief strength of the Island) and to take order for the fortifying and repair thereof. Which having done he first secured the Men of War and the three *French* Barks, under the command of that Castle; and then gave leave to Sir *Henry Palmer* and the rest of the sea Captains to take their pleasures in Forraging and scowring all the Coasts of *France*, which lay near the Islands, commanding them to attend him on the Saturday following. Next he gave liberty to all the *French* which he had taken the day before, whom he caused to be landed in their own Countrie, to their great rejoycing, as appeared by the great shout they made when they were put into some long boats at their own disposing. The three Barks still remaining untouched in the state they were, save that some wines were taken out of them for his Lordships spending. On Sunday *March* 8. it was

ordered,

ordered, that the people of the Town of St. *Hellers* should have their divine offices in that Church performed so early, that it might be left wholly for the use of the *English* by nine of the clock, about which time his Lordship attended by the Officers and Souldiers in a solemn Military pompe (accompanied with the Governours of the Town and chief men of the Island) went toward the Church, where I officiated Divine Service according to the prescript form of the Church of *England*, and after preached on those words of *David, Psal.* 31. 51. *viz. Offer unto God thanksgiving*, &c. with reference to the good successe of our Voyage past, and hopes of the like mercies for the time to come. The next day we made a Journey to *Mount Orgueil*, where we were entertained by the Lady *Carteret* (a Daughter of Sir *Francis Dous* of *Hampshire*) And after Dinner his Lordship went to take a view of the Regiment of Mr. *Josuah de Carteret, Seignieur de la Trinity*, mustering upon the Green upon *Havre de Bowle* in the Parish of *St. Trinitie*. On Tuesday, *March* the 10. his Lordship took a view of the Regiment of Mr. *Aron Misservie* Col. and on Wednesday, *March* the 11. went unto St. *Oen*, where we were feasted by Sir *Philip de Carteret*, whose Regiment we likewise viewed in the afternoon. The Souldiers of each Regiment very well arrayed, and not unpractised in their Armes; but such, as never saw more danger then a Training came to. On Thursday his Lordship went into the *Cohu* or Town-hall, attended by Sir *John Palmer* the Deputy Governour, Sir *Philip de Carteret*, the Justices, Clergy, and Jurors of the Island, with other the subordinate Officers thereunto belonging: where being set, as in a Parliament or Sessions, and having given order for redresse of some grievances by them presented to him in the name of that people, he declared to them in a grave and eloquent speech the great care which his Majesty had of their preservation in sending Men, Money, Armes, and Ammunition to defend them against the common Enemies of their peace and
con-

consciences; assuring them that if the noise of those preparations did not keep the *French* from looking towards them, his Majesty would not fail to send them such a strength of Shipping, as should make that Illand more impregnable then a wall of Brasse; in which regard he thought it was not necessary for him to advise them to continue faithfull to his Majesties service, or to behave themselves with respect and love towards those Gentlemen, Officers, and common Souldiers, who were resolved to expose themselves (for defence of them, their Wives and Children) to the utmost dangers. And finally, advising the common Souldiers to carry themselves with such sobriety and moderation, towards the natives of the Countrey, (for as for their valour towards the enemies he would make no question) as to give no offence or scandall by their conversation. This said, the Assembly was dissolved, to the great satisfaction of all parties present; the night ensuing and the day following being spent for the most part in the entertainments of rest and pleasures.

The only businesse of that day was the disposing of the three Barks which we took in our Journey, the goods whereof having before been inventoried and apprized by some Commissioners of the Town, and now exposed to open sale, were for the most part, bought together with the Barks themselves by that very *Holland man of warre*, whom they had hired to be their Convoy: Which gave me such a Character of the mercenary and sordid nature of that people, that of all men living, I should never desire to have any thing to do with them, unlesse they might be made use of (as the *Gibeonites* were) in *hewing wood, and drawing water for the use of the Tabernacle*; I mean in doing servile offices to some mightier State which would be sure to keep them under.

On Saturday, *March* the 14. having spent the greatest part of the morning in expectation of the rest of our Fleet, which found better imployment in the Seas then they could in the Haven, we went aboard the Merchants ship, which before I spake of, not made much lighter by the unlading of the one halfe of the Ammunition which was left at *Jersey*, in regard that the 200 foot which should have been distributed in the rest of the ships, were all stowed in her. Before night, being met by the rest of our Fleet, we came to Anchor neer St. *Pier-port* or St. *Peters Port* within the Bay of *Castle Cornet*, where we presently landed. The Castle divided from the Town and Haven, by the inter-currency of the Sea; in which respect we were fain to make use of the Castle-hall in stead of a Chappell. The way to the Town Church being too troublesome and uncertain to give us the constant use of that, and the Castle yeelding no place else of a fit capacity for the receiving of so many as gave their diligent attendance at Religious exercises.

On Monday, *March* the 16. our Fleet went out to Sea againe, taking the *Charles* with them for their greater strength, which to that end was speedily unladen of such ammunition as was designed for the use of that Island.

The whole time of our stay here was spent in visiting the Forts, and Ports, and other places of importance, taking a view of the severall Musters of the naturall Islanders, distributing the new come Souldiers in their severall quarters, receiving the services of the Gentry, Clergy and principall Citizens; and finally in a like meeting of the States of the Island, as had before been held in *Jersey*.

Nothing considerable else in the time of our stay, but that our Fleet came back on Wednesday, *March* 25. which hapned very fitly to compleat the triumph of the Friday following, being the day of his Majesties most happy Inauguration; celebrated in the Castle, by the Divine Service for that day, and after by a noble Feast, made by him for the chief men of the Island; and solemnized without the Castle by 150 great shot, made

made from the Castle, the Fleet, the Town of St. *Peters Port*, and the severall Islands, all following one another in so good an order, that never Bels were rung more closely, nor with lesse confusion.

Thus having given your Lordship a brief view of the course of our Voyage; I shall next present you with the sight of such observations, as I have made upon those Islands at my times of leasure; and that being done, hoise sail for *England*.

Chap. I.

(1) *Of the convenient situation*, *and* (2) *condition of these Islands in the generall.* (3) Alderney, (4) *and* Serke. (5) *The notable stratagem whereby this latter was recovered from the* French. (6) *Of* Guernzey, (7) *and the smaller Isles neer unto it.* (8) *Our Lady of* Lehu. (9) *The road, and* (10) *the Castle of* Cornet. (11) *The Trade, and* (12) *Priviledges of this people.* (13) *Of* Jarsey, *and* (14) *the strengths about it.* (15) *The Island why so poor and populous.* (16) Gavelkind, *and the nature of it.* (17) *The Governours and other the Kings Officers.* *The* (18) *Politie, and* (19) *administration of Justice in both Islands.* (20) *The Assembly of the* Three Estates. (21) *Courts* Presidiall *in* France *what they are.* (22) *The election of the Justices,* (23) *and the Oath taken at their admission.* (24) *Of their* Advocates *or* Pleaders, *and the number of them.* (25) *The number of* Atturneys *once limited in* England. (26) *A Catalogue of the Governours and Bailiffs of the Isle of* Jarsey.

TO begin then with the places themselves, the Scene and Stage of our discourse, they are the only remainders of our rights in *Normandy*: unto which Dukedome they did once belong. *Anno* 1108. at such time as *Henry* I. of *England* had taken prisoner his Brother *Robert*, these Islands as a part of *Normandy*, were annext unto the

English

English Crown, and have ever since with great testimony of faith and loyalty, continued in that subjection. The sentence or arrest of confiscation given by the Parliament of *France* against King *John*, nor the surprisall of *Normandy* by the *French* forces, could be no perswasion unto them to change their Masters. Nay when the *French* had twice seized on them, during the Reign of that unhappy Prince, and the state of *England* was embroyled at home, the people valiantly made good their own, and faithfully returned unto their first obedience. In aftertimes as any war grew hot between the *English* and the *French*, these Islands were principally aimed at by the enemy, and sometimes also were attempted by them, but with ill successe. And certainly, it could not be but an eye sore to the *French*, to have these *Isles* within their sight, and not within their power; to see them at the least in possession of their ancient enemy the *English*; a Nation strong in shipping, and likely by the opportunity of these places to annoy their trade. For if we look upon them in their situation, we shall find them seated purposely for the command and Empire of the Ocean. The Islands lying in the chief trade of all shipping from the Eastern parts unto the West, and in the middle way between St. *Malos* and the river *Seine*, the only trafick of the *Normans* and *Parisians*. At this St. *Malos*, as at a common *Empory* do the Merchants of *Spain* and *Paris* barter their Commodities; the *Parisians* making both their passage and return by these Isles, which if wel aided by a smal power from the Kings Navy, would quickly bring that entercourse to nothing. An opportunity neglected by our former Kings in their attempts upon that Nation, as not being then so powerfull on the Seas as now they are, but likely for the future to be husbanded to the best advantage, if the *French* hereafter stir against us. Sure I am, that my Lord of *Danby* conceived this course of all others to be the fittest, for the impoverishing if not undoing of the *French*; and accordingly made proposition by his Letters to the Councell, that a squadron of eight Ships (viz. five of the *Whelpes*, the *Assurance*, the *Adventure* and the *Catch*) might be employed about these Islands for that purpose. An advice which had this Summer took

took effect, had not the Peace between both Realms, been so suddenly concluded.

Of these, four only are Inhabited, and those reduced only unto two Governments; *Jarsey* an entire Province as it were within it self; but that of *Guernzey* having the other two of *Alderney* and *Serke* dependant on it. Hence it is, that in our Histories, and in our Acts of Parliament, we have mention only of *Jarsey* and of *Guernzey*, this last comprehending under it the two other. The people of them all live as it were in *libera custodia*, in a kind of free subjection; not any way acquainted with Taxes, or with any levies either of men or money. In so much, that when the Parliaments of *England* contribute towards the occasion of their Princes, there is alwayes a proviso in the Act, "That this grant of Subsidies "or any thing therein contained, extend not to charge the "inhabitants of *Guernzey* and *Jarsey*, or any of them, of, for "or concerning any Mannors, Lands, and Tenements, or "other possessions, Goods, Chattels, or other moveable "substance, which they the said Inhabitants, or any other "to their uses, have within *Jarsey* and *Guernzey*, or in any "of them, &c. These priviledges and immunities (together with divers others) seconded of late dayes with the more powerfull band of Religion, have been a principall occasion of that constancy, wherewith they have persisted faithfully in their allegiance, and disclaimed even the very name and thought of *France*. For howsoever the language which they speak is *French*, and that in their originall, they either were of *Normandy* or *Britagne*; yet can they with no patience endure to be accounted *French*, but call themselves by the names of *English-Normans*. So much doth liberty, or at the worst a gentle yoak, prevail upon the mind and fancy of the people.

To proceed unto particulars, we will take them as they lie in order, beginning first with that of *Alderney*, an Island called by *Antonine*, *Arica*, but by the *French* and in our old Records known by the name of *Aurigny* and *Aurney*. It is situate in the 49 degree between 48 & 52 minutes of that degree, just over against the Cape or promontory of the *Lexobii*, called at this time by the Mariners the *Hogue*. Distant from this

this Cape or Promontory three leagues only, but thirty at the least from the nearest part of *England*. The aire healthy, though sometimes thickned with the vapours arising from the Sea. The soil indifferently rich both for husbandry and grasing. A Town it hath of well-near an hundred families, and not far off, an haven made in the manner of a semicircle, which they call *Crabbie*. The principall strength of it, are the high rocks, with which it is on every side environed, but especially upon the South; and on the East side an old Block-house, which time hath made almost unserviceable. The chief house herein belongeth unto the *Chamberlains*, as also the dominion or Fee-farme of all the Island, it being granted by Queen *Elizabeth* unto *George* the son of Sir *Leonard Chamberlain*, then Governour of *Guernzey*, by whose valour it was recovered from the *French*, who in Queen *Maries* dayes had seized upon it. Neer unto the Fort or Block-house afore mentioned, a great quantity of this little Island is overlaid with sand, driven thither by the fury of the Northwest-winde. If we believe their Legends, it proceeded from the just judgement of God upon the owner of those grounds, who once (but when I know not) had made booty and put unto the Sword some certain *Spaniards*, there shipwracked.

Four leagues from hence, and to the Southwest and by west, lyeth another of the smaller Islands, called *Serke*; six miles in circuit at the least, which yet is two miles lesser in the whole compasse then that of *Alderney*. An Isle not known at all by any name amongst the Antients, and no marvail, for till the fifth of Queen *Elizabeth* or thereabouts, it was not peopled. But then, it pleased her Majesty to grant it for ever in Fee farme to *Helier de Carteret*, vulgarly called *Seigneur de St. Oen*, a principall Gentleman of the Isle of *Jarsey*, and Grandfather to Sir *Philip de Carteret* now living. By him it was divided into severall estates, and leased out unto divers Tenants, collected from the neighbour Islands, so that at this day it may contain some forty housholds; whereas before it contained only a poor hermitage, together with a little Chappell appertaining to it; the rest of the ground serving as a Common unto those

of

of *Guernzey* for the breeding of their Cattell. For strength it is beholding most to nature, who hath walled it in a manner round with mighty rocks, there being but one way or ascent unto it, and that with small forces easie to be defended against the strongest power in Christendome. A passage lately fortified by the Farmers here, with a new platforme on the top of it, and thereupon some four pieces of Ordinance continually mounted. In this Island, as also in the other, there is a Bailiff and a Minister, but both of them subordinate in matter of appeal unto the Courts and *Colloquies* of *Guernzey*.

During the reign of the late Queen *Mary*, who for her husband *Philips* sake, had engaged her self in a war against the *French*; this Island then not peopled, was suddenly surprized by those of that Nation, but by a Gentleman of the Netherlands, a subject of King *Philips* thus regained, as the story much to this purpose is related by Sir *Wal. Raleigh*. The *Flemish* Gentleman with a small Bark came to Anchor in the road, and pretending the death of his Merchant, besought the *French* that they might bury him in the Chappell of that Island, offering a present to them of such commodity as they had aboard. To this request the *French* were easily entreated, but yet upon condition that they should not come on shoar with any weapon, no not so much as with a knife. This leave obtained, the *Fleming* rowed unto the shoar with a Coffin in their Skiffe for that use purposely provided, and manned with Swords and Arcubushes. Upon their landing, and a search so strict and narrow, that it was impossible to hide a pen-knife; they were permitted to draw their Coffin up the Rocks, some of the *French* rowing back unto the Ship to fetch the present, where they were soon made fast enough and laid in hold. The *Flemings* in the mean time which were on land, had carryed their Coffin into the Chappell, and having taken thence their weapons, gave an alarme upon the *French*, who taken thus upon the suddain, and seeing no hopes of succour from their fellowes, yeelded themselves, and abandoned the possession of that place. A stratagem to be compared, if not preferred, unto any of the Ancients; did not that fatall folly reprehended once by
Tacitus,

CHAP. I. *the Estate of* Guernzey *and* Jarsey. 297

Tacitus, still reign amongst us, *Quod vetera extollimus recentium incuriosi*; that we extoll the former dayes, and are carelesse of the present.

Two leagues from *Serke* directly Westward, lyeth the chief Island of this Government, by *Antonine* called *Sarnia*; by Us and the *French* known now by the name of *Garnzey*, or of *Guernzey*. Situate in the 49 degree of Latitude, between the 39 and 46 minutes of that degree, eight leagues or there-abouts from the coast of *Normandy*, and well-neer in an equall distance from *Alderney* and *Jarsey*. The forme of it, is much after the fashion of the Isle of *Sicily*, every side of the triangle being about nine miles in length, and 28 in the whole compasse. In this circuit are comprehended ten Parishes, whereof the principall is that of St. *Peters* on the Sea, as having a fair and safe peer adjoyning to it for the benefit of their Merchants, and being honoured also with a Market, and the *Plaidery* or Court of Justice. The number of the Inhabitants is reckoned neer about twenty thousand, out of which there may be raised some two thousand able men; although their trained Band consists only of twelve hundred, and those, God knows, but poorly weaponed. The aire hereof is very healthfull, as may be well seen in the long lives both of men and women; and the earth said to be of the same nature with *Crete* and *Ireland*, not apt to foster any venemous creature in it. Out of which generall affirmation, we may do well to except *Witches*, of whom the people here have strange reports, and if an Ox or Horse perhaps miscarry, they presently impute it to *Witchcraft*, and the next old woman shall straight be hal'd to Prison. The ground it self, in the opinion of the Natives, more rich and battle then that of *Jarsey*; yet not so fruitfull in the harvest, because the people addict themselves to merchandise especially, leaving the care of husbandry unto their hindes. Yet Bread they have sufficient for their use; enough of Cattell both for themselves and for their ships; plenty of Fish continually brought in from the neighbour seas, and a Lake on the Northwest part of it, neer unto the sea, of about a mile or more in compasse, exceeding well stored with Carpes, the best that ever mortall eye beheld, for tast and bignesse.

Q q Some

Some other Isles yet there be pertaining unto this Government of *Guernzey*, but not many nor much famous. Two of them lie along betwixt it and *Serke*, viz. *Arme*, and *Jet-how*, whereof this last serveth only as a Parke unto the Governour, and hath in it a few fallow Deer, and good plenty of Conies. The other of them is well-neer three miles in circuit, a solitary dwelling once of Canons regular, and afterwards of some Fryers of the Order of St. *Francis*, but now only inhabited by Pheasants, of which amongst the shrubs and bushes, there is said to be no scarcity. The least of them, but yet of most note, is the little Islet called *Lehu*, situate on the North side of the Eastern corner, and neer unto those scattered rockes, which are called *Les Hanvaux*, appertaining once unto the Dean, but now unto the Governour. Famous for a little Oratory or Chantery there once erected and dedicated to the honour of the Virgin *Mary*, who by the people in those times, was much sued to by the name of our Lady of *Lehu*. A place long since demolished in the ruine of it, *Sed jam periere ruinæ*, but now the ruines of it are scarce visible, there being almost nothing left of it but the steeple, which serveth only as a seamarke, and to which as any of that party sail along, they strike their top sail. *Tantum religio potuit suadere*, such a Religious opinion have they harboured of the place, that though the Saint be gone, the wals yet shall still be honoured.

But indeed, the principall honour and glory of this Iland, I mean of *Guernzey*, is the large capaciousnesse of the harbour, and the flourishing beauty of the Castle; I say the Castle, as it may so be called by way of eminency, that in the vale, and those poorer trifles all along the Coasts, not any way deserving to be spoken of. Situate it is upon a little Islet just opposite unto *Pierpert* or the Town of St. *Peter*, on the Sea; to which, and to the peere there it is a good assurance, and takes up the whole circuit of that Islet whereupon it standeth. At the first it was built upon the higher part of the ground only, broad at the one end, and at the other, and bending in the fashion of an horne, whence it had the name of *Cornet*. By Sir *Leonard Chamberlaine* Governour

Governour here in the time of Queen *Mary*, and by Sir *Thomas Leighton* his successour in the reign of Queen *Elizabeth*, It was improved to that majesty and beauty that now it hath, excellently fortified according to the moderne art of war, and furnished with almost an hundred piece of Ordinance, whereof about sixty are of Brasse. Add to this, that it is continually environed with the Sea, unlesse sometimes at a dead-low water, whereby there is so little possibility of making any approaches neer unto it, that one might justly think him mad, that would attempt it. And certainly it is more then necessary that this place should be thus fortified, if not for the safety of the Island, yet at the least for the assurance of the Harbour. An harbour able to contain the greatest Navy that ever sailed upon the Ocean; fenced from the fury of the winds by the Illes of *Guernzey*, *Jet-bow*, *Serke* and *Arule*, by which it is almost encompassed; and of so sure an anchorage, that though our Ships lay there in the blustering end of *March*, yet it was noted that never any of them slipped an anchour. Other Havens they have about the Island, viz. *Bazon*, *L'Aucresse*, *Fermines* and others; but these rather landing places to let in the Enemy, then any way advantageous to the trade and riches of the people. A place not to be neglected in the defence of it; and full of danger to the *English* State and Trafick, were it in the hands of any enemy.

Upon the notable advantage of this harbour, and the conveniency of the Peer so neer unto it, which is also warranted with six peece of good Canon from the Town; It is no marvell if the people betake themselves so much unto the trade of Merchandise. Nor do they trafick only in small boats between St. *Malos* and the Islands, as those of *Jarsey*; but are Masters of good stout Barks, and venture unto all these neerer Ports of Christendom. The principall commodity which they use to send abroad, are the works and labours of the poorer sort, as Wast-cotes, Stockins, and other manufactures made of wool, wherein they are exceeding cunning; of which wooll to be transported to their Island in a certain proportion, they lately have obtained a licence of our Princes. But there accreweth a further benefit unto this people, from their harbour then their own trafick, which is the continuall concourse and resort of Merchants thither, especially upon the noise or being of a War. For by an antient priviledge of the Kings of *England*, there is with them in a manner a continuall truce; and lawfull it is both for *French* men and for others, how hot soever the war be followed in other parts, to repair hither without danger, and here to trade in all security. A priviledge founded upon a Bull of Pope *Sixtus* IV. the 10 year, as I remember, of his Popedom; *Edward* IV. then reigning in *England*, and *Lewis* XI. over the *French*: by virtue of which Bull, all those stand *ipso facto* excommunicate, which any way molest the Inhabitants of this Isle of *Guernzey*, or any which resort unto their Island, either by Piracy or any other violence whatsoever. A Bull first published in the City of *Constance*, unto whose Diocesse these Islands once belonged, afterwards verisyed by the Parliament of *Paris*, and confirmed by our Kings of *England* till this day. The copy of this Bull my self have seen, and somewhat also in the practise of it on record; by which it doth appear, that a man of war of *France* having taken an *English* ship, and therein some passengers and goods of *Guernzey*; made prize and prisoners of the *English*, but restored those of *Guernzey* to their liberty and to their own.

And now at last after a long passage, and through many difficulties, we are Anchored in the Isle of *Jersey*; known in the former ages, and to *Antonine* the Emperor, by the name of *Cesarea*. An Island situate in the 49 degree of Latitude, between the 18 and 24 minutes of that degree; distant 5 leagues only from the Coast of *Normandy*, 40 or thereabouts from the neerest parts of *England*, and 6 or 7 to the South east from that of *Guernzey*. The figure of it will hold proportion with that long kind of square, which the *Geometricians* call *Oblongum*; the length of it from West to East 11 miles, the breadth 6 and upwards, the whole circuit about 33. The aire very healthy and little disposed unto diseases, unlesse it be unto a kinde of Ague in the end of Harvest, which they call *Les Settembers*. The soil sufficiently fertile in it self, but most curiously manured, and of a plentifull small increase unto the Barn; not only yeelding Corne enough for the people of the Island, but sometimes also an ample surplusage, which they barter at St. *Ma'os* with the *Spanish* Merchants. The Countrey generally swelling up in pretty hillocks, under which lie pleasant Vallies, and those plentifully watered with dainty Rils or Riverets; in which watery commodity, it hath questionlesse the precedency of *Guernzey*.

Both Islands consist very much of small Inclosure, every man in each of them, having somewhat to live on of his own. Only the difference is, that here the mounds are made with ditches & banks of earth cast up, well fenced and planted with severall sorts of apples, out of which they make a pleasing kinde of Sider, which is their ordinary drink; whereas in *Guernzey* they are for the most part made of stones, about the height and fashion of a *Parapet*. A matter of no small advantage in both places against the fury of an enemy, who in his marches cannot but be much annoyed with these Incumbrances, and shall be forced to pay deerly for every foot of ground which there he purchaseth.

For other strengths this Island is in part beholding unto Nature, and somewhat also unto Art. To Nature which hath guarded it with Rocks, and Shelves, and other shallow places very dangerous; but neither these, nor those of Art, so serviceable and full of safety, as they be in *Guernzey*. Besides the landing places, here are more, and more accessible, as namely the Bay of St. *Oven*, and the Havens of St. *Burlade*, *Beule*, St. *Katharines*, with divers others. There is, indeed, one of them, and that the principall, sufficiently assured; on the one side by a little *Blockhouse*, which they call *Mount St. Aubin*; and on the other by a fair Castle, called the Fort *Elizabeth*. The Harbour it self is of a good capacity, in figure like a semicircle or a crescent, and by reason of the Town adjoyning, known by the name of the Haven of St. *Hilaries*. On that side of it next the Town, and in a little Islet of it self is situate the Castle, environed with the Sea at high water, but at an ebb easily accessible by land; but yet so naturally defended with sharpe Rocks and craggy clifts, that

though

though the accesse unto it may be easie, yet the surprizall would be difficult. It was built not long since by our late Queen of famous memory, at such times as the Civill warres were hot in *France* about Religion, and the Kings Forces drawn downwards towards *Normandy*. Furnished with 30 pieces of Ordinance and upwards; and now, upon the preparations of the *French*, there are some new works begun about it, for the assurance of that well. On the East side, just opposite and in the view of the City of *Constantia*, there is seated on an high and craggy rock, a most strong Castle, and called by an haughty name *Mount Orgueil*; of whose founder I could learn nothing, nor any other thing which might concern it in matter of antiquity, save that it was repaired and beautified by *Henry* V. It is for the most part the inhabitation of the Governour, who is Captain of it; stored with about some forty pieces of Ordinance, and guarded by some five and twenty wardours. A place of good service for the safety of the Island; if perhaps it may not be commanded, or annoied by an hill adjoyning, which doth equall, if not overtop it.

This Island, as before we noted, is some 33 miles in compasse, comprehending in it 12 Parishes, whereof the principall is that of S. *Hilaries*. A Town so called from an antient Father of that name, and Bishop of *Poystiers* in *France*, whose body they suppose to be interred in a little Chappell neer unto the Fort *Elizabeth*, and consecrated to his memory. But of his buriall here, they have nothing further then tradition, and that unjustifiable; for St. *Jerome* telleth us, that after his return from *Phrygia*, whereunto he had been confined, he dyed in his own City; and we learn in the *Roman Martyrologie*, that his *Obit* is there celebrated on the 13 of *January*. The chief name the which this Town now hath, is for the conveniency of the Haven, the Market there every Saturday, and that it is honoured with the *Cohu* or *Sessions house* for the whole Island. The other Villages lie scattered up and down, like those of *Guernzey*, and give habitation to a people very painfull and laborious; but by reason of their continuall toyle and labour, not a little affected to a kinde of melancholy surlinesse incident to plough men.

Those

Those of *Guernzey* on the other side, by continuall converse with strangers in their own haven, and by travailing abroad being much more sociable and generous. Add to this, that the people here are more poor, and therefore more destitute of humanity; the children here continually craving almes of every stranger; whereas in all *Guernzey* I did not see one begger.

A principall reason of which poverty, I suppose to be their exceeding populousnesse, there being reckoned in so small a quantity of ground, neer upon thirty thousand living souls. A matter which gave us no small cause of admiration; and when my Lord of *Danby* seemed to wonder, how such a span of earth could contain such multitudes of people, I remember that Sir *John Payton* the Lieutenant Governour, made him this answer, viz. That the people married within themselves like Conies in a burrow; and further, that for more then thirty years they never had been molested either with Sword, Pestilence, or Famine.

A second reason of their poverty (add also of their numbers) may be the little liking they have to Trafick; whereby as they might have advantage to improve themselves, and employ their poor; so also might that service casually diminish their huge multitudes, by the losse of some men, and diverting others from the thought of marriage.

But the main cause, as I conceive it, is the tenure of their Lands, which are equally to be divided amongst all the Sons of every Father, and those parcels also to be subdivided even *ad infinitum*. Hence is it, that in all the Countries you shall hardly finde a field of Corne of larger compasse then an ordinary Garden; every one now having a little to himself, and that little made lesse to his posterity. This Tenure our Lawyers call by the name of *Gavel-kinde*; that is, as some of them expound it, *Give all-kinne*, because it is amongst them all to be divided. For thus the Law speaking of the customes of *Kent*, in the 16 Chap. *De prærogativa Regis*. *Ibidem omnes hæredes masculi participabant hæreditatem eorum, & similiter fæminæ; sed fæminæ non participabunt cum viris*. A tenure which on
the

the one side hath many priviledges, and on the other side as many inconveniences.

For first, they which hold in this Tenure, are free from all customary services, exempt from wardship, at full age when they come to 15 years, and if they please, they may alienate their estates either by gift or sale, without the assent or knowledge of the Lord. But which is most of all, in case the Father be attaint of Felony or Murder, there is no *Escheat* of it to the Lord; the whole Estate, after the King hath had *Diem annum & vastum*, descending on the Heires. *Et post annum & diem terræ & tenementa reddentur, & revertentur proximo hæredi cui debuerant descendisse, si felonia facta non fuisset*; so the Lawyers.

On the other side, by this means their estates are infinitely distracted, their houses impoverished, the Kings profits in his Subsidies diminished, and no little disadvantage to the publick service, in the finding of Armours for the Wars. Whereupon, as many Gentlemen of *Kent* have altered by especiall Acts of Parliament, the antient Tenure of their Lands, and reduced it unto *Knights service*; so is it wished by the better sort of this people, and intended by some of them, that their Tenure may be also altered and brought into the same condition. A matter of no little profit and advantage to the King, and therefore without difficulty to be compassed.

By this Tenure are their estates all holden in every of the Islands, except 6 only which are held in Capite; whereof 4 in *Jarsey*, and 2 in *Guernzey*, and those called by the names of *Signeuries*. The *Signeuries* in *Jarsey* are first, that of *St Oen*, anciently belonging to the *Cartereto*; and that of *Ressell*, bought lately of Mr. *Dominick Perin*, by Sir *Philip de Carteret* now living. 3. That of *Trinity*, descended upon Mr. *Joshua de Carteret* in the right of his Mother, the heir generall of the L' *Emprieres*. And 4. That of *St. Marie*, vulgarly called *Lammarez*, descended from the *Paines* unto the Family of the *Du Maresque* who now enjoy it. Those of *Guernzey*, as before I said, are two only; *viz.* that of *Aumerile*, and that of *De Sammarez*; both which have passed by way of sale through divers hands, and now at last

CHAP. I. *the Estate of Guernzey and Jarsey.*

last are even worne out almost to nothing. The present owners, *Fashion* and *Androes*, both of them *English* in their parentage.

The chief Magistrates in both these Isles, for as much as concernes the defence and safety of them, are the Governours; whose office is not much unlike that of the Lord Lieutenants of our shires in *England*, according as it was established by King *Alfred*, revived by *Henry* III. and so continueth at this day. These Governours are appointed by the King, and by him in times of warre, rewarded with an annuall pension payable out of the Exchequer; but since the encrease of the domaine by the ruine of Religious houses, that charge hath been deducted; the whole Revenues being allotted to them in both Islands for the support of their estate. In Civill matters they are directed by the *Bailiffs* and the *Jurates*; the *Bailiffs* and other the Kings Officers in *Guernzey*, being appointed by the Governour; those of *Jarsey* holding their places by Patent from the King.

The names of which Officers, from the highest to the lowest, behold here as in a Tablet, according as they are called in each Island.

GUERNZEY.

The Governour	the Earl of *Danby*.
The Lieutenant	*Nath. Darcell*.
The Bailiffe	*Aymes de Carteret*.
The Provost	
The Kings Advocate	*Pet. Beauvoir*.
The Comptroller	*De la Marsh*.
The Receiver	*Carey*.

JARSEY.

JARSEY.

The Governour	Sir *John Peyton*, Sen.
The Lieutenant	Sir *John Peyton*, Jun.
The Bailiffe	Sir *Philip de Carteret*.
The Vicompt	*Hampton*.
Le Procureur	*Helier de Carteret*.
The Advocate	*Messerney*.
The Receiver	*Dison*.

By those men, accompanied with the Justices or Jurates, is his Majesty served, and his Islands governed; the places in each Island being of the same nature, though somewhat different in name. Of these in matters meerly Civill, and appertaining unto publick justice, the Bailiffe is the principall; as being the chief Judge in all actions both criminall and reall. In matter of life and death, if they proceed to sentence of condemnation, there is requisite a concurrence of seven Jurates together with the Bailiffe; under which number so concurring, the Offender is acquited. Nor can the Countrey finde one guilty, not taken, as we call it, *in the matter*; except that 18 voices of 24 (for of that number is their *Grand Enquest*) agree together in the verdict. Personall actions, such as are Debt and Trespass, may be determined by the *Bailiffs*, and two only are sufficient; but if a triall come in right of Land and of Inheritance, there must be three at least, and they decide it. For the dispatch of these businesses, they have their Termes, about the same time as we in *London*; their Writs of Arrest, Appearance and the like, directed to the *Vicompt* or *Prevost*; and for the tryall of their severall causes, three severall Courts or Jurisdictions, *viz.* the Court *Criminall*, the Court of *Chattel*, and the Court of *Heritage*. If any finde himself agrieved with their proceedings, his way is to appeal unto the *Councell-Table*. Much like this forme of Government, but of later stampe, are those Courts in *France*, which they call *Les Seiges Presideaux*, instituted for the ease of the people by the former Kings, in divers Cities of the Realme, and since confirmed *anno* 1551 or thereabouts. Wherein there is a *Bailiffe*, attended by twelve *Assistants* (for the most part) two *Lieutenants*, the one criminall and the other civill, and other officers; the office of the *Bailiffe* being to preserve the people from wrong, to take notice of Treasons, Robberies, Murders, unlawfull assemblies, &c. and the like.

In this order, and by these men, are all such affaires transacted which concern only private and particular persons; but if a businesse arise which toucheth at the publick, there is summoned by the Governour a *Parliament*, or *Convention* of the three *Estates*. For however *Aristotle* deny in the first of his *Politicks*, τὸ οὐδὲν διαφέρειν μεγάλης οἰκίας, ἢ μικρᾶς πόλιν, that a great houshold nothing differs from a little City, yet certainly we may affirme that in the art of Government, a little Empire doth nothing differ from a greater; whereupon it is, that even these little Islands, in imitation of the greater Kingdomes have also their *Conventus ordinum*, or assembly of the *States*; viz. of the *Governour* as chief, the *Bailiffe* and *Jurates* representing the nobility, the *Ministers* for the Church, and the severall *Constables* of each Parish for the Commons. In this assembly generall, as also in all private meetings, the *Governour* takes precedence of the *Bailiffe*, but in the Civill Courts and pleas of law, the *Bailiffe* hath it of the *Governour*.

In this Assembly they rectifie such abuses as are grown among them, appoint Deputies to solicite their affairs at Court, resolve on publick contributions, &c. and among other things, determine the election of the *Justices*. For on the vacancy of any of those places, there is notice given unto the people in their severall Parishes on the next Sunday, after the morning exercise; and there the people, or the major part of them, agree upon a man. This nomination at the day appointed for the Assembly of the *States* is returned by the *Constables* of each Village, out of whom so named, the whole body chuseth him whom they think most serviceable for that Magistracy. This done, the new *Jurate* either then immediately, or at the next sitting of the Justices, shall be admitted to his place and office; having first taken an Oath for the upright demeanour of himselfe, in the discharge of his duty, and the trust reposed in him. The tenour of which Oath, is as followeth.

"YOU Mr. *N N.* since it hath pleased God to call "you lawfully to this charge, shall swear and "promise by the faith and troth which you owe to "God, well and truely to discharge the Office of a *Ju-* "*rate* or *Justiciar*, in the Court Royall of our Sove- "raigne Lord the King of *England*, *Scotland*, *France* and "*Ireland*, &c. in this Isle of *Jarsey*; whose Majesty, next "under God, you acknowledge to be supreme Gover- "nour in all his Realmes, Provinces, and Dominions, "renouncing all strange and forain powers. You shall "defend the rights both of his Majesty and Subjects. "You shall uphold the honour and glory of God, and "of his pure and holy word. You shall administer true "and equall Justice, as well to the poor as to the rich, "without respect of persons; according to our Lawes, "Usages and Customes, confirmed unto us by our pri- "viledges, maintaining them together with our Liber- "ties and Franchises, and opposing your selfe against "such as labour to infringe them. You shall also pu- "nish and chastise all Traitours, Murderers, Felons, "Blasphemers of Gods holy name, Drunkards and o- "ther scandalous livers, every one according to his de- "sert; opposing your self against all seditious persons "in the defence of the Kings Authority, and of his "Justice. You shall be frequently assistent in the Court, "and as often as you shall be desired, having no law- "full excuse to the contrary, in which case you shall "give your *proxie* to some other Justice, giving your ad-
"vise,

"vise, counsell, and opinion according to the since-
"rity of your conscience. You shall give reverence and
"due respect unto the Court. And shall defend, or
"cause to be defended, the rights of Widowes, Orphans,
"Strangers, and all other persons unable to help them-
"selves. Finally, in your verdict (or the giving your
"opinion) you shall regulate and conforme your self to
"the better and more wholesome counsell of the *Bai-*
"*liffe* and *Justices.*

"*All which you premise to make good upon your*
"*conscience.*

A way more compendious then ours in *England*, where the *Justices* are fain to take three Oaths, and those founded upon three severall Statutes, as *viz.* that concerning the discharge of their office, which seemeth to be founded on the 13. of *Richard* II. Cap. 7. That of the *Kings Supremacy*, grounded on the first of Queen *Elazabeth* Cap. 1. And lastly, that of *Allegiance*, in force by virtue of the Statute 3. *Jac.* Cap. 4. Of these *Justices* there are twelve in all in each Island; of whose names and titles in the next Chapter.

The other members of the *Bailiffes* Court, are the *Advocates* or *Pleaders*, whereof there be six onely in each Island; this people conceiving rightly, that multitudes of *Lawyers* occasion multitudes of businesse; or according to that merry saying of old *Haywood*, *The more Spaniels in the field, the more game.* Of these advocate, two of them which are (as we call them here in *England*) the Kings *Atturney* or *Solliciteur*, are called *Advocati stipulantes*, the others *Advocati postulantes.* Yet have they not by any order confined themselves to this number, but may enlarge them according to occasion, though it had not been a *Solecisme* or a novelty, were the number limited. For it appeareth in the Parliament Records, that *Edward* the first restrained the number both of *Counsellers* and *Atturneys* unto 140 for all *England*, though he also left authority in the *Lord Chief Justice* to enlarge it, as appeareth in the said Records, *Anno* 20. *Rotul.* 5. *in dorso de apprenticiis & attornatis*, in these words following. D. *Rex injunxit Job. de Metingham* (he was made chief Justice of the Common Pleas in the 18 of this King) *& sociis suis quod ipsi per eorum discretionem provideant & ordinent certum numerum in quolibet Comitatu, de melioribus & legalioribus, & libentius addiscentibus, sec. quod intellexerint quod curiæ suæ & populo de regno melius valere poterit*, &c. *Et videtur regi & ejus concilio quod septies viginti sufficere poterint. Apponant tamen præfati justiciarii plures, si viderint esse faciendum, vel numerum anticipent,* &c. Thus he wisely and happily foreseeing those many inconveniences which arise upon the multitudes of such as apply themselves unto the Lawes, and carefully providing for the remedy.

But of this, as also of these Islands, and of their manner of Govenment, I have now said sufficient; yet no more then what may fairly bring your Lordship on to the main of my discourse and Argument, *viz.* the Estate and condition of their Churches.

I shall here only adde a Catalogue of the *Governours* and *Beiliffs* of the Isle of *Jarsey* (for of those of *Guernzey*, notwithstanding all my paines and diligence I could finde no such certain constat) which is this that followeth.

CHAP. I.   *the Estate of Guernzey and Jarsey.*   311

A Catalogue of the *Governours* and Bailiffs of *Jarsey*.

Bailiffs.		Governours.
1301	Pierre Vigoure.	Edw. II. Otho de Grandison Sr. des Isles.
1389	Geofr. la Hague.	Edw. III. Edm. de Cheynie Gard des Isles.
1345	Guill. Hastings.	Thom. de Ferrer. Capt. des Isles.
1352	Rog. Powderham.	
1363	Raoul L. Empriere.	
1367	Rich de St. Martyn.	
1368	Jean de St. Martyn.	
	Rich le Peill.	
1370	Jean de St. Martyn.	
	Jean Cokerill.	
1382	Tho. Brasdefer.	Hen. IV. Edw. D. of York.
1396	Geofr. Brasdefer.	V. Jean D. of Bedford. 1414.
1405	Guill. de Laick.	
1408	Tho. Daniel.	VI. Hum. D. of Glocester. 1439.
1414	Jean Poingt dexter.	
1433	Jean Bernard Kt.	
1436	Jean l' Empriere.	
1444	Jean Payne.	
1446	Regin. de Carteret.	
1453	Jean Poingt dexter.	Edw. IV. Sir Rich. Harliston.
1462	Nicol. Mourin.	
1485	Guill. de Harry Angl.	Hen. VII. Mathew Baker Esq;
1488	Clem. le Hardy.	Tho. Overey Esq;
1494	Jean Nicols.	David Philips Esq;
1496	Jean l' Empriere.	
1515	Hel. de Carteret.	Hen. VIII. Sir Hugh Vaughan.
1524	Helier de la Rocq.	Sir Antony Utterell.
		1526. Rich.

Bailiffs.	Governours.
1526 Rich Mabon.	
1528 Jasper Penn. Angl.	
1562 Hostes Nicolle.	Edw. VI. Edw. D. of Somerf. L Protect.
Jean du Maresque	Cornish.
Geo. Pawlet, Angl.	Ma. R. Sir Hugh Pawlet.
1516 Jean Herault Kt.	Eliza. R. Sir Aimer Paulet.
1622 Guill. Parkhurst.	Sir Antho. Pawlett.
16 Philip de Carteret Kt.	Sir Walt. Raleigh.
now living ann. 1644.	Jac. Sir Joh. Peiton. S. a Cross ingrailed O
	Car. Sir Tho. Jermin, now living

Further then this I shall not trouble your Lordship with the Estate of these Islands in reference either unto Naturall or Civill Concernments. This being enough to serve for a foundation to that superstructure, which I am now to raise upon it.

CHAP.

Chap. II.

(1) *The City and Diocese of* Constance. (2) *The condition of these Islands under that Government.* (3) *Churches appropriated what they were.* (4) *The* Black Book *of* Constance. (5) *That called* Domesday. (6) *The suppression of* Priours Aliens. (7) Priours Dative, *how they differed from the* Conventualls. (8) *The condition of these Churches after the suppression.* (9) *A* Diagram *of the Revenue then allotted to each severall Parish, together with the* Ministers *and* Justices *now being.* (10) *What is meant by* Champarte *desarts and* French querrui. (11) *The alteration of Religion in these Islands.* (12) *Persecution here in the days of Queen* Mary. *The Authors indignation at it, expressed in a Poeticall rapture.* (13) *The Islands annexed for ever to the Diocese of* Winton, *and for what reasons.*

But before we enter on that Argument, The estate and condition of their Churches, a little must be said of their Mother-City, to whom they once did owe Canonicall obedience. A City, in the opinion of some, once called *Augusta Romanduorum,* and after took the name of *Constance* from *Constantine the great*, who repaired and beautified it. Others make it to be built in the place of an old standing campe, and that this is it which is called *Constantia castra* in *Ammian. Marcellinus, Meantesq; protinus prope castra Constantia funduntur in Mare, lib.* 15. To leave this controversie to the *French*, certain it is, that it hath been

(1) The City

and

and yet is a City of good repute; the County of *Constantine* (one of the seven *Bailiwicks* of *Normandy* being beholding to it for a name.)

Diocese of Constance.

As for the Town it self, it is at this day accounted for a *Ventè*, but more famous for the Bishoprick; the first Bishop of it, as the *Roman Martyrologie* (and on the 23, if my memory fail not, of *September*) doth instruct us, being one *Paternus*. *Du Chesne* in his book of *French Antiquities*, attributes this honour to St. *Ereptiolus*; the man, as he conjectures, that first converted it into the faith: his next successors being St. *Exuperance*, St. *Leonard*, and St *Lo*; which last is said to have lived in the year 472. By this account it is a City of good age; yet not so old but that it still continues beautifull. The Cathedrall here one of the fairest and well built pieces in all *Normandy*, and yeelding a fair prospect even as far as to these Islands. The Church, it may be, raised to that magnificent height, that so the Bishop might with greater ease survey his Diocese. A Diocese containing antiently a good part of Countrey *Constantine*, and these Islands where now we are.

(2) The condition of these Islands under that Government.

For the better executing of his Episcopall jurisdiction in these places divided by the Sea from the main body of his charge, he had a *Surregat* or *Substitute*, whom they called a *Dean*, in each Island one. His office consisting, as I guesse at it by the jurisdiction, of that of a *Chancellour* and an *Archdeacon*, mixt; it being in his faculty to give institution and induction, to give sentence in cases appertaining to Ecclesiasticall cognisance, to approve of Wils, and withall to hold his visitations. The revenue fit to entertain a man of that condition; viz. the best benefice in each Island, the profits arising from the Court, and a proportion of tithes allotted out of many of the Parishes. He of the Isle of *Guernzey* over and above this, the little Islet of *Lehu*, of which in the last Chapter; and when the houses of *Religion*, as they called them, were suppressed, an allowance of an hundred quarters of Wheat, *Guernzey* measure, paid him by the Kings receiver for his Tithes. I say *Guernzey* measure, because it is a measure different from ours; their quarter being no more then five of our bushels or thereabouts. The
Ministery

Ministery at that time not answerable in number to the Parishes, and those few very wealthy; the *Religious houses* having all the Prediall tithes appropriated unto them; and they serving many of the Cures, by some one of their own body licenced for that purpose.

Now those Churches, or Tithes rather, were called *Appropriated* (to digresse a little by the way) by which the Patrons *Papali authoritate intercedente*, &c. the Popes authority intervening, and the consent of the King and *Diocesan* first obtained, were for ever annexed, and as it were incorporated into such *Colledges*, *Monasteries*, and other foundations as were but sparingly endowed. At this day being irremediably and ever aliened from the Church; we call them by as fit a name, *Impropriations*.

(3) Churches appropriated what they were.

For the rating of these Benefices, in the payment of their first fruits and tenths or *Annats*, there was a note or taxe in the Bishops Register, which they called the *Black book* of *Constance*: like as we in *England*, the *Black book* of the *Exchequer*. A Taxe which continued constantly upon Record till their disjoyning from that Diocese, as the rule of their payments and the Bishops dues. And as your Lordship well knowes, not much unlike that course there is alwayes a Proviso in the grant of *Subsidies* by the *English Clergie*; "That the rate, taxation, valuation, and esti-"mation now remaining in Record in his Majesties "Court of Exchequer, for the payment of a perpetuall "*Disme* or Tenth granted unto King *Henry* the VIII. of "worthy memory, in the 26 year of his Reign, concer-"ning such promotions as now be in the hands of the "Clergie, shall onely be followed and observed. A course learnt by our great Prelates in the taxing of their Clergie, from the example of *Augustus*, ἐν ᾗ ἀπογραφὴ ἐοικυίαις, in his taxing of the World. For it is reported of him by *Co. Tacitus*, that he had written a book with his owne hand, *in quo opes publicæ continebantur*, wherein he had a particular estimate of all the Provinces in that large Empire; what Tributes and Imposts they brought in, what Armies they maintained, &c. and what

(4) The black book of Constance.

Sf 2 went

went also in Largesse and Pensions out of the publick finances.

(5) That of Doomsday.

This Providence also exactly imitated by our *Norman* Conquerour, who had taken such a speciall survey of his new purchase, that there was not one hide of Land in all the Realme, but he knew the yearly Rent and owner of it; how many plow-lands, what Pastures, Fennes and Marishes; what Woods, Parkes, Farmes and Tenements were in every shire, and what every one was worth.

This *Censuall Roll*, the *English* generally call *Doomesday book*, and that as some suppose, because the judgement and sentence of it was as impossible to be declined as that in the day of *doome*. *Sic cum orta fuerit contentio de his rebus quæ illic continentur cum ventum fuerit ad librum, ejus sententia infatuari non potest, vel impune declinari;* so mine Authour. Others conceive it to be corruptly called the Book of *Doomes-day*, for the Book of *Domus dei*, or the *Domus-dei book*, as being by the Conquerour laid up in the *Maison dieu* or Gods-house in *Winchester*. A book carefully preserved, and that under three Keyes in his Majesties Exchequer, not to be looked into under the price of a Noble; nor any line of it to be transcribed without the payment of a groat. *Tanta est authoritas vetustatis;* So great respect do we yeeld unto antiquity.

(6) The suppression of Priors Aliens.

But to return again to my Churches whom I left in bondage under their severall *Priories*, and other the *Religious houses*. I will first free them from that yoak which the superstition of their *Patrons* had put upon them. So it was, that those *Houses of Religion* in these Islands, were not absolute foundations of themselves; but dependent on, and as it were the appurtenances of, some greater Abby or Monastery in *France*. In this condition they continued till the beginning of the Reign of King *Henry* the V. who purposing a war against the *French*, thought fit to cut of all helpes and succours as they had from *England*, at that time full of *Priors Aliens*, and strangers possess'd of

Bene-

CHAP. II.   *the Estate of* Guernzey *and* Jarsey.

Benefices. To this end it was enacted, *viz.* "Whereas "there were divers *French men* beneficed and preferred to "Priories and Abbies within this Realm, whereby the trea- "sures of the Realm were transported, and the counsels of "the King, and the secrets of the Realm disclosed unto the "Kings enemies to the great damage of the King and of the "Realm, that therefore all *Priors Aliens*, and other *French men* "beneficed, should avoid the Realm, excepet only *Priors Con-* "*ventuals*, such as have institution and induction: and this also "with a Proviso, that they be *Catholick*, and give sufficient "surety that they shall not disclose the counsels of the King "or of the Realm; so the Statute ; Hen 5. *cap.* 7. This also noted to us by *Pol. Virgil ad Reip. commodum sancitum est ut post hæc ejusmodi externis hominibus nullius Anglicani sacerdotii possessio traderetur.* Upon which point of statute the *Britons* belonging to the Queen *Dowager*, the widow once of *John de Montfort* Duke of *Bretagne*, were also expelled the Land by Act of Parliament, 3 *Hen.* 5. *cap.* 3. By this means the *Priors Aliens* being banished, their possessions fell into the Kings hands, as in *England* so also in these Islands; and their houses being all suppressed they became an accession to the patrimony Royall, the *demaine*, as our Lawyers call it, of the Crown.

These *Priors Aliens* thus exiled, were properly called *Priors Dative*, and removeable; but never such Aliens never so removeable, as they were now made by this Statute. What the condition of these *Priors* was, and wherein they differed from those which are called above by the name of *Priors Conventuals*; I cannot better tell then in the words of another of our Statutes, that namely of the 27 of *Hen.* 8. *cap.* "The Parliament had given unto the King, all Abbies, "Priories and Religious houses whatsoever, not being above "the value 200 *l.* in the old rent. Provided alwayes "(saith the letter of the Law) that this Act, *&c.* shall not "extend nor be prejudiciall to any Abbots or Priors of "any Monastery or Priory, *&c.* for or concerning such "Cels of Religious houses appertaining or belonging to "their Monasteries or Priories; in which Cels the Priors "or other chief Governours thereof, be under the obedi- "ence of the Abbots or Priors to whom such Cels be-

(7) *Priors dative*, how they differed from *Conventuals*.

"long.

"long. As the *Monke* or *Canons* of the Covent of their Mo-
"nasteries or Priories, and cannot be sued by the Lawes
"of this Realm, or by their own proper names for the
"possessions or other things appertaining to such Cels,
"whereof they be Priors and Governors; but must sue and
"be sued in, and by the names of the Abbots and Priors to
"whom they be now obedient, and to whom such Cels be-
"long, and be also Priors or Governours *dative* or *re-*
"*moveable* from time to time, and accomptez of the profits of
"such Cels, at the only will and pleasure of such of the
"Abbots and Priors, to whom such Cels belong, &c. This once
the difference between them, but now the *criticisme* may be
thought unnecessary.

(8) The condition of these Churches after that suppression.

To proceed, upon this suppression of the Priors and others the Religious houses in these Islands, and their Revenue falling unto the Crown; there grew a composition between the Curates and the Governours about their tithes, which hath continued hitherto unaltered, except in the addition of the Deserts, of which more hereafter. Which composition in the proportion of tithe unto which it doth amount, I here present unto your Lordship in a brief *Diagramme*, together with the the names of their Ministers and Justices now beng.

JARSEY.

CHAP. II. *the Estate of Guernzey and Jarsey.* 319

JARSEY.

(9) The Diagram.

Parishes.	Ministers.	Revenues.	Justices.
St. Martins	Mr. Bandinell sen. the Dean.	The 3 of the kings tithe.	Josuah de Carteret Seign. de Trinite.
St. Hillaries	Mr. Oliver the Sub-dean or Commissary.	The 10 of the kings tithe.	Dan du Maresque seign de Sammarez.
St. Saviours.	Mr. Essart.	The Deserts and 22 acres of Gleb.	Ph. L' Emprire Sr. de Dilament.
St. Clements.	Mr. Paris.	The 8 and 9 of the kings tithe.	Ph. de Carteret Sr. de Vinchiles de Laut.
St. Grevill'es.	Mr. de la Place.	The 8 and 9, &c.	Eli. du Maresque Sr. de Vinchiles abas.
St. Trinities.	Mr. Mollet.	The Deserts and the 10 of the kings tithe.	Eli. de Carteret Sr. de la Hagne.
St. Johns.	Mr. Brevin.	The Deserts, &c.	Joh. L' Emprire Sr. des augrace.
S. Lawrences.	Mr. Prinde.	The Deserts, &c.	Aron Messervie.
St. Maries.	Mr. Blanchivell, jun.	The 3 sheaf of the Kings tithe.	Ben. la cleche Sr. de Longueville.
St. Owens.	Mr. La clocke.	The Deserts, &c.	Jo. Harde.
St. Burlads.		The 8 and 9, &c.	Abr. Herod.
St. Peters.	Mr. Grueky.	The Deserts, &c.	Ph. Mirret.

Note that the taking of the 8 and 9 sheafe is called *French querrui*; as also that an acre of their measure is 40 Perches long and one in breadth, every Perche being 21 foot.

GUERNZEY.

GUERNZEY.

Parishes.	Ministers.	Revenues.	Justices.
*St.Pierre-porte. *St. Peters on the Sea.	M. de la March	The 7 of tithe and champarte.	Tho. Andrewes Sr. de Sammariz.
St. Martins.	Mr. de la Place	The like.	Pet. Carey sen.
La Forest.	Mr. Picote.	The 9 of tithe and champarte.	John Fautrat Sr. de Coq.
Tortevall } Mr. Fautrat.		The 3 of tithe and champarte.	Joh. Bonamy.
S. Andrews }		The 4 of, &c.	Joh. Ketville.
†St. Pierre du Bois. †St. Peters in the Wood.	Mr. Perchard.	The 3 of the tithe only.	James Guile Sr. des Robais.
St. Saviours		The Desert and the tenths in all 600 sheafes.	Tho. Blundell.
Chastell.	Mr. Panisee.	The 9 of the tithe only.	Pet. de Beauvoyre Sr. des Granges St. Mich.
St. Michael in the vale } St. Sampson }	Mr. Millet.	The 4 of the Kings tithe only. The like.	Pet. Gosselin. Josias Merchant.
Serke.	Mr. Brevin.	20 l. stipend and 20 quarters of corn.	Pet. Carey jun.
Alderney.	Mr. Mason.	20 l. stipend.	

Note that the Parish called in this *Diagram*, *La Forest*, is dedicated as some say, to the *holy Trinity*; as other to St. *Margaret*, that which is here called *Tortevall*, as some suppose unto St. *Philip*, others will have it to St. *Martha*; but that of *Chastell* to the hand of the blessed Virgin, which is therefore called in the Records, our *Ladies Castle*. Note also, that the Justices or Jurates are here placed, as near as I could learn, according to their Seniority, not

CHAP. II. *the Estate of* Guernzey *and* Jarsey. 321

not as particularly appertaining to those Parishes against which they are disposed.

For the better understanding of this *Diagram*, there are three words which need a commentary, as being meerly Aliens to the *English* tongue, and hardly *Denizens* in *French*. Of these, that in the *Diagrams* called the *Deserts*, is the first. A word which properly signifieth a Wildernesse, or any wast ground from which ariseth little profit. As it is taken at this present and on this occasion, it signifieth a field which formerly was laid to waste, and is now made arable. The case this: At the suppression of the *Priors Aliens* and the composition made betwixt the Curates and the Governours, there was in either Island much ground of small advantage to the Church or to the owner, which they called *Les Deserts*. But the Countreys after growing populous, and many mouths requiring much provision, these Deserts were broke up and turned into tillage. Hereupon the Curates made challenge to the tithes, as not at all either intended or contained in the former composition. The Governours on the other side alleadging custome, that those grounds had never paid the Tithe, and therefore should not. Nor could the *Clergy* there obtain their rights untill the happy entrance of King *James* upon these Kingdoms. A Prince of all others a most indulgent father to the Church. By him and by a letter Decretory from the Counsell, it was adjudged in favour of the Ministery; the Letter bearing date at *Greenwich* June the last, *anno* 1608. subscribed T. *Ellesmere* Canc. R. *Salisbury*, H. *Northampton*, E. *Worcester*, T. *Suffolke*, *Exeter* Zouch, Wotton, Cesar, Herbert. A matter certainly of much importance in the consequence, as making known unto your Lordship how easie a thing it is in the authority royall to free the Church from that tyranny of *custome* and *prescription* under which it groweth.

The next of these three words to be explained, is in the note *French Querrui*, which in the note is told us to be the 8 and 9 sheaf; by which account or way of tithing, the Minister in 50 sheafs receiveth 6, which is one sheaf more then the ordinary tithe. The word corrupted, as I

(10) What is meant by *Deserts*,

French *Querrui*, and by conceive,

T t

conceive, from the *French* word *Charrue*, which signifieth a Plough, and then *French querrui* is as much as Plough-right, alluding to the custome of some Lords in *France*, who used to give their husbandmen or villains, as a guerdon for their toyle, the 8 and 9 of their increase.

Champart.

As for the last, that, *viz.* which the *Diagram* calleth *Champart*, it intimates in the origination of the word, a part or portion of the field, that which the Lord in chief reserved unto himself.

In *Guernzey* it is constantly the 12 sheaf of the whole crop, the Farmer in the counting of his sheafes casting aside the 10 for the King, and the 12 which is the Champart, for the Lord.

Now here in *Guernzey* (for those of the other Isle have no such custome) there is a double *Champart*, that namely *Du Roy*, belonging to the King, whereof the Clergy have the tithe, and that of St. *Michael en leval*, not titheable. The reason is, because at the suppression of the Priorie of St. *Michael*, which was the only *Religious house* in these Islands, which subsisted of it self; the Tenants made no tendry of this *Champart*, and so it lay amongst *concealments*. At the last, Sir *Thomas Leighton* the Governour here recovered it unto the Crown by course of Law, and at his own charges; whereupon the Queen licenced him to make sale of it, to his best advantage, which accordingly he did.

(11) The alteration of Religion in these Islands.

For the Religion in these Islands, it hath been generally such as that professed with us in *England*, and as much varied. When the *Priors Aliens* were banished *England* by King *Henry* V. they also were exiled from hence. Upon the demolition of our Abbeys; the Priory of St. *Michael*, and that little Oratory of our *Lady of Lebu*, became a ruine. The *Masse* was here also trodden down whilest King *Edward* stood, and raised again at the exaltation of Queen *Mary*. Nay even that fiery tryall, which so many of Gods servants underwent in the short Reign of that misguided Lady, extended

tended even unto these poor Islanders; and that, as I conceive, in a more fearfull tragedy, then any, all that time presented on the Stage of England. The story in the brief is this;

Katharine Gowches a poor widow of St. Peters-parte in *Guernzey*, was noted to be much absent from the Church, and her two daughters guilty of the same neglect. Upon this they were presented before *Jaques Amy* then Dean of the Island, who finding in them, that they held opinions contrary unto those then allowed, about the Sacrament of the Altar, pronounced them *Hereticks* and condemned them to the fire. The poor women on the other side pleaded for themselves, that that Doctrine had been taught them in the time of King *Edward*; but if the Queen was otherwise disposed, they were content to be of her Religion. This was fair, but this would not serve; for by the Dean they were delivered unto *Elier Gosselin* the then Bailiffe, and by him unto the fire, *July* 18. *Anno Dom.* 1556. One of these daughters, *Perotine Massey* she was called, was at that time great with childe; her husband, which was a Minister, being, in those dangerous times, fled the Island; in the middle of the flames and anguish of her torments, her belly brake in sunder, and her child, a goodly boy, fell down into the fire, but was presently snatched up by one *W. House* one of the by-standers. Upon the noise of this strange accident, the cruell Bailiffe returned command, that the poor Infant must be cast again into the flames; which was accordingly performed; and so that pretty babe was borne a Martyr, and added to the number of the *Holy Innocents*. A cruelty not paralleld in any story, not heard of amongst the Nations. But such was the pleasure of the Magistrate, as one in the Massacre of the younger *Maximinus*, viz. *Canis pessimi ne catulum esse relinquendum*; that not any issue should be left alive of an Heretick Parent.

(11) Persecution here in the dayes of Q. Mary.

The horrror of which fact stirred in me some Poeticall Fancies (or Furies rather) which having long lien dormant, did break out at last, indignation thus supplying those suppressed conceptions.

Si natura negat, dabit indignatio versum.

Holla ye pampred Sires of Rome, *forbear*
To act such murders, as a Christian ear
Hears with more horrour, then the Jews *relate*
The dire effects of Herods *fear and hate,*
When that vilde Butcher, caus'd to cut in sunder
Every Male childe of two years old and under.

These Martyrs in their cradles, from the womb
This pass'd directly to the fiery tomb;
Baptiz'd in Flames and Bloud, a Martyr born,
A setting sun in the first dawn of morn:
Yet shining with more heat, and brighter glory
Then all Burnt-offerings *in the Churches story.*

Holla ye pampred Rabines of the West,
Where learnt you thus to furnish out a Feast
With Lambs of the first minute? What disguise
Finde you to mask this horrid Sacrifice?
When the old Law so meekly did forbid,
In the Dams milk to boil the tender Kid.

What Riddles have we here? an unborn birth,
Hurried to Heaven, when not made ripe for Earth;
Condemned to die before it liv'd, a twin
To its own mother; not impeached of sin,

Yet doom'd to death, that breath'd but to expire,
That scap'd the flames to perish in the fire.

Rejoyce ye Tyrants of old times, your name
Is made lesse odious on the breath of fame,
By our most monstrous cruelties; the Males
Slaughtered in Egypt, *waigh not down these scales.*
A Fed to equall this no former age
Hath given in Books, or fancie on the Stage.

This fit of indignation being thus passed over, I can proceed with greater patience to the rest of the story of this Island, which in brief is this:

That after the death of Queen *Mary*, Religion was again restored in the reformation of it to these Islands. In which state it hath ever since continued in the main and substance of it; but not without some alteration in the circumstance and forme of Government. For whereas notwithstanding the alteration of Religion in these Islands they still continued under the Diocese of *Constance*, during the whole Empire of King *Henry* the VIII. and *Edward* the VI. yet it seemed good to Queen *Elizabeth* upon some reasons of State, to annex them unto that of *Winton*.

(13) The Islands annexed for ever unto the Diocese of *Winton*, and so what Reason

The first motive of it was, because that Bishop refused to abjure the pretended power which the Pope challengeth in Kingdomes, as other of the *English* Prelates did; but this displeasure held not long. For presently upon a consideration of much service and intelligence which might reasonably be expected from that Prelate, as having such a necessary dependence on this Crown, they were again permitted to his jurisdiction.

At the last, and if I well remember, about the 12 year of that excellent Ladies Reign, at the perswasion of Sir *Amias Paulet*, and Sir *Tho. Leighton* then Governours, they were for ever united unto *Winchester*. The pretences that so there might a fairer way be opened to the *reformation* of Religion; to which that Bishop was an enemy, and that the secrets of the State might not be carryed over into *France*, by reason of that entercourse which needs must be between a Bishop and his Ministers. The truth is, they were both resolved to settle the *Geneva* discipline in every Parish in each Island; for which cause they had sent for *Snape* and *Cartwright*, those great incendiaries of the *English* Church to lay the ground-work of that building. Add to this that there was some glimmering also of a Confiscation in the ruine of the Deanries; with the spoyles whereof they held it fit to enrich their Governments. Matters not possible to be effected, had he of *Constance* continued in his place and power. But of this more in the next Chapter.

Chap. III.

(1) *The condition of* Geneva *under their Bishop.* (2) *The alteration there both in* Politie, *and* (3) *in Religion.* (4) *The state of that Church before the coming of* Calvin *thither.* (5) *The conception,* (6) *birth, and* (7) *growth of the* New Discipline. (8) *The quality of* Lay-elders. (9) *The different proceedings of* Calvin, (10) *and* Beza *in the propagation of that cause.* (11) *Both of them enemies to the Church of* England. (12) *The first entrance of this platforme into the Islands.* (13) *A permission of it by the Queen and the Councell in St.* Peters *and St.* Hilaries. (14) *The letters of the Councell to that purpose.* (15) *The tumults raised in* England *by the brethren.* (16) Snape *and* Cartwright *establish the new Discipline in the rest of the Islands.*

THus having shewed unto your Lordship the affairs and condition of these Churches till the Reformation of Religion; I come next in the course of my designe, unto that Innovation made amongst them in the point of Discipline. For the more happy dispatch of which businesse, I must crave leave to ascend a little higher into the story of change, then the introduction of it into those little Islands. So doing, I shall give your Lordship better satisfaction, then if I should immediately descend upon that Argument; the rather because I shall deliver nothing in this discourse not warranted to be by the chief

(1) The condition of Geneva under their Bishop.

chief contrivers of the Discipline. To begin then with the first originall and commencement of it; so it is that it took the first beginning at a City of the *Allobroges* or *Savoyards*, called *Geneva*, and by that name mentioned in the first of *Cesars* Commentaries. A Town situate at the end of *Lacus Lemannus*, and divided by *Rhodanus* or *Rhosne* into two parts. Belonging formerly in the Soveraignty of it to the Duke of *Savoy*; but in the profits and possession to their Bishop and homager of that Dukedome. To this Bishop then there appertained not only an Ecclesiasticall jurisdiction, as Governour of the Church under the Archbishop of *Vienna*, in *Daulphinoys* his Metropolitane; but a jurisdction also temporall, as Lord and Master of the Town under the protection of the Duke of *Savoy*. This granted by the testimony of *Calvin* in his Epistle unto Cardinall *Sadolet*, dated the last of *August* 1539. *Habebat sane* (saith he) *jus gladii, & alias civilis jurisdictionis partes*; but as he conceived, I know not on what grounds, *Magistratui ereptas*, fraudulently taken from the Civill Magistrate.

(2) The alteration there both in Religion,

In this condition it continued till the year 1528. when those of *Berne*, after a publick disputation held, had made an alteration in Religion. At that time *Viret* and *Farellus*, men studious of the Reformation had gotten footing in *Geneva*, and diligently there sollicited the cause and entertainment of it. But this proposall not plausibly accepted by the Bishop, they dealt with those of the lower rank, amongst whom they had gotten most credit, and taking opportunity by the actions and example of those of *Berne*, they compelled the Bishop and his Clergy to abandon the Town, and after proceeded to the reforming of his Church. This also avowed by *Calvin* in his Epistle to the said Cardinall, *viz*. That the Church had been reformed and setled before his coming into those quarters by *Viret* and *Farellus*, and that he only had approved of their proceedings, *Sed quia que a* Vireto *&* Farello *facta essent, suffragio meo comprobavi*, &c. as he there hath it.

and

(1) in Polity.

Nor did they only in that tumult alter the Doctrine and orders of the Church, but changed also the Government of the Town, disclaiming all alleagiance either to their Bishop or their Duke, and standing on their own liberty as a free City. And for this also they are indebted to the active counsels of *Farellus*. For thus *Calvin* in his Epistle to the Ministers of *Zurich*, dated the 26 of *November* 1553. *Cum hic nuper esset frater noster* Farellus, *cui se totos debent*, &c. and anone after, *Sed deploranda est senatus nostri cæcitas, quod libertatis suæ patrem*, &c. speaking of their ingratitude to this *Farellus*.

The power and dominion of that City thus put into the hands of the common people, and all things left at liberty and randome, it could not be expected that there should any discipline [be] observed, or good order in the Church. The Common-councell of the Town disposed of it as they pleased; and if any crime which antiently belonged to Ecclesiasticall jurisdiction, did hap to be committed, it was punished by order from that Councell. No censures Ecclesiasticall, no sentence of Excommunication thought on at that time, either here at *Geneva*, or in any other of the popular Churches. *Si quidem excommunicationi in aliis Ecclesiis nullus locus*, as *Beza* hath it in the life of *Calvin*. And the same *Calvin* in his Epistle to the Ministers of *Zurich* affirmes no lesse in these words, *viz. Nec me latet pios & doctos esse homines, quibus sub principibus Christianis non videtur esse necessaria Excommunicatio*; so he. (4) The estate of that Church before the coming of *Calvin* thither.

Thus was it with the Church and City of *Geneva* at the first coming of *Calvin* to them; a man of excellent abilities, and one that had attained a good repute in many places of the *French* dominions. Not finding that assurance in the Realm of *France*, he resolved to place himselfe at *Basil* or at *Strasburg*. But taking *Geneva* in his way, upon the importunity of *Farellus*, he condescended to make that place the scene of his endeavours, and his assent once known, he was admitted straight to be one of their ordinary preachers and their Divinity reader. *Mens. Aug. anno* 1536. This done he presently negotiates with the people, publickly to abjure the Papacy: nor so only, but (as *Beza* hath it in his life) *Quod doctrinam & disciplinam capitibus aliquot comprehensam admitterent*; that they also should give way to such a discipline, which he and his associates had agreed on. A matter (5) The conception.

U u

matter at the last effected, but not without much difficulty, and on the 20 of *July*, anno 1537. the whole City bound themselves by oath accordingly; which discipline of what quality it was I cannot learn: sure I am, it had no affinity with that in use amongst the ancients. For thus himself in his Epistle above mentioned unto *Sadolet*, *Disciplinam qualem vetus habuit Ecclesia apud nos non esse* [*dicis*]; *neq; nos diffitemur*.

(6) The Birth and

The Discipline hitherto was only in conception, before it came unto maturity, and ready for the birth, the people weary of this new yoak began to murmur, and he resolutely bent not to vary from his first purpose, was in that discontentment banished the Town, together with *Farellus* and *Coraldus* his colleagues, anno 1538. Three years, or thereabouts he continued in this exile, being bountifully entertained at *Strasburg*; from whence with unresistible importunity he was again recalled by that unconstant multitude. A desire to which by no means he would hearken, unlesse both they and all their Ministers would take a solemn oath to admit a compleat forme of discipline, not arbitrary, not changeable; but to remain in force for ever after. Upon assurance of their conformity herein, he returns unto them like an other *Tully* unto *Rome*; and certainly we may say of him as the Historian of the other, *Nec quisquam aut expulsus est invidiosius, aut receptus lætius.* On the 13 of *September*, 1541. he is admitted into the Town; and now (there being strength enough to deliver) the Discipline such as he had contrived it, was established on the 20 of *November* following.

(7) Growth of the new Discipline.

This new Discipline thus borne into the world, was yet crush'd almost in the growth of it, by the faction of *Perinus* at that time Captain of the people, and of great power among the many. Twelve years together, but yet with many lucid intervals, did it struggle with that opposition, and at the last was in a manner ruined and oppressed by it. For whereas the Consistory had given sentence against one *Berteliet*, even in the highest censure of *Excommunication*, the Common-councell not only absolved him from that censure, but foolishly decreed, That Excommunication

munication and *Absolution* did properly belong to them. Upon this he is again resolved to quit the Town; but at last the Controversie is by joynt consent referred unto the judgement of four Cities of the *Switzers*. Then did he labour in particular to consider of it, not as a matter of ordinary consequence, but (as in his said Epistle to those in *Zurich*) *De toto Ecclesiæ hujus statu*, &c. such as on which the whole being of that Church depended. In the end he so contrived it, that the answer was returned to *Geneva*, *Nil contra tentandum*; that they should not seek to alter what was so well established; and hereupon they were all contented to obey. By which means this Infant-discipline, with such variety of troubles born and nursed, attained unto a fair and manly growth, and in short space so well improved, that it durst bid defiance unto Kings and Princes.

The chief means by which this new Platforme was admitted in *Geneva*, and afterwards desired in other places, was principally that parity and equality, which it seemed to carry, the people being as it were a double part in it, and so advanced into the highest Magistracy. For so the cunning Architect had contrived it, that for every pillar of the Church, there should be also two Pillasters, or rather underproppers of the people. *Non solos verbi Ministros sedere judices in consistorio; sed numerum duplo majorem, partim ex minori senatu, partim ex majori delige*; so he in his Remonstrance unto them of *Zurich*, affixed to his Epistle. These men they honour with the name of *Elders*, and to them the charge is specially committed of inquiring into the lives of those within their division, viz. *Sitne domus pacata & recte composita*, &c. as the Epistle to *Gasp. Olivianus* doth instruct us. By which device there is not only a kind of satisfaction given to the multitude, but a great deal of envie is declined by the Ministery; which that curious and unneighbourly inquisition would otherwise derive upon them. And certainly, were there in these *Elders*, as they call them, a power only of information, the device might be so much the more allowable. But that such simple

(8) The quality of Lay-Elders.

wretches should caper from the shop-board upon the Bench, and there be interessed in the weightiest causes of the Church, *Censure* and *Ordination* is a monster never known among the *Antients*. Especially considering, that the mindes of these poor *Laicks*, is all the while intent upon their penny; and when the Court is risen they hasten to their shops as *Quinctius* the *Dictator* did in *Florus* to his plough, *Ut ad opus relictum festinasse videantur.*

(9) The different proceeding of *Calvin*.

The businesse thus happily succeeding at *Geneva*, and his name continually growing into higher credit; his next endevour was to plant that government in all places which with such trouble had been fitted unto one. Certainly we do as much affect the issue of our braines as of our bodies, and labour with no lesse vehemency to advance them. And so it was with him in this particular, his after-writings tending mainly to this end, that his new Platforme might have found an universall entertainment. But this modestly enough, and chiefly by way of commendation. Two examples only shall be sufficient, because I will not be too great a trouble to your Lordship in the collection of a tedious Catalogue. *Gasper Olevianus* a Minister of the Church of *Tryers*, by his Letters bearing date the 12 of *April*, anno 1560. giveth notice unto *Calvin* of the State of their affaires; and withall that he found the people willing to condescend unto a Discipline. *Calvin* in his answer presents him with a summary of that platforme, raised lately at *Geneva*, and then closeth with him thus, *Compendium hoc satis putavi fore ex quo formam aliquam conciperes, quam præscribere non debui. Tu quod putabis utile istic fore,* &c. In this he doth sufficiently expresse his desire to have his project entertained; in that which followeth he doth signifie his joy that the world had made it welcome. An epistle written to a certain *Quidam* of *Polonia*, dated the year 1561. Wherein he doth congratulate the admission of the Gospell (as he cals it) in that Kingdom. And then, *Hæc etiam non pœnitenda gaudia accessis, cum audio disciplinam cum Evangelii professione conjunctam,* &c. thus he.

But

But *Beza* his successour goeth more plainly to the businesse, and will not commend this project to the Churches, but impose it on them. This it was, that made him with such violence cry down the *Hierarchie* of the Church, the plague of Bishops, as he cals it. *Hanc pestem caveant qui Ecclesiam salvam cupiunt*, &c. *Et ne illam quæso unquam admittas* (he speaketh it unto *Cnoxe*) *quantumvis unitatis retinendæ specie*, &c. *blandiatur.* This was it which made him reckon it as a note essentiall of the Church * without which it was not possible to subsist; a point so necessary, *Ut ab ea recedere non magis quam ab religionis ipsius placitis, liceat. Epist.* 83. that it was as dangerous to depart from this, as from the weightiest mysteries of Religion. This in a word was it which made him countenance those turbulent spirits, who had so dangerously embroyled our Churches, and prepared it unto ruine; but of them and their proceedings more anone.

(10) *Beza* in the propagation of that cause.

* V. cap. 5. n.

And certainly it was a matter of no small grief and discontent unto them both, that when so many Churches had applauded their invention, the Church of *England* only should be found untractable. Hereupon it was that *Calvin* tels the *English* Church in *Franckford* (in his Epistle to them *anno* 1555) how he had noted in their publick Liturgy, *Multas tolerabiles ineptias*, many tolerable vanities; *sacis Papisticæ reliquias*, the relicks of the filth of Popery: and that there was not in it *ea puritas quæ optanda foret*, such piety as was expected. Hereupon it was that *Beza* being demanded by the brethren, what he conceived of some chief matters then in question; returned a *Non probamus* to them all. The particulars are too many to be now recited, and easie to be seen in the 120 of his Epistles, the Epistle dated from *Geneva, anno* 1567. and superscribed, *Ad quosdam Anglicarum ecclesiarum fratres super nonnullis in Ecclesiasticis politiis controversis.*

(11) Both of these enemies to the Church of *England*.

Yet at the last they got some footing, though not in *England*, in these Islands which are members of it, and as it were the Suburbs of that City. The means by which it

(12) The first entrance of these Partisans into these Islands.

it entred, the resort hither of such *French Ministers* as came hither for support in the times of persecution and the Civill wars, *anno* 1561. and 62. Before their coming that forme of prayer was here in use which was allowed with us in *England*. But being as all others are, desirous of change, and being also well encouraged by the Governors, who by this means hoped to have the spoyle of the poor *Deanries*; both Islands joyned together in alliance or confederacy to petition the Queens Majesty for an approbation of this Discipline, *anno* 1563.

(13) A permission of it by the Queen, &c.

The next year following, the Seignieur *de St. Oen,* and *Nich. de Soulmont* were delegated to the Court, to sollicite this affaire; and there they found such favour, that their desire received a gracious answer, and full of hope they returned unto their homes. In the mean time the Queen being strongly perswaded that this design would much advance the Reformation in those Islands, was contented to give way unto it in the Towns of St. *Peters-port,* and of St. *Hilaries,* but no further. To which purpose there were Letters Decretory from the Councell directed to the *Bailiff,* the *Jurates,* and others of each Island; the tenor whereof was as followeth.

(14) The Letters of the Councell to that purpose.

"AFter our very hearty commendations unto you.
"Where the Queens most excellent Majesty under-
"standeth that the Isles of *Guernzey* and *Jarsey* have anti-
"enly depended on the Diocese of *Constance,* and that there
"be certain Churches in the same Diocese well reformed,
"agreeably throughout in Doctrine as is set forth in this
"Realm; knowing therewith that they have a Minister
"which ever since his arrivall in *Jarsey,* hath used the like
"order of Preaching and administration, as in the said
"Reformed Churches, or as it is used in the *French* Church
"at *London*; her Majesty for divers respects and conside-
"rations moving her Highnesse is well pleased to admit
"the same order of Preaching and Administration to be
"continued at St. *Heliers*, as hath been hitherto accustomed
"by

CHAP. III. *the Estate of* Guernzey *and* Jarsey.   335

"by the said Minister. Provided always that the residue
"of the Parishes in the said Isle, shall diligently put apart
"all superstitions used in the said Diocese; and so con-
"tinue there the order of Service ordained and set forth
"within this Realm, with the injunctions necessary for that
"purpose; wherein you may not fail diligently to give
"your aides and assistance, as best may serve for the ad-
"vancement of Gods glory. And so fare you well. From
"*Richmond* the 7 day of *August*, Anno 1565. Subscri-
"bed,

  N. Bacon. Will. Northamp. R. Lecester.
  Gul. Clynton. R. Rogers. Fr. Knols.
  William Cecil.

 Where note, that the same Letter, the names only of the places being changed, and subscribed by the same men, was sent also unto those of *Guernzey* for the permission of the said Discipline in the haven of *St. Peters*. And thus fortified by authority they held their first Synod according to the constitutions of that platforme on the 22. of *September*, and at St. *Peters-porte* in *Guernzey*, anno 1567.

 By this means, by this improvident assent (if I may so call it) to this new discipline in these Islands; her Majesty did infinitely prejudice her own affaires, and opened that gap unto the Brethren, by which they had almost made entrance unto meer confusion in this state and Kingdome. For whereas during the Empire of Queen *Mary*, *Goodman*, *Whittingham*, *Gilbie* and divers others of our Nation, had betook themselves unto *Geneva*, and there been taught the *Consistorian practises*; they yet retained themselves within the bounds of peace and duty. But no sooner had the Queen made known by this assent that she might possibly be drawn to like the Platforme of *Geneva*; but presently the Brethren set themselves on work to impose those new inventions on our Churches. By *Genebrard* we learn in his *Chronologie*, *ortos Puritanos anno* 1566. and that their first
               Belweather

(15) The tumults raised in *England* by the Brethren.

Belweather was called *Sampson*; a puissant Champion doubtlesse in the cause of *Israel*. By our own Antiquary in his Annals it is referred *ad Annum* 68. and their Leaders were *Coliman*, *Fudson*, *Bellingham* and *Benson*. By both it doth appear that the brethren stirred not here, till the approbation of their Discipline in those Islands, or till the execution of it, in their first Synod. No sooner had they this incouragement, but they presently mustered up their forces, betook themselves unto the quarrell, and the whole Realme was on the suddain in an uproar. The Parliaments continually troubled with their *Supplications*, *Admonitions* and the like; and when they found not there that favour which they looked for, they denounce this dreadfull curse against them, *That there shall not be a man of their seed that shall prosper to be a Parliament man, or bear rule in England any more.* The Queen exclaimed upon in many of their Pamphlets, her honourable Counsell scandalously censured as opposers of the Gospell. The Prelates every were cryed down as *Antichristian, Petty-popes, Bishops of the Devill, cogging and cousening knaves, dumb dogs, enemies of God,* &c. and their Courts and Chanceries the *Synagogues of Satan*. After this they erected privately their *Presbyteries* in divers places of the Land; and cantoned the whole Kingdome into their severall *Classes* and divisions; and in a time when the *Spaniards* were expected, they threaten to petition the Queens Majesty with 100000 hands. In conclusion what dangerous counsels were concluded on by *Hacket* and his *Apostles*, with the assent and approbation of the Brethren, is extant in the Chronicles. A strange and peevish generation of men, that having publick enemies unto the faith abroad, would rather turn the edge of their Swords upon their Mother and her children. But such it seemeth was the holy pleasure of *Geneva*; and such their stomach not to brook a private opposition.

Cumq; superba feret Babylon spolianda trophæis,
Bella geri placuit, nullos habitura triumphos.

Yet

Yet was it questionlesse some comfort to their souls, that their devices, however it succeeded ill in *England*, had spred it self abroad in *Guernzey* and in *Jarsey*, where it had now possession of the whole Islands. For not content with that allowance her Majesty had given unto it, in the Towns of St. *Peters* and St. *Hillaries*; the Governours having first got these Isles to be dissevered from the Diocese of *Constance*, permit it unto all the other Parishes. The better to establish it, the great supporters of the cause in *England*, *Snape* and *Cartwright* are sent for to the Islands; the one of them being made the tributary Pastor of the Castle of *Cornet*, the other of that of *Mont-orguel*. Thus qualified forsooth they conveene the Churches of each Island, and in a Synod held in *Guernzey*, anno 1576. the whole body of the Discipline is drawn into a forme. Which forme of Discipline I here present unto your Lordship, faithfully translated according to an authentick copy, given unto me by Mr. *Painsee* Curate of our Ladies Church of *Chastell* in the Isle of *Guernzey*.

CHAP. IV.

The Discipline Ecclesiasticall, *according as it hath been in practise of the Church after the* Reformation *of the same, by the* Ministers, Elders, *and* Deacons *of the Isles of* Guernzey, Jarsey, Serke, *and* Alderney; *confirmed by the authority and in the presence of the Governours of the same Isles in a Synod holden in* Guernzey *the* 28 *of* June 1576. *And afterwards revived by the said* Ministers *and* Elders, *and confirmed by the said Governers in a Synod holden also in* Guernzey *the* 11, 12, 13, 14, 15, *and* 17 *dayes of* October 1597.

CHAP. I.

Of the Church in Generall.

Article I.

1. THe Church is the whole company of the faithfull, comprehending as well those that bear publick office in the same, as the rest of the people.

II.

2. No one Church shall pretend any superiority or dominion over another; all of them being equall in power, and having one only head *CHRIST JESUS.*

3. The

III.

3. The Governours of the *Christian* Church where the Magistrates professe the Gospell, are the Magistrates which professe it, as bearing chief stroke in the Civill Government; and the Pastors and Overseers [or *Superintendents*] as principall in the Government Ecclesiasticall.

IV.

4. Both these jurisdictions are established by the law of God, as necessary to the Government and welfare of his Church; the one having principally the care and charge of mens bodies and of their goods; to govern them according to the Laws, and with the temporall Sword; the other having cure of souls and consciences, to discharge their duties according to the Canons of the Church, and with the sword of Gods word. Which jurisdiction ought so to be united, that there be no confusion, and so to be divided, that there be no contrariety; but joyntly to sustain and defend each other, as the armes of the same body.

CHAP. II.

Of the Magistrate.

THe *Magistrate* ought so to watch over mens persons and their goods; as above all things to provide that the honour and true worship of God may be preserved. And as it is his duty to punish such as offend in Murder, Theft, and other sins against the second Table; so ought he also to correct Blasphemers, Atheists and Idolaters, which offend against the first; as also all those which contrary to good order and the common peace, addict themselves to riot and unlawfull games; and on the other side he ought to cherish those which are well affected, and to advance them both to wealth and honours.

CHAP. III.

Of Ecclesiasticall functions in generall.

Article I.

1. OF Officers Ecclesiasticall, some have the charge to teach or instruct, which are the *Pastors* and *Doctors*; others are as it were the eye to oversee the life and manners of Christs flock, which are the *Elders*; and to others there is committed the disposing of the treasures of the Church, and of the poor mans Box, which are the *Deacons*.

II.

2. The *Church officers* shall be elected by the *Ministers* and *Elders*, without depriving the people of their right; and by the same authority shall be discharged, suspended and deposed, according as it is set down in the Chapter of Censures.

III.

3. None ought to take upon him any function in the Church without being lawfully called unto it.

IV.

4. No *Church officer* shall or ought to pretend any superiority or dominion over his companions, *viz.* neither a Minister over a Minister, nor an Elder over an Elder, nor a Deacon over a Deacon; yet so, that they give reverence and respect unto each other, either according to their age, or according to those gifts and graces which God hath vouchsafed to one more then another.

V.

5. No man shall be admitted to any office in the Church, unlesse he be endowed with gifts fit for the discharge of that office unto which he is called; nor unlesse there be good testimony of his life and conversation; of
which

which diligent enquiry shall be made before his being called.

VI.

6. All those which shall enter upon any publick charge in the Church, shall first subscribe to the confession of the faith used in the reformed Churches, and to the Discipline Ecclesiasticall.

VII.

7. All those which are designed for the administration of any publick office in the Church, shall be first nominated by the *Governours*, or their Lieutenants; after whose approbation they shall be proposed unto the people, and if they meet not any opposition, they shall be admitted to their charge within fifteen dayes after.

VIII.

8. Before the nomination and admission of such as are called unto employment in the Church, they shall be first admonished of their duty; as well that which concerneth them in particular, as to be exemplary unto the people, the better to induce them to live justly and religiously before God and man.

IX.

9. Although it appertain to all in generall to provide that due honour and obedience be done unto the Queens most excellent Majesty, to the *Governours*, to their Lieutenants, and to all the officers of Justice; yet notwithstanding they which bear office in the Church, ought chiefly to bestir themselves in that behalf, as an example unto others.

X.

10. Those that bear office in the Church, shall not forsake their charge without the privity and knowledge of the *Consistory*, and that they shall not be dismissed, but by the same order by which they were admitted.

XI.

11. Those that bear office in the Church, shall employ themselves in visiting the sick, and such as are in prison, to administer a word of comfort to them, as also to all such as have need of consolation.

XII.

12. They shall not publish that which hath been treated in the *Consistory, Colloquies,* or *Syneds,* either unto the parties whom it may concern, or to any others, unlesse they be commanded so to do.

XIII.

13. They which beare office in the Church, if they abstain from the *Lords Supper,* and refuse to be reconciled, having been admonished of it, and persisting in their error, shall be deposed, and the causes of their deposition manifested to the people.

CHAP. IV.

Of the Ministers.

Article I.

1. THose which aspire unto the *Ministery*, shall not be admitted to propose the word of God, unlesse they be indued with learning, and have attained unto the knowledge of the Greek and Hebrew tongues, if it be possible.

II.

2. The *Ministers* shall censure the *proponents*, having first diligently examined them in the principal points of learning requisite unto a *Minister*. And having heard them handle the holy Scriptures, as much as they think necessary, if they be thought fit for the Ministery, they shall be sent unto the Churches then being void, to propose the Word of God three or four times, and that bare-headed. And if the

Churches

Churches approve them, and desire them for their Pastors, the *Coloquie* shall depute a *Minister*, to give them institution by *the imposition of hands*.

III.

3. The *Ministers* sent hither or resorting for refuge to these Isles, and bringing with them a good testimony from the places whence they came, shall be employed in those Churches which have most need of them, giving and receiving the *band of association*.

IV.

4. They which are elected and admitted into the *Ministery*, shall continue in it all their lives, unlesse they be deposed for some fault by them committed. And as for those which shall be hindred from the encreasing of their Ministery, either by sicknesse or by age, the honour and respect due unto it, notwithstanding shall be theirs.

V.

5. The *Ministers* which flie hither as for refuge, and are employed in any Parish during the persecution, shall not depart from hence untill six moneths after leave demanded; to the end, the Church be not unprovided of a *Pastor*.

VI.

6. The *Ministers* shall visite every houshold of their flockes, once in the year at the least; but this at their discretion.

VII.

7. The *Ministers* shall propose the Word of God, every one in his rank, and that once every moneth; in such a place and on such a day as shall be judged most convenient.

VIII.

8. If there be any which is offended at the Preaching of any *Minister*, he shall repair unto the said *Minister* within four and twenty houres for satisfaction. And if he cannot

not receive it from the *Ministers*, he shall addresse himselfe within eight dayes to the *Consistory*; in default whereof his information shall not be admitted. If any difference arise, the *Ministers* shall determine of it at their next conference.

CHAP. V.

Of Doctors and of School-masters.

Article I.

1. The office of a *Doctor* in the Church is next unto the *Pastors*. His charge is to expound the Scripture in his Lectures, without applying it by way of Exhortation. They are to be elected by the *Colloquie*.

II.

2. The *School-masters* shall be first nominated by them, to whom the right of nomination doth belong, and shall be afterwards examined by the *Ministers*; who taking examination of their learning, shall also informe themselves of their behaviour; as viz. whether they be modest, and not debauched; to the end, that may be an example to their Scholars, and that they by their ill Doctrine, they bring not any Sect into the Church. After which examination if they are found fit for the institution of youth, they shall be presented to the people.

III.

3. They shall instruct their Scholars in the fear of God, and in good learning, in modesty and civility, that so their Schooles may bring forth able men, both for the Church and Common-wealth.

IV.

4. They shall instruct them in *Grammar*, *Rhetorick* and *Logick*, and of *Classicke* authors, in the most pure both for learning and language; for fear lest children reading
lascivious

V.

5. If they perceive any of their Scholars to be towardly and of good hope, they shall advise their Parents to bring them up to the attainment of good learning; or else shall obtain for them of the *Governours* and *Magistrates*, that they maintain them at the publick charge.

VI.

6. They shall cause their Scholars to come to Sermons and to Catechismes, there to answer to the Minister; and they shall take their places neer the *chaire*, to be seen of all, that so they may demean themselves orderly in the Church of God.

VII.

7. The *Ministers* shall oversee the *School-masters*, to the end that the youth be well instructed; and for this cause shall hold their *Visitations* twice a year, the better to understand how they profit. If it be thought expedient, they may take with them some one or two of the neighbour *Ministers*.

CHAP. VI.

Of the Elders.

Article I.

1. THe *Elders* ought to preserve the Church in good order, together with the Ministers; and shall take care especially that the Church be not destitute of Pastors, of whom the care shall appertain to them to see that they be honestly provided for. They shall watch also over all the flock, especially over that part of it committed to them by the *Consistory*; diligently employing themselves to admonish and reprehend such as are faulty,

ty, to confirme the good, and reconcile such as are at difference.

II.

2. They shall certifie all scandals to the *Consistory*.

III.

3. They shall visit (as much as in them lyeth) all the housholds in their division, before every communion; and once yearly with the Minister, to know the better how they behave themselves in their severall families. And if they finde among them any refractory and contentious persons which will not be reconciled, to make a report of it to the *Consistory*.

IV.

4. They shall assemble in the *Consistory* with the Ministers; which *Consistory* shall be holden, if it may be, every Sunday, or any other day convenient, to handle causes of the Church. And those of them which are elected to go unto the *Colloquies* and *Synods* with the Ministers, shall not fail to goe at the day appointed.

CHAP. VII.

Of the Deacons.

Article I.

1. THe *Deacons* shall be appointed in the Church to gather the benevolence of the people, and to distribute it according to the necessities of the poor, by the directions of the *Consistory*.

II.

2. They shall gather these benevolences after Sermons, faithfully endevouring the good and welfare of the poor; and if need require, they shall go unto the houses of those men which are more charitably enclined, to collect their bounties.

3. They

III.

3. They shall distribute nothing without direction from the *Consistory*, but in case of urgent necessity.

IV.

4. The almes shall be principally distributed unto those of the faithfull, which are naturall Inhabitants; and if there be a surplusage, they may dispose it to the relief of strangers.

V.

5. For the avoiding of suspicion, the *Deacons* shall keep a register both of their Receipts and their disbursements, and shall cast up his accounts in the presence of the Minister, and one of the Elders.

VI.

6. The *Deacons* shall give up their accounts every Communion day; after the evening Sermon, in the presence of the Ministers, the Elders, and as many of the people as will be assistant; who therefore shall have warning to be there.

VII.

7. They shall take order that the poor may be relieved without begging; and shall take care that young men fit for labour be set unto some occupation; of which they shall give notice to the officers of Justice, that so no person be permitted to go begging from door to door.

VIII.

8. They shall provide for those of the poor which are sick or in prison, to comfort and assist them in their necessity.

IX.

9. The shall be assistant in the *Consistory* with the *Ministers* and *Elders*, there to propose unto them the necessities of the poor, and to receive their directions; as also in the election of other *Deacons*.

X.

10. There ought to be *Deacons* in every Parish, unlesse the *Elders* will take upon them the charge of collecting the almes, and distributing thereof amongst the poor.

The Liturgie of the Church, wherein there is contained the preaching of the Gospell, the administration of the Sacraments, the Laws of Marriage, the Visitation of the Sick, and somewhat also of Buriall.

CHAP. VIII.

Of the Preaching of the Gospell.

Article I.

1. THe people shall be assembled twice every Sunday in the Church, to hear the *Preaching* of the *Gospell*, and to be assistant at the publick prayers. They shall also meet together once or twice a week, on those dayes which shall be thought most convenient for the severall Parishes; the Master of every houshold bringing with him those of his family.

II.

2. The people being assembled before Sermon, there shall be read a Chapter out of the *Canonicall* books of Scripture only, and not of the *Apocrypha*; and it shall be read by one which beareth office in the Church, or at the least, by one of honest conversation.

III.

3. During the prayer, every one shall be upon his knees, with his head uncovered. Also during the singing of the *Psalmes*, the administration of the Sacraments; and whilest the Minister is reading of his text, every one shall be *uncovered*, and shall attentively observe all that is done and said.

4. The

IV.

4. The Ministers every Sunday after dinner shall *Catechize*, and shall choose some text of Scripture sutable to that section which they are to handle; and shall read in the beginning of that exercise the said text, as the foundation of the Doctrine contained in that Section.

V.

5. The Church shall be locked immediately after Sermon and the publick prayers, to avoid superstition; and the benches shall be orderly disposed, that every one may hear the voice of the Preacher.

VI.

6. The Churches being dedicated to Gods service, shall not be imployed to prophane uses; and therefore intreaty shall be made to the Magistrate, that no *Civill Courts* be there holden.

CHAP. IX.

Of Baptisme.

Article I.

1. THe Sacrament of *Baptisme* shall be administred in the Church, after the Preaching of the Word, and before the *Benediction*.

II.

2. The Parents of the Infants, if they are not in some journey, shall be near the Infant, together with the *Sureties*, to present it unto God; and shall joyntly promise to instruct it, according as they are obliged.

III.

3. No man shall be admitted to be a *Surety* in holy *Baptisme*, which hath not formerly received the Communion, or which

which is not fit to receive it, and doth promise so to do upon the next conveniency, whereof he shall bring an attestation if he be a stranger.

IV.

4. They which intend to bring an Infant unto holy *Baptisme*, shall give competent warning unto the Minister.

V.

5. The Minister shall not admit of such names as were used in the time of *Paganism*, the names of *Idols*, the names attributed to God in Scripture, or names of office, as *Angell*, *Baptist*, *Apostle*.

VI.

6. In every Parish there shall be kept a Register of such as are *Baptized*, their *Fathers*, *Mothers*, *Sureties*, and the day of it; as also of *Marriages* and *Funerals*, which shall be carefully preserved.

CHAP. X.

Of the Lords Supper.

Article I.

1. THe *holy Supper* of our Lord *Jesus Christ* shall be celebrated four times a year, viz. at *Easter* or the first Sunday of *Aprill*, the first Sunday of *July*, the first Sunday of *October*, and the first Sunday of *January*, and that after the Sermon, in which expresse mention shall be made of the businesse then in hand, or at least a touch of it in the end.

II.

2. The manner of it shall be this, The Table shall be set in some convenient place near the Pulpit; the people shall communicate in order, and that *sitting*, as is most conformable to the first institution; or else *standing*, as is accustomed in some places; the men first, and afterwards the

the women; none shall depart the place untill after *Thanks-giving* and the *Benedi&i.n*.

III.

3. They which intend to be *communicants*, shall first be catechized by the Minister, that so they may be able to render a reason of their faith. They ought also to understand the *Lords Prayer*, the *Articles of their belief*, the *Ten Commandements*, or at the least the substance of them. They shall also abjure the Pope, the Masse, and all superstition and Idolatry.

IV.

4. No man shall be admitted to the *Lords Supper*, which is not of the years of discretion, and which hath not a good testimony of his life and conversation, and which will not promise to *submit himself unto the Discipline*.

V.

5. If any be accused before the *Justice* to have committed any crime, he shall be admonished to forbear the *Supper* untill he be acquitted.

VI.

6. The Minister shall not receive any of another Parish without a testimony from the *Pastor*, or if there be no Pastor, from one of the *Elders*.

VII.

7. They which refuse to be reconciled, shall be debarred the *Communion*.

VIII.

8. The people shall have warning fifteen dayes at the least before the *Communion*, to the end they may be prepared for it.

IX.

9. Besides the first examination which they undergoe, before they are partakers of the *Lords Supper*, every one shall again be Catechized, at the least once a year, at the best conveniency of the Minister, and of his people.

CHAP.

CHAP. XI.

Of Fasts and Thanksgiving.

Article I.

1. THe publick *Fasts* shall be celebrated in the Church when the *Colloquie* or the *Synod* think it most expedient, as a day of rest; in which there shall be a Sermon both in the morning and the afternoon, accompanyed with Prayers, reading of the Scripture, and singing of Psalmes; all this to be disposed according to the occasions and causes of the *Fast*, and by the authority of the Magistrate.

II.

2. Solemn *Thanksgiving* also shall be celebrated after the same manner as the Fast, the whole exercise being sutable to the occasion of the same.

CHAP. XII.

Of Marriage.

Article I.

1. ALL contracts of *Marriage* shall be made in the presence of Parents, Friends, Guardians, or the Masters of the parties, and with their consent, as also in the presence of the Minister, or of an *Elder*, or a *Deacon*, before whom the contract shall be made, with invocation on the name of God, without which it is no contract. And as for those which are *sui juris*, the presence of the Minister, or of the *Elders*, or of the *Deacons*, shall be also necessary for good orders sake. And from a promise thus made, there shall be no departing.

II.

2. Children and such as are in Wardship, shall not make any promise of *Marriage*, without the consent of their Fathers

Fathers and Mothers, or of their Gardians in whose power they are.

III.

3. If the Parents are so unreasonable as not to agree unto a thing so holy, the *Consistory* shall give them such advice as is expedient; to which advice if they not hearken, they shall have recourse unto the Magistrate.

IV.

4. They also which have been *Married* shall owe so much respect unto their Parents, as not to *marry* again without their leave; in default whereof they shall incur the censures of the Church.

V.

5. No stranger shall be affianced without licence from the Governours or their Lieutenants.

VI.

6. The degrees of *consanguinity* and of *affinity* prohibited in the word of God, shall be carefully looked into, by such as purpose to be *marryed*.

VII.

7. Those which are affianced, shall promise, and their Parents with them, that they will be *marryed* within 3 moneths after the contract, or within 6 moneths in case either of them have occasion of a Journey; if they obey not, they shall incur the censures of the Church.

VIII.

8. The *Banes* shall be asked successively three Sundayes in the Church, where the parties do inhabit; and if they *marry* in another Parish, they shall carry with them a testimony from the Minister by whom their *Banes* were published; without which they shall not *marry*.

IX.

9. For the avoiding of the abuse and profanation of the Lords-day, and the manifest prejudice done unto the Word of God, on those dayes wherein *Marriage* hath been solemnized; it is found expedient, that it be no longer solemnized upon the Sunday, but upon some Lecture dayes which happen in the week only.

X.

10. If any purpose to forbid the *Banes*, he shall first addresse himself unto the Minister, or two of the *Elders*, by whom he shall be appointed to appear in the next *Consistory*, there to alleadge the reasons of his so doing, whereof the *Consistory* shall be judge. If he appeal from thence, the cause shall be referred unto the next *Colloquie*.

XI.

11. Those which have too familiarly conversed together before their *espousals*, shall not be permitted to marry before they have made confession of their fault: if the crime be notoriously publick, before the whole congregation; if lesse known, the *Consistory* shall determine of it.

XII.

12. Widowes which are minded to *re-marry*, shall not be permitted to contract themselves untill six moneths after the decease of their dead husbands; as well for honesties sake, and their own good report, as to avoid divers inconveniences. And as for men, they also shall be admonished to attend some certain time, but without constraint.

CHAP. XIII.

Of the Visitation of the sick.

Article I.

1. Those which are afflicted with *sicknesse*, shall in due time advertise them which bear office in the Church; to the end, that by they them may be *visited* and comforted.

2. Those

II.

2. Those which are *sick* shall in due time be admonished to make their *Wils*, while as yet they be in perfect memory, and that in the presence of their Minister or Overseer, or other honest and sufficient persons, which shall witnesse to the said *Wils* or *Testaments*, that so they may be approved and stand in force.

CHAP. XIV.

Of Buriall.

Article I.

1. THe *Corps* shall not be carryed, nor *interred* within the Church, but in the Church-yard only, appointed for the *buryall* of the faithfull.

II.

2. The Parents, Friends and Neighbours of the *deceased*, and all such whom the Parents shall intreat, as also the *Ministers*, if they may conveniently (as members of the Church and Brethren, but not in relation to their charge no more then the *Elders* and the *Deacons*) shall accompany the body in good fashion unto the *grave*. In which action there shall neither be a Sermon, nor Prayers, nor sound of Bell, nor any other ceremony whatsoever.

III.

3. The bodies of the *dead* shall not be interred without notice given unto the *Minister*.

IV.

4. The bodies of those which die *excommunicate*, shall not be interred among the faithfull without the appointment of the Magistrate.

CHAP. XV.

Of the Church censures.

Article I.

1. ALL those which are of the Church, shall be subject unto the *censures* of the same; as well they which bear office in it, as they which have none.

II.

2. The sentence of *Abstention* from the *Lords Supper*, shall be published only in case of *Heresie, Schisme*, or other such notorious crime, whereof the *Consistory* shall be judge.

III.

3. Those which receive not the *Admonitions* and *Reprehensions* made unto them in the word of God, which continue hardned without hope of returning into the right way, after many exhortations; if otherwise they may not be reclaimed, shall be *excommunicate*: wherein the proceeding shall be for three Sundayes together, after this ensuing manner.

IV.

4. The *first Sunday* the people shall be exhorted to pray for the offender, without naming the person or the crime.

V.

5. The *second Sunday* the person shall be named, but not the crime. The third, the person shall be named, his offence published, and himself be *excommunicate*. Which sentence shall stand in force as long as he continueth in his obstinacy.

VI.

6. Those which are *excommunicate*, are to be cast out of the bosome of the Church, that they may neither be admitted unto publick Prayer, nor to the Preaching of the Gospell.

7. They

VII.

7. They which bearing publick office in the Church, become guilty of any crime, which in a private person might deserve an *Abstention* from the *Lords table*, shall be suspended from their charge; and they which are found guilty of any crime, which in a private person might merit *excommunication*, shall be deposed.

VIII.

8. In like manner, those which are convict d of such a fault, by reason whereof they be thought unfit to exercise their functions to the edification of the Church, shall be deposed.

IX.

9. If the offender repent him of his sin, and demand *absolution* of the *Consistory*, they shall diligently informe themselves of his conversation; whereupon there shall be notice of it given unto the people the Sunday before he be admitted, and shall make acknowledgment, to be restored unto the peace of the Church.

X.

10. The second Sunday he shall be brought before the Pulpit, and in some eminent place, where he shall make *confession* of his sin; demanding pardon of God, and of the Church with his own mouth, in confirmation of that which the Minister shall say of his repentance.

CHAP. XVI.

Of Ecclesiasticall Assemblies for the rule and government of the Church.

Article I.

1. IN all *Ecclesiasticall Assemblies*, the Ministers shall preside as well to collect the suffrages as to command silence, to pronounce sentence according to the plurality of voices,

as also to denounce the *censures*; unto which himself as well as others shall be subject.

II.

2. The *censures* shall be denounced with all meeknesse of spirit.

III.

3. The *Ecclesiasticall Assemblies* shall commence and end with prayer and thanksgiving; this is to be done by him that is then President.

IV.

4. All they which are there *assembled*, shall speak every one in his own order, without interrupting one another.

V.

5. None shall depart the place without licence.

VI.

6. All matters of *Ecclesiasticall cognisance* shall be there treated and decided according to the word of God, without encroaching upon the civill jurisdiction.

VII.

7. If there happen any businesse of importance, which cannot be dispatched in the lesser *Assemblies*, they shall be referred unto the greater. In like manner, if any think himself agrieved by the lesser Assemblies, he may appeal unto the greater. Provided, that nothing be handled in the greater Assemblies, which hath not been formerly treated in the lesser, unlesse in case only of *remission*.

VIII.

8. There shall be kept a *Register* of all things memorable done in the *Assemblies*; and a *Scribe* appointed in each of them for that purpose.

IX.

9. The *Ecclesiasticall Assemblies* in the main body of them shall

shall not intermeddle with businesse appertaining to the *Civill Courts*; notwithstanding that, they may be members of the same as private persons, but this not often, *viz.* when there is a businesse of great consequence to be determined.

X.

10. He that is banished from the *Lords table*, or suspended from his office by one *Assembly*, shall be readmitted only by the same.

CHAP. XVII.

Of the simple or unmixt Assembly, which is the Consistory.

Article I.

1. THe *Consistory* is an *Assembly* of the *Ministers* and *Elders* of every Church, for the government of the same, for superintendency over mens manners, and their doctrine; for the correction of vices, and the incouragement of the good. In this there may be assistants both the *Deacons* and the *Proponents*, those *viz.* which are nominated to be *Ministers*, the better to fashion them unto the Discipline and guidance of the Church.

II

2. The *Consistory* shall be *assembled* every Sunday, or any other day and time convenient, to consult about the businesse of the Church.

III.

3. No man shall be called unto the Church without the advice of the *Minister* and two *Elders* at the least, in case of necessity; and every *Elder* or *Sexton* shall give notice unto those of his division, according as he is appointed.

4. The

IV.

4. The *Elders* shall not make report unto the *Consistory* of any secret faults, but shall observe the order commanded by our *Saviour*, *Mat.* 18. Reproving in secret such faults as are secret.

V.

5. Neither the *Minister* nor the *Elder* shall name unto the *Consistory* those men of whose faults they make report, without direction from the *Consistory*.

VI.

6. The *censures* of the *Consistory* shall be denounced on some convenient day before every *Communion*; at which time they shall also passe their opinions on the *Schoole-master*.

VII.

7. The *Consistory* shall make choice of those which go to the *Colloquie*.

VIII.

8. The correction of crimes and scandals appertains unto the *Consistory*, so far as to *excommunication*.

IX.

9. In *Ecclesiasticall* businesse the *Consistory* shall make enquiry into such crimes as are brought before them, and shall adjure the parties in the name of God to speak the truth.

CHAP. XVIII.

Of Assemblies compound, viz. the Colloquies and the Synods.

Article I.

1. IN the beginning of the *Assembly*, the Ministers and Elders which ought to be assistant, shall be called by name.

II.

2. The persons appointed to be there, shall not fail to make their appearance, upon pain of being *censured* by the next Assembly, unto which they shall be summoned.

III.

3. The Articles of the precedent *Assembly* shall be read before they enter upon any businesse, to know the better how they have been put in execution. And at the end of every *Assembly*, the *Elders* shall take a copy of that which is there enacted, that so they may all direct themselves by the same rule.

IV.

4. In every *Assembly* there shall be one appointed for the *Scribe*, to register the acts of the *Assembly*.

V.

5. In the end of every *Assembly*, there shall a favourable censure passe, of the *Consistories* in generall, of the *Ministers* and *Elders* which shall be there assistant; and principally of that which hath been done in the *Assembly*, during the Sessions.

VI.

6. The sentence of *Excommunication* shall be awarded only in these *Assemblies*.

VII.

7. The Justices shall be entreated to intermit the course of pleading, both ordinary and extraordinary, during the *Colloquies* and the *Synods*; to the end, that those which ought to be assistant, may not be hindred.

CHAP. XIX.

Of the Colloquie.

Article I.

1. THe *Colloquie* is an Assembly of the *Ministers* and *Elders* delegated from each severall Church in either *Island*, for the governance of those Churches, and the advancement of the Discipline.

II.

2. The *Colloquies* shall be assembled four times a year, *viz.* ten dayes before every Communion; upon which day the word of God shall be proposed, according to the forme before established, Chap. Of *Ministers*.

III.

3. The Ministers of *Alderney* and *Serke* shall make their appearance once yearly at the least, at the *Colloquie* of *Guernzey*; but for that one time it may be such as shall most stand with their convenience.

IV.

4. The *Colloquie* shall make choice of those which are to go unto the *Synod*, and shall give unto them Letters of credence.

CHAP. XX.

Of the Synod.

Article I.

1. THe *Synod* is an Assembly of *Ministers* and *Elders* delegated from the *Colloquies* of both Islands.

II.

2. The *Synod* shall be assembled from two years to two years

years in *Jarsey* and *Guernzey* by turnes, if there be no necessity to exact them oftner; in which case those of that Isle where the *Synod* is thought necessary, shall set forwards the businesse by the advice of both *Colloquies*.

III.

3. There shall be chosen in every *Synod*, a *Minister* to moderate in the Assembly, and a *Clerk* to register the acts.

IV.

4. The Minister of the place where the Assembly shall be holden, shall conceive a prayer in the beginning of the first Session.

V.

5. The *Colloquies* shall in convenient time, mutually advertise each other in generall of those things; which they have to motion in the *Synod*; to the end that every one may consider of them more advisedly. Which said advertisement shall be given before the *Colloquie*, which precedeth the *Synod*, in as much as possible it may. And as for matters of the lesser consequence, they shall be imparted on the first day of the Session.

The Conclusion.

Those Articles which concern the *Discipline*, are so established, that for as much as they are founded upon the word of God, they are adjudged immutable. And as for those which are meerly *Ecclesiasticall*, *i. e.* framed and confirmed for the commodity of the Church, according to the circumstance of persons, time and place; they may be altered by the same authority, by which they were contrived and ratifyed.

THE END.

Chap. V.

(1) *Annotations on the* Discipline. (2) *No place in it for the Kings* Supremacy. (3) *Their love to* Parity, *as well in the State as in the Church.* (4) *The covering of the head a sign of liberty.* (5) *The* right hands of fellowship. (6) Agenda *what it is, in the notion of the Church; The intrusion of the Eldership into Domestical affairs.* (7) *Millets case.* (8) *The brethren superstitions in giving names to children.* (9) *Ambling Communions.* (10) *The* holy Discipline *made a a third note of the Church.* (11) *Marriage at certain times prohibited by the* Discipline. (12) *Dead bodies anciently not interred in Cities.* (13) *The Baptism of Bels.* (14) *The brethren under pretence of* scandal, *usurp upon the* civil Courts. (15) *The* D.scipline *incroacheth on our Church by stealth.* (16) *A caution to the Prelates.*

Sic nata Romana *superstitio; quorum ritus si percenseas, ridenda quam multa, multa etiam miseranda sunt*: as in an equal. case, *Minutius.* This is that *Helena* which lately had almost occasioned τὸ συγχυρῆσι τὴν Ἑλλάδα to put all the cities of our *Greece* into combustion: This that *Lemanian Idol*, before which all the Churches of the world, were commanded to fall down and worship: this that so holy *Discipline*, so essential to the constitution of a Church, that without it, Faith and the Sacraments were to be judged unprofitable. *Egregiam vero laudem & spolia ampla.* How infinitely are we obliged to those most excellent contrivers, that first exhibited unto the world so neat a model of

Church

Church Government! with what praises must we celebrate the memory of those, which with such violent industry endevoured to impose upon the world, these trim inventions! But this I leave unto your Lordship to determine: proceeding to some scattered Annnotations on the precedent text; wherein I shall not censure their devices, but expound them.

Cap. 1. 3. *As bearing chief stroke in the Civil Government.*] For in the Government *Ecclesiastical*, they decline his judgement as incompetent: An excellent instance whereof we have in the particular of *David Blacke*, a Minister of *Scotland*, who having in a Sermon traduced the person and government of the King: was by the King commanded to appear before him. But on the other side, the Church revoked the cause unto their *tribunal, & jussit eum judicium illud declinare,* saith mine Author. True it is, that in the next chapter they afford him power to correct *Blasphemers, Atheists,* and *Idolaters*: but this only as the executioners of their decrees; and in the punishment of such whom their assemblies have condemned. On the other side, they take unto themselves, the designation of all those, which bear publick office in the Church: Chap. 3 7. The appointing and proclaiming all publick fasts: Chap. 11. 1. The presidency in their Assemblies: Chap. 16. 1. The calling of their Councels: Chap. 19. 20. Matters in which consists the life of Soveraignty. No marvell then if that party so much dislike the *Supremacy* of Princes in causes Ecclesiastical: as being *ex diametro* opposed to the *Consistorian* Monarchy. A lesson taught them by their first *Patriarch* in his Commentaries on the 7. chapter of the Prophet *Amos*, vers. 13. in these words, and in this particular. *Qui tantopere extulerunt Henricum Angliæ* (understand the 8. of the name) *certe fuerunt homines inconsiderati: dederunt enim illi summam rerum omnium potestatem; & hoc me graviter semper vulneravit.* Afterwards he is content to permit them so much power as is granted them in the 2 chapter of this Book of *Discipline*: but yet will not have then deal too much in *spiritualities.* He (saith he) *summopere requiritur a regibus, ut gladio quo præditi sunt, utantur, ad cultum dei asserendum. Sed interea sunt homines inconsiderati, qui faciunt eos, nimis spirituales.* So he, and so his followers since.

Chap. 3. 4. *No Church officer shall or ought to pretend any superiority or dominion over his companions.*] And in the chapt. 1. 2. *No one Church shall pretend, &c.* And this indeed, this parity is that which all their projects did so mainly drive at: these men conceiving of *Religion* as *Philosophers* of friendship; *cum amicitia semper pares aut inveniat, aut faciat*: as in *Minutius*. A *parity* by those of this party so earnestly affected in the Church; the better to introduce it also into the State. This was it which principally occasioned *G. Buchanan* in the Epistle before his libellous Book *De jure regni*, to reckon those common titles of Majesty and Highnesse, usually attributed unto Princes, *inter barbarismos Aulicos*, amongst the solecisms and absurdities of Courtship. This was it, which taught *Pareus* and the rest that there was a power in the Inferiour Magistrates to restrain the person of the Prince; and in some cases to depose him. This was it, which often moved the *Scottish* Ministery to put the sword into the hands of the multitude: and I am verily perswaded that there is no one thing which maketh the brethren so affected to our Parliaments, as this, that it is a body, wherein the Commons have so much sway.

Chap. 3. 6. *Shall first subscribe to the confession of the Faith used in the reformed Churches*] But the reformed Churches are very many, and their confessions in some points very different. The *Lutheran* Confessions are for *consubstantiation* and *ubiquity*: the *English* is for *Homilies*, for *Bishops*, for the *Kings Supremacy*: and so not likely to be intended. The confession then here intended, must be that only of *Geneva*, which Church alone is thought by some of them to have been rightly and perfectly reformed.

Chap. 4. 1. *To propose the Word of God.*] The fashion of it, this; such as by study have enabled themselves for the holy Ministery; upon the vacancy of any Church, have by the

Colloquie

Colloque, some time appointed, to make trial (as they call it) of their gift. The day come, and the Colloque assembled, they design him a particular place of Scripture, for the ground of his discourse: which done, and the *proponent* (for so they term him) commanded to withdraw, they passe their censures on him, every one of them in their order: If they approve of him, they then send him also to *propose* unto the people, as in the second Article.

Chap. 4. 2. *And that bareheaded*] And this it may be, because *Candidates*; peradventure, because not yet initiated. For themselves having once attained the honour to be *Masters in Israel*; they permit their heads to be warmly covered: a thing not in use only by the Ministers of the *Geneva* way; but (as my self have seen it) among the Priests and *Jesuites*. I know the putting on of the hat is a sign of liberty; that the *Laconians* being made free Denizens of *Lacedemon*, would never go into the battail, *nisi pileati*, without their hats: and that the Gent. of *Rome* did use to manumit their slaves, by giving them a cap; whereupon *ad pileum vocare*, is as much as to set one free. Yet on the other side, I think it little prejudicial to that liberty, not to make such full use of it, in the performance of those pious duties. True it is, that by this book of *Discipline* the people are commanded to be *uncovered*, during the Prayers, the reading of the Text, the singing of the Psalmes, and the administration of the Sacraments. Chap. 8 3. But when I call to minde, that S. *Paul* hath told us this, 1 Cor. 11. *That every man praying or prophecying with his head covered dishonoureth his head*: I shall applaud the pious modesty of the *English* ministery; who keep their *heads uncovered*, as well when they prophecy as when they pray.

To give them institution by imposition of hands.] A ceremony not used only in the *Ordination* (if I may so call it) of their Ministers, but in that also of the *Elder* and of the *Deacons*: persons meerly *Laical*. But this In mine opinion very improperly: for when the Minister whose duty it is, instals them in their charge; with this solemn form of words he doth perform it. *Je t' impose les mains, &c. viz.* I lay mine

hands.

hands upon you in the name of the *Consistory*; by which imposition of hands you are advertised, that you are set apart from the *affairs of the world &c.* and if so, how then can these men receive this *imposition*, who for the whole year of their charge, imploy themselves in their former occupations, at times; and that expired, return again unto them altogether? A meer mockage of a reverent ceremony.

Chap. 4. 5. *Giving and receiving the hand of Association.*] An ordinance founded on that in the 2. to the *Gal.* 5. viz. *They gave unto me and* Barnabas *the right hands of fellowship*: An embleme, as it is noted by *Theod. Beza*, on the place, of a perfect agreement and consent in the holy faith; *Quod Symbolum esset nostræ in Evangelii doctrina summæ consensionis*: and much also to this purpose that of learned *Chrysostome*; Μάρυσι ᾖ κ̣ τὸ ἐκείνων αὐτῷ, κ̣ τὸ αὐτῷ ἐκείνων: This phrase of speech borrowed, no question, from the customes of those times; wherein the giving of the hand, was a most certain pledge of faith and amity. So *Anchises* in the third book of *Æneids Dextram dat juveni, atq; animum præsenti pignore firmat*: so in another place of the same author; *Jungimus hospitio dextras. Commissaq; dextera dextræ*, in the Epistle of *Phillis* to *Demophoon*. Whereupon it is the note of the *Grammarians*, that as the front or fore-head is sacred to the *Genius*; and the knees to mercy: so is the right hand consecrated unto faith. But here in *Guernzey* there is a further use made of this ceremony; which is an *abjuration* of all other arts of preaching, or of government, to which the party was before accustomed: and an absolute devoting of himself to them, their ordinances and constitutions whatsoever. So that if a Minister of the Church of *England* should be perchance received among them: by this *hand* of *association*, he must in a manner condemn that Church of which he was.

Chap. 5. 5. *That they maintain them at the publick charge.*] A bounty very common in both Islands: and ordered in this manner; the businesse is by one of the Assembly expounded to the *three Estates*, viz. that *N. N.* may be sent abroad to the Universities of *France* or *England*, and defrayed

frayed upon the common purse. If it be granted, then must the party bring in sufficient sureties to be bound for him; that at the end of the time limited, he shall repair into the Islands, and make a proffer of his service in such places, as they think fit for him; if they accept it, he is provided for at home: if not, he is at liberty to seek his fortune.

Chap. 6. 3 *How they behave themselves in their several families*] By which clause the Elders authorised to make enquiry into the lives and conversations of all about them: not only aiming at it by the voice of fame, but by tampering with their neighbours, and examining their servants. It is also given them in charge, at their admission into office; to make diligent enquiry, whether those in their division, have private prayers both morning and evening in their houses; whether they constantly say grace, both before meat and after it; if not, to make report of it to the *Consistory*. A diligence, in my minde, both dangerous and sawcy.

Chap. 8. 1. *To be assistant at the publick prayers*] The publick prayers here intended, are those which the Minister conceives according to the present occasion: beginning with a short confession, and so descending to crave the assistance of Gods Spirit in the exercise, or Sermon then in hand. For the forme, the *Geneva* Psalter telleth us, that it shall be left *alla discretion du Ministre*, to the Ministers discretion: the form of *Prayers*, and of Marriage, and of administration of the Sacraments, there put down; being *types* only and examples, whereby the Minister may be directed in the general. The learned *Architect* which took such great pains in making the *Altare Damascenum*, tels us in that piece of his, that in the Church of *Scotland* there is also an *Agenda*, or form of prayer and of ceremony: but for his part having been 13 years a Minister, he never used it. *Totos ego tredecem annos quibus functus sum Ministerio, sive in Sacramentis, & iis quæ extant in agenda, nunquam usus sum*: and this he speaks as he conceives it, to his commendation. Where by the way, *Agenda*,

Bbb (it

(it is a word of the latter times) is to be understood for a set form in the performance of those ministerial duties, *quæ statis temporibus agenda sunt*, as mine Author hath it. In the *Capitular* of *Charles* the great, we have mention of this word *Agenda*, in divers places: once for all, let that suffice in the 6 book, *Can*. 234. *viz Si quis Presbyter in consulto Episcopo, Agendam in quolibet loco celebrare voluerint; ipse honori suo contrarius extitit.*

Chap. 8. 5. *The Churches shall be locked immediately after Sermon*] The pretence is as it followeth in the next words, *to avoid superstition*: but having nothing in their Churches to provoke superstition; the caution is unnecessary. So destitute are they all both of ornament and beauty. The true cause is, that those of that party are offended with the antient custome of stepping aside into the *Temples*, and their powring out the soul in private prayer unto God: because forsooth it may imply, that there is some secret vertue in those places more then in rooms of ordinary use; which they are peremptory not to give them.

Chap. 9. 1. *After the preaching of the word*] And there are two reasons why the Sacrament of Baptism should be long delayed: the one because they falsly think, that without the preaching of the word there is no Sacrament: the other to take away the opinion of the *necessity* of holy *Baptism*; and the administration of it in private houses in case of such *necessity*. In this strictnesse very resolute, and not to be bended with perswasions, scarce with power. At our being in the Isle of *Guernzy*, the Ministers presented unto his Lordship a catalogue of grievances against the civill Magistrate. And this among the rest, that they had entermedled with the administration of the Sacraments. This certainly *visum crimen* C. *Cæsar, & ante hoc tempus inauditum*: but upon examination it proved only to be thus. A poor man of the Vale had a childe born unto him weak and sickly; not like to live till the publick exercise; whereupon he desires *Millet* the Incumbent there, that he would Baptize it: but after two or three denials made, the poor man

com-

complained unto the *Bailiffes* by whom the Minister was commanded to do his duty. This was all, *& crimine ab uno disce omnes.*

Chap. 9. 5. *Names used in Paganism*] Nor mean they here, such names as occur in Poets, as *Hector, Hercules, &c.* though names of this sort occurre frequently in S. *Pauls* Epistles: but even such names as formerly have been in use amongst our ancestors; as *Richard, Edmund, William,* and the like. But concerning this behold a story wherein our great contriver *Snape* was a chief party, as I finde in the book called *Dangerous positions,* &c. verified upon the oath of one of the brotherhood. *Hodkinson* of *Northampton,* having a childe to be baptized, repaired to *Snape* to do it for him: and he consented to the motion, but with promise, that he should give it some name allowed in Scripture. The childe being brought, and that holy action so far forwards, that they were come to the naming of the childe, they named it *Richard*: which was the name of the Infants Grandfather by the Mothers side. Upon this a stop was made, nor would he be perswaded to baptize the childe; unlesse the name of it were altered: which when the Godfather refused to do, he forsook the place, and the childe was carried back unchristned. To this purpose, but not in the same words, the whole history. But if the name of *Richard* be so *Paganish*, what then shall we conceive of these; *The Lord is near, More-tryall, Joy-again, Free-gift, From-above,* and others of that stamp? are they also extant in the Scripture?

Chap. 10. 2. *And that sitting &c. or standing &c.*] In this our *Synodists* more moderate, then those of the *Netherlands,* who have licensed it to be administred unto men, even when they are walking. For thus *Angelocrator* in his *Epitome* of the *Dutch Synods,* cap. 13. art. 8. viz. *Liberum est stando, sedendo, vel eundo, cœnam celebrare, non autem geniculando*: and the reason, questionlesse, the same in both; οὐ ἀρτολατρείας periculum; for fear of bread-worship. I had before heard sometimes of *ambling Communions*; but till I met with that *Epitome,* I could not stumble on the meaning. A strange and stubborn

stubborn generation; and stiffer in the hams, then any *Elephant*: such as will neither *bow* the *knee* to the *Name* of *Jesus*, nor kneel to him in his Sacraments.

Chap. 10. 4. *which will not promise to submit himself unto the Discipline*] A thing before injoyned in the subscription to it, upon all such as take upon them any publick office in the Church: but here exacted in the submission to it of all such as desire to be Communicants. The reason is, because about that time it seemed good unto the brethren to make the *holy Discipline*, as essential to the being of a Church, as the preaching of the word and administration of the Sacraments; and so essential, that no Church could possibly subsist without it. For thus *Beza* in his Epistle unto *Cnoxe*, Anno 1572. *Magnum est Dei munus quod unam & religionem puram, & εὐταξίαν, (doctrinæ viz: retinendæ vinculum) in Scotiam intulistis. Sic obsecro & obtestor, hæc duo simul retinete, ut uno amisso alterum diu permanere non posse, semper memineritis.* So he *Epist.* 79. According unto which Doctrine Mr. *Dela-Marshe*, in his new Catechism, which lately by the authority of the *Colloquie*, he imposed upon the Churches in the Isle of *Guernzy*: hath joyned this *holy Discipline*, as a chief note, together with the others.

Chap. 12. 9. *That it be no longer solemnized upon the Sunday*] Wherein (so scarcely did the same Spirit rule them both) the *Dutch Synodists* have shewed themselves more moderate, then these contrivers, they having licensed marriage on all daies equally; except such as are destinate to the *Lords Supper*, and to solemn fasts; *Quovis die matrimonia confirmari & celebrari poterunt, modo concio ad populum habeatur: exceptis cænæ diebus, & jejunio sacratis.* Cap. ult. art. 8. By both of them it is agreed that marriage be celebrated on such daies only, on which there is a Sermon: and if the Sermon be any thing to the purpose, I am content they should expect it. Only I needs must note with what little reason these men and their abettors have so often quarrelled our Church, for the restraint of marriage, at some certain seasons: whereas they think it fit, at some times to restrain it in their own. Well
fare

fare therefore our neighbours of the Church of *Scotland*: men very indifferent both for the time, and for the place. For the time; *Nullum tempus tam sacrum quod ejus celebratione polluatur:* and for the place, *immo & in prætorio vel quovis loco publico--&c. & extra sacra & publicum conventum totius ecclesiæ.* So they, that made the *Altare Damascenum.* p. 872. 865. 866.

Chap. 14. 1. *The Corps shall not be carried or interred within the Church*] Which prohibition, whether it hath more in it of the *Jew* or of the *Gentile,* is not easie to determine. Amongst the *Jewes* it was not lawful for the Priest to be present at a Funeral; or for the dead corps to be interred within the camp: and on the other side, it was by Law in *Athens,* and in *Rome* forbidden, either to burn their dead, or to bury them within their Cities. *In urbe ne sepelito neve urito,* saith the Law of the 12 *Tables*; nor do I see for what cause this generation should prohibit the dead bodies entrance into the Church, and to permit it in the Church-yards. If for the avoiding of superstition, it is well known, that not the Church only, but the Church-yards are also consecrated. The reason why they will not bury in the Church is only their desire and love of *parity* ; the Church will hardly be capacious enough to bury all: and since by death and nature all are equall, why should that honour be vouchsafed unto the rich, and not unto the poor? Out of this love of *parity* it is, that in the next article, they have forbidden *Funeral Sermons*; wherein the *Dutch Synods,* and those men most perfectly concur; as appeareth in that collection, cap. 11. 5. For if such Sermons be permitted, the common people will be forsooth aggrieved, and think themselves neglected: *Ditiores enim hoc officio cohonestabuntur, neglectis pauperibus.*

Chap. 14. 2. *Nor any prayers, nor sound of bell*] The last for love of *parity*; but this for fear of superstition. For prayers at the burial of the dead, may possibly be mistook, for prayers for the dead; and so the world may dream perhaps of *Purgatory.* The silencing of bels is somewhat juster, because that musick hath been superstitiously and foolishly imployed in former times, and in this very case at Funerals. It is well known with what variety of ceremonies they were baptized and consecrated (as in the Church of *Rome* they still are) by the Bishops. Whereby the people did conceive a power inherent in them, not only for the scattering of tempests, in which cases they are also rung amongst them: but for the repulsing of the *Devil* and his Ministers. Blessings which are intreated of the Lord for them, as appeareth by one of those many prayers, prescribed in that form of *consecration*; by the *Roman Pontifical*, viz. *ut per sactum illorum procul pellantur omnes insidiæ inimici, fragor grandinum, procellæ turbinum, &c.* Whilest therefore the people was superstitious in the use of *bels*, the restraint of them was allowable: but being now a matter only of solemnity, it argueth no little superstition to restrain them.

Chap. 16. 6. *Without encroaching on the civil jurisdiction*] And well indeed it were, if this clause were intended to be observed: for in the 17. chap. and 8. art. it is decreed, that the correction of crimes and scandals appertaineth unto the *Consistory*. What store of grist, the word *Crime*, will bring unto their mills, I leave unto your Lordship to interpret: sure I am, that by this of *scandal*, they draw almost all causes within their cognizance. A matter testified by his late most excellent Majesty in a Remonstrance to the Parliament: *viz.* that the *Puritan* Ministers in *Scotland* had brought all causes within their jurisdiction; saying, that it was the Churches office to judge of *scandal*, and there could be no kinde of fault or crime committed, but there was a *scandal* in it, either against God, the King, or their neighbour. Two instances of this, that counterfeit *Eusebius, Philadelphus* in his late Pamphlet against my Lord of St. *Andrewes*, doth freely give us. Earl *Huntley* upon a private quarrel had inhumanely killed the Earl of *Murray*. For this offence his Majesty upon a great suit, was content to grant his pardon: *Ecclesia tamen Huntileum jussit sub dirorum pænis, ecclesiæ satisfacere*; but yet the Church (in relation to the *scandall*) commanded him under the pain of of *Excommunication*, to do penance. Not long after the said Earl *Huntly* and others of the *Romish faction*, had enterprised against the peace and safety of the Kingdome. The King resolved to pardon them for this also: *Ecclesia autem excommunicationis censura pronuntiavit*: but the Church pronounced against them the dreadful sentence of *Anathema*; so little use is there of the civil Magistrate, when once the Church pretends a *scandal*.

Chap. 17. 9. *And shall adjure the parties in the Name of God*] And shall *adjure*, i. e. They shall *provoke* them, or Induce them to confession, by using or Interposing of the Name of God: for thus *adjuration* is defined to us by *Aquinas* Secunda secundæ qu. 9. in Axiom. *Adjurare, nihil aliud est* (saith he) *nisi creaturam aliquam divini nominis, aut alterius cujuspiam sacræ rei interpositione, ad agendum aliquid impellere*: the parties, and those not such as give in the informations, for that is done in private by the *Elders*: but such of whose Ill fame Intelligence is given unto the *Consistory*. If so, then would I fain demand of the contrivers, with what reason they so much exclaim against the oath *ex officio judicis*, used by our Prelates in their *Chancellaries*: since they themselves allow it in their *Consistories*. But thus of old, as it is in *Horace, de Arte*.

Cæcilio Plautoq; dedit Romanus, ademptum
Virgilio Varioque.

Concluf. *They are adjudged to be Immutable*] And no marvail, if as the brethren and their *Beza* think, it be so essential to the Church, that no Church can possibly subsist without it: If so essential, that we may as warrantably deny the written Word, as these inventions. But certainly, what ever these think of it; the founder of this plat-form thought not so: when thus he was

per-

perswaded, that the ordering of the Church of God, for as much as concernes the form of it, was left to the discretion of the Ministers. For thus himself in his Epistle ad *Neocomenses*, dated 1543. viz. *Substantiam disciplinæ ecclesiæ exprimit disertis verbis Scriptura: forma autem ejus exercendæ, quoniam a Domino præscripta non est, a ministris constitui debet pro ædificatione.* Thus he: and how dare they controll him? Will they also dare to teach their Master?

Thus have I brought to end those Annotations, which I counted most convenient, for to expresse their meaning in some few passages of this new plat-form; and to exemplifie their proceedings. A larger Commentary on this Text had been unnecessary: considering both of what I write, and unto whom. Only I needs must note, that as the erecting of these fabricks in these Islands was founded on the ruine of the *Deanries*: so had the birth of this device in *England* been death unto the Bishopricks. No wonder then if those which principally manage the affairs of *holy Church*, so busily bestir themselves in the destroying of this viper: which by no other means can come into the world, then by the death and ruine of his mother. Yet so it is, I know not whether by destiny, or some other means; I would not think; but so it is: that much of this new plat-form hath of late found favour with us; and may in time make entrance to the rest. Their Lecturers permitted in so many places, what are they, but the *Doctors of Geneva*? save only that they are more factious and sustain a party. And what the purpose and design of this, but so by degrees to lessen the repute of such daies as are appointed *holy* by the Church; and fasten all opinion to their daies of preaching? By whose authority stand the *Church-wardens* at the Temple doors (as I have seen it oft in *London*) to collect the bounty of the hearers: but only by some of their appointments, who finde that duty (or the like) prescribed here unto the *Deacons*, cap. 1. 2.

I

I could say somewhat also of our *ordinary Fasts*, how much they are neglected every where: and no Fast now approved of, but the *solemn*. Nay we have suffered it of late to get that ground upon us; in the practise at the least: that now no common businesse must begin without it. Too many such as these I fear, I could point out unto your Lordship, did I not think that these already noted were too many. A matter certainly worthy of your Lordships care, and of the care of those your Lordships partners in the *Hierarchie*: that as you suffer not these new *Inventions*, to usurp upon our Churches by violence; so that they neither grow upon us, by cunning or connivence.

Chap. VI.

(1) *King James how affected to this Platform.* (2) *He confirmes the* Discipline *in both Iflands.* (3) *And for what reasons.* (4) *Sir* John Peyton *sent Governour into* Jarzey. (5) *His Articles against the Ministers there.* (6) *And the proceedings thereupon.* (7) *The diftracted eftate of the Church and Miniftery in that Ifland.* (8) *They referre themfelves unto the King.* (9) *The Inhabitants of* Jarzey *petition for the* English *Difcipline.* (10) *A reference of both parties to the Councell.* (11) *The reftitution of the* Dean. (12) *The* Interim *of Germanie what it was.* (13) *The* Interim *of* Jarzey. (14) *The exceptions of the Miniftery againft the* Book of Common-prayer. (15) *The eftablifhment of the new* Canons.

IN this ftate and under this Government continued thofe Iflands till the happy entrance of King *James* upon the Monarchy of *England*. A Prince of whom the brethren conceived no fmall hopes, as one that had continually been brought up by and amongft thofe of that faction: and had fo oft confirmed their much defired *Presbyteries*. But when once he had fet foot in *England*, where he was fure to meet with quiet men, and more obedience: he quickly made them fee, that of his favour to that party, they had made themfelves too large a promife. For in the conference at *Hampton Court*, he publickly profeffed, that howfoever he lived among *Puritans*, and was kept for the moft part as a ward under them; yet ever fince he was of the age of ten

years

years old, he ever disliked their opinions: and as the Saviour of the world had said, *though he lived among them, he was not of them.* In this conference also, that so memorized Apophthegm of his Majesty: *No Bishop*, no King: and anon after, My Lords the Bishops (saith he) *I may thank ye, that these men (the Puritans) plead thus for my Supremacy.* Add to this, that his Majesty had alwaies fostred in himself a pious purpose, not only of reducing all his Realms and Dominions into one uniform order and course of discipline; which thing himself avoweth, in his Letters Patents unto those of *Jarzey*: but also to establish in all the reformed Churches, if possibly it might be done; together with unity of Religion, and uniformity of devotion. For which cause he had commanded the *English Liturgie* to be translated into the *Latine*, and also into most of the national Languages round about us: by that and other more private means, to bring them into a love and good opinion of our Government: which he oftentimes acknowledged to *have been approved by manifold blessings from God himself.* A heroick purpose, and worthy of the Prince from whom it came.

This notwithstanding, that he was enclined the other way; yet upon suit made by those of these Islands, he confirmed unto them their present orders, by a Letter under his private Seal, dated the 8. of *August* in the first year of his reign in *England*; which Letters were communicated in the Synod at St. *Hilaries* the 18. of *September*, 1605. the Letter written in the *French* Tongue; but the tenor of them was as followeth:

"*James* by the Grace of God, King of *England*, *Scotland*,
"*France* and *Ireland*, &c. unto all those whom these pre-
"sents shall concern, greeting: Whereas we our selves and
"the Lords of our Councell have been given to understand,
"that it pleased God to put it into the heart of the late
"Queen our most dear sister, to permit and allow unto the
"Isles of *Jarzey* and *Guernsey* parcel of our *Dutchy* of *Norman-*
"*dy*, the use of the Government of the *reformed Churches* in
"the said *Dutchy*, whereof they have stood possessed until our
"coming to this Crown: for this cause we desiring to fol-
"low

"low the pious example of our said Sister in this behalf, as
"well for the advancement of the glory of Almighty God,
"as for the edification of his Church; do will, and ordain,
"that our said Isles shall quietly enjoy their said liberty in
"the use of the *Ecclesiastical Discipline* there now established:
"forbidding any one to give them any trouble or impeach-
"ment, as long as they contain themselves in our obedience,
"and attempt not any thing against the pure and sacred
"Word of God. Given at our Palace at *Hampton Court* the
"8. day of *August*, Anno Dom. 1603. and of our reign in
"*England* the first.

Signed above *James R.*

The reasons which moved this Prince to assent unto a form of Government, which he liked not; was partly an ancient rule and precept of his own, viz. That *Princes at their first entrance to a Crown ought not to innovate the government presently established*. But the principal cause indeed, was desire not to discourage the *Scots* in their beginnings: or to lay open too much of his intents at once unto them. For since the year 1595. his Majesty wearied with the confusions of the *Discipline* in that Church established; had much busied himself in restoring their antient place and power unto the Bishops. He had already brought that work so forwards, that the *Scottish Ministers* had admitted of 13 Commissioners (which was the antient number of the Bishops) to have suffrage in the *Parliament*; and to represent in that Assembly the body of the Clergy: and that their place should be perpetual. Thus far with some trouble, but much art, he had prevailed on that unquiet and unruly company: and therefore had he denied the Islanders an allowance of their *Discipline*; he had only taught the *Scottish Ministery* what to trust to. An allowance whereof he after made especial use in his proceedings with that people. For thus his Majesty in a Declaration concerning such of the *Scottish Ministers*, as lay attainted of High Treason, *Anno* 1606. viz. " And as we have
" ever regarded carefully how convenient it is to maintain
" every Countrey in that form of Government which is
" fittest and can best agree with the constitution thereof;
" and

CHAP. VI. *the Estate of* Guernzey *and* Jarsey. 381

"and how dangerous alterations are without good advice
"and mature deliberation; and that even in matters of or-
"der of the Church, in some small Island under our Do-
"minions, we have abstained from suffering any alterati-
"on; So we doubt not, &c as it there followeth in the words
"of the Declaration.

On these reasons, or on some other not within the power of my conjecture; this Discipline was permitted in these Islands: though long it did not continue with them. For presently upon his Majesties comming to the Crown, Sir *Walter Raleigh* then Governor of *Jarsey* was attaint of Treason: on which attaindure this with others of his places, fell actually into the Kings disposing: upon this variancy, it pleased his Majesty to depute the present Governor Sir *John Peiton*, to that office: A Gentleman not over forward in himself, to pursue the projects of the *Pawlets* his predecessors, (for Sir *W. Raleigh* had but a little while possessed the place) and it may well be furnished also with some secret instructions from the King, not to be too indulgent to that party. Whether that so it was or not, I cannot say: Sure I am that he omitted no opportunity of abating in the *Consistorians* the pride and stomach of their jurisdiction. But long it was not before he found a fit occasion to place his battery against those works; which in the Island there they thought impregnable. For as in the ancient proverb, *Facile est invenire baculum ut cædas canem*: it is an easie thing to quarrell one, whom before hand we are resolved to baffle. The occasion this. The Curate of S. *Johns* being lately dead, it pleased the *Colloquie* of that Island, according to their former method; to appoint one *Brevin* to succeed him: against which course, the Governor, the Kings Attorney and other the officers of the Crown protested; as prejudicial to the rights and profits of the King. Howbeit, the case was over-ruled; and the *Colloquie* for that time carried it: hereupon a bill of Articles was exhibited unto the Councel against the Ministers, by *Peiton* the Governor, *Marret* the Attorney, *now one* of the Jurates, and the rest: as *viz.* that they had usurped the Patronage of all benefices in the Island; that thereby they admitted men to
livings

livings without any form of presentation; that thereby they deprived his Majesty of Vacancies and first-fruits; that by connivence (to say no worse of it) of the former Governors, they exercised a kinde of arbitrary jurisdiction, making and disannulling lawes at their own uncertain liberty; whereupon they most humbly besought his Majesty to grant them such a discipline, as might be fittest to the nature of the place, and lesse derogatory to the Royal *Prerogative*.

This Bill exhibited unto the Councell, found there such approbation, that presently Sir *Robert Gardiner*, once chief Justice, (as I take it) in the *Realm of Ireland*; and *James Huffey* Doctor of the Lawes; though not without some former businesse; were sent into the Islands. Against their coming into *Jersey*, the Ministers of that Island had prepared their Answer; which in the general may be reduced to these two heads; *viz*. That their appointment of men into the Ministery, and the exercise of Jurisdiction being principal parts of the Church Discipline; had been confirmed unto them by his Majesty. And for the matter of First-fruits, it was a payment which had never been exacted from them; since their discharge from him at *Constance*; unto whom in former times they had been due. Upon this answer the businesse was again remitted unto the King, and to his Councell; by them to be determined upon the comming of their Deputies: the Committees not having (as they said) a power to determine it; but only to instruct themselves in the whole cause, and accordingly to make report. Other matters within the compasse of their Commission, and about which they were said principally to be sent over, were then concluded: all which hapned in the year 1608. Immediately upon the departure of these Commissioners; and long before their Deputies had any faculty to repair unto the Court: a foul deformity of confusion and distraction had overgrown the Church and *Discipline*. In former times all such as took upon them any publick charge either in Church or Common-wealth, had bound themselves by oath to cherish and maintain the *Discipline*: that oath is now disclaimed as dangerous and unwarrantable. Before it was their custome

stome to exact *subscription* to their platform, of all such as purposed to receive the *Sacrament*: but now the Kings *Attorney*, and others of that party, chose rather to abstain from the Communion; nay even the very *Elders* silly souls, that thought themselves as *Sacrosancti* as a *Roman Tribune*: were drawn with proces into the civil courts; and there reputed with the vulgar. Nor was the case much better with the *Consistory*: the *Jurates* in their *Cohu* or Town-hall, relieving such by their authority, whom that *Tribunal* had condemned or censured. *A pravis ad præcipitia*. Such is the inhumanity of the world, that when once a man is cast upon his knees, every one lends a hand to lay him prostrate. No sooner had those of the lower rank, observed the Ministers to stagger in their chairs; but they instantly begin to wrangle for the Tithes: and if the Curate will exact his due; the Law is open, let them try the Title. Their Benefices, where before accounted as exempt and priviledged, are brought to reckon for *first fruits* and *tenths*: and those not rated by the book of *Constance*, but by the will and pleasure of the Governor. Adde unto this, that one of the *Constables* preferred a Bill against them in the *Cohu*: wherein the Ministers themselves were *indicted* of *hypocrisie*; and their government of *tyranny*. And which of all the rest was the greatest of their miseries; it was objected that they held secret meetings and private practises against the Governor: yea such as reflected also on the King.

In this confusion and distresse they were almost uncapable of counsel. They applyed themselves in the next *Colloquie* unto the Governor, that he would please to intercede for them to his Majesty: but him they had so far exasperated by their clamours, that he utterly refused to meddle for them. Nor did the Ministers, as I conjecture, propound it farther to him, then by way of due respect: as little hoping that he should bend himself for their relief; whom they so often had accused to be the cause of all this trouble. At last they are resolved to cast themselves upon the grace and favour of the King; and for that cause addressed themselves and their desires unto the Earl of *Salisbury*, a man, at that time of special credit with the King, being also *Lord High Trea-*

Treasurer, and chief Secretary. This their addresse as he took in special good regard; so did he also seem to advise them for the best: his counsel, that they should joyn unto them those of *Guernzey*, in the perusing of their *Discipline*, and the correcting of such things most stomacked by the Civil Magistrates: and after, both together to refer themselves unto his Majesty. A counsel not to be despised in the appearance: but yet (as certainly he was of a fine and subtil wit) of exceeding cunning. For by this means the businesse not yet ripe, and the King scarce master of his purposes in *Scotland*; he gains time farther to consider of the main: and by ingaging those of *Guernzey* in the cause, they also had been subject to the same conclusion: But subtil as he was, he found no art to protract the fatal and inevitable blow of death; for whilest his Clients busily pursued this project, in reviewing of their platform, he yeelded up himself unto the grave, *March* 24. *anno* 1612. upon report whereof, they layed by the prosecution of that businesse; referring of it to the mercy of some better times.

This comfort yet they found in their addresse unto the Court, that things at home were carried on in a more fair and quiet course: but long they would not suffer themselves to enjoy that happinesse. The Parish of S. *Peters* being void, *Messervy* was presented to it by the Governour: one that had spent his time in *Oxenford*, and had received the Orders of the Priesthood from the Right Reverend Doctor *Bridges*, then Bishop of that Diocesse. A matter so infinitely stomacked by the *Colloquie*, that they would by no means yeeld to his admission: not so much because of his presentation from the Governor, as of his ordination from the Bishop. For now they thought *Annibalem ad portas*, that Popery began again to creep upon them: and therefore they resolved to fight it out, *tanquam de summa rerum*, as if the whole cause of Religion were in danger. M. *sserny* howsoever enjoyed the profits of the living; and a new complaint was made against them to the Councel: In which complaint, there also was intelligence given unto their Lordships, that the inhabitants generally of the Isle, were discontented with the *Discipline* and guidance of the
Church:

Church: and that the most of them would easily admit the form of *English* Government; that some of them did desire it. The matter thus grown ready for an issue, and his Majesty desirous to bring all things to the most peaceable and quiet end; both parties were commanded to attend at Court: the Governor and secular states, to prosecute their suit, and make good their intelligence; the Ministers to answer the complaints, and tender their proposals. Hereupon the Governor and those of the laity delegated to the Court, *Marret* the *Attorney*, and *Meſſerʋy* the new Parson of St. *Peters*: by whom the people sent a formal Petition to his Majesty, signed by many of their hands; and to this purpose, viz. that he would be pleased to establish in their Island, the book of Common-prayers; and to settle there among them some Ecclesiastical Officer, with *Episcopal* jurisdiction. On the other side, there were deputed, for the Ministers, Mr. *Bandinell*, the now Dean; *Oliveis*, the now Sub dean; *Effart*, the Curate of St. *Saviours*; and *De la place*, then Curate of St. *Maries*. To whom this also was specially given in charge, that with all industry they should oppose whatsoever innovation (as they called it) might be proposed unto them: and resolutely bear up for the present *Discipline*.

Immediately upon their appearance at the Court, both parties by his Majesty were referred to the Council: and by them again to my Lord Archbishop of *Canterbury*, the Lord *Zouche*, and Sir *John Herbert*, then principal Secretary. Before them the cause was privately argued by the Deputies of both parties: and the desires of the Governor and of the people, constantly impugned by the Ministers. But as it alwaies hapneth that there is no confederacy so well joyned, but one member of it may be severed from the rest; and thereby the whole practise overthrown: so was it also in this businesse. For those which there sollicited some private businesse of theGovernors, had finely wrought upon the weaknesse or ambition of *De la place*; bearing him in hand, that if the Government of the Church were altered, and the office of the Dean restored; he was for certain resolved

resolved upon to be the man. Being fashioned into this hope, he speedily betrayed the counsels of his fellowes; and furnished their opponents at all their enterviews, with such intelligence as might make most for their advantage. At last the Ministers not well agreeing in their own demands, and having little to say in the defence of their proper cause, whereto their answers were not provided beforehand; my Lord of *Canterbury* at the Councel-table thus declared unto them the pleasure of the King and Councell: *viz.* that for the speedy redresse of their disorders, it was reputed most convenient to establish among them, the authority and office of the Dean; that the book of Common-prayer being again printed in the *French* should be received into their Churches; but the Ministers not tyed to the strict observance of it in all particulars: that *Messerny* should be admitted to his benefice; and that so they might return unto their charges.

This said, they were commanded to depart, and to signifie to those from whom they came, they full scope of his Majesties resolution; and so they did. But being somewhat backward in obeying this decree, the Councel intimated to them by Sir *Phil. de Carteret* their Agent for the Estates of the Island; that the Ministers from among themselves, should make choice of three learned and grave persons, whose names they should return unto the board: out of which his Majesty would resolve on one to be their Dean. A proposition which found among them little entertainment. Not so much out of dislike unto the dignity, for they were most of them well contented with the change: but because every one of them conceived hopefully of himself to be the man, and all of them could not be elected; they were not willing to prejudice their own hopes, by the naming of another. In the mean time, Mr. *David Bandinell* then Curate of *St. Maries,* either having or pretending some businesse unto *London*; was recommended by the Governor as a man most fit to sustain that place and dignity. And being also approved by my Lord of *Canterbury* (as certainly he is a man of good abilities) as a person answerable to the Governors commendations; he was established in that office by Letters Patents from his Majesty, dated the 8. of *March, anno* 1619. and was invested with all such rights as formerly had been inherent in that dignity: and that both in point of profit; and also in point of jurisdiction. For whereas formerly the Dean was setled in the best benefice in the Island, that *viz.* of St *Martins*; and had divers portions of tithes out of every of the Parishes: the said St. *Martins* was allotted to him, upon the next avoidance; and the whole tithes of St. *Saviours* allowed him, in consideration of his several parcels. And whereas also at the suppression of the *Deanry*, the Governor had taken into his hands the probate of Testaments, and appointed unto civil Courts the cognizance of Matrimoniall causes and of tithes: all these again were restored unto him, and forever united to this office.

For the executing of this place, there were some certain Articles, or rather Canons drawn and ratified to be in force till a perfect draught of Ecclesiastical constitutions could be agreed on: which it pleased his Majesty to call the *Interim*. And this he did in imitation of *Charles* the 5. which Prince, desirous to establish peace and quietnesse in the Church of *Germany*; and little hoping that any Councel would be summoned soon enough to determine of the differences then on foot: composed a certain mixture of opinions, in favour of each party; which he endevoured to obtrude upon that people: the compilers of it, *Julius Pflugius, Michael Sidonius*, and *Isleblus*: the time when, *anno* 1594. the name of it the *Interim*: a name given unto it by the Emperor, *eo quod præscriberet formulam doctrinæ & ceremoniarum in religione in terra tenendam, quoad de universa re religionis concilio publico definitum esset*: so the historian of the Councell. In like manner, did it please his Majesty as himself tels us in the next chapter: "In the *interim*, untill he "mought be fully informed what Lawes, &c. were meet and "fit to be established for the good government of the said "Island in causes Ecclesiastical, &c. to grant commission, &c. "to exercise the Ecclesiastical Jurisdiction there according "to

"to certain instructions signed with our royal hand, to con-
"tinue only untill we might establish, &c. as it followeth
in the Original. By this *Interim* there was a clause in force,
whereby it was permitted to the Ministers not to bid ho-
lydaies, or use the Crosse in Baptism, or wear the Surplice, or to exact it of the people that they kneel at the
Communion. In other matters it little differed from the
Canons afterwards established, and now in being in that
Island.

Thus fortified with power, and furnished with instructions, home cometh the new *Dean* into his Countrey: and
in a frequent assembly of the *three Estates*, takes full possession of his place, and office. Nor found he any opposition,
till he began to exercise his Jurisdiction; At what time
Sir *John Herault*, then *Bayliffe* of the Island, and to whom
his Majesty had given the title of St. *Saviour*; not pleased to
see so many causes drawn from his *Tribunal*, made head
against him. But this disgust was quickly over-blown; and
the Bailiffe for four years suspended by his Majesty from
the executing of his office. This done, his fellow Ministers
were called together, and he imparted unto them his instructions. All of them seeming well contented with the Jurisdiction (*De la place* excepted) who much impatient (as
commonly the miscarrying of our hopes as much torments
us, as the losse of a possession) to see himself deluded, forsook the Countrey. But to the *Liturgie* they thought they
had no cause to give admission; nay that they had good
cause unto the contrary: *viz.* as not being desired
by them in their addresse; and having been for fifty
years at least a stranger in the Islands: a thing also much
stomacked and opposed by many learned men in *England*;
and not imposed as yet upon the *Scotts*, which people in so
many other particulars, had been brought unto conformity with the *English*. In the end, having six moneths
allowed them to deliberate, *frangi pertinaciam suam passi sunt*;
they were content to bend and yeeld unto it, upon such
qualifications of it, as in the instructions were permitted. A
duty carelessly discharged and as it were by halfs, by many of

them;

them; those *viz* of the ancient breed, which have so been wedded to a voluntary frame and fabrick of devotion: but punctually observed by those of the lesser standing, as having good acquaintance with it here in *England*; and not possessed with any contrary opinion, whereby it might be prejudiced. And now there wanted nothing to perfect the intentions of his Majesty; and to restore unto the Island, the ancient face and being of a Church: but only that the *Policy* thereof was something temporary and not yet established in the rule and Canon. But long it was not, ere this also was effected: and a fixt Law prescribed of Government *Ecclesiastical*. Which what it is, by what means it was agreed on, how crossed, and how established; his Majesties own Letters Patents can best instruct us: and to them wholly I referre the honour of the relation.

Chap. VII.

The Canons and Constitutions Ecclesiasticall for the Church Discipline of Jarsey: *together with the Kings Letters Patents for the authorising of the same.*

"JAMES by the grace of God King of *England*, Scot-
"land, *France* and *Ireland*, defender of the faith, &c.
"To our right trusty and well beloved Counseller
"the reverend father in God *Lancelot* Bishop of *Winton*, and
"to our trusty and well beloved Sir *John Peyton* Knight,
"Governour of the Isle of *Jarsey*; and to the Governour
"of the said Isle for the time being, and to the *Bailiffe* and
"*Jurates* of the said Isle for the time being; to whom it
"shall or may appertain, Greeting. Whereas we held it
"fitting heretofore upon the admission of the now *Dean* of
"that Island unto his place, in the *Interim*, untill we might
"be fully informed what Lawes, Canons, or Constitutions
"were meet and fit to be made and established for the good
"government of the Island in causes Ecclesiasticall, appertai-
"ning to Ecclesiasticall jurisdiction; to command the said
"Bishop of *Winton*, Ordinary of the said Island to grant
"his Commission unto *David Bandinell* now *Dean* of the same
"Island, to exercise the *Ecclesiasticall jurisdiction* there accor-
"ding to certain instructions signed with our royall hand,
"to continue only till we might establish such Constituti-
"ons, Rules, Canons and Ordinances, as we intended to
"settle for the regular government of that our Island in all
"Ecclesiasticall causes, conformed to the Ecclesiasticall go-
"vernment established in our Realm of *England*, as near as
"conveniently might be. And whereas also to that our pur-
"pose

"pose and pleasure was, that the said *Dean* with what con-
"venient speed he might, after such authority given unto
"him as aforesaid, and after his arrivall into that Island,
"and the publick notice given of that his admission unto
"the said office, should together with the Ministers of this
"our Island, consider of such Canons and Constitutions as
"might be fitly accomodated to the circumstances of time, and
"place, and persons whom they concern; and that the same
"should be put in good order, and intimated by the *Gover-
"neur, Bailiffe* and *Jurates* of that our Island; that they
"might offer to us and our Councell such acceptions, and
"give such reformations touching the same, as they should
"think good. And whereas the said *Dean* and Ministers
"did conceive certain Canons, and presented the same un-
"to us on the one part, and on the other part the said
"*Bailiffe* and *Jurates* excepting against the same, did send
"and depute Sir *Philip de Carteret* Knight, *Joshuah de Carte-
"ret* and *Philip de Carteret* Esquires, three of the *Jurates* and
"Justices of our said Isle; all which parties appeared before
"our right trusty and well beloved Counsellers, the most
"reverend father in God the Lord Archbishop of *Canterbury*,
"the Right reverend father in God the Lord Bishop of
"*Lincolne* Lord Keeper of the Geat Seal of *England*, and the
"Right reverend father in God the said Lord Bishop of
"*Winton*, to whom we granted commission to examine the
"same; who have have accordingly heard the said parties
"at large, read and examined, corrected and amended the
"said Canons, and have now made report unto us under
"their hands, that by a mutuall consent of the said De-
"puties and *Dean* of our Island, they have reduced the said
"Canons and Constitutions Ecclesiasticall, into such order,
"as in their judgements may well stand with the estate of
"that Island.

"Know ye therefore, that we out of our Princely care
"of the quiet and peaceable government of all our Domi-
"nions, especialy affecting the peace of the Church, and the
"establishment of true Religion, and *Ecclesiasticall discipline*,
"in one uniforme order and course throughout all our
"Realms and Dominions, so happily united under us as
"their

"their Supreme Governor on earth in all causes, as well
"Ecclesiasticall as Civill: Having taken consideration of
"the said Canons and Constitutions thus drawn as afore-
"said, do by these deputies ratifie, confirme and approve
"thereof.

"And farther, we out of our Princely power and regall
"authority, do by these Patents signed and sealed with our
"royall Signet, for us, our heirs and successors, will with
"our royall hand, and command that these Canons and
"Constitutions hereafter following, shall from henceforth
"in all points be duly observed in our said Isle, for the
"perpetuall government of the said Isle in causes Ecclesiasti-
"call; unlesse the same, or some part or parts thereof,
"upon further experience and tryall thereof by the mutuall
"consent of the Lord Bishop of *Winton* for the time being,
"the *Governour*, *Bailiffs* and *Jurates* of the said Isle, and of the
"*Dean*, and *Ministers*, and other our Officers in the said Isle
"for the time being, representing the body of our said Isle,
"and by the royall authority of us, our heirs and successors
"shall receive any additions or alterations as time and occa-
"sion shall justly require. And therefore we do farther will
"and command the said Right reverend father in God *Lance-
"lot* now Lord Bishop of *Winton*, that he do forthwith, by
"his Commission under his Episcopall seal, as *Ordinary* of
"the place, give authority unto the said now *Dean* to exer-
"cise *Ecclesiastical jurisdiction* in our said Isle, according to
"the said Canons and Constitutions thus made and establi-
"shed, as followeth.

Canons

Canons and Constitutions Ecclesiasticall, treated, agreed on, and established for the Isle of *Jarsey*.

CHAP. I.

Of the Kings Supremacy, and of the Church.

Article I.

1. AS our duty to the Kings most excellent Majesty requireth, it is first ordained, That the *Dean* and Ministers having care of souls, shall to the utmost of their power, knowledge and learning, purely and sincerely, without any backwardnesse or dissimulation, teach, publish and declare, as often as they may, and as occasion shall present it self; that all strange, usurped and forain power (for as much as it hath no gound by the law of God) is wholly, as for just and good causes taken away and abolished; and that therefore no manner of obedience or subjection within any of his Majesties Realms and Dominions, is due unto any such forain power; but that the Kings *power* within his Realms of *England, Scotland* and *Ireland,* and all other his Dominions and Countries, is the highest power under God, to whom all men, as well inhabitants, as born within the same, do by Gods Law owe most loyalty and obedience, afore and above all other power and Potentates in the earth.

II.

2. Whosoever shall affirme and maintain that the Kings Majesty hath not the same authority in causes *Ecclesiasticall*, that the godly Princes had amongst the *Jews* and the *Christian Emperours* in the *Church primitive,* or shall impeach in any manner the said *Supremacy* in the said causes.

III. IV.

3. Also whosoever shall affirme that the Church of *England* as it is established under the Kings Majesty is not a true and *Apostolicall* Church, purely teaching the Doctrine of the Prophets and Apostles. 4. Or shall impugne the Government of the said Church by *Archbishops, Bishops* and *Deans*, affirming it to be *Antichristian*, shall be *ipso facto* Excommunicated, and not restored but by the *Dean* sitting in his Court, after his repentance and publick *recantation* of his errour.

CHAP. II.

Of Divine Service.

Article I.

1. IT is injoyned unto all sorts of people that they submit themselves to the *Divine service* contained in the book of *Common prayers* of the Church of *England*. And for as much as concerns the Ministers, that they observe with uniformity the said *Liturgie* without addition or alteration; and that they suffer not any *Conventicle* or *Congregation* to make a sect apart by themselves, or to distract the Government Ecclesiasticall established in the Church.

II.

2. The Lords day shall be sanctified by the exercises of publick prayer, and the hearing of Gods word. Every one also shall be bounden to meet together at an hour convenient, and to observe the order and decency in that case requisite; being attentive to the reading or preaching of the Word; kneeling on their knees during the Prayers, and standing up at the Belief; and shall also testifie their consent in saying *Amen*. And further, during any part of *Divine service* the Church-wardens shall not suffer any interruption or impeachment to be made by the insolence and practice of any person, either in the Church or Church-yard.

3. There

III.

3. There shall be publick exercise in every Parish on Wednesdays and Fridays in the morning, by reading the *Common prayers*.

IV.

4. When any urgent occasion shall require an extraordinary *Fast*, the *Dean* with the advice of his Ministers shall give notice of it to the *Governour* and Civill Magistrate; to the end, that by their authority and consent it may be generally observed, for the appeasing of the wrath and indignation of the Lord by true and serious repentance.

CHAP. III.

Of Baptism.

THe Sacrament of *Baptism* shall be administred in the Church with fair water according to the institution of *Jesus Christ*, and without the limitation of any dayes. No man shall delay the bringing of his child to *Baptism* longer then the next Sunday or publick Assembly, if it may conveniently be done. No person shall be admitted to be a Godfather, unlesse he hath received the Lords Supper; nor shall women alone (*viz.* without the presence of a man among them) be admitted to be Godmothers.

CHAP. IV.

Of the Lords Supper.

Article I.

1. THe *Lords Supper* shall be administred in every Church four times a year; whereof one to be at *Easter*, and the other at *Christmas*; and every Minister in the administration of it, shall receive the Sacrament himself, and after give

give the Bread and wine to each of the *Communicants*, using the words of the *institution* of it.

II.

2. The Masters and Mistresses of Families shall be admonished and enjoyned to cause their children and Servants to be instructed in the knowledge of their salvation; and to this end shall take care to send them to the ordinary *Catechizing*.

CHAP. V.

Of Marriage.

Article I.

1. NO man shall *marry* contrary to the degrees prohibited in the word of God, according as they are expressed in a table made for that purpose in the Church of *England*, on pain of *nullity* and *censure*.

II.

2. The *Banes* of the parties shall be asked three Sundays successively in the Churches of both parties; and they of the Parish where the Marriage is not celebrated, shall bring an attestation of the bidding of their *Banes* in their own Parish. Neverthelesse in lawfull cases there may be a *Licence* or dispensation of the said *Banes*, granted by the authority of the *Dean*, and that upon good caution taken, that the parties are at liberty.

III.

3. No separation shall be made *a thoro & mensa*, unlesse in case of Adultery, cruelty, and danger of life duly proved; and this at the sole instance of the parties. As for the maintenance of the woman during her divorce, he shall have recourse to the Secular power.

CHAP.

CHAP. VI.

Of Ministers.

Article I.

1. NO man that is unfit to teach, or not able to preach the word of God shall be admitted to any Benefice within the Isle, or which hath not received *imposition of hands*, and been ordained according to the forme used in the Church of *England*.

II.

2. None of them, either *Dean* or *Minister*, shall at the same time hold two *Benefices*, unlesse it be in time of vacancy; and only the Natives of the Isle shall be advanced to these preferments.

III.

3. The *Ministers* every Sunday after morning prayer, shall expound some place of holy Scripture; and in the afternoon, shall handle some of the points of Christian Religion, contained in the Catechism in the Book of Common-prayers.

IV.

4. In their Prayers they shall observe the titles due unto the King, acknowledging him the Supreme governour under *Christ*, in all causes, and over all persons as well Ecclesiasticall as Civill: recommending unto God the prosperity of his person and royall posterity.

V.

5. Every *Minister* shall carefully regard that modesty and gravity of apparell which belongs unto his function; and may preserve the honour due unto his person; and shall be also circumspect in the whole carriage of their lives to keep themselves from such company, actions and haunts,

which may bring unto them any blame or blemish. Nor shall they dishonour their calling by Gaming, Alehouses, Usuries, guilds, or occupations not convenient for their function; but shall endevor to excell all others in purity of life, in gravity and virtue.

VI.

6. They shall keep carefully a Register of Christnings, Marriages and Burials, and shall duely publish upon the day appointed to them the Ordinances of the Courts, such as are sent unto them, signed by the *Dean*, and have been delivered to them fifteen dayes before the publication.

VII.

7. The *Ministers* shall have notice in convenient time of such *Funerals* as shall be in their Parishes; at which they shall assist, and shall observe the forme prescribed in the book of Common-prayers. No man shall be interred within the Church, without the leave of the *Minister*, who shall have regard unto the quality and condition of the persons, as also unto those which are benefactours unto the Church.

CHAP. VII.

Of the Dean.

Article I.

1. THe *Dean* shall be a Minister of the word, being a Master of the Arts or Graduate at the least in the Civill Lawes, having ability to exercise that office; of good life and conversation, as also well affected to Religion, and the service of God.

II.

2. The *Dean* in all causes handled at the Court, shall demand

mend the advice and opinion of the Ministers which shall then be present.

III.

3. There shall appertain unto him the cognisance of all matters which concern the service of God, the preaching of the Word, the administration of the *Sacraments, Matrimoniall* causes, the *examination* and censure of all *Papists, Recusants, Hereticks, Idolaters,* and *Schismaticks,* persons perjured in causes Ecclesiasticall; *Blasphemers,* those which have *recourse to Wizards, Incestuous persons, Adulterers, Fornicators, ordinary drunkards,* and *publick profaners* of the *Lords days*; as also the profanation of the Churches and Church-yards, misprisions and offences committed in the Court, or against any officers thereof in the execution of the mandats of the Court; and also of Divorces and separations *a thoro & mensa*; together with a power to censure and punish them according unto the Lawes Ecclesiasticall, without any hindrance to the power of the Civill Magistrate in regard of temporall correction for the said crimes.

IV.

4. The *Dean* accompanied with two or three of the Ministers, once in two years shall visite every Parish in his own person, and shall take order, that there be a Sermon every visitation day, either by himself, or some other by him appointed. Which *Visitation* shall be made for the ordering of all things appertaining to the Churches, in the service of God, and the administration of the Sacraments: as also that they be provided of *Church-wardens,* that the Church and Church-yards, and dwellings of the Ministers be kept in reparations. And farther, he shall then receive information of the said *Church-wardens,* or in their default of the Ministers, of all offences and abuses which need to be reformed; whether in the Minister, the officers of the Church, or any other of the Parish. And the said *Dean* in lieu of the said visitation, shall receive 4 s. pay out of the Treasures of the Church for every time.

5. In

V.

5. In the vacancy of any Benefice either by death or otherwise, the *Dean* shall give present order, that the profits of it be sequestred; to the end, that out of the revenue of it, the Cure may be supplyed; as also that the widow and children of the deceased may be satisfied according to the time of his service, and the custome of the Isle; excepting such necessary deductions as must be made for *dilapidations* in case any be. He shall also give convenient time to the widow of the deceased, to provide her of an house, and shall dispose the residue unto the next Incumbent; for which the Sequestrator shall be accomptant.

VI.

6. In the same case of vacancy, if within six months the Governour do not present a *Clerk* unto the Reverend father in God the Bishop of *Winton*, or if that See be void, to the most Reverend father in God the Archbishop of *Canterbury*, to be admitted and instituted to the said Benefice; then shall the *Dean* give notice of the time of the vacancy unto the said Lords the Bishop and Archbishop, whereby it is in the lapse, that so it may be by them *collated*. And then if any one be offered to them, the *Dean* shall give a testimony of the Demeanure and sufficiency of the party to be approved by them, before he put him into actuall possession of the said Benefice.

VII.

7. The *Dean* shall have the Registring and *Probate* of *Testaments*; which be approved by the seal of his office, and afterwards enregistred. He shall also have the registring of the Inventories of the moveable goods of *Orphanes*, which he shall carefully record, to give copies of them at all times, and as often as he is required. Also he shall give letters of administration of the goods of *Intestates*, dying without heirs of their body to the next of kindred.

8. They

VIII.

8. They which have the keeping of the Will, whether he be *Heir*, *Executor*, or any other, shall transcribe and bring it unto the *Dean* within one moneth; in default whereof he shall be brought by processe into the Court, and be constrained to pay double charges. And the said *Dean* for the said *Testaments*, *Inventories* and *Letters* of administration, shall have such fees, as are specified in a Table for this purpose.

IX.

9. All *legacies* moveable, made unto the Church, the Ministers, Schools, or to the poor, shall be of the cognisance of the *Dean*, but upon any opposition made concerning the validity of the Will, the Civill Courts shall determine of it between parties.

X.

10. It shall appertain unto the *Dean* to take cognisance of all detention of tithes consecrated to the Church, of what kinde so ever they be, which have been payed unto the Ministers, and which they have enjoyed or had in possession for the space of forty years; and every person convicted of withholding or fraudulently detaining the said tithes, shall be adjudged to make restitution, and shall pay the cost and charges of the party. And for the preservation of all rights, tithes, rents, lands and possessions belonging to the Church, there shall be a *Terrice* made by the Bailiffe and Justices assisted by the *Dean* and the Kings Atturney.

XI.

11. The *Dean* shall have also power to make a Deputy or *Commissary* which shall supply the place and office of the *Dean*, as far as his Commission shall extend; whereof there shall be an *authentick* copy in the rails of the said Court.

Fff   CHAP.

CHAP. VIII.

Of the Overseers or Church-wardens.

Article I.

1. THe next week after *Easter*, the Minister and people of every parish shall make choice of two to be *Church-wardens*, discreet men, of good life and understanding, able to read and write, if such may be had. But if the people cannot agree on such a choice, then shall the Minister name one and the Parishioners another, by the major part of their voices; which two shall be after sworn in the next Court, and there advertised of their duties.

II.

2. Their duty shall be to see that the Churches and Church-yards be not abused by any profane and unlawfull actions; as also not to suffer any *excommunicated* person to come into the Church, after the sentence hath been published in that Parish; they shall also carefully present from time to time those which neglect the publick exercises of Divine service, and the administration of the Sacraments; and generally all crimes of Ecclesiasticall cognisance; which said presentations they shall exhibite under their hands; nor shall they be constrained to present above twice a year.

III.

3. They shall have care particularly that the Churches be well repaired, and the Church-yard well fenced; and shall see that all things appertaining to the Church, the administration of the word and Sacraments, from time to time may be provided. As *viz.* a *Bible* of the best translation, and the largest letter; the book of *Common-prayers* both for the Minister, as also for the Clerk or Sexton of the Parish; one Parchment book to Register the Christnings, Marriages and Burials; a decent *Communion table,*

table, with a Carpet to cover it during Divine service; the Fonts for *Baptism*, cups and vessels dedicated to that use, together with a fair linnen cloth, and a coffer wherein to put the said utensils; also a trunk or chest for the peoples alms, a cloth and cushion for the pulpit. They shall also provide bread and wine for the the *Communion*; and shall see that the seats and benches be well fitted for the conveniency of the Minister and of the people, with the advice and counsell of the Minister, and shall look to the rents and revenues of the Churches treasure.

IV.

4. The said Church-wardens shall be enjoyned to keep a good and true accompt both of their disbursments or receipts, and of the employment which they have made of the money issuing out of the Church-treasury, which shall from time to time be published according to the custome, and of that also which is remaining in the hands of them, or of the Overseers of the poor. They shall employ the said treasure in things necessary and fitting for the Church and the common good, guiding themselves by the direction of their Minister, and the principall of the parish in such extraordinary matters as concern the Parish. In case of publick businesse, the assembly of the Estates shall prescribe them, what they think expedient for the common profit; and before they quit their charge, they shall give notice to the Parishioners in the *Easter* week to hear their accounts, which shall passe under the hands of the Minister and the chief of the Parish; if any of the said Parishioners or others shall refuse to pay the moneys which they owe to the said treasury; the said Church-wardens and Overseers or any of them, shall prosecute the law against them. In case of any controversie about the said accounts or abuse to be reformed, the *Dean* and Minister of the Parish where the said controversie or abuse shall be, together with the Bailiffe and Justices shall determine of it as is most convenient.

5. The

V.

5. The said Church-wardens on the Sunday during Divine service shall search in places suspected for games or riot, and having the Constables for their assistants, shall search also into Alehouses, and houses of misdemeanor.

VI.

6. They shall be carefull, that there be no detention or concealment of any thing appertaining to the Church, and shall also seise into their hands all goods and legacies moveable given unto the Church, or to the poor, according to the custome of the Country.

CHAP. IX.

Of the Collectors and Sides-men.

THere shall be two *Collectors* for the poor appointed in every Parish, which also shal discharge the place of *Sidesmen* or Assistants; who shall be chosen as the *Church-wardens* are, and shall take an oath to carry themselves well in the said office, and to give an account of their Stewardship twice a year, before the Minister and the Parishioners, *viz.* at *Easter* and at *Michaelmas*.

CHAP. X.

Of Clerks and Sextons.

Article I.

1. THe *Clerks* and *Sextons* of Parishes shall be chosen by the Minister and the principall of the Parish; men of the age of twenty years at the least, of good life and conversation, able to read fairly, distinctly, and understandingly, and to write also, and fitted somewhat for the singing of the Psalmes, if it may be.

II.

2. Their charge is, by the ringing of a Bell, to call the people to Divine service, and the hearing of the Word, at the proper and ordinary hours; to keep the Church locked and clean, as also the Pulpit and the seats, to lay up the Books and other things belonging to the Church committed to their trust, to provide water against the Christnings, to make such proclamations as are enjoyned them by the Court or by the Minister. And shal receive their stipend and wages by the contribution of the Parishioners, be it in Corn or money, according to the custome of the place.

CHAP. XI.

Of School masters.

Article I.

1. There shall be a *School master* in every Parish, chosen by the Minister, Church wardens, and other principall persons therein, and afterwards presented unto the *Dean* to be licenced thereunto. Nor shall it be lawfull for any one to take upon him this charge, not being in this manner called unto it. The Ministers shall have the charge of visiting the *Schooles*, to exhort the Masters to their duty.

II.

2. They shall accustome themselves with diligence and painfulnesse to teach the children to read and to write, to say their prayers and to answer in the Catechismes; they shall instruct them in good manners, they shall bring them unto Sermons, and to Common-prayers, and there see them quietly and orderly demean themselves.

CHAP. XII.

Of the Court Ecclesiasticall.

Article. I.

1. THe *Court* shall be holden every Munday, in the year, observing the same vacations as the *Courts Civill.*

II.

2. At every Session, in the beginning of it, the names of the Assessors shall be inrolled, the day, the moneth and the year, and the decrees perused.

III.

3. After judgment and sentence given in the main matter, the costs of the parties, and the wages of the officers shall be awarded by censure Ecclesiastick.

IV.

4. There shall be two *Procters* duely sworn unto the Court, to the end, the people may proceed formally and juridically, without any confusion or surprise. And the *Register* (being also sworn) shall faithfully record the sentences pronounced, and give copies of the Acts to such as do require it.

V.

5. The Kings *Atturney*, or in his absence the *Sollicitor*, shall be assistant in the Court from time to time in the awarding of punishment, or censure upon all causes of *crime* and *scandall.*

VI.

6. For the serving of citation and summons, the *Dean* shall swear the *Sextens* of every Parish, together with an *Apparitour*, which shall truly discharge themselves in giving

copies

copies of the originall proces and citation unto those whom it concerns, or in the absence of the party, to his servants. In which proces and citations, the causes of their appearance shall be expressed.

VII.

7. If the party will not be found, as either hiding himself, or using any other collusion, the citation shall be affixed (in case that he have never an house) on the Church door of the Parish where he dwelleth, and that upon a Sunday.

VIII.

8. If it come unto the notice of the *Dean* by the report of honest men, that any one hath doth live notoriously scandalous, he shall advertise the Minister and Church-wardens of the Parish, to the end, that being thus informed, they may present such persons as merit to be punished, or censured.

IX.

9. Upon good notice of a crime committed by any of the Ministers, the *Dean* after two warnings or admonitions, shall proceed to the reforming of him, by the advice and consent of two of his brethren, even unto *suspension* and *sequestration*. And in case he continue refractory, the *Dean* by the consent of the major part of Ministers, shall proceed to *deprivation*.

X.

10. No *commutation* shall be made in lieu of penance, without great circumspection, and regard had unto the quality of the persons and circumstances of the crime. And the *commutation* shall be inrolled in the Acts of the Court, to be imployed upon the poor, and in pious uses; whereof an account shall be given according to the Register.

11. After

XI.

11. After the first default, the non-appearance of the party again cited shall be reputed as a contempt; if being after peremptorily cited, he doth not appear, then shall they proceed against him by *excommunication*; and if before the next Court day he endevour not to obtain *absolution*, they shall proceed to the publishing of the sentence of the minor *excommunication*, which shal be delivered to the Minister of the Parish to be read upon some solemn day and in the hearing of the greater part of the Parishioners. The party still continuing in his *contumacy*, they shall then proceed unto the major *excommunication*; whereby he shall be excluded *a sacris & societate fidelium*. If this bring him not unto obedience and acknowledgement within the space of forty dayes, then shall the *Dean* by his certificate *authentick* give notice unto the Bailiff and *Justices* of the said *contumacy*, requiring their assistance to seise on him, and commit him prisoner to some sure place till he be humbled, and shall give surety that he will submit unto the ordinance of the Church; and before that he be absolved, he shall be bound to defray the costs and charges of the suit.

XII.

12 In cases of *incontinency* upon presentment of the Church-wardens, together with the *probabilities* of a common *fame*, *scandall* and presumptions in this case requisite, the party shall undergo the purgation upon oath, or else shall be reputed as convict.

XIII.

13. In causes of *Adultery*, at the instance of the party, the proceedings shall go on advisedly by good proofs and informations, even to evidence of the crime objected; and if the matter or evidence of fact be clear, they may proceed to separation *a thoro & mensa*.

XIV.

14. He that shall offend in point of calumny and diffamation,

tion, shall make acknowledgment of the injury according to the exigence of the case, provided that the businesse be followed within the compasse of the year, and that the matter of it be of Ecclesiasticall cognisance in the crimes above recited.

CHAP. XIII.

Of Appeales.

Article I.

1. Appeales in causes Ecclesiasticall shall be heard and determined by the reverend father in God the Bishop of *Winton* in person, and if that See be void, by the most reverend father in God, the Archbishop of *Canterbury* in person.

II.

2. All *Appeales* shall be exhibited within fifteen dayes after notice taken of the sentence, and the party shall be constrained to take or write out the whole proces, as it is upon the Register or Rols of Court; which Acts of the said Court shall be delivered to him in forme and time convenient, under the seal of the office, and the *Appellant* shall pursue the action within a year and a day, *aut sententiæ latæ stare compellitur.*

III.

3. It shall not be lawfull to appeal untill after the *definitive* sentence, unlesse in these two cases, viz. either when the *Interlocutory* is such as puts an end unto the businesse, or else when the said *Interlocutory* being obeyed brings such irreparable damage to the party, that he cannot help himself by his *Appeal.*

Ggg

A Table of the Fees appertaining to the *Dean* and his Officers in all causes Ecclesiasticall.

FOr the proving of a Will where the goods of the deceased exceed not the value of five pound. To the Dean o. To the Register for writing and recording it 6 d.

For the approving of a Will above the value of 5 l. To the Dean 2 s. To the Register or Notary 1 s.

For a Letter of *administration* where the goods of the deceased exceed not the value of 5 l. *de claro*. To the Dean o. To the Register for writing it 6 d.

For a Letter of *administration* above that value. To the Dean. 1 s. To the Register 1 s.

For the registring an *Inventory* of the goods of *minors*, where the said *inventory* exceedeth not the value of 5 l. To the Dean o. To the Register 4 d.

For the registring of *Inventories* exceeding the value of 5 l. To the Dean 2 s. To the Register 1 s.

For an *authentick* copy of the said *Wils, Inventories* or *Letters of administration.* To the Dean for his seal 6 d. To the Register 6 d.

For processe compulsory to bring in the Wils 1 s.

For Licences of marriage. To the Dean 3 s.

For the sequestration of the profits of a Benefice. To the Dean 6 s.

For the induction of a Minister. To the Dean 3 s.

For proces and citations. To the Dean 2 d. ob. To the Notary 1 d. qa. To the Apparitor for serving the Proces and Citations 3 d. To the Sexton for serving a Citation within the Parish 1 d. qa.

For absolution from the *minor excommunication.* To the Dean 1 s. To the Notary 2 d. ob. To the Apparitor 2 d. ob.

For absolution from the *major excommunication.* To the Dean 2 s. To the Notary 2 d. ob. To the Apparitor 6 d.

In causes *Litigious*, the party overthrown shall pay the fees and duties of the Officers, and for the *authentick* writing. To the party 4 d. as also to every witnesse produced in Court 4 d.

To

To the Proctors of the Court for every cause they plead 6 d.
To the Notary for every instrument entred in the Court 1 d. qa.
To him for every first default in Court 1 d. qa.
To him in case of *contumacy* 4 d.

"According whereunto it is ordained that neither the
"*Dean* nor his successors, nor any of his officers, either directly
"or indirectly, shall demand, exact, or receive of the Inhabi-
"tants of the said Isle, any other fees or duties, then such as
"are specified in the table above written. And it is further
"ordained, that whatsoever hath been done or put in exe-
"cution in the said Isle, on any causes, and by virtue of any
"Ecclesiasticall jurisdiction, shall be forthwith abrogated;
"to the end, that it may not be drawn into example by the
"said Dean, or any of his successors in the times to come,
"contrary to the tenure of these Canons at this present made
"and established; but that all their proceedings be limited
"and fitted to the contents of the said Canons and Consti-
"tutions Ecclesiasticall. Also that there be no hindrance
"or impeachment made by the Civill Magistrate unto the
"said *Dean* and his successors in the peaceable execution of
"the said jurisdiction contained in the said Canons, as being
"nothing prejudiciall to the priviledges and customes of
"the said Isle, from which it is not our purpose at all to
"derogate. Given (as before said) under our signet at our
"Court at *Greenwich*, on the last day of *June*, in the year of
"our Reign of *England*, *France* and *Ireland*, the one and twen-
"tieth, and of *Scotland* the six and fiftieth.

Chap. VIII.

(1) *For what cause it pleased his Majesty to begin with* Jarsey. *(2) A representation of such motives whereon the like may be effected in the Isle of* Guernzey. *(3) The indignity done by a Minister hereof to the Church of* England. *(4) The calling of the Ministers in some reformed Churches how defensible.* (5) *The circumstances both of time and persons how ready for an alteration.* (6) *The grievances of the Ministery against the Magistrates.* (7) *Proposals of such means as may be fittest in the managing of this design.* (8) *The submission of the Author and the work unto his Lordship. The conclusion of the whole. Our return to* England.

I Now am come unto the fourth and last part of this discourse, intended once to have been framed by way of suit unto your Lordship, in the behalf of the other Island not yet weaned from the breasts of their late mother of *Geneva*. But finding that course not capable of those particulars which are to follow; I chose rather to pursue that purpose by way of declaration. My scope and project, to lay before your Lordship such reasons which may encite you to make use of that favour which most worthily you have attained to with his Majesty, in the reduction of this Isle of *Guernzey* to that antient order by which it formerly was guided, and wherein it held most conformity with the Church of *England*. Before I enter on with argument, I shall remove a doubt which might be raised about

this

this businesse; as *viz*. For what cause his late most excellent Majesty proceeded to this alteration in one Island, not in both; and being resolved to try his forces on the one only; why he should rather sort out *Jarsey*. A doubt without great difficulty to be cleared. For had his Majesty attempted both at once, the Ministers of both Islands had then communicated counsels, banded themselves in a league, and by a mutuall encouragement continued more peremptory to their old *Mumpsimus*. It is an ancient principle in the arts of Empire, *Divide & impera*; and well noted by the *State-historian*, that nothing more advantaged the affaires of *Rome* in *Britaine*, then that the natives never met together to reason of the common danger. *Ita dum singuli pugnabant, universi vincebantur*. And on the other side his Majesty foresaw for certain, that if one Island once were taken off, the other might with greater ease be perswaded to conforme. Being resolved then to attempt them single, there was good reason; why he should begin with *Jarsey* first, as unto which he was to send a new Governour, not yet ingaged unto a party, and pliable to his instructions. Whereas Sir *Tho. Leighton* still continued in his charge at *Guernzey*, who having had so main a hand in the introduction of the Platforme, could not be brought with any stomach to intend an alteration of his own counsels.

But not to lose my self in the search of Princes counsels, which commonly are too far removed from vulgar eyes, let us content our selves with knowing the event; which was, that by his means the Isle of *Jarsey* was reduced unto a Discipline conformable to that of *England*, and thereby an easie way for the reforming also that in *Guernzey*. For the accomplishment of which designe, may it please your Lordship to take notice of these reasons following, by which it is within my hopes, your Lordship possibly may be perswaded to deal in it. *A Jove principium.*

And here (as in a Christian duty I am bound) I propose unto your Lordship in the first place, the honour which will redound unto the Lord in this particular, by the restoring of a *Discipline* unto the smallest *Oratory* of his Church,

which

which you assure your self to be most answerable to his holy word, and to the practice of those blessed spirits the *Apostles*. For why may not I say unto your Lordship, as *Mardocheus* once to *Hester*, though the case be somewhat different, *Who knoweth whether you be come unto these dignities, for such a time as this?* And why may it not be said of you even in the application unto this particular designment, *That unto whom so much is given, of him also shall much be required?* Private exployts and undertakings are expected even from private persons. But God hath raised up you to publick honours, and therefore looks that you should honour him in the advancement and undertaking of such counsels as may concern his Church in publick. And certainly, if (as I verily perswade my self) your counsels tend unto the peace and glory of the Church; the Church, I mean, whereof you are so principall a member: You shall not easily encounter with an object, whereon your counsels may be better busied. So strangely do these men disgrace your blessed Mother, *and lay her glory in the dust*. Two instances hereof I shall present unto your Lordship to set the better edge on your proceedings, though otherwise I had forborne to meddle with particulars. It pleased his Majesty for the assurance of these Islands, to send into each of them two Companies of Souldiers, which were equally distributed. But such was the peevish obstinacy of one of the Ministers of this *Guernzey*, that he would not allow their Minister to read prayers unto them in his Church, at such times when himself and people did not use it. At last on much entreaty he was contented to permit it, but with expresse condition, that he should not either read the *Litany*, or administer the *Communion*. Since when, as often as they purpose to receive the Sacrament, they have been compelled to ferry over to the Castle, and in the great hall there celebrate the holy *Supper*. As little is our Church beholding to them in her *Festivals*, as in her *Liturgie*. For whereas, at the Town of St. *Peters* on the Sea, they have a Lecture every Thursday, upon which day the Feast of Christs Nativity was solemnized with us in *England, anno* 1623. the same party chose rather to put off the Sermon

for

for that time, then that any the smal lest honour might reflect upon the day. *O curvæ in terris animæ, & cœlestium inanes.* An opposition far more superstitious then any ceremony, observation of a day, though meerly *Jewish.*

Next to the honour due to God and to his Church, is that which all of us are obliged to tender to our Princes, as being Gods by office, and *nursing fathers* of that Church whereof they are. Therefore I represent in the next rank unto your Lordship a consideration of the honour which you shall here in do unto your Kings. To the one, your late Master of happy memory, who gave you first his hand to guide you unto greatnesse, in the pursuit of his intendments. So glorious were the purposes of that Heroick Prince, for the secure and flourishing tranquillity of Gods holy Church, that certainly it were impiety if any of them be permitted to miscarry. To the other our now gratious Soveraign, who hath doubled the promptions conferred upon you by his father; in being an author to him of those thoughts which may so much redound unto his glory; the rather, because, in case his Majesty should find a time convenient to go forward in his Fathers project, of reducing all the Churches *Protestant* unto one *Discipline,* and *Liturgie;* there might not an objection thwart him, drawn from home. Otherwise it may perhaps be us'd to him by some of those which do not fancy the proposall, as *Demades* once to *Philip,* ὅτι πρῶν καὶ σεσαυκὼ πλέγμα κινδύνῳ τ' Ἐνάλιε, &c. That first he might do well to compose the differences in his own dominions, before he motion a conformity to others. At the least, he may be sure to look for this reply from *Scotland,* when ever he proposeth to them the same businesse. The Ministers of *Jarsey,* as before I have shown your Lordship, denyed admission to the book of Common-prayer, as not imposed upon the *Scots;* with better reason may the *Scots* refuse to entertain it, as not imposed on those of *Guernzey.*

Besides the honour due to God, the Church, and to the King, there is an honour next in order to the calling of the Priest. A calling, as much stomached in generall by all that party, so most especially reviled by those amongst our selves for *Antichristian,* tyrannous, a divelish ordinance, a bastardly govern-

government, and the like. Nor do I think that those of *Guernzey* are better affected to it, though more moderate in professing their dislike: for did they but approve the hierarchy of Bishops, they would not then proceed so unwarrantably as now they do, in the ordination of their Ministers. I cal it unwarrantable proceeding, because the lawful and ordinary door of entrance unto the Ministery, was never shut unto this people; and therefore their preposterous entry upon this sacred calling, either by the *back-door* or by the *window*, the more unanswerable. Whereas it may be pleaded in the behalf of those in some parts beyond the seas, that they could not meet with any Bishops which would give them *ordination*, unlesse they would abjure the Gospell as they then profest it, and therefore that necessity compelled them to the private way of *imposing hands* on one another. In which particular, the case of some reformed Churches, may not unfitly be resembled unto that of *Scipio*, as it is related to us in the third book of *Valerius Max. cap. 7.* upon some want of money for the furtherance of the necessary affaires of state, he demanded a supply from the common treasury. But when the *Questor* pretending that it was against the Lawes, refused to open it, himself a private person, seised the Keyes, *Patefacto ærario legem utilitati cedere coegit*; and over-ruled the Law by the advancement of the Weal publick. In like manner (which is I think the most and best that can be said in this behalf) to promote the reformation of Religion, many good men made suit to be supplyed out of the common treasury, to be admitted to the preaching of the word according to the ordinary course of *ordination*; which when it was denied them by the *Questors* or *Prelates* of those dayes; they chose rather to receive it at the hands of private and inferior Priests, then that the Church should be unfurnished. This may be said for them, which in excuse of those of *Guernzey* can never be alleadged; whose continuall recourse unto these *private keyes* is done upon no other reason then a dislike of that high calling to which your Lordship is advanced; which therefore you are bound, if not to punish in them, yet to rectifie.

 Two other reasons yet there are which may invite your Lordship to this undertaking, though not so weighty or of
that

that importance as the former. The one, that the remainders of that party here at home, may not be hardned in their obstinacy; the other, that those of *Jarsey*, be not discouraged in their submission and conformity. I have already shewn unto your Lordship, that the brethren here in *England*, never made head against the Church, till the permission of plat-forme in these Islands. After which, with what violence they did assaile the hierarchy, what clamours they continually raised against the Prelates, what superstitions and impieties they imputed to our *Liturgy; notius est quam ut stylo egeat*, is too wel known to be related. If so, then questionless it cannot but confirme them in their new devices, to see them still permitted to this Isle. Nor can they think themselves but wronged, that still they are contrould and censured for the maintenance of that discipline, which is by Soveraign authority allowed and licensed; though in other places, yet in the same dominions. And on the other side, your Lordship may conceive how just a cause of discontent and of repining it may be to those of *Jarsey*; when they shall dayly hear it thundred from the Coasts of *France*, that faintly they have sold themselves to bondage; whereas the faithfull zelots in the Isle of *Guernzey*, doe still preserve themselves in liberty. *Vel neutrum flammis ure, vel ure duos*, as the Lover in *Ausonius*.

From my first rank of motives here presented to your Lordship, which I may most properly call *motives necessary*, and in respect unto the cause; I come next to those of an other quality, which I call *motives of conveniency*, and in relation to the time. For questionlesse the time is at this present more convenient for the accomplishment of this work, then ever we may hope to see hereafter; whether we consider it in reference unto our Kingdome, or to the *Discipline* it self, or to the Governour, or to the people of both sorts, the Clergy and the Magistrates.

For first, there is at this instant, an established peace between it and *France*, concluded on while we were in these Islands, and published immediately on our coming home; which Realm only carryeth a covetous and watchfull eye upon those Islands. Were it between us, as it lately was, nothing but wars and depredations; the alteration then perhaps might be unsafe, it being alwayes dangerous to discontent or charge that Nation, upon whose loyalty we must rely. Nor can I tell unto what desperate and undutifull practises, the furious heat of some few Preachers may possibly excite a multitude; when come the worst that can, there is an enemy at hand that will subscribe to any articles. But now tis peace, and how long peace will hold, is not easie to determine, depending as it doth, upon the will and pleasure of another.

If, in the second place, we look upon the *Discipline* it self, we shall find it well prepared, and ready for a change. For whereas it is ordered in their *Canons* (if I so may call them) that the errours of the *Consistory* shall be corrected by the *Colloquie*, those of the *Colloquie*, by the *Synod*; by the departure of *Jarsey* from them, they have no way of further *Synods*, and therefore no redresse of grivances. So then either the sentence of the *Colloquie* must be unalterable, which is expresly contrary to the platforme; or else there must be granted some other *jurisdiction* to have power above them, whereby their censures may be moderated. The first of these would estate their *Colloquies* in a tyranny more prevalent and binding, then the chair of *Rome* so much complained of. The other openeth a way for the entrance of *Episcopall* authority, for the admission of *Appeals*, for the directions of their proceedings. Add hereunto, that at this time they have a noble Governour, no friend I am assured to any of that party; and such a one which gladly would resign those rights of old belonging to the *Deanry*, when ever it shall please his Majesty to restore that dignity unto the Island. A Peer so perfectly known unto your Lordship and to all the Kingdom, that I need not say more of him, then that which once *Velleius* did of *Junius Blæsus*, *Vir nescias an milior Castris, vel melior toga*. It were a matter of no ordinary study to determine, whether he be more able in the *Campe* or *Senate*.

But in alterations, such as these, the fancy and affection of the people is principally to be attended, as those whom such mutations most properly concern; wherein I find all things made ready to your Lordships hand, if you vouchsafe to set it forwards. The Magistrates and more understanding people of the Isle, offended with the severe and unsociable carriage of
the

the *Consistories*, especially of late, since the unlimited Empire of the *Colloquie* hath made that government unsufferable. Before they had enough to keep themselves from censure, and their houses from the diligence of *Consistoriall* spies; when yet there was an higher Court wherein there was some hope of remedy. But there being none to appeal from in the *Consistory*, but those which wil condemn them in the *Colloquie*; they undergo the yoak with much clamour, but with more stomach. A stomach which eftsoones they spare not to disgorge upon them, as often, *viz.* as they come within the compasse of their Courts, either in way of punishment or censure. On the other side the Ministers exclaime against the Magistrates, as presuming too far above their latchet; pretending that by them their *Discipline* hath been infringed, their priviledges violated, and their Ministery interrupted. Matters that have not been repined at only in a corner, but publickly presented as on the Theater, and complained of to their Governours. For at my Lord of *Danbies* being there, they articled against the Magistrates for invading, the *Ecclesiasticall jurisdiction*; as *viz.* that they take upon them to dissolve *contracts* made in the presence of the Minister, and with an invocation of the name of God, which in judgment of the *Discipline* (*Chap.* 12. 1.) are *undissoluble*. That they had intermedled with the administration of holy *Baptisme*, a duty meerly spirituall. That they had seised upon the treasures of the Church in some places, and disposed of them at their pleasure. That they had caused the Ministers to be imprisoned, and there detained them for a long time, to their great discomfort, and the hazard of their *flocks*. And lastly that they had deprived them of the liberty of Natives in denying them their suffrages for the election of the *Curates*. Other grievances there were, but these the principall. True it is, that upon due examination of particulars, it did appear that the Magistrates had more reason in their actions, then the Ministers in their complaints. But not having been accustomed to the like usage, they do esteem it a thraldome so incompetent and unsupportable, that I perswade my self they sooner would resolve to yeeld to any course, then have their doings crost by that *tribunall*. Sure I am, when they found so small redresse for these (as they conceived) great oppressions, they made petition to his Lordship to bethink himself on some other way for their relief, and laboured to procure me to be their Mediator to his Lordship in it.

These circumstances also happily concurring, portend, in my opinion, as great an alteration in this state *Ecclesiasticall*, as the conjunction of some powerfull Planets doth sometimes upon the temporall. And if your Lordship should be wanting now unto present opportunity, it may be such a confluence of preparatives and helps may hardly be met withall hereafter. Presuming therefore, that your Lordship will not neglect the advantage offered, I should next proceed unto those means which might best be used in the effecting of this work; but what were this but to read a lecture of the wars to *Hannibal*, to play a part on the Stage in the sight of *Roscius*? For whether your Lordship shall think most fit to treat first of it with my Lord the Governour, that he may make plain the way before you, and facilitate the businesse; or whether it may be thought most proper, that some negotiate with the people and the *Jurates*, to commence a suit in this behalf unto the Councell; or whether that the Ministers themselves, in this conjuncture of time, oppressed, as they conceive it, by the Civill Magistrates encroaching on them, may not with great facility be perswaded to sollicite for a change; who can so well determine as your Lordship, whom long experience and naturall abilities have made perfect in these arts? Only let me beseech your Lordships leave to enjoy mine own folly, and for a while to act my part, to read my lecture, though *Hannibal* and *Roscius* be in presence.

At such time as by the Ministers his Lordship was petitioned to resolve upon some course for their relief; they made request to me to sollicite for them their desires, to be a remembrancer for them to his Lordship. To which I answered, that I could direct them in a way which should for ever free them from that yoak which so much they feared, and if they would vouchsafe to see my Chamber, I would there impart it. A motion not made unto the wals, or lost in the proposall; for down unto my Lodging they descended, and there we joyned our selves in Councell. The Petitioners were five in number,

viz.

CHAP. VIII. *the Estate of Guernzey and Jarsey.* 421

viz. De la March, Millet, Perchard, Picote, and *De la Place*; my self alone, and not provided (save in Wine and Sider) for their entertainment. But as *Lactantius* in an equall case, *Necesse est, ut me causa bonitas faciat eloquentem*, presuming on the goodnesse of my cause, but more upon their ignorance, I was resolved to bid them battail. Immediately upon the opening of the Counsell, I was importuned my opinion; whereto I freely made them answer, the only course whereby they might subsist entire and free from bondage, was to address themselves to his Majesty for the restitution of the *Dean.* But this say they is Physick worse then the disease; and thereupon the battails began to joyn with greater violence; with violence it was, and therefore (as we are instructed in *Philosophy*) of no long continuance; for presently upon the first encounter their ranks were broken, and their forces disunited. *Picote* for his part protested, that he had alwayes been an enemy to *Lay Elders*, and that he could not see by what authority of Scripture they were permitted in the Churches. *Ferchard* was well enough content, that the dispensing of the poor mans box might be committed unto others, and that the *Deacons* as being a degree or step unto the Ministery, might be employed about the treasures of salvation. *Millet* stood silent all the while, and as I think reserved himself to try the fortune of another day. *De la March* and *De la Place* (this *De la Place* is he who abandoned *Jarsey* upon his failing of the *Deanship*) what they could not make good by reason, supplied by obstinacy. In my life I never knew men more willing to betray a cause, or lesse able to maintain it. My inference hereupon is this, that if his Majesty should signifie unto them, that it is his royall pleasure, to admit a *Dean* among them, or else repair unto the Court to give a reason of their refusall; they sooner would forsake and quit their cause, then either be resolved to agree about it, or venture to defend it. If I were sure to make no use of *Logick*, till these men shal run the hazard of a *disputation*, I would presently go and burn my *Aristotle*.

To draw unto an end, for I have been too tedious to your Lordship. Before I pluck off my disguise and leave the stage whereon I act, I could me thinks add somewhat here about the choicing of a man most fit for this authority. In which

Hhh 3 parti-

particular, as I stand well affected to *Perchard*, for a moderate and quiet man, so hath he also a good repute in all the Island, both for his vein of Preaching, his liberall hospitality, and plausible demeanor. Or if your Lordship think a forainer more fit, there being now the Parish of St. *Saviours* void, and so full room for that *induction*, I durst propose to you *Olivier* of *Jarsey*; a man which I perswade my self, I may say safely, not inferiour unto any of both Islands in point of Scholarship, and well affected to the *English* form of Government. Add to this that already he is acquainted with the nature of the place, as having executed the office of the *Commissary* or *Subdean*, ever since the introduction of the charge, and therefore not to seek in the managing and cariage of his jurisdiction. But good God! what follies do we dayly run into, when we conceive our selves to be disguised, and that our actions are not noted? It is therefore high time for me to unmaske my self, and humbly crave your Lordships pardon, that under any habit I should take upon me to advise. A further *plaudite* then this I do not seek for, then that you will vouchsafe to excuse my boldnesse, though not allow it: the rather because a zeal unto the beauteous uniformity of the Church did prompt me to it. But this, and this discourse, such as it is, I consecrate unto your Lordship; for whose honour, next under Gods, I have principally pursued this argument. For my self, it will be unto me sufficient glory, that I had any, though the least, hand in such a pious work; and shall be happy, if in this, or in any other your Lordships counsels for the Churches peace, I may be worthy of imployment. Nor need your Lordship fear, that in the prosecution of this project, you may be charged with an innovation. To pursue this purpose is not to introduce a *novelty* but to restore a *Discipline*, to revive the perfect service of God, which so long hath been, to say the best of it, in a *Lethargy*, and to make the *Jerusalem* of the *English Empire*, like a *City which is at unity within it self.*

Sic nova dum condis, revocas (vir summe) priora;
Debentur quæ sunt, quæque fuere tibi.
Si priscis servatur honor te Præside, templis;
Et casa tam culto sub Jove numen habet.

    Thus (Reverend Lord) to you,
    Churches both old and new
Do owe themselves; since by your pious care
New ones are built, and old ones in repaire.
    Thus by your carefull zeal
    Unto the Churches weal,
As the old *Temples* do preserve their glories,
So private houses have their *Oratories*.

It is now time to acquaint your Lordship with the successe and safety of our return; all things being done and fully setled for the peace and security of those Islands, which was the only cause of our voyage thither. Concerning which, your Lordship may be pleased to know in a word, that the crosnesse of the winds and roughnesse of the water, detained us some dayes longer in *Castle Cornet*, then we had intended; but at the last, on Thursday *Aprill* 2. being *Maundy Thursday*, *anno* 1629. we went aboard our Ships, and hoised sail for *England*. It was full noon before we were under sail, and yet we made such good way, that at my waking the next morning, we were come neer the Town of *Peal*, and landed safely the same day in the Bay of *Teichfeild*, where we first took Ship; his Lordship being desirous to repose himself with the said Mr. *Bromfeild*, till the Feast of *Easter* being passed over might render him more capable to pursue his Journey.

And now I am safely come into my Countrey, where according to the custome of the Antients, I offer up my thanksgiving to the God of the waters, and testifie before his Altars the gratefull acknowledgement of a safe voyage and a prosperous return, blessings which I never merited.

> ———*Me tabula sacer*
> *Votiva paries indicat uvida*
>   *Suspendisse potenti*
> *Vestimenta maris Deo.*

> My *Votive Table* on the Sacred wall
>   Doth plainly testifie to all,
>   That I those *gratefull vowes* have paid,
> Which in the tumults of the *deep* I made,
>   To him that doth the Seas command,
>   And holds the waters in his hand.

The End of the Last Book, and the Second Journey.

www.ingramcontent.com/pod-product-compliance
Lightning Source LLC
Chambersburg PA
CBHW070159240426
43671CB00007B/494